This is a cogent and well written exposition of the complex nature of the public policy process. It is a process shot through with differing values and self interest. Yet, as the book rightly argues seeking policy solutions to complex problems is a crucial part of the political realm. A key strength of the book is the way it combines theoretical analysis and a discussion of some of the key policy challenges of today.

Hugh Atkinson, *London South Bank University, UK*

In *Public Policy and Private Interest* Jim Chandler gives the public policy textbook a much needed make-over. Chandler covers a wide range of thinkers, concepts and debates expertly and with a welcome lightness of touch. The book will be an invaluable text for any undergraduate or masters level public policy course.

Jonathan Davies, *De Montfort University, UK*

Public Policy and Private Interest

Public Policy and Private Interest explains the complexities of the policy making process in a refreshingly clear way for students who are new to this subject. The key topics it explains are:

- how policy originates, is refined, legitimised, implemented, evaluated and terminated in the forms of theoretical models of the policy process;
- which actors and institutions are most influential in determining the nature of policy;
- the values that shape the policy agenda such as ideology, institutional self-interest and resource capabilities;
- the outcome of policies, and why they succeed or fail;
- the main policy theories including the very latest insights from network theory and post-modernism;
- how national policy is influenced by globalisation.

The text is fully illustrated throughout with a broad range of national and international case studies on subjects such as the banking crisis, the creation of unitary authorities and global environmental policy and regulation.

Combining both a clear summary of debates and theories in public policy and a new and original approach to the subject, this book is essential reading for students of public policy and policy analysis.

J.A. Chandler is Emeritus Professor of Local Governance in the Faculty of Organisation and Management at Sheffield Hallam University, UK. He has published extensively in the field of public policy and administration with a particular emphasis on local governance.

Routledge Textbooks in Policy Studies

This series provides high-quality textbooks and teaching materials for upper-level courses on all aspects of public policy as well as policy analysis, design, practice and evaluation. Each text is authored or edited by a leading scholar in the field and aims both to survey established areas and present the latest thinking on emerging topics.

The Public Policy Primer
Managing the policy process
Xun Wu, M Ramesh, Michael Howlett and Scott Fritzen

Designing Public Policies
Principles and instruments
Michael Howlett

Making Policy Work
Peter John

Analyzing Public Policy
2nd edition
Peter John

Public Policy and Private Interest
Ideas, self-interest and ethics in public policy
J.A. Chandler

Public Policy and Private Interest
Ideas, Self-interest and Ethics in Public Policy

J.A. Chandler

Routledge
Taylor & Francis Group

LONDON AND NEW YORK

First published 2017
by Routledge
2 Park Square, Milton Park, Abingdon, Oxon OX14 4RN

and by Routledge
711 Third Avenue, New York, NY 10017

Routledge is an imprint of the Taylor & Francis Group, an informa business

British Library Cataloguing in Publication Data
A catalogue record for this book is available from the British Library

Library of Congress Cataloging in Publication Data
A catalog record for this book has been requested

ISBN: 978-0-415-55831-0 (hbk)
ISBN: 978-0-415-55832-7 (pbk)
ISBN: 978-1-315-29529-9 (ebk)

Typeset in Times New Roman
by Taylor & Francis Books

Printed and bound by CPI Group (UK) Ltd, Croydon, CR0 4YY

Contents

List of illustrations   vi
Preface   vii
Acknowledgement   ix
Abbreviations   x

1 Introduction   1

2 The legacy of the 'scientific' origins of Policy Studies   10

3 Subjective approaches   23

4 Policy, ideology and ideas   34

5 Self-interest   50

6 Ethics and public policy   65

7 Policy and power   80

8 Public policy in autocracies   91

9 Liberal democracy   103

10 Networks and the Advocacy Coalitions Framework   115

11 Getting policy on the agenda   130

12 Evaluation and validation   142

13 Refining policy towards legitimation   156

14 Implementation   168

15 Policy evolution   179

16 Success and failure   192

17 Deliberative policy making   203

18 Conclusion   217

Glossary   224
Bibliography   227
Index   239

List of Illustrations

Figures

2.1   Easton's political system   18
10.1 AFC restructured   122
14.1 Stages of the dependent variables of the implementation process   173
15.1 Tensions between governing elites and civil society   183
15.2 Stacey diagram of complex policy making   189
15.3 A fitness landscape   190

Tables

3.1   Lowi's policy typology: Types of coercion, types of policy and types
      of politics   30
3.2   Core social motives   31
5.1   Political engagement in the United Kingdom   52
10.1 Policy communities and networks   117

Preface

This study is intended to complement many of the current standard texts on public policy by taking a more subjective rather than a positivist approach to the processing of public policy. There are many texts in print concerning public policy which provide excellent material for developing an understanding of theories in the sub-discipline of public policy. Why then write a further text book on the subject? Although this study sets out the major theories relating to the study of public policy from the conscious development of this study in the 1930s to the present day, it also seeks to widen the theoretical and subjective approach to the discipline and bring the study closer to the wider disciplinary interests of the social sciences.

An underlying argument in this study is that many discussions on public policy have become too self-referential and inward looking and therefore become rather detached from wider sociological and political theory. Too often studies of the subject refer to analysis drawn from a rather limited palette of evidence and theories that have grown around policy studies as opposed to the more all-encompassing range of social studies theories. Perhaps of greatest concern is that policy studies as a subject area has paid too little attention to policy outcomes especially in regard to the extent to which subjective values shape their output and content. This tendency too often neglects to relate policy analysis to ideological values and even less to issues concerning self-interest and ethics. The policy studies genre is also largely focused on liberal democratic systems as opposed to policy making within autocratic frameworks that, as shall be discussed in this study, make up many of the institutional structures that form the basis of liberal democratic political systems. There is also a tendency in many texts on public policy to be shaped predominantly on critical discussion of theories that have been established specifically within the framework of policy studies rather than the wider theoretical models of social, political or economic behaviour within the broad social sciences. Thus, for example, theories of the state, social revolt and revolution or political alienation are rarely fully incorporated into the sub-discipline of public policy. Many writers in the post-modern traditions such as Foucault or critical realists such as Habermas, who have much to say relating to public policy, also tend to be overlooked.

A few comments may be useful concerning the use of examples in this study and its design. I have provided within the text examples and case studies illustrating public policy practice in liberal democracies and autocracies in boxes. I have largely concentrated in the discussions on policy making within liberal democracies on examples from the United States and Britain. This is to concentrate on regimes that are likely to be most familiar to the potential readership of this study and on political systems with which I have most familiarity. Both countries also are exemplars of differing approaches to the institutional structuring of liberal democracies that are in turn based on differing ideological value systems. Such a style also avoids scattering examples among a wide range of liberal democracies that may have few common features.

Acknowledgement

Many thanks are due to the many individuals who have contributed to my ideas that have formed the basis of this study and have also helped in my research. This also includes Sheffield Hallam University which continues to provide me with access to the research facilities following my retirement from full time lecturing. Particular thanks go to colleagues who have read versions of the book and provided me with comments on its progress. These include Neil Barnett, Dr Robert Jones, John Kingdom and Ralph Spence. Dr Becky Jubb was particularly helpful in the design of some of the diagrams in the study. I must also thank my wife Krys and family members who encourage me to continue writing.

Abbreviations

ACF	Advocacy Coalitions Framework
BCE	Before the Common Era
BSE	Bovine spongiform encephalopathy ('Mad cow disease')
CIA	Central Intelligence Agency
EU	European Union
FBI	Federal Bureau of Investigation
ISIS	Islamic State of Iraq and Syria
NGO	Non-government Organisation
NHS	National Health Service (United Kingdom)
NPM	New Public Management
OFSTED	Office for Standards in Education, Children's Services and Skills
QUANGO	Quasi-Autonomous Non-government Organisation
MP	Member of Parliament (United Kingdom)
USA	United States of America
USSR	Union of Soviet Socialist Republics
WMD	Weapons of Mass Destruction

1 Introduction

There are many sound texts on the policy process that discuss the theory and practice of how policy problems emerge on to the agenda of governments and how these governments deliberate and refine a solution to issues that leads to a policy outcome. Such studies also discuss how policy once promulgated is put into practice and evaluated and how it may then evolve or be terminated. The importance of any public policy is, however, for most citizens not primarily about how it is made but the consequences of its content to them as individuals. In liberal democracies, our decision on how to vote is dependent largely on the policies put forward by contending political parties. For many of us the choice we make is based on self-interest for our own well-being and that of our family or closest friends. It may also encompass a wider altruistic concern for the well-being of humanity in general. Self-interest and even more certainly altruism are often guided by established beliefs and inclinations that can be bound up as ideological and ethical values, that is, established systems of thought concerning how ideally society should be shaped.

Beliefs, emotions and values are personal to the individual. These preferences are not subject to scientific verification based on evidence, but on the experience and genetic make-up of each individual, that creates their view of the world and, more crucially, what they desire within that world. As shall be explained later this personal view of the world is not a subject that in any logical scientific sense can be judged to be right or wrong. Our policy preferences are, as a result, not so much based on positivist certainties but on our subjective values that, whilst they may be rational for us as an individual, may be irrational for others. As such, subjective beliefs are not subject to being regarded as true or false even though they may for many be either admirable or repulsive.

Policy emerges through the struggles between those in positions of power to secure their preferences. It is argued in this work that the content of public policy is a reflection of the combination of ideological and ethical values and self-interest. Usually, policy is the result of compromises made within groups rather than by any single individual. This struggle to control the process is fought within the institutional setting of governments, whether they are termed democratic or autocratic, but it is not so much the institutions that are central to how policy is made. It shall be argued in this study that the distance between democratic and autocratic policy making is not as sharply defined as many would like to believe.

The Chinese Republic within thirty years moved from being a command economy communist state to a nation guided by capitalist values without any major change in the institutional structures of its government (Moise, 2008). Similarly in Britain, a social democratic state in which the central and local governments owned a large slice of the productive industries of the state and the majority of social care services has been changed since the 1980s into a regime in which the private sector dominates the productive and social care services even though there has been little change within the constitutional arrangements of the United Kingdom. What has changed is the ideological and ethical values of those who governed these regimes.

At the heart of liberal democracies and autocracies are small conclaves of politicians, businessmen, financiers and media moguls who dominate most political systems and struggle against one another to ensure their values determine the content of the policy process. In this context these systems do not differ that greatly from the policy making that can be observed in autocracies as powerful barons struggle to either depose or gain the attention of the ruling monarch. The satirical content of sit-coms such as 'Yes Minister' or 'The Thick of It' is not too dissimilar to the power games illustrated in Hilary Mantel's (2009; 2015) novels of the rise and fall of Thomas Cromwell in Tudor England. This is, however, not to argue that liberal democracies are no different from oligarchies. Liberal democracies are generally far more liberal than autocracies by allowing freedom of ideas and assembly but in the long term economic freedom creates within such states serious inequalities in the resources necessary to gain power which ensures they are less than democratic in the sense that popular opinion is the dominant driver of the policy process.

Due to the irrationality of our subjective values and emotions, let alone the complexity of the policy process and the lack of certainty concerning the information we have of our world, the most powerful positivist rational thinkers require luck as well as judgement to achieve results that favour their personal view of how the world should be shaped. Such a view contrasts with the development of policy studies from the 1930s that originally sought to discover methodologies that could through scientific analysis find the optimum answer to any policy problem. The development of policy studies by the 1950s began to move away from such false optimism and discussed how policy ideas arrived on the political agenda, were refined by governments, on occasion implemented and then either gained widespread acceptance, remained controversial issues or were abandoned. This approach was, nevertheless, still guided by broadly positivist thinking that the social sciences could forward theories of how policies developed by considering evidence based on the observation of how the many elements within the policy making process were played out in differing institutional settings and in relation to differing policy subjects. Public policy must, however, be valued not only in terms of the efficiency and effectiveness of its outputs or the differing institutional hurdles it must surmount before it can be implemented and evaluated. Policy must also be considered in terms of whether decisions are fair and just for those individuals whose behaviour must be guided by that policy and made in the interest of the majority rather than that of the policy makers. The positivist approach cannot fully explain why the policies take the forms that they do, nor whether the decisions collectively make any sense in terms of effectiveness, let alone morality or justice. A complete discussion of policy making must analyse the extent to which subjective ideological views on society and morality colour the policy process and also the extent to which self-interest rather than the interest of citizens determines the content of policy and the structure of power that determines its direction. It is, therefore, the subjective element of the policy process that will be placed in the foreground of this study, in order to view policy making and development from an alternative perspective.

Defining public policy

Policy making is an activity that seeks to generate order out of the chaos of both natural events and the unintended accidents that result from uncoordinated and self-interested human actions. James Anderson (1975: 3) succinctly defined the policy process as 'a purposive course of action followed by an actor or set of actors in dealing with a problem or matter of concern'. An essential feature of policy, as opposed to the wider issue of politics, is that it is about the planning, implementation, and consequences of deliberate efforts to resolve problems or seize opportunities affecting a country or a society, or, outside the realm of the public sector, a business or even a family. Policy involves attempts to rationally resolve conflict and politics can be defined as the study of conflict.

At the root of policy making is, therefore, the application of human rationality. Rationality should not, however, be identified with the search for an ideal truth and a commonality of ideas and behaviour. If everyone had exactly the same values in life there would be no need to study policy and indeed the idea of policy would be meaningless. A termite hill is full of the interacting beasties that are biologically programmed to take on specific roles within their colony and have little reasoning power to be able to diverge from the routines they have evolved over millions of years. Their genetic programming is to build a lasting and stable colony. The capacity for humans, and indeed some animals and birds, that have different objectives and wants from other members of their species, means that policy is shaped from the cooperation, struggles and compromises between self-conscious individuals with very different ideas as to what is important both to them and to others. Policy thus concerns the emotional intelligence that we learn to use in order to secure an acceptable standard of life to enable us to live and work together (Fischer 2009: 191–2). The seventeenth century philosopher Thomas Hobbes, following his experience of the English Civil War, argued that, although we might be said as humans to have rights to do as we please, if we use these rights without concern for others we will as individuals be in constant conflict with one another. As a consequence 'the life of man: (is) solitary, poore, nasty brutish and short' (Hobbes 1965: 65). Policy making is the element of the political, social and economic activity that seeks to prevent the chaos that could exist in society if we did not work together to plan how we should co-ordinate our activities. Bernard Crick (1962: 141) argued that politics 'is a way of ruling in divided societies without undue violence' but it is policy that ensures through deliberation that this may be achieved.

Whilst public policy is a political phenomenon it must not be simplistically seen as only the clearly legitimised output of governments as codified in legislation, official government papers or statements from political leaders. What is said by specific politicians or bureaucrats may not signify their real intentions and emotions. Many policy aims, especially those connected with personal self-interest such as the desire to reach the highest levels of political power, are frequently and for obvious strategic reasons, never stated. Hidden within the accretion of policy outcomes are often decisions that were once controversial but have now engrained in the values and actions of members of a civil society that they are not noticed as elements of public policy. There are also many levels of society connected with policy development and processes that simmer below the surface of civic society that can eventually boil over in volcanic eruptions of revolt against established policy decisions or the whole social order determining those who can advocate or as policy gate keepers steer the policy system.

The public element in public policy

Policy is developed by businesses, social groups and even in families but the analysis of public policy making is focused largely on how governments or sub-government agencies develop, refine, implement and validate their strategies. Some definitions of public policy, such as the widely quoted but all-encompassing statement by Thomas Dye (1995: 2), that it is 'what governments do, why they do it, and what difference it makes' are, therefore, rather wide of the mark. Certainly policy studies must consider governments' impact, but many dramatic political events are not in themselves policy decisions and many policies, however well planned, do not have the outcome that was intended.

> The First World War did not, in itself, begin as an act of policy. None of the combatant nations began 1914 with the policy intention that they would wage war on one another. Each had individual foreign policies that were the outcome of their deliberations on where the best interest of their nations lay in terms of alliances and defensive arrangements but when faced with a sudden diplomatic crisis these arrangements were so lacking in any harmony that the differences in policy led to an unplanned and unwanted conflict (Hobsbawm 1987: 322–4).
>
> In contrast the Second World War is arguably a consequence of policy, at least as far as Germany was concerned, as the National Socialist Government of Adolf Hitler established a strategy to increase the territorial boundaries of the German State. This consciously adopted policy may not have been developed with the ultimate aim of fighting wars but the consequences certainly led to the 1939 to 1945 conflict, at least in Europe (Bullock 1990: 525–6).

Public policy is concerned with the making and the outcome of deliberations by governments and government agencies. There are within private sector businesses or not for profit non-government organisations (NGOs) complex frameworks for making policy, which, in many respects, parallel the operations of public bodies. General Motors, Barclays Bank or the charity OXFAM must, just like the British government, devise policies in order to fulfil their objectives. The development of their policies follows the patterns of progression and can be analysed using the same models that are discussed in this study. In some respects, however, the study of business policy making or business strategy is a more simplistic process than that faced by a national government. Given that the prime goal for many private businesses is to make a profit, such organisations are not faced with the more complex task of balancing a range of aims and objectives, such as ensuring a growing economy whilst securing social equity, security for citizens and preservation of freedom.

Whilst governments forge public policy, they are not independent entities whose actions emanate from a closed circle of politicians and bureaucrats. Even the most centralised of autocracies are organisations shaped in their actions by the impact of the external world on their values and interests. Within open pluralist liberal democracies the actions of the government are a reflection of the interplay of an array of decision makers of whom many may not be public sector employees let alone be in the core executive of central government. The structure of a pluralist society is by definition composed of many centres of influence in relation to specific areas of human activity that are designed to support private rather than the general interest. The concerns of these agencies must be co-ordinated with the many other segments of society if they are to prosper. Privately owned businesses, for example, whilst not part of government, can have a major influence on public policy. The economist Milton Friedman argued that the only duty of a business manager is to make a profit for his or her shareholders and ensure they keep to the law and the established customs of the country in which they operate (Friedman 1970). This is an extraordinarily insular view of the role of business in policymaking as Friedman assumes that governments make laws and that law making is not the role of a business. A moment's reflection on the policy making process in the United States should reveal that multi-national businesses are constantly lobbying the Presidential Office or Congress for changes in the law to secure their interests and that businesses are a major source of funding to secure the election of Presidents and Congressmen.

> Decisions to repair the damage caused in 2008 by the failure of multi-national banks were not resolved solely by deliberations within the governments of the most industrialised states but emerged after intense discussion and debate between the chief executives of major banking houses and their national governments in order to forge a policy that could rescue the liquidity of world finance (Brown 2010: 50–66).

Apart from businesses there are a wide range of agencies that are neither privately nor publicly owned that help determine policies that affect us, the public. These include the many NGOs, sometimes referred to as third sector organisations, that are active in pluralist societies. Some of these bodies can be described as charities involved partly with the support of volunteers in altruistically raising funds to secure aid for the underprivileged, destitute or unprotected. Many interests represent members of professional or business organisations. An increasingly important influence on national governments are major global institutions of governance such as the United Nations or the International Monetary Fund. As shall be shown throughout this study, this is not a book solely about decision making within government but it is also about decision making that affects what governments and their public agencies decide.

The breadth and scope of policy as a concept

Public policy can be viewed as operating on a number of levels although in reality each level at its boundaries slowly merges into the next level. On the smallest scale, that can be termed the micro level, policy is concerned with techniques for resolving specific issues, for example, how to secure a balanced budget within a publicly owned hospital. It may at its widest, or macro, level be depicted as involving issues on a large and all-encompassing scale, such as global strategies to combat climate change. Both micro and macro level theories are constantly relevant to the study of public policy but the study may best be described as occupying a meso-level of analysis, which relates to the middle ground of social activity. As a study pitched at a micro level, policy making is not centrally concerned with small scale decision making. A policy must not be confused with any sort of decision no matter how trivial. Policy frequently involves decisions on complex issues that may engage the mobilisation of a range of agencies, public, private and voluntary as well as a commitment by individual citizens. If policies are to work as a whole, they must often encompass a considerable number of separate political decisions, many taken at a micro level. To be effective, these must be compatible with one another and closely interlinked. As a deliberate set of decisions a policy is not normally a spur of the moment intention but a strategy for action that may often evolve and change. Policies are decisions that are intended to guide action for the foreseeable future and can be visualised as containers in which are packed many smaller boxes of decision making which contribute to the policy as a whole.

> The decision made by the Coalition Government in Britain in 2013 to develop a high-speed rail network was a major and potentially very costly policy decision. It is also a decision that will involve over time many contributory policy decisions such as determining contracts for building the rolling stock or for a local community whether its members contest compulsory purchase orders for land.

At the opposite extreme, policy studies does not seek to develop over-arching macro-theory to explain and justify a whole range of social actions. As such, policy should not be confused with ideology even though, as is argued in this book, it can be greatly affected by ideological concerns. Many people, and in particular the movers and shakers of political action, have, at some time in their career, developed or attached themselves to an ideological view point that sets out the framework that guides the direction of their decision making. In normal political discourse, ideology is, however, differentiated from policy. Policy decisions, as opposed to ideological positions, relate to more specific problems that concern a particular issue. Ideology may guide the policy maker as to how they should deal with the problem, but an ideological position is a set of ideas that shape the values and preference of the decision maker and is not usually focused on a specific issue.

> Governments, with increasing urgency during the last twenty years, have to address how they are to fulfil the demands for energy within a state on a sustainable non-polluting basis. An ideologically 'deep green' political actor will address this policy very differently from a New Right ideologist who believes that economic market forces will ensure technology will be found to resolve the problem. Deep green ideology leads to a resolution of the problem through radical cutting back of our rate of consumption of the Earth's resources that may involve the promotion of much more austere life styles (Dobson 2007: 42–6). A New Right market orientated ideologist is likely, in contrast, to consider that there is no need to develop public policy on sustainability and they should continue to lavishly consume the Earth's resources to satisfy our personal needs and desires since the unfettered economic decisions of individuals will determine the best answers for all concerned.

Policy studies are concerned to develop theories on how such decisions are made and how they evolve once they are put into practice rather than being an explanatory narrative of how a specific policy came into being and its subsequent history. Many historical studies concentrate on a particular policy issue and dissect all aspects of how that policy came about or was implemented. Although regarded as a great, if controversial, study of history A. J. P. Taylor's (1969) account of the origins of the First World War is in a sense a meticulous analysis of how a number of governments chose the path to conflict. Taylor did not, however, ask in general how policy is made or attempt to build up theoretical generalisations on how policy develops or is evaluated. In contrast, Graham Allison (1971) analysed the history of the Cuban Missile Crisis, but through that study drew out general theoretical ideas about how policy is made during key periods of conflict between nations. Such a study is sometimes referred to as policy analysis. Within this envelope are divisions that have emerged as writers seek to discuss more specific activities within the policy process. These include policy implementation that studies how policies once formed and legitimated by government are put into practice. A further widely used sub-division is policy evaluation that considers how effective a policy may be in terms of its efficiency, its capacity to meet its objectives or, though less frequently, its ethical consequences. Other studies may also concentrate on how a policy emerges on to the political agenda, or analyse the institutional framework in which public policy is processed.

Public policy, given its association with government, is often classified in university syllabuses or publishers' lists of textbooks as a sub-division of the discipline of political studies. However, the content of policy decisions is not solely a matter of politics, that is the resolution of conflict, but will frequently be concerned with economic and social ideas and may often require an understanding of basic scientific and engineering matters. Indeed as will be discussed in the following chapter, early studies of policy were in part aimed at removing the awkward political element based on self-interest in decision making in the hope that dispassionate scientific rigour could be applied to the resolution of policy issues. However, as Michael Hill (2014: 4) observes 'suggestions for taking "politics" out of policy making disregard the fact that politics is much more than simply the interplay of politicians'. The study of public policy like most divisions within the social sciences, including politics, is inter-disciplinary in that it requires an understanding of the many functional divisions in the social sciences, and on occasion the humanities, through philosophy and ethics, as well as the physical sciences.

There is, however, a central political dimension in the study of public policy. Since policy making usually, but not necessarily, involves conflict and the necessity to make compromises within a society, the resultant outcome of such differences involves the resolution of power relationships within society. The distribution of power within any society is, however, based on the sociological arrangement and beliefs within a society. It is also related to the material resources held by individuals and groups and hence policy has within it an essential economic element. Related to these factors is an individual's knowledge and understanding to enable them to enforce their views on others or convince them of their ideas. However, within any study of the social sciences that is aimed at developing understanding that can achieve practical outcomes that shape society and as a consequence how we, as individuals, conduct our lives, it is also necessary to understand how we ought to behave as humans. As such, public policy must have a central concern with philosophical understanding and in particular the branch of philosophical discourse concerning ontology, that is the meaning of being and life, and hence the moral and ethical dimensions of how individuals should behave to each other and to the natural creation that surrounds them.

The structure of the book

This study differs from many texts on public policy by emphasising at its starting point that the central essence of public policy making is the expression of prevailing patterns of moral and ethical attitudes in society. Policy outcomes are the result of clashes between individuals and groups that have differing beliefs on how a social system ought to be organised and how, if at all, it ought to evolve. As shall be discussed in greater detail in the following chapter, education, particularly in Western culture, has become dominated by positivist modes of thought which require explanations of behaviour based on scientific paradigms of thinking that assume that the world we perceive is similar to that perceived by others. Even though we may consciously seek to deceive others for our own advantage, from a positive perspective, the world as it appears to us represents a universal truth. In contrast to this paradigm, this study begins with discussions on what may be termed, in contrast to the positivist stance, a subjectivist view, that is, a position in which we should not believe that the aims, hopes and objectives of individuals are any more valid and therefore true than those that are wholly opposed to them.

The grounding for this position will be developed in Chapters 2 and 3 and creates a rather different starting and finishing point to understanding public policy from many standard texts on the subject. It will emphasise that policies originate not from some problem that appears to be forced on a society from some external physical event or social movement, but from the capacities of individuals, often working uneasily with others, to put into practice their beliefs and motives for securing their self-imagined position within the society or societies that they feel is important to their well-being. These emotions and motives have for simplicity been divided into ideology (Chapter 4), that is systematic beliefs in the physical and social structure of society, then attitudes concerned with self-interest (Chapter 5), that is our concern to develop ourselves and those close to us and finally the role of ethics (Chapter 6), that is beliefs concerning how we ought to behave to one another. These passions may overlap but often can be imperatives that create serious dilemmas for individuals and group development. They create within societies what may broadly be termed their political culture, that is the sum total of how they may be characterised by conflict or by a dominant mode of thought and hence common attitudes to what may be seen as a policy problem or an opportunity for developments that require policy judgements. This groundwork for the origins of public policy is discussed in Chapter 7.

The development of the following chapters shifts its focus from considering the motives and beliefs that originate policy to the issue of power and the institutional, social and economic resources that enable certain groups to secure many of their social aims for their well-being. As a corollary many others may lack the capacity to secure what they may believe is their hopes for life and must accept subordinate positions in society that allow the policies of others to determine their experience. To a large extent this structuring of society in terms of securing policies that are beneficial or destructive is based, as discussed in Chapters 8 to 10, on the power relationships in any society and especially within nations and the apparatus for world governance. The first of these chapters reviews policy making systems in the many variants of autocratic and oligarchic states while Chapter 9 reviews the extent to which policy making in liberal democracies can also be viewed as in the main an oligarchic process. How far do individuals living in differing circumstances with unequal access to resources of wealth or knowledge and subjective understanding become subordinated to the success of small elites who develop their greater hold over resources of power to dominate policy making to secure their own interests? In this context, Chapters 9 and 10 discuss the extent to which liberal democracies that claim to operate the most ethical and equitable arrangements for society can in practice achieve these goals in contrast to more overtly autocratic societies. These chapters, therefore, critically review twentieth and twenty-first century positivist views on the working of liberal democracy and conclude that liberal democracies may be more liberal in terms of human rights and freedom than autocracies but many aspects of their policy making structures and behaviour are, in terms of democracy, not too far removed from autocratic practice.

Chapters 11 to 14 continue the debates on power, motives and policy through analysing the policy process. Chapter 11 considers how policy innovations originate and become an active issue on the agenda of governments. Integral to the practice of policy is also the issue of how far public policy can be evaluated, which is discussed in Chapter 12, given that most policies require evaluation as to their possible effectiveness before rather than after their implementation. The reality of policy advocacy is, however, rarely if ever a matter of scientific method and, in as much as it is rational, it is rational for some but by no means all in society. Politicians, it will be argued, in many cases are not concerned to scientifically evaluate in a dispassionate positivist manner policy outcomes rather than attempting to validate policies in the context of their self-interest and ideological values. The following chapter considers how policy ideas that have entered the purview of governance are refined and legitimated or, as is often the case, swept into the long grass. Chapter 14 then considers policy implementation and hence the fortunes of policies once they are legitimated and Chapter 15 continues this theme by discussing the cycles of evolution through which public policies progress or fade away. Following the discussion of the policy process, Chapter 16 considers how far and in what sense can any policy be said to have been a success or a failure. The penultimate chapter then analyses whether, on the basis of the discussion on policy attitudes and power, there is any possibility that we can craft better forms of understanding that may create more democratic and fair structures for public policy outcomes within a foreseeable future. The key area for debate is the claims of subjectivist writers that in theory at least it may be possible to develop through the acceptance of an ethical practice for discourse and discursive resolution of policy conflicts a more fair and humane approach to decision making. In the final chapter the central arguments of the book will be summed up in a conclusion.

2   The legacy of the 'scientific' origins of Policy Studies

How public policy should be developed and implemented will have been discussed as soon as societies began to emerge. Ancient Greek philosophers encompassed policy issues in their musings on politics. Aristotle observed, circa 333 BCE, that:

> Poverty is the cause of the defects of democracy. That is the reason why measures should be taken to ensure a permanent level of prosperity. This is in the interest of all classes, including the prosperous themselves; and therefore the proper policy is to accumulate any surplus revenue in a fund, and then to distribute this fund in block grants to the poor. The ideal method of distribution, if a sufficient fund can be accumulated, is to make such grants sufficient for the purchase of a plot of land: failing that, they should be large enough to start men in commerce or agriculture.
> (Aristotle, Barker 1946: 268–9)

Tradition and religious beliefs as well as common sense played a part in the structuring in the earliest times of organised human society of what could be regarded as public policy. Much of this discourse will have involved lessons drawn from what dominant members of a society thought they had experienced and also from the myths, legends and suppositions of how their society was created (see for example Beard 2015: 53–130). Public policy as a subject that is viewed as a sub-discipline within the extensive field of social studies has, however, relatively recent origins. Whilst some may argue that the earlier essays in the emerging field are now out of date and superseded and require but a passing acknowledgement, the development of policy studies is of interest as, despite considerable evolution in terms of depth and sophistication, much contemporary writing on the subject still bears an imprint of the ideas of the pioneers who popularised the subject area

The origins of policy analysis reflect the growth of social scientific thought that began in France in the thought of Saint-Simon and Comte and in Britain from Locke, Hume and Bentham. It was argued by the eighteenth century Scottish philosopher, historian and economist David Hume (1962: 125–30) that we may, with a high degree of certainty, regard some ideas to be factually true, from inference derived from the expectation that we can reason through repeated observation that an event will always happen following a preceding event, such as a billiard ball striking another ball leads both to move away from each other. Truth through mathematical proofs can also appear certain by the application of deductive logic. The capacity of humans to develop scientific theories of how the material world, and we as human beings, behave, is based on the application of logic and inference. Those who claim to develop their view of the world on this basis are using positivist thinking. Positivists argue that there is a physical world external to us that we can recognise and understand through our senses and rational interpretation using scientific thought. In contrast it has for a long time been realised that preferences, motives and emotions are not phenomena that can in any factual sense be regarded as either right or wrong. It may, of course, be a fact that someone has a preference to ignore all evidence about the impact of global warming on future generations, but whether they are morally right or wrong to think that cannot be subject to positivist scientific assessment. The eighteenth century Scottish philosopher David Hume argued preferences cannot be subject to being proven by either deductive or inferential logic as either good or bad:

> It is not contrary to reason to prefer the destruction of the whole world to the scratching of my finger. It is not contrary to reason for me to choose my total ruin, to prevent the least uneasiness to an Indian or person wholly unknown to me.
>
> (Hume 1962, 128)

Following the development of scientific methodology, many liberal theorists argued that the religious and metaphysical ideas that had developed a grounding for landed elites to dominate society should be replaced by an analysis of social development based on the methodology of the natural sciences. In as much as science could be applied to resolving problems such as disease or increasing wealth through harnessing new sources of energy such as steam or electricity, it could be possible to discern social principles for establishing a more efficient and rational arrangement for society. Psychology and economics in particular are widely studied as social sciences using this approach. A scientific methodology was deeply embedded in the minds of economists and more specifically those who leant towards mathematically based econometric analysis. In the early twentieth century leading economists such as John Maynard Keynes or Paul Samuelson argued that in this branch of social sciences proven policy decisions could be developed given the established acquisitive habits of commercialised man. It was a short step from economics, psychology and management theory to the application of scientific methodology to society as a whole to create social sciences in disciplines such as political studies. Some positivist thinkers may feel they have circumvented the problem of subjectivity by arguing that repeated observation of human behaviour shows that all rational people will act in predictable ways. In the 1930s an influential methodological practice termed behaviourism became fashionable, arguing that social studies should be based on evidence gained through observing the actions and environmental circumstances of individuals and, through interviews and questionnaires, how they thought about the world. The patterns of behaviour and thought could then be correlated with their situation within the environment and, using statistical techniques, the probability that an environmental factor was associated with social behaviour and beliefs could be revealed and then be subject to theoretical explanation.

By the late nineteenth and early twentieth century as politicians and bureaucrats became increasingly concerned about the efficiency and effectiveness of the output of government policy, the possibility of administrative, as opposed to political, science was given prominence in the United States and Britain. The academic Woodrow Wilson, later to become President of the United States, was a prominent campaigner for reforming what were widely seen to be corrupt political practices in state and federal government without undermining the liberty and republican ethos of the political system. Wilson (1887) argued that whilst the content of policy decisions was a subjective matter that was the province of politicians, the administration of these policies should be regarded as a science. Woodrow Wilson observed, rather dramatically, that:

> If I see a murderous fellow sharpening a knife, clearly I can borrow his way of sharpening the knife without borrowing his intention to commit murder with it; and so if I see a monarchist dyed in the wool managing a public bureau well, I can learn his business methods without changing one of my republican spots. He may serve his king; I will continue to serve the people; but I should like to serve my sovereign as well as his. By keeping this distinction in view, – that is, by studying administration as a means of putting our own policies into convenient practice as a means of making what is democratic politic towards all administratively possible towards each – we are on perfectly safe ground and can learn without error what foreign systems have to teach us.
>
> (Woodrow Wilson 1887: 200)

Writing in a climate of economic growth fuelled by scientific principles, Woodrow Wilson had little need to spell out his vision, as behind many of these developments lay the growing hegemony among professionals of the scientific method. These ideas were paralleled in the context of management by, for example, Henri Fayol whose major thoughts extolled the value of hierarchic corporate structure with each element in the pyramid having specialised tasks. In the United States, F.W. Taylor (1911) attempted to measure scientifically the conditions and practices of industrial workers that could secure the most efficient use of labour. By the 1930s in the United States and Britain, the application of social science was an important influence on the emerging interest of policy studies. There were influential schools of thought promoting public scientific management, of which Luther Gulick, an advisor on administrative efficiency to Franklin Roosevelt, was arguably the most prominent exponent. His ideas were based on the principles of:

- A separation between politics and administration
- Administration can be made into a science
- Principles of administration can be discovered that are analogous to physical laws
- These principles ensure how the goals of economy and efficiency are realised.

(Thomas 1978: 6)

Gulick, as a sound social scientist, did not see these principles as scientific in the strict sense of being a predictable set of rules such as in the disciplines of physics or chemistry but considered they were nevertheless the most rational means to guide the approach of policy makers. Whilst politicians may pronounce on the goals to be achieved based on un-testable value statements, the bureaucrat should as far as possible methodically seek the best strategies to fulfil the politicians' demands.

Simultaneously in Britain there developed a debate led largely by distinguished civil servants and politicians such as Richard, later Viscount, Haldane, concerning the extent to which there could be a science of administration that would enable public decision making to be conducted effectively and efficiently. Haldane was instrumental in 1922 in founding the Royal Institution for Public Administration and a year later the journal *Public Administration* which devoted most of its articles to issues that would now fall under the remit of public policy or public management. Followers of these ideas such as Lyndall Urwick, Oliver Sheldon or Josiah Stamp sought to establish what became referred to as organisation theory as a rational, if not wholly scientific methodology proposing templates through which management of decision making could arrive at efficient and practically applicable conclusions. These theories also had underlying moral aims that tended to differentiate each theorist. Stamp, for example, enlisted the enactment of Christian principles as a fundamental aim of organisation outcomes, whilst Haldane and Sheldon emphasised service to society and the state (Thomas 1978: 138–97). The movement favouring a theory of organisation was, however, to be gradually superseded by a more robust development of theories concerning public policy and private management.

Several writers (Parsons 1995: 18–20; Howlett and Ramesh 2003: 3; John 1998: 3; De Leon 2006: 39) place the pioneering work of Harold Lasswell as the starting point for policy studies as a new sub-discipline as opposed to a science of administration.

The United States polymath scholar Harold Lasswell (1902–1978) taught political studies prior to the Second World War at the University of Chicago and moved during the conflict to become Director of War Communications research at the United States Library of Congress. After 1945 he taught politics, largely based at Yale University. He showed a wide interest in the social sciences in general and psychology in particular and also in the development of systems theory approaches to social issues. His definition of political science as 'Who gets what, when and how' is still widely quoted.

During the 1940s Lasswell realised the importance of a multi-disciplinary approach to policy development and firmly popularised this idea in his many writings. Lasswell's theories were being devised within an optimistic culture that believed in the capacity of humans to resolve many of their problems by the application of scientific ideas. In many of his works on the subject he refers not so much to policy studies but to the possibility of policy sciences (Lasswell 1951: 4; Lerner and Lasswell 1951; Parsons 1995: 18–20). Although much influenced by the possibilities inherent in social sciences, Lasswell was also aware that both personal and ideological values motivated policy making but he believed this should not serve as a barrier to establishing systems and behaviours that could lead to better founded and effective policy decisions. He became after the 1940s an influential advocate for the development of a greater understanding of the policy process for the good of mankind, if not a science of policy development and analysis (Parsons 1995: 18–19). In his 1956 address to the American Political Studies Association, of which he was then the president, Lasswell urged the profession to become the policy scientists of democracy (Farr, Hacker and Kazee 2006: 580).

It is not too difficult to find examples of public policy decisions of vital importance to humanity that have been largely processed with relatively little controversy or the need for coercion. The elimination throughout the world of deadly diseases such as smallpox shows that, where there is near universal consensus among all nationalities and social groups within society, a serious problem can be solved by proven technology established by scientific research and evaluation that is easily affordable in terms of financial and manpower resources.

With the creation of globalised agencies such as the World Health Organization and the capacity of wealthy countries to provide aid and some expertise to poorer nations after 1945, several deadly and highly infectious diseases have been declared extinct. Similar procedures are now in use for the containment of the Ebola virus and much headway has been made towards the treatment of the complex grouping of AIDS viruses.

There are, however, relatively few policy problems which can be resolved that may fit the conditions that depend on widespread consensus on the policy aims and a clearly proven, affordable and effective means to secure policy goals. There is by no means consensus within mass society even on scientific evidence and many technological achievements are for some too expensive for them to be readily adopted in spite of the advantages they may bring. Most policies, however, are not contingent on technology but concern subjective issues on which aims and procedures are subject to serious conflict and are so complex they may have repercussions that are impossible to predict.

Simon and bounded rationality

After the Second World War, a new generation of writers concerned with ensuring efficient administrative practice began to debate the limits of rationality in policy making around the models and principles devised by theorists such as Gulick and Lasswell. Leading this field was a former student of Lasswell, Herbert A. Simon.

Simon (1916–2001) was born in Milwaukee, Illinois and was educated at the University of Chicago where he was tutored by, among others, Harold Lasswell. After obtaining his doctorate he subsequently taught and undertook research in a number of universities. Although having a wide range of interests from computer studies to psychology he was awarded the Nobel Prize for economics in 1978 largely for his work on decision making and policy.

Simon argued that in practice it would be impossible to reach completely rational solutions for determining the best methods to secure specific policy aims, given the complexity of most social, economic and political problems as a consequence of both procedural logical problems and psychological issues. The politicians and bureaucrats who must design policy have, argued Simon, neither the understanding, nor the time, nor the resources to follow a fully rational path. All we can do is to resolve a policy problem as rationally as possible by first clarifying the nature of the problem and then reviewing all possible policies that may resolve the issue.

Procedural issues concerning the development of policy first must be concerned not only with finding the 'means to an end' of resolving a problem but ensuring this is achieved as efficiently as possible from the choices known to the policy makers. To use Simon's example, we may want to build a bridge across a river but we also need to bring in issues of which design may be more economic or efficient. 'Rational decision making always requires the comparison of alternative means in terms of the respective ends to which these may lead' (Simon 1976: 65). A second issue is that pursuing one particular aim may compromise other values. Can the government attempt to reduce alcoholism through taxation by demanding that supermarkets raise the price of cheaply produced lager without offending people's right to freedom? A third procedural issue is that of setting priorities. If we spend billions of dollars on landing a man on the moon will this divert resources from goals such as finding a cure for all cancers? Moreover, the consequences of certain decisions cannot be revoked and may set in train changes in the environment and society that lead to the need for further decisions (Simon 1976: 62–6). Securing satisfactory decisions despite these problems also requires attention to three central tenets (Simon 1976: 240–4). First, decision makers must ensure that they or their agents have the required skills to complete a task. The efficient completion of a building, Simon argues, needs skilled bricklayers and it is essential for such a policy that training is given to those involved in this task. Secondly, the policy maker must be fully dedicated to the goal of efficiently undertaking a decision and needs to be focused on the goals of the whole organisation and not on his or her interest in their particular section of the business. Thirdly, the decision makers must ensure they are, as much as possible, fully informed about the situation with which they are dealing.

The psychological issues that undermine any semblance of complete scientific rationality present further reasons that undermine the capacity to create perfect policies. First, it is impossible to gain all the knowledge needed to resolve most complex problems and any novel application of ideas even in relatively simple circumstances can never be evaluated until a later date. Simon (1976: 80–109) was also aware of a string of failings given the way the human brain functions. We have a limited capacity to analyse a problem, in part, because there are serious limits to how far individuals can retain and then process complex data. We are also always making decisions within a specific organisational environment that are shaped by unquestioned habits and customs that will bias our attitude to factual data.

Since we lack intellectual resources and the time to make fully rational policy choices, it is necessary for decision makers to choose a more limited range of policy options for consideration. This is a process that Simon terms 'bounded rationality', in which, within our limited capacities, we seek to make decisions that seem to be the best possible under the circumstances of knowledge, resources and time. Thus:

> The individual can be rational in terms of the organization's goals only to the extent that he is able to pursue a particular course of action, he has a correct conception of the goal of the action, and he is correctly informed about the conditions surrounding his action.
>
> (Simon 1976: 241)

The final result is unlikely to be the perfect answer to the issue but one that, using Simon's (1997: 118) term, 'satisfices', that is, gives the best solution that can be achieved under practical limitations of knowledge, time and research capacities. Essentially Simon argues that, whilst policy can never be made with complete certainty, we can at least rationally pursue methods of policy development that are most likely to reach the best policy:

> The central concern of administrative theory is with the boundary between rational and non-rational aspects of human social behaviour. Administrative theory is

peculiarly the theory of intended and bounded rationality – of the behaviour of human beings who satisfice because they have not the wits to maximize.

(Simon 1976: xxviii; see also Simon 1997: 118)

What Simon's critique of the earlier theories on policy studies importantly reveals is that it is far from being a subject that can be regarded as a science, given its complexity and the subjective element of its content.

Muddling through

Many policy theorists were greatly influenced by Simon. Most do not deny the basic dichotomy between non-factual statements of value and the potential capacity through the application of deduction and induction to reach a correct means of achieving a specific aim. They do, however, differ in how far it may be possible to approach rational decision making structures and, more emphatically, the steps we need to take in order to develop the means to secure policy goals. An important critique of Simon's theory, developed by Charles E. Lindblom, was that in practice policy makers do not normally review all the options open to them as rationally as is possible. Policy makers instead review existing policies to ensure they can be adapted to new demands and circumstances. Lindblom argued that policy usually does not, at least in liberal democracies, change in revolutionary steps but through gradual incremental change to existing policies (Braybrooke and Lindblom 1963: 62–5). Organisations establish small scale reviews of the existing demands and problems related to a particular policy that cannot stretch to a wholesale intellectual sweep of the policy area. Lindblom's model is often termed as 'muddling through', in which policy advocates seek to resolve immediate pressing demands by taking small incremental steps to existing policies in the hope that they may to some degree alleviate the problem.

Whilst it is tempting to see Lindblom's earlier views on incrementalism as an opposing critique of the rational decision making of Simon, this is, as Hogwood and Gunn (1984: 60) and John (1998: 35) observe, rather misleading. Much of Simon's work is devoted to showing there are serious limits to the extent to which policy making could be undertaken in a rational manner. Simon's view of bounded rationality and satisficing and Lindblom's incrementalism are both responses to the general problems connected with the capacity of any collection of public bodies to review all possible solutions to complex problems. In as much as there is clear water between the two theorists, it relates to the extent to which policies can be subject to thorough review or are more susceptible to cost effective systems of policy refinement. In practice, governments adopt both strategies depending on the issue involved and their attitude towards the problem.

The incrementalist approach to policy making has been criticised as an essentially conservative theory in that it suggests that change is only possible through slow evolutionary steps. This objection sees Lindblom's early work as pursuing the eighteenth century Tory philosophy of Edmund Burke (1790) or in the twentieth century Michael Oakshott's (1962) objections to revolutionary change, since human beings could never estimate the consequences of root and branch reformism. This is, however, a mistaken view of Lindblom's ideological position as his later writing shows that he is far from a supporter of the inequalities within liberal democratic societies or of the view that market forces are the answer to solving social problems (Lindblom and Woodhouse 1993).

A further criticism of the incremental model is that from time to time organisations, both public and private, undertake radical reviews of policy. At the heart of such an objection is the issue of when a policy change can be regarded as more a revolutionary rather than an incremental change. Clearly it is impossible to set exact criteria in this context. However, regime change, such as the fall of the monarchy in Russia in 1917 and its replacement following civil war by the communist state led by Lenin, can hardly be seen as an incremental change. Revolutionary change is, nevertheless, in respect to more discreet policy changes within stable liberal democracies infrequent, but not impossible, as shall be discussed in later chapters.

One of the most influential attacks on the muddling through model was developed by Yehezkel Dror who has been a major advocate of following Lasswell's call for a better analytical framework to guide policy making. Incrementalism, argued Dror (1964: 154), is only possible in limited circumstances in which policy makers are in broad agreement and there is a high level of continuity in thinking regarding a problem and the available means to deal with the issue. Even in a highly stable nation such as the United States these conditions are not always present. Changes in values, as in the case of racial segregation, or new circumstances such as the economic slump that ushered in the New Deal policy of President Franklin Roosevelt, can result in radical changes in policy. Dror (1964) argues that the bounded rationality approach still had considerable merit and developed what became an eighteen-stage schema of factors that needed to be taken into account in the development of policy. Central to his ideas is that policy makers should take on board the issue of values in such a way that these normative decisions could be analysed as rationally as possible. Policy makers should consider a wide range of policies to deal with a pressing issue and estimate the pay offs and risks of specific approaches. Introducing evaluation in terms of what ought to be done would also involve more 'blue sky' thinking among policy analysts that could overcome the limitations of conservative incrementalism. Thought must also be given to the operationalisation of policy that would involve testing and monitoring ideas and learning through experience.

A further influential theory seeking to develop rationality in policy development is the mixed scanning model developed by Amitai Etzioni (1968: 282–8) which suggested that policy makers initially must review the range of most likely options necessary to solve a problem and then use more incrementalist detailed searches to refine and develop policy on the information made available by the earlier strategic view of possibilities. Etzioni illustrates the model through a military metaphor of commanders reviewing the field of battle to try to get an overview of enemy strength and the objectives of the forthcoming struggle and then passing orders to units in the field to work their way incrementally to their perceived objective. He also observes how weather forecasts survey the broad patterns of weather fronts before homing in on the details of the most influential elements of the overall picture, such as the potential development of a hurricane.

Systems theory and the policy process

Paralleling much of the debate on whether there could be a science of policy rather than simply attempts to muddle through were approaches to public policy that took their template from systems theory and functionalism. Many earlier studies of public policy, partly based on the ideal of developing a scientific approach to the subject, began to view the subject as a functional system in which the development of policy progressed as a consequence of pressures to resolve social problems placing demands on government who then responded by creating policy outputs. This was illustrated in the 1950s by David Easton's seminal model of the functions of a political system which became an important structural element in the image of the political process and more especially policy development as illustrated in Figure 2.1.

The model does, however, have serious limit actions especially concerning what goes on within, what detractors termed the 'black box' at the centre of the decision making model that is the government. The original portrayal of the political system is moreover very simplistic and has been further refined by later theorists. Bill Jenkins argues 'that public policy is best understood by considering the operation of a political system in its environment and examining how such a system maintains itself and changes over time' (Jenkins 1978: 21).

The development of policy analysis also coincided with a now seldom credited view of social sciences, functional theory, which, taking a biological analogy, suggested that for a system to operate as a whole an organisation needs to perform a number of functions that can form the identifiable bases for understanding the whole system. Systemising the flow of policy led to attempts to understand the policy process as a cycle of functions that were too often taken to be seen as consecutive stages. Harold Lasswell (1971) is often seen as initiating this approach (Jenkins 1978: 16; De Leon 1999: 20), nominating seven stages in a decision making process as:

- Intelligence
- Promotion
- Prescription
- Invocation
- Application
- Termination
- Appraisal.

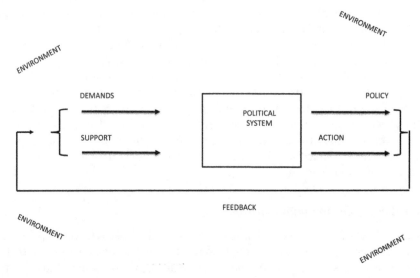

Figure 2.1 Easton's political system
(Adapted from Easton 1965: 32)

This functional approach, more than the Easton style systems models, became an important structuring resource for some subsequent studies of public policy. Hogwood and Gunn (1984: 4), for example, developed the following list which they used to discuss the elements of the policy process in the remainder of their text:

- Deciding to decide (issue search or agenda setting)
- Deciding how to decide (issue filtration)
- Issue definition
- Forecasting
- Setting objectives and priorities
- Options analysis
- Policy implementation, monitoring and control
- Evaluation and review
- Policy maintenance, succession or termination.

The exercise of identifying stages in policy making is now unfashionable as it was realised that policy development is far from being a linear consecutive process. Peter John (1998: 22–7) and Hal Colebatch (2002: 126) argue that many of the stages that were identified in the policy cycle do not develop in sequence but are an ever present consideration throughout many, if not all, stages of the policy process. Sabatier and Jenkins-Smith's (1993) Advocacy Coalitions Framework (ACF) also implies that policy formation is more complex than is depicted by diagrams that suggested a flow of policy ideas. Evaluation of the effectiveness of policy is, for example, usually undertaken during the tabling and refinement of emerging policies given that suggested ideas are rarely proposed by policy advocates, let alone undertaken by governments, without considerable research to ascertain whether they are workable and a better alternative to existing conditions or alternative suggestions. Government ministers and senior civil servants would be feeble minded creatures if they did not think through the problems that might allow citizens to circumvent their policies and, thus, build into their strategies arrangements that anticipate how the policy might be put into practice.

> The first Government of Mrs Thatcher naively thought that local government would at their command follow their preferred policies of cutting public expenditure but, in the early 1980s, they found their attempts to get local authorities to spend less were constantly thwarted. They later began carefully drawing up legislation that was far more watertight in ensuring that local governments would obey the government even to the extent of forcing local authorities to collect the widely reviled poll tax (Chandler 2007: 244–46).

To be fair to the proponents of the stages model, Jenkins (1978: 16) and Hogwood and Gunn (1984: 4) for example observe that the stages in their models did not necessarily follow one another in a chronological order rather than occurring simultaneously. 'This list is not intended as a straightforward description of what actually happens to every issue; rather it is a framework for organizing our understanding of what happens' (Hogwood and Gunn 1984: 4). It is difficult to escape using idealised descriptions of any social process, if we are to untangle the many strands of actions, institutional structures and thoughts and motives that compose complex social systems. The abstraction of a policy cycle that can be divided into functions is not in itself untenable and can form a useful framework to help facilitate description and understanding of the policy process. Policies do have a beginning when social and environmental circumstances evolve to create a problem or opportunity for public action to be taken and pass through identifiable processes before their adoption or termination. It is possible to discern functions within civil society that determine what is to be viewed as a policy problem of sufficient weight that it must be recognised as such by government. Governments have a function in bringing together potential answers to issues that become part of their active agenda. These include activities such as evaluation and validation of policy ideas and securing the legitimation of a fully fledged policy proposal. Once a policy has been legitimised, public or private organisations dependent on its edicts have the function of ensuring the policy is implemented and also, in many cases, reviewing whether it is successful in meeting the government's aims. This period of evaluation may then lead to renewed demands for further policy ideas that may feed back into the machinery of policy development in order to either keep the policy on the track intended by a government or, especially if governments change, to terminate an initiative and replace it with a radically different idea.

It is, however, possible to take such models of the policy process too far as a particularly useful explanatory device for modelling how in practice the policy is made and evolves. The tendency to see the issue of policy in this way has generated and continues to generate rather too many systemic charts of the specific functions or inputs into a system of government that may illustrate the institution or pressures or sequences that can be used to describe the process. In practice these attempts at best establish categories that can be used to describe in a simplified way the policy process without giving sufficient attention to policy content and emotional attitudes and the sources of power that make public policy a real issue in citizens' lives.

Subjective behaviour: the elephant in the room

The most intractable disqualification of policy studies becoming a science is the problem that, as discussed in the introduction, decisions are usually founded on the subjective beliefs of policy advocates. Few policies are such that there are widely agreed solutions to a policy problem, given that, if there is widespread consensus on an issue, it will have long since not been viewed as an active problem but become one of the many often unrealised assumptions about how we should behave. Relatively little is said however about the policy content or the motives of those who promote policy even though policy is for political actors in essence not about procedures but about its content. All too frequently many policy theorists suggest that as subjective values of individuals are not rational, at least in the scientific sense of being preferences incapable of being found to be true or false, policy analysis must omit consideration of these elements. Public policy can be theorised and its development improved by studying how a policy problem, once it is clearly defined by a government, can be resolved so that the policy aims of the government can be achieved in practice. Simon states in an afterword to the last edition of *Administrative Behaviour* that:

> We can summarize the conclusions we have reached with respect to a science of administration. In the first place, an administrative science, like any science, is concerned with purely factual statements. There is no place for ethical assertions in

the body of a science. Whenever ethical statements do occur, they can be separated into two parts, one factual and one ethical and only the former has any relevance to science.

(Simon 1997: 360)

Such an approach remains engrained in much of the present writing on public policy. Knill and Tosun (2012: 3), for example, observe that in their study 'we adopt a positivist approach ... because in our view it is most suitable for attaining descriptive knowledge of the real world and therefore shedding light on causal mechanism'. The tendency of many studies on public policy is to omit any subjective consideration of the content of policy but to concentrate on seeking to explain how public policy is processed. In many earlier studies this project was based around breaking up the procedure into manageable chunks of consecutive policy stages.

A further element in this descriptive analysis of the policy system is the hope that, as Lasswell or Simon suggest, given a particular policy problem, the operation of the policy system could ensure that the difficulty was resolved by the most efficient and effective means possible at each stage in the policy process from the numerous alternatives open to discussion. Policy evaluation and the measure of its success was thus based on assessing whether the outcome of the policy actually approximated to the practice of the policy solution within society without causing any substantial collateral damage (Etzioni 1964: 4). The actual content of the policy in terms of whether it was ethical it was not, as a subjective issue, possible to question, given that from a positivist perspective matters of feeling and opinion were not open to scientific judgement.

A second more modern trend is to see policy development not so much as a set of processes and the product of conflict within society as differing interests struggling or at times working in alliance with one another to ensure that their chosen policies are legitimated and widely accepted within the political system. As shall be discussed in later chapters much of this work is based on the development of theories of the liberal democratic state concerning the extent to which policy is formed and accepted through the trade-offs and also coincidence of mutual concerns between organised coalitions of interest groups within open pluralist societies. Policy, therefore, tends to evolve in fits and starts to resolve the problems faced by any society through, in liberal democracies, discourse between the many organisations and individuals interested in the issue to secure the best policy outcomes for the good of society. However, this largely positivist discussion of the operations of liberal democracy in resolving policy content lacks much of an ethical edge that questions how far the policy content that is produced by such activity is at all equitable or desirable for humanity as a whole or determined in a wholly democratic manner. It may be argued that there are individuals who have rather personal and not universally admired motives but in liberal democracies the power of public opinion ensures that such individual ideas are never fulfilled and that the will of the majority dominates. However, as shall be discussed later in this study we cannot presume that liberal democracies ensure that all citizens have an equal voice in determining policy. In practice policy making in liberal democracies such as Britain, France or the United States is made predominantly in small autocratic conclaves in which certain well-resourced and favoured interests dominate the setting of the agenda. It will be argued within this study that debate and conflict concerning policy content should be seen as the starting point of policy development and indeed is one of the most central *raisons d'être* for policy. As such it is policy content both in terms of its publicly communicated aims and also the privately held aims of its advocates that should be seen as the defining issue that determines the structure and processes of policy development and its outcomes for the lives of citizens.

Conclusion

This chapter has sketched the development of public policy as an academic discipline in the twentieth century, and shown through the analysis of Simon, Lindblom and Dror that the subject cannot be fully understood as a science of administration that can provide predictable and rational answers to policy problems. A consequence of this reasoning has been that in its origins the study of public policy was seen as largely an analysis of the process by which policy was developed rather than what formed the content of policy. This tendency has been attenuated by many more recent theories on policy but it has nevertheless left a legacy on how the subject is discussed by theorists as a positivist if not wholly scientific study that has the starting point and, for some, an end point in the processes through which policy emerges from its social and ethical context and is then refined to become the institutionalised political decisions by the state that are then subsequently implemented and evaluated only to be often restructured and further refined or abandoned in practice. Within this framework it is possible to develop some ideas on how the development of a policy may progress, given a specific aim among policy makers, through bounded judgements, a measure of luck and a preparedness to stop digging further into the pits created by a failing policy. However, such an approach omits serious discussion of the subjective content of public policy and the motives that are vital to its creation and development.

3   Subjective approaches

The preceding chapter has shown that most policy issues are too complex to be solved simply by a scientific approach. The aims and content of any policy are largely subjective, that is statements on the feelings and motives of individuals as opposed to positivist statements that the universe appears and operates exactly how everyone perceives it. In this chapter it is argued that although the use of positivist thought can at best only partially explain the policy process let alone its content, this does not mean that it is impossible to rationally understand public policy. Subjective ideas may be described and classified and, if not firmly felt by everyone, are not impossible to understand. They are, moreover, established as will be shown below on the basis of rational thought.

The rational basis of subjective values

It is pointed out in the preceding chapter that scientific thought involves aspects of rational thought but is far from being the only process that determines how we use reason. Policy making can never be logical since individuals have differing likes and wants and hence aspirations towards different goals in life. Hume's argument that moral judgements are statements of preferences and can never as such be given a justification grounded on logic or observable fact was, in the nineteenth century, accepted by Utilitarian philosophers such as Jeremy Bentham (see Parekh 1973) and John Stuart Mill (1861) and in the twentieth century reinforced in many philosophical studies by positivist thinkers such as Wittgenstein (1958), Karl Popper (1957) or A. J. Ayer (1936) who is credited by Simon (1997: 55–6) as a major influence for his critique of a science of policy.

Policy can, nevertheless, be argued to be based on rational ideas to achieve desired mutual aims and it is essential to explain what rationality entails, at least for the arguments advanced here. Rational thought relates to our capacity to use our facility to reason to justify what we should believe, including how we, and others, should act. As such rationality should not be confined only to thinking that requires us to use 'logic' or 'inference' and hence positivist scientific methodology to develop our ideas, and we can, as Simon observes, discuss rationality in various contexts. 'A decision may be called "objectively" rational if *in fact* it is the correct behaviour for maximizing given values in a given situation. It is "subjectively" rational if it maximizes attainment relative to the actual knowledge of the subject' (Simon 1997: 85). We develop by a rational process many ideas and preferences that are peculiar to ourselves, although they may be shared and appreciated by others. These include moral choices on how far we should do all we can to help others or satisfy our own interests.

A central issue for any social theorist, and this includes policy analysts, is how, if at all, we can, in the sense outlined above, rationally seek to understand subjective variables. We cannot escape the problems of uncertainty by simply refusing to make policy decisions. When faced with a challenge, to do nothing may in itself be a policy decision. It would, moreover, be highly irrational to attempt to resolve a policy problem by selecting a number of random ideas and piecing these together to make a policy. Policy making is a task that is laid upon us as rational human beings. Rationality is the development and acceptance of ideas based on evidence and/or theory which, although in many cases may not be subject to proof, can help us to achieve our desires, that ideally, for many, are in harmony and agreement, with others. It therefore makes sense to use evidence and understanding of our desires to try to attain the most rational answers to policy issues that circumstances and time permit. Indeed human civilisation is founded and sustained by our capacity to develop rational forms of behaviour and institutions that ensure we are not living in a chaotic world of conflict as shown in Hobbes' nightmare scenario of society governed solely by self-interest.

Policy ideas it may be argued stem from creations in the mind of policy makers. They are reflections of the social environment and genetic make up of the policy activist as they are perceived by individuals to create problems or opportunities for themselves and whoever or whatever they care about. They are the starting point of any policy which cannot exist without being a set of thoughts and impulses generated within our minds. Without such ideas, the formal institutional framework and the informal networks of associations needed to forward policy would have no relevance or meaning. Since policy must have some content, even if it is to do nothing in the face of some problem, and policies must also encapsulate the motives and beliefs of individuals, it is necessary to consider how we can make appropriate rational judgements that cannot in any logical sense be regarded as right or wrong.

The broad term 'subjectivism' can encapsulate a wide range of positions that have been used to theorise our perceptions of the world. At the further shores of subjectivism is a view that the external world is a product of an individual's thought and that it is possible for all individuals to perceive the world very differently from one another. Few thinkers adopt the viewpoint that there is no external reality, although many such as Plato and Descartes have speculated about whether this is a possibility. Most broadly subjectivist thinkers such as the idealist philosopher Immanuel Kant or contemporary theorists such as Jürgen Habermas, Pierre Bourdieu or Roy Bashkar argue from differing perspectives that there is probably a fixed reality external to us but much of this cannot be clearly revealed by our senses and experiences.

The extent to which subjective values pervade the development of public policy may be demonstrated if we analyse the nature of what is seen as a policy problem. Many studies of public policy see the process as a means through which policy is developed in order to overcome a problem in society although it may be pointed out in passing that many policy proposals are not necessarily seeking to resolve some negative problem but, for their advocates, are hoping to take advantage of an opportunity. This may be, for example, developing greater efficiency in tax collection following advances in information technology. Whether there is seen to be either a problem requiring a resolution or an advantage to be gained from any policy proposal may be founded on some factual understanding gained from logic and experience but will, in all cases, also depend on the personal preference of those who either support, oppose, or are indifferent to the idea. Moreover, even policy problems that appear to be widely accepted may not be experienced and acted on in the same way by policy advocates.

Everyone wants on the surface to bring an end to the outbreaks of deadly diseases such as Ebola but to achieve this aim there are many factors that motivate individuals as regards how it may be achieved. Some altruistic individuals put their lives at risk to visit the countries where the disease is endemic to work in hospitals to nurse those brought low by the virus. Others, such as investors in pharmaceutical businesses, may pursue the aim of eliminating the problem by developing vaccines against Ebola in order to make a profit for their company and employment for themselves. Indeed for some the upsurge in the malady is not a problem but an opportunity to expand their wealth as well as gaining praise and a sense of fulfilment through their scientific vocation.

Given that the elimination of a disease may on the surface be a widely held aim, but nevertheless may harbour very different motives, more widely disputed issues will contain even greater nuances of subjective attitudes that may determine how these issues are problematised in as much as they are seen as a problem at all.

The policy by the Blair Government to ban fox hunting was successfully put into law because of its many interpretations of the importance of and need for this legislation. For Prime Minister Tony Blair (2010: 304–6) it was largely seen as a means to clear from his policy agenda an issue in which he had little interest both to satisfy backbench supporters of a ban on hunting with hounds and to appease the supporters of hunting. The pro-hunting lobby realised that the wording of the legislation was such that it was difficult to interpret what exactly might constitute hunting with hounds whilst the supporters of a ban were supporting the idea from a mixed variety of sentiments including a dislike of the hunting upper classes or sympathy for telegenic furry wildlife.

For many key decision makers resolving policy problems is not so much concerned with a policy in itself but a wider concern to ensure that they can retain power in the face of pressures from their potential supporters. As a consequence of the differing views as to whether there is a policy problem, there are also many answers as to how the problem should be resolved. Very rarely, if at all, can the content of a policy initiative have the same meaning to every individual who is aware of the proposal. Moreover, the many perceptions of what a policy means will frequently change for each individual with the passage of time and the arrival of new circumstances that impinge on its content.

The weasel world of language

A broadly based position within the subjective genre is that language is a crucial concern for any attempt to gain some understanding of the world, let alone to communicate our vision to others. For such writers, how we use language is the key to epistemology, that is a theory of knowledge. What we claim to be our knowledge of the world and our understanding of other people's ideas are predominantly transmitted through language. This creates serious epistemological problems. If language is subjective, even if we are speaking the same language, do you mean the same thing or view the same world as others?

> Does the colour 'grey' look the same and mean the same for everyone or, with more relevance to policy, does the term 'democracy' for example mean the same as it does for everyone using the English language?

This question was posed in the early twentieth century by Ludwig Wittgenstein (1958) and has become a central issue both in positivist and subjective theory. It is now widely accepted that words cannot over time be argued to have a definitive meaning. This is in part because they evolve in popular culture to have differing meanings from earlier usages. For older generations of English speakers an 'icon' referred to Russian religious paintings usually on wooden panels, and not, as is the case today, any cultural product such as a building or song that is widely regarded as both famous or typical of its makers. 'Ultimate' similarly meant chronologically the last or furthest occurrence of an object or action rather than its present use to label an object or performance as the best.

Not only does the meaning of words change, they may also have quite different meanings in different contexts. Wittgenstein (1958: 32–6) pointed out how a word like 'games' is impossible to define succinctly as it can be used to describe a range of human activities from organised sports such as a major league football match to a simple pastime for a child like throwing a ball at a wall and catching it. The meaning of a word is determined as much by the context in which it is used as any formal ascription of meaning in a dictionary. We generally understand the difference between someone saying 'I am going to the football game tomorrow' and an irate comment, 'what game do you think you are playing' from a person who doubts the stated motives and integrity of a rival to his policy proposals.

Where some subjectivist writers may part company with positivism is to argue that how words are used within any context also determines how people view the world and react to others as a consequence of their interpretation of words. In his earlier writing, the French post-modernist writer Michel Foucault (see Smart 2002: 19–26) observed how individuals regarded as mentally ill were treated as largely unconstrained individuals, then as criminals subject to imprisonment and later as individuals who were subjected to surveillance by authority. The idea of madness, as such, not only changed but this also determined the position in society of individuals thought to be mad. Reality is, therefore, at any time a construction of relationships of power, and is likely to change for many inexplicable reasons and hence it can be inferred policy is a highly capricious statement of power relationships that is almost impossible to explain.

> It has become commonplace in the last few years in the current British news-media to use the term 'tax payers' money' to refer to resourcing government policies. For example, a commentator on the increase in expenditure on two new aircraft carriers being built for the Royal Navy suggests that this is not providing 'tax payers with a sound return for their money'. Even if we leave aside the question of how much of a government's expenditure is derived from taxation, such a use of the term 'tax payers'

in this context can be subject to a number of connotations in respect to the nature of government. The comment can be read that the government is not using taxable income efficiently and perhaps that tax payers will need to pay more than they need for the policy to be implemented. However, it also suggests that those who do not pay tax or receive more income from the government than they pay in indirect taxation, for example the unemployed, those on low wages or students, should not be considered as having a concern for the issue of national defence. Such usage commodifies government as a provider from which we purchase services rather than an ethically based institution to protect all its citizens and ensure basic rights and a fair distribution of wealth and opportunities.

At an extreme end of this subjectivist position, when dealing with a complex social picture there develop so many complexities in our imagination that individual views of the world are inconsistent and there is no way of assuring ourselves as to what the truth may be. The French post-modernist theorist Jacques Derrida maintained that in consequence there can be no truths other than a multitude of truths in regard to any understanding of social phenomena (Drolet 2004: 23). Such a view suggests that policy statements are positions that have different meanings to individuals and cannot be seen to have any definite meaning in relation to the external world. In order to understand some of these meanings it is necessary for followers of Derrida to engage in a process of critical reconstruction that would review the possible implications and motives within policy statements. An interesting consequence of Derrida's argument is that any decision, and hence policy, is unwise or even an exercise in madness as it is inevitably a step into the unknown (Reynolds 2004: 47–8). There are many possible decisions that could be relevant to determining a policy and given that a choice must be made and can never be wholly obvious, the policy maker is always making an 'undecidable leap beyond all prior preparations for the decision' (Reynolds 2004: 47).

By no means all critical social theorists accept the rather bleak and potentially anarchic position of Derrida. The importance of language in our understanding and subsequent behaviour that had stemmed from Wittgenstein's philosophy was further developed by members of what came to be called the Frankfurt School of critical thought under the direction of theorists such as Theodore Adorno and later Jürgen Habermas. Critical theorists such as Habermas generally accepted that language is interpreted subjectively but argued that this does not mean that we are necessarily imprisoned in our own thoughts (Habermas 2001: 144–50). Since we communicate with others through language there exists an element of common understanding and commonality in language. Craig Calhoun (1995: 50) sums up this approach by observing that 'People are not self-identical in any simple sense because each is constituted as a person in relation to others and through participation in more or less impersonal but social processes such as language'.

The critical realist tradition that descends from Kantian philosophy provides a more workable view of the juxtaposition between subjectivist and positivist theory in terms of the use of language. Habermas consciously follows a moral position that emerged with the European enlightenment in the seventeenth century when social and political thinkers began arguing that rational thought was possible and could lead to a universal understanding of how the universe was created, organised and operated. This possibility is however difficult to achieve, especially in areas such as ethics and aesthetics.

Society is riven by a multitude of differences between groups characterised in numerous ways. People's moral ideas and tastes may differ because of nationality and national characteristics. Socialists also argue that class, defined in terms of economic relationships or cultural behaviour, creates major differences between people. A concern of post-modern and critical social theorists is to determine what constitutes such differences, how far they can be reconciled and for ethical theory, whether they ought to be reconciled. There are several approaches to these problems that have major implications to the structure of society. If a deep and comprehensive understanding between individuals is the key to an effective society, it may be argued that groups with similar cultural values should develop separately from one another, as for example independent nations, or as separate classes. However, exclusivity creates huge differences between and within nations and also the creation of what many may argue to be immoral ethical disparities in living standards and life chances. How far, therefore, ought there to be dialogue and the means to secure meaningful understanding between different groups? These issues will be revisited in later chapters but it is necessary at this stage to consider how critical theorists consider policy making may be developed and shaped within the context of a differentiated society.

Interpretive understanding

Emphasis on public policy as a subjective process is inherent in theories of interpretive methodology which seeks in the social sciences to understand the complex meanings that attach to social behaviour and emotions and the resultant institutions and customs. As a consequence the interpretive approach eschews analysis through the construction of models of social behaviour and institutional structures rather than trying to understand the social meanings that create a constantly changing social structure. Such an approach develops an insight into how we can understand how policy changes over time through seeking to develop narratives that provide a satisfying and convincing story of the developmental history of political and social phenomena. The approach is, moreover, not simply confined to the analysis of the meaning of words but can be applied to the meaning given to concrete objects such as architecture (Yanow 1995). Pursuing the evolution of social systems thus requires the development of narratives, that is bringing an understanding of the meaning of subjective ideas to construct explanations or better still stories that underlie institutional and cultural behaviour. As Bevir and Rhodes (2003: 25) observe:

> Our concept of a narrative points to the need to decentre institutions and practices. By so doing, narratives reveal the diversity of beliefs and traditions on which institutions rest. They also show the contingent and changing nature of institutions as they are constantly recreated through particular action.

As with many classifications of methodological and ontological approaches to society, interpretive analysis has been defined in rather different ways by differing theorists. Indeed such a tendency underlines one of the central points of the subjectivist contention, that the same word may have different meanings for individuals and can conjure up different emotions and actions. At one extreme the idea may cover all approaches to subjective analysis and, for example, include phenomenological thought that regards all our actions as mind games as opposed to reality. In this study, however, following the current use of interpretive methodology within much recent policy and political studies material, the approach may be regarded as one which corresponds with positivist evidence where there is a clear place for such beliefs within any social narrative (Bevir and Rhodes 2006: 29). As Dvora Yanow (2000: 5) observes:

> Interpretive methods are based on the presupposition that we live in a social world characterized by the possibilities of multiple interpretations. In this world there are no 'brute data' whose meaning is beyond dispute. Dispassionate, rigorous science is possible – but not the neutral, objective science stipulated by traditional analytical methods (as represented by the scientific method). As living requires sensemaking and sensemaking entails interpretation, so too does policy analysis.

As a methodology this approach does however raise a number of questions in terms of developing widely accepted understanding of the explanation for policy and the policy process. Developing narratives of social phenomena, even if the 'facts' of the case may appear to be beyond dispute by observers, can lead to a number of differing but plausible stories. The technique, therefore, requires an inductive process of analysis using coherent evidence based on theoretical constructs from data concerning observation of human behaviour in similar circumstances.

Subjective classifications

The use of subjective categorisation of the forms and processes within policy making has been a significant element in the earlier approaches to public policy analysis even within the writings of the most enthusiastic proponents of developing a policy science, such as Lasswell. This is embedded largely in the classification of processes and outputs in the policy process that are necessary to divide the subject area up into bite-sized components that can help provide a model for how a complex and inter-related system can work. There is considerable value and indeed necessity for such a classificatory approach. However, for many theorists, the subjective nature of this activity is not sufficiently realised and given a concern to avoid what was more obviously subjective emotional debate on ideology or ethics they began to embed much of the writing on the area in increasingly limited illustrations of organisational and functional structuring of the policy process, to the detriment of concern for content. Attempts at classifying the stages of the policy process were frequent within the earlier years of the study and by the 1950s many studies adopted a functional stages approach to creating the chapters of textbooks on the subject area.

Classifying output and content

The subjective elements of public policies may have an underlying role in creating a problem in this context since many of the motives that drive policy decisions are inextricably mixed both between groups advocating and opposing policy change or even within the minds of individuals concerned with public policy development. Attempts were developed in the 1960s and 1970s to classify policy with some regard to content by relating the form of political conflict arising from policy ideas. Theodore Lowi put forward a classification of policy types on the basis of the view that 'policies determine politics' (Lowi 1972: 299) and that politics provides different routes through which citizens may be coerced within a state to accept policy. Policy can be enforced by directly impinging on the behaviour of individuals by sanctions if they do not comply with a demand, whilst others can be controlled by the manipulation of general rules, such as the levels of taxes on income or sales. Moreover, such actions may be secured by rather remote means such as operating a marketing strategy to ensure the implementation of the policy or by immediate intervention through direct contact with the individual by, for example, imposing fines for improper conduct. Lowi considered that the juxtaposition of these variables creates a different system of politics which as outlined in Table 3.1 creates four modes of policy: distributive, constituent, regulative and redistributive.

A not dissimilar and rather simpler classificatory framework developed by James Q. Wilson (1989) is based on the assumption that the politics of policy development concerns the issue of who feels they are gaining or losing by a policy. He develops a matrix around the extent to which the benefits and the costs of a policy are concentrated on the lives of specific groups in society or, like the British National Health Service, available to all. Where both the costs and benefits of a policy are concentrated, politics is a battle between the gaining and losing interests but where the costs are concentrated but the benefits are diffuse, politics for Wilson is entrepreneurial.

A not dissimilar set of distinctions can be derived from the neo-Marxist perspectives of, for example, James O'Conner (1973) concerning the role of the state in developing potentially conflicting areas of policy content between the need to create capital through production and to provide redistributive welfare payments to ensure that those who produce have the health and living condition to remain loyal to the state and capable of producing output. These may also be linked to theories from Claus Offe (1984) on the tensions with the state and civil society on how to manage both redistributive and productive roles of the state.

There are, as with most classifications of social phenomena, objections to these models on the grounds of the lack of clear definition and overlapping nature of their parameters. They may also be criticised from a subjective position for their assumption that politics is for all individuals a coercive process rather than being a means in which many individuals recognise that they must make sacrifices and lose a certain degree of personal freedom in order to ensure compliance with ethical principles of fairness and their dependence on cohesion within society as opposed to conflict and individualism. Coercion it may be argued is necessary to ensure the individuals who feel they are

Table 3.1 Lowi's policy typology: Types of coercion, types of policy and types of politics

Likelihood of coercion	Applicability of coercion	
	Individual conduct decentralised, local	*Environment of conduct centralised, 'systems' level*
Remote	Distributive policy (e.g. Tory 19th century land policies, tariffs and subsidies)	Constituent policy (e.g. Setting up a new agency, propaganda)
Immediate	Regulative policy (e.g. elimination of sub-standard goods, unfair competition, fraudulent advertising)	Redistributive policy (e.g. progressive income tax, social security)

Source: Adapted from Lowi 1972: 300.

losers in a policy arrangement conform to the policy, but it is as much the consent of the many to a policy rather than the dissent of a few that secures its development. Wilson's classification is also oblivious to the wider subjective values behind many policies that may not be providing any material gains or losses in terms of resources for citizens but are matters of cultural belief such as arguments over women's rights or religious practice.

The structuring of policy content or the policy process requires at least some serious attention to the motives of policy advocates although it is by no means simple to identify subjective values with any clarity. As in the case of developing a classificatory framework for the policy process as a sequence of events, it is impossible to clearly abstract one type of motive from another in regard to an individual's thoughts and feelings. This is even more the case with determining, as observed earlier in this chapter, the reasons why a policy is adopted and how it is shaped by a policy actor, given that there may be several very different motives involved in their advocacy. These can for example be a mix of ideas that they believe if adopted may promote the common good, but also motives to gain greater standing in their society if they are recognised as being the central player in bringing the policy to fruition and these values may also be curbed or advanced with reference to their ethical preferences. There are within the domain of social psychology many attempts to define and understand the motives and emotions to which we may be subject. The well known Maslow (1970) pyramid of self-realisation in which we begin by seeking food and shelter in order to preserve our lives and then seeking love, self-esteem and finally self-awareness still has much relevance to the policy of the individuals. A more recent framework for determining the basic drivers of motivation developed by Susan Fiske (2010: 14–26) provides a useful starting point for this analysis of public policy by emphasising that a key concern for almost all human beings is to have a sense of belonging, by which she means association with and interaction with others. As outlined in Table 3.2 this need provides a motive to understand our relationships and to control our position in society. In accord with such understanding we need to enhance our self-image and the view of others concerning our worth. This also is a reflection of the extent to which we can trust those within the communities that affect us.

In terms of our relationship with public policy such a framework may be usefully developed by re-casting the motives identified by Fiske to fit the language and resultant imagery used within conventional political studies literature. Thus we can appreciate the need for belonging as indicative within the policy process of the essential need for

Table 3.2 Core social motives

Fiske's Core Motives	Needs consequent on Fiske's core motives	Typology of motive in this study
Understanding	Need for shared meaning	Ideology
Self-enhancing	Need for self-worth	Self-interest
Trusting	Need to see others as basically benign	Ethics and altruism
Controlling	Need to control behaviour and outcomes	Power

Source: Adapted from Fiske, 2010: 16

policy activists to create and join interest groups if they are to forward their ideas, given that any successful policy outcome requires consensus among those subject to the requirements of its content. The elements that can create the need for developing the collective interests that steer and legitimate policy are built from attempts to understand our world and our reaction to the consequent social environment. They may in the context of political discourse be seen as ideology. Within the framework of ideology is also the development of an understanding of how far we can control our position within society and hence those elements of ideology relating to power relations in terms of democratic or authoritarian values. Separable from ideological concerns, although often greatly affecting our ideological viewpoint, is what Fiske terms the self-enhancing motive that politically may be seen as self-interest, that is a motive to enhance the wealth and happiness of ourselves as individuals or the well-being of those closest to us, namely our family and close friends.

Fiske finally identifies trust as a 'need for viewing others as basically benign' (Fiske 2010: 16). Within a public policy perspective the issue of trust may be crucial for large-scale social cohesion but is far from certain. Trust may seen as somewhat analogous to the idea of a civic culture, which Edward Banfield (1958) and later Putnam (1994) identified as a central requirement for an effective, stable polity. In many socio-political studies this concept may be seen as a counterweight to trust founded on self-interest, in which trust only extends to family relations and close supporters. Such limited forms of trust can be a central element in patron–client relationships that evolve to benefit a small community of clients owing allegiance to a specific leader as opposed to a wider civic society. Francis Fukuyama (1995) has argued that the capitalist liberal democratic state has emerged in regimes where there is a high expectation of trust between individuals who are not closely related or known to one another and contrasts this with the difficulties in establishing an effective economy and political system where trust does not extend beyond small familial patron–client groups. Trust for others when operationalised through understanding builds into our practical view of ethics and morality and hence our expectations on how we ought to behave to others. Thus, this motive may be more usefully translated as part of our expression of moral and ethical values.

From this analysis of motives we can for simplicity identify three central motives that operate in an uneasy conflict within our minds to create the dilemmas as much as the solutions to our attitudes towards our own policy preferences and those that are imposed by or accepted from others. These may be seen as our ideological understanding of society and our position and capacities to shape our position within that society. Intertwined with this concern are our motives from the two often conflicting demands on our consciousness, that of developing our own self-interest and the demands to follow an ordered ethical set of values such that we expect others to adopt towards us. This framework is illustrated in Table 3.2 mapping the motives identified by Fiske to those developed in this study.

Whilst it is possible to classify motives that are central to our social psychology, it is also important to realise that the capacity and methods of realising these motivations will be different for each individual as a consequence of their emotional values. Certain individuals will be, for example, driven by personal ambition to control others and to secure substantive self-esteem from a wide population. In contrast the psychology of some actors will be more modest and many will prefer to accept from others their guiding ideological values and be also prepared to accept control by others. The extent to which what may be termed extrovert and submissive dispositions will probably be in part a consequence of their genetic make-up, but will also be characterised by the social institutions and civic culture in which they are brought up. A further issue that will characterise human motives towards the public policy process is the rationalisation by an individual concerning the material and psychological costs of investment in gaining greater understanding of the outside world and ourselves to make it worthwhile to seek an active, let alone dominant role in the policy process at any specific level of social interaction. This issue will be discussed in later chapters and in the more prosaic language of political science concerns the factors that determine who opts out of the public policy process leaving the issue to those who strive for leadership roles in society. It will also require consideration of the formal institutional factors and less formal ideological divisions in society that create much greater costs in any polity for some individuals to become at all active within policy development. Policy content and the conduct of the policy process will be a reflection of ideological, ethical and self-interested concerns but in varying degrees, not so much for the many in society but the well-resourced and genetically suitably adapted few.

Conclusion

It is argued in this chapter that any understanding of public policy and how it is processed cannot be based solely on positivist statements and theory given that the motives and emotions that drive policy initiatives as well as their content are based on subjective values. This does not, however, exclude any rational approach to understanding but requires a different approach to rationality. It requires an acceptance that what may be of value to certain policy activists may not be of value to others and hence many policies cannot be condemned or praised as intrinsically right or wrong but can be understood in the context and through the personal characteristics, as much as they can be revealed, of policy activists. The next three chapters explore further this ground and also consider the impact of these subjective drivers that form the content of public policy before considering the distribution and use of power within a political system that determines which of many policy ideas emerge from a maelstrom of content and motives and how, following policy legitimation, it is implemented and validated and evolves.

4 Policy, ideology and ideas

Ideologies or fragments of ideological beliefs often determine perceptions as to whether there is a policy problem or opportunity and the willingness either to support, and implement, a policy initiative or to oppose and undermine its development. According to the Italian thinker Antonio Gramsci ideologies 'create the terrain on which men move, acquire consciousness of their position (and) struggle' (Gramsci 1971: 337). Ideology is, however, a contested concept that has many definitions. In populist sentiment ideology can be used as a pejorative term that condemns organised political views as dangerous and divisive excesses that underpin the rationale for authoritarian non-pluralist governments. However, as used by political researchers it is a term that can encompass both authoritarian views of political systems and also those that support democratic representative systems such as the predominant values within the United States or Britain. As a normatively neutral description it can simply be defined as 'any more or less coherent systems of beliefs or views on politics and society' (Leach 1991: 10).

Ideology in the twenty-first century

There has been a fashionable trend to claim that the strife between left and right wing policies is to be consigned to the history books. In 1960 Daniel Bell completed his influential work *The End of Ideology* in which he argued that the development of democracy in Western states signalled the end of ideological conflict. Francis Fukuyama (1992) has argued that capitalist democracy was gradually spreading throughout the world and would become the dominant and accepted mode of social development. In Britain efforts to bridge the gap between socialism and capitalism during the Blair Governments led to the idea of a Third Way in politics that they hoped would become the dominant framework for society (Giddens 1998). Such essays do not, however, presage the end of ideology, let alone the end of history, but more the suggestion that a specific ideology will dominate thinking on public policy. What these studies in various ways suggest is that ideologically everyone will, whether consciously or unconsciously, accept a world based on a capitalist society allowing widespread political freedom but retaining a measure of state regulation to protect individuals' property and also compensate, through state aid, those who are unable to support themselves. If this were to be the future, then all policy problems would accept without much, if any, conscious thought a range of ideas to fit in with the liberal democratic framework. Thus, any study of policy analysis could effectively accept the platform on which policy is devised and practised and move to discussion of the more detailed methods of developing policy within the scope of the accepted ideological value system.

Domination by a single ideology still seems some way in the future if it ever can be or should be obtained. There remain a significant number of non-liberal democratic autocracies and oligarchies in the world. Major states, such as China or Russia, may increasingly support the values of capitalism but are far more cautious over admitting pluralist democratic principles. Nationalism remains in almost all nations a significant value that differentiates one community and its political and cultural practices from other societies. New ideological values such as environmentalism and feminism still divide many societies and religious beliefs remain, as in the Middle East, a major factor in political thought. Moreover, the concept of liberal democracy enfolds different values ranging from demands for participative and discursive democracy to libertarianism and representative democratic systems. Whilst there may be a greater ideological divide between autocratic and democratic thought than, for example, liberal and participative democracy, divisions can be just as intense within each movement.

In practice, most policy makers develop their ideas with a palette of notions that have little defensible justification and have little connection with one another. Few policy actors can frame a comprehensive ideology such as are found in, for example, the works of Karl Marx or Friedrich von Hayek. Some policy actors who claim allegiance to the ideas of a specific author or named ideological positions will have a well-rounded, clear understanding of their adopted ideological stance, but many ideologies that are cited as the motive for policy often derive from untested or irrational beliefs and for many politicians may be internally inconsistent.

Within the United States the ideological defence of the rights of man as laid out in the Constitution was never honoured in practice before the Civil War outlawed slavery and subsequently it was not until 1920 that women received the vote and until the 1970s that racial segregation was ruled as unlawful by the Supreme Court.

The concern of the coalition government led by David Cameron to restrict immigration does not sit easily with the concept of a free economy. Similarly the attitude prevalent since the Thatcher Governments and held by both the Conservative and the New-Labour wing of the Blair and Brown Governments favouring privatisation rather than state ownership as a means of creating economic growth and efficiency is highly questionable. The failure of the private banks that brought the most serious economic recession since the 1930s might suggest that the theory that the private sector free from any state control is inevitably more efficient than the public sector needs some revision. Similarly in Britain the failures of Yorkshire Water, Rail Track or the Rover Car Company might suggest that privatised industries may at times surpass the public sector in their capacity to destroy an industry.

Ideological values espoused by politicians tend to appear in the land of theory rather than methodical practice in a large part because of the influence of self. However, it is, as the following section outlines, unrealistic to gloss over the substantial role that ideologies perform as an important means of determining not just the content of policy but how it is processed and implemented.

The impact of ideology on policy

Ideology, like morality, can be an essential motive behind the framing of policy content and how it is to be processed even though few policy makers are wholly ideologically driven and are inclined, or required, to temper their ideals of the good state with the realisation that they must work with others who do not necessarily share their views. Irrespective of whether ideological beliefs are consciously built up by an individual or simply picked up in the street or taken from parents, the system of values shapes not only the likely reaction of an individual to a policy problem but, more fundamentally, the manner in which they recognise policy problems or opportunities and how they approach the issue of how they may resolve a problem.

Ideology firstly shapes attitudes on what should be seen as problems or opportunities and hence greatly colours the policy agenda. This point may be illustrated by the following reflection on health policy and environmental politics in the United States.

For libertarian Republicans it is not the role of the state but that of the individual to provide for their health care. This predominant view in the earlier twentieth century ensured a system of health care that was predominantly available only for those with sufficient incomes to afford the costs of doctors and other health professionals. Democratic thought was since Roosevelt's New Deal evolving towards a greater partnership of state and citizens to ensure welfare provision as the last resort to those in need. By the 1960s there was sufficient ideological grounding supporting the Kennedy and Johnston Administrations to establish federal and local state funded support through Medicare and Medicaid to subsidise health care costs to respectively the elderly and the poor. Subsequent Democratic Party Presidents have attempted, not always successfully, to further develop state support for health care on European models of national insurance. The on-going debate has in essence been largely fought on the ideological issues of the role of the modern state in subsidising the less fortunate in society. For libertarian Republicans the most serious social problem of government regulation of health care is preventing what they see as dangerous interference by the state in the personal lives of citizens.

Environmental policy proponents embracing green ideological values see the effects of global warming through the use of fossil fuels as a major threat to civilisations throughout the world. In the United States during the Presidency of George W. Bush many Republican New Right economists denied that global warming was a serious threat to society and even if they conceded that there was a problem, did not see this as a central issue for the public sector given their belief that human ingenuity and the response of free individuals to the economic problems of dwindling fossil fuel reserves will ensure that the long-term problem of global warming will be resolved through the operation of the competitive market economy.

Ideological positions secondly structure the scope of the policy search by ensuring that certain possibilities are never entertained. The rational approach to policy making argues that policy makers select for serious consideration only those policies that appear to be viable in terms of resolving policy problems. In practice, however, policy problems are in many cases determined by the ideological position of the policy elites who have the power to determine political change rather than consideration of the most efficient or effective way of resolving a problem. In terms of Etzioni's concept of mixed scanning, ideology can be a central factor. If ideological issues are at the centre of what are seen as high order policy making processes policy agents immediately concentrate on the more incremental policy alternatives within the framework of their acceptable ideological value range (Etzioni 1967: 389). A strong ideological outlook effectively rules out numerous courses of action and concentrates the mind on those policy avenues that are consistent with the preferred value system.

In Britain the Labour Government led by Gordon Brown forwarded policies to resolve the national debt crisis following the banking collapse of 2008 by growing the economy and raising taxation from the wealthier citizens rather than dramatically cutting welfare expenditure. In contrast the more right wing Conservative–Liberal Democrat coalition led by David Cameron followed New Right values and cut welfare benefits and public expenditure at the risk of slowing economic growth in order to tackle the debt crisis. Both the Brown and Cameron policies may resolve the problem but the radically differing policy options they put forward have little to do with technical decisions on the most efficient ways of paying off the nation's debt as opposed to the ideological values of following more re-distributive social democrat values as opposed to a public choice view of shrinking the state's involvement in helping the less well off.

Thirdly, ideological considerations will not only determine the preferred content of policy solutions but will also be a significant factor in determining the personnel that are employed to find solutions. In autocracies of either an extreme right or left wing orientation membership of a single ideologically orientated political party may serve as the only avenue to positions of authority within an all pervasive public sector. Thus, in Soviet Russia power rested with the Politburo which was the inner cabinet of the leadership of the Communist Party. In pluralist states the role of ideology is evident within the informal but central machinery of the dominant party systems. In Britain, the prime minister and cabinet are composed of the leaders of the political party, or occasionally parties, that have won the majority of seats in Parliament and can, consequently, expect legislative support for their decisions. Power lies within the leadership of an organisation that has evolved around a broad ideological stance towards policy making. A frequent question raised by Mrs Thatcher when considering whether a politician or advisor should be appointed to a policy role was whether he or she was 'one of us' (Young 1989: xiii).

A fourth function of ideological values in the creation and process of policy is that the ideological views of policy advocates will lead them in most circumstances to seek technical support and advice from those who accept their general view of the world. If free to make the choice a policy entrepreneur will seek out the support of fellow travelling interests.

The Redcliffe-Maud Commission established in 1966 to enquire into the possibilities of a root and branch restructuring of local government in Britain, was composed of personnel from largely local and central government circles who had similar views to those of the Local Government Minister Richard Crossman on the need to abolish most smaller local authorities in order to greatly streamline the structure of the prevailing local government system (Chandler 2007: 197).

However, advice and technical expertise only from those within a policy elite's ideological tent is not always possible and on many occasions governments are obliged to consider the values of opposing ideological interests. A governing party may, for example, wish to demonstrate for public consumption that they are leaving no stone unturned in order to seek a solution to a problem but then subsequently ignore or find fault with their advice.

The ideology of policy shapers will also be a major factor within a political system that determines the scope and direction of public as opposed to private sector policy. New Right political theory argues that government and hence the public sector should be kept at a minimum level. From this perspective the study of public policy may at best be seen as a necessary but potentially unprofitable and dangerous activity for the liberty of citizens. This direction results in an important genre of studies which attempt to show that the public policy process must constantly be subject to control from a vigilant parliament and the executive of the state, to ensure it does not overstep the boundaries of what ought to be a private matter. At the opposite ends of the left–right ideological scale socialist values require equality of opportunity and rewards. For many socialists this can only be achieved by extensive intervention by the state. Socialist governments will consider that private sector businesses create some of the worst problems for the society as they are argued to be a source of inequality rather than being the solution to an ideal society. Thus, whenever control over a government changes from leaders supporting a particular ideological position on the role of the state and the boundaries between private and public enterprise there can be a substantial shift in what is seen as public policy.

In Britain the accession to power after the end of the Second World War of the first majority Labour Government under the leadership of Clement Attlee ushered in a major change in the role of the state. Following social democratic ideological principles Attlee had presided over the nationalisation of a wide swathe of industries, distributing essential resources such as gas, electricity and transport to the public sector. The ideology that brought about the expanded role of the state was, in part, accepted by the following Conservative Governments between 1951 and 1974. It was not until the emergence of the Thatcher Government after 1979 that the ideology of what was referred to as the mixed economy welfare state began to be reversed by the new New Right ideology of Conservative Governments and also through Blair's concept of New Labour and the Third Way.

In most stable states governments will be pervaded by the dominant ideology concerning the processes of governance that shape how policy can be made and by whom it may be made. Autocrats will construct an ideological myth around their importance to the state and ensure that those who show no support for these values are rapidly removed from not only the policy making process but, in the most totalitarian of states, life itself. In liberal democracies there are similarly powerful conventions that ideologically structure the ladder of opportunity to shape policy. The chosen consensus in most Western liberal democracies against the participative democratic theory from Rousseau's *Social Contract* published in 1762 (Rousseau 1966) to Carolyn Pateman (1970) and Benjamin Barber (1984) ensures support for highly centralised national governance and the tendency to rely on networks for creating policy decisions.

A final impact of ideology is not so much about a direct impact on policy ideas themselves but on the way in which policy analysts choose to depict the policy process. How far academic analysis on policy has shaped the way in which politicians and interests shape policy may be open to question but how academics, including the author of this volume, approach the subject is in most cases founded on their personal ideological values. Whilst most social scientists maintain they operate in a political neutral climate, this is, from a subjective perspective, difficult to sustain. Many discussions of policy in liberal democracy are perhaps too oblivious to the strength of elitist arguments and imprison their models of policy development within what has become the ideological straitjacket of the myths that are popularised concerning the liberal democratic system to the exclusion of critical theory and strong democracy approaches to the subject.

Ideological content

As suggested in the opening chapter of this book, it is important in any study of public policy to discuss not only how policy is processed in political systems but how the values and attitudes of the public in general and policy advocates and gate keepers in particular shape policy content. An understanding of ideology as well as the role of self-interest and ethics is therefore essential to gain a comprehensive view of how in different political systems public policy takes the form that is imposed, if not necessarily followed, by its subjects. It is, however, clearly impossible here to review all forms of systematic political and social ideologies, let alone more specific political ideas, before launching into a broader discussion on how ideology may colour not just the content but the procedures for policy enhancement. Nevertheless to understand the arguments presented in this study it may be useful to sketch some of the central ideological dispositions that determine policy ideas. As this is not a work solely dedicated to the study of ideology, reference to some of the many substantive works on the subject will be a useful complement to facilitate an understanding of public policy.

Any discussion of ideology is beset by a problem of how to categorise different sets of political beliefs, largely because many political views are never held within societies as all-encompassing and clearly defined sets of ideas. The blueprints of many ideologies are largely described through the works of revered writers on both political and moral theory, whose views are seen to express a specific view of society. Rarely, however, are ideologies, as practised, exactly as suggested by their founders. For example, Engels commented in a letter written in the 1890s that Karl Marx told him in relation to 'French "Marxists" of the late seventies: "All I know is that I am not a Marxist"' (Marx and Engels 1962b: 486).

Each generation continuously evolves the inspirations of specific thinkers just as much as public policy is a set of evolving practices. Moreover, as indicated in the preceding chapter, the extent to which a policy activist may pursue their initiatives solely with reference to a specific motive is open to question. Many professions of loyalty and belief in a specific ideology may be complicated by the presence of self-interested motives.

A further complication concerning a clear definition of ideology is the presence of what may be termed partial ideologies, such as feminism or environmentalism which colour the values of more comprehensive ideologies usually by merging one set of ideas into an existing set of beliefs. Whilst some ideologies can appear to be all-encompassing, several recent studies of ideology have seen concerns such as feminism or the green movement presented as an ideological concern even though they do not normally bring together all aspects of a supporter's political thought. A strong enthusiast for feminism can, for example, be attached to either a New Right or a socialist ideological view concerning the distribution of resources within a community. In civil society outside the small coterie of those greatly concerned with policy development, ideologies are, moreover, not so much well thought out systems of ideas but rather moods or dispositions that colour an individual's or society's direction of thought. An individual may, for example, have very strong views concerning immigration overriding any other pretence at political thought and these values can impel them to support political movements hostile to immigration regardless of whatever values such a party may hold. There is, therefore, a difficult to define boundary between a firmly held political, economic or social idea and a comprehensive joined up view of social beliefs. The following sections will, therefore, outline the predominant ideologies that set in their structure a more comprehensive view of political, economic and social values relevant to public policy content and then more briefly outline what may be thought of as partial ideologies that may determine a central focus for policy action or inaction but must be tempered in different ways through the impact of more comprehensive ideological themes such as equality or personal freedom.

Religious belief

Societies from very early times will have developed widely accepted stories, legends and customs to maintain cohesion and at times a belligerent identity against other social groups who appeared to be a threat to their well-being or present an opportunity for plunder. How far the ancient Greeks for example actually believed in the Gods atop Mount Olympus may be open to question, but these legends will have served as a means of defining how individuals should relate to their society.

Religion still remains in some modern societies an important framework that determines how society should be organised and hence can serve as the fount of public policy content and processes. Religions can create strong political ideologies, as in Britain in the 1640s, when the nation was engaged in a civil war based, at least in part, on the divisions between protestant and catholic values. Today, in the Middle East, competing versions of Muslim thought can determine very different approaches to ideas on the role of the state. There are, of course, major distinctions and also similarities between religious beliefs that can on occasion have a major bearing on policy content. On the whole, however, many strongly religious activists, whether Muslims, Jews, Hindus or Christians, will be influenced by other more secular beliefs, such as an enthusiasm for equality among Quakers as opposed to the libertarian values of many United States Christian fundamentalists. The bitter feuds and civil wars that have created, and still create, mayhem in many regions of the world that are fought in the name of religion, in reality may conceal differences based on nationalism or between socialist and capitalist values.

Conservatism

Conservative values are for many individuals an emotional disposition rather than a firm and rationally developed belief. There is a tendency for some people to be content with their position in society and not to seek change. However, for many it is concern for the unknown future rather than contentment with their situation that drives them to support conservative values, through what Zygmunt Bauman (2006) has described as a climate of fear. This creates a disposition to avoid radical change to their lifestyle as it may lead to unknown or even well identified pitfalls and dangers rather than personal growth and pleasure. In such cases there may be in the making of policy strong opposition to change from the devil we know to the devils we do not know.

This tendency in the nineteenth century was given more rational substance by historically minded theorists such as Edmund Burke who argued, following the evidence of terror and bloodshed in the French Revolution, that any radical transformation of a society following an untested intellectualised formula would be likely to end in a loss of order and a spiral into violence and extremism. While not opposed to the need for any society to change, this must be undertaken in an ordered piecemeal manner that pragmatically evaluates social problems rather than developing overarching metatheories requiring wholesale root and branch reorganisation. These values continued to be supported in the nineteenth century by politicians such as Benjamin Disraeli who believed that society should be governed by the most able and cultured leaders who were steeped in a strong set of moral values that required them to aid the hard working though less intellectual poor (see for example, the morals of his novels *Sybil* (1981) and *Coningsby* (1948)). In the twentieth century Michael Oakeshott (1962) has cogently argued for the importance of respecting traditional values as these encapsulate the wisdom of many generations rather than the more fallible ideals developed by a specific thinker such as Marx or Mill and Bentham. In this respect, Conservatives differ substantially from the ideals of liberalism or those of the New Right. Robert Scruton (2001a) is currently a strong advocate for this position.

Liberalism

The dominant secular ideology of the age of industrial commerce and capitalism can be encapsulated in the ideology of liberalism, that argued, against the authoritarian dominance of monarchy and aristocracy, that all individuals were born equal before the law and should be as free as possible from state interference. Protest against rule by aristocrats was endemic in many earlier societies and may be a sub-text in religions such as Christianity. However in Western Europe it was not until the seventeenth century that liberalism became more coherently established as ideological thought. Following the protestant rebellion against Charles I in England in the civil wars of the 1640s, groups such as the Levellers and the Diggers emerged to proclaim the then radical idea that all individuals were born equal and should be politically free to voice their opinions. After James II was obliged to flee the country following his attempts to return England to the catholic faith, protestant theorists such as John Locke (1924) had the capacity to publicise the widely developing view that kings could not govern by divine right and that sovereignty could be centred on the right of all citizens to freedom of life, liberty, speech and the ownership of property.

These values emerged in a society where manufacturing and commerce began to rival the ownership of landed estates as the most important form of capital and hence wealth. Similarly, in France theorists such as Montesquieu argued against the policy of a weakening monarchy by suggesting government should be based on a balance of powers between the classes and institutions of the state. The insistence of an aristocratic landowning class seeking to keep at bay the unregulated growth of industry led to the 1789 revolution and the downfall of the aristocracy. In Britain a less violent revolution led to the eclipse of aristocratic power centred in the House of Lords and the development of a dominant House of Commons that by the late nineteenth century was controlled by industrialists and bankers as much as the owners of great estates. The United States had in the War of Independence overthrown aristocratic domination by English landed interests in 1783 to found a Federal state that allowed freedom from controls over commerce from both external and internal interests.

The liberal ideology that justified the supplanting of landowning and aristocracy with democratic liberalism demanded that the state, and thus the public sector, should ensure that each person had as much freedom as possible by establishing laws that safeguarded each individual's right to life and the property they acquired through their own or their ancestors' efforts. In order to ensure the state was not dominated by a self-interested hereditary monarchy and aristocracy, a wider electorate would democratically have the right to vote for a parliament that would on their behalf establish the policies that could guarantee political and economic freedom. In reality early liberal states such as Britain and the United States were far from liberal and excluded participation of women and the many imported immigrants, sometimes serving as slaves. The foundations of liberalism also promoted new divisions of wealth and influence in 18th and nineteenth century societies and allowed a merchant and manufacturing class, the bourgeoisie, to begin to dominate policy making in the newly created liberal political systems.

The exclusion of over half the populations of many supposedly liberal states from any involvement in public policy making was only painfully reversed in the twentieth century and still has some way to go before securing equality between the sexes or the elimination of racism. The development in most Western capitalist states of the principle of one person one vote and the associated freedoms of communication and assembly to press for ideological and policy change led to the concept of the liberal democratic state which is widely viewed as the ideal polity. However, as will be a recurring theme in this study, it can be questioned whether such arrangements within capitalist societies can be both fully liberal and at the same time sufficiently democratic to allow citizens equal opportunity to influence public policy outputs.

Socialism

The introduction of *laissez faire* liberal ideology fuelled the increasing dominance of capitalism in Western Europe. This led to inequalities of wealth and power which began to be challenged by the new industrial working proletariat and fellow-travelling intellectuals in socialist ideologies. By 1900 the most influential streams of these ideas were attributed to Karl Marx and Friedrich Engels, anarchists such as Bakunin or, in a more measured and less revolutionary style, social democrats. Socialism at the Marxist extreme pushed for major changes in the distribution of power by maintaining that every individual should have the same life chances as could be enjoyed by the wealthy. This would be possible once industrial production had become so efficient a mechanism that it could supply each person with what they desired in life and that such desires would be sufficient for people's needs, rather than desires for unnecessary luxuries that in a capitalist society were for the bourgeoisie symbolic of their claimed superiority over the proletariat. Public policy generated democratically at state and local level would provide, as listed in the *Communist Manifesto* (Marx and Engels 1962a), the social necessities of education and health care and support when misfortune put individuals in need. To achieve such an aim it was necessary for the poor and the middling classes to combine to bring about the demise of a relatively small group of capitalists who dominated government within an industrial society. Marx considered that the capitalist mode of production contained contradictions that would over time lead to its destruction. Among these problems was a view that unregulated economic competition would ensure that most entrepreneurs would be forced out of the market by a few powerful players, leading to a situation in which a small elite would dominate a much larger group of exploited workers who, once conscious of their subordinate position, would be sufficient in their overwhelming number to overthrow their economic masters. This point would be reached only when the technological capacity in the world had created the potential for providing for the needs and desires of every member of society. Rather than a crude insistence on absolute equality, Marx suggested that society would ensure distributive justice under the principle of 'from each according to their ability and to each according to their needs' (Marx and Engels 1962c: 24). The state would be simply a means to administer such a system and cease to be the centre of power as the need for competition was removed. Public policy under this vision would cease to be political and an object of struggle between interests but simply a matter of establishing technical solutions to deal with problems that may affect the production and distribution of goods and services for all. Even more radically, anarchists argued over the possibilities of removing the state altogether as such an entity was in the final analysis the fount of all inequalities and conflict.

In practice the more extreme ideas for supplanting the private sector through a proletarian revolution did not take place in the most industrialised states, as Marx and Engels predicted, but in the twentieth century in the less technologically advanced, if resource rich, states of Russia and China where extremist ideas channelled through largely agrarian based revolutions against decaying monarchies founded totalitarian states led by autocrats or oligarchies who drove forward industrialisation at the expense of personal freedom (Moore 1966). In these communist regimes the intellectual leaders of revolt in the name of equality fortified their positions of power not by running down the power of the liberal state but by enhancing its dominance to ensure the leaders of rebellion could maintain their control over all aspects of society.

New Liberalism to social democracy

Within most European states in the twentieth century and, although to a lesser degree, the United States, the inequalities of the classical liberal state were challenged, not so much by Marxism, but by what may be termed a New Liberal or Social Democratic ideology. By the late nineteenth century liberal theorists such as John Stuart Mill and Thomas Hill Green began to evolve liberal and socialist ideas into what was termed New Liberalism. They accepted the idea of legal equality of citizens but also looked to the state not just to protect personal property but also to provide through redistributive taxation sufficient resources to allow the poorer majority the resources of education, acceptable homes and health care to be able to use their natural abilities to their full potential. These ideas were taken up in the early twentieth century more forcibly by more radical liberal thinkers in Britain such as L.T. Hobhouse and Sydney and Beatrice Webb who paved the way for the introduction of early welfare orientated policies following the Liberal landslide General Election victory of 1906. Similarly, throughout mainland Europe socialist politicians and thinkers, such as Jean Jaures, who do not attract today the attention of the media and public imagination as more revolutionary minded socialists such as Trotsky or Lenin do, began to popularise the possibility that socialism could be developed within a democratic framework without the necessity of violent revolution and wars between nations. This change could be brought about by extending the franchise to every citizen within the state rather than only to those white males who owned property or extensive capital. Higher rates of re-distributive taxation could provide free education and welfare services to the poor and also protected workers from the periodic crises in economic production. By the mid-twentieth century the disruption of two world wars and the exposure of different classes and sexes to each other's lifestyles and levels of competence ensured that for many the dominant ideology of West European countries was a predominantly social democratic vision. Welfare support for the under-privileged channelled through the state with the assistance in some regimes of the private sector or charitable organisations was widely accepted.

In Britain these policies led to the development by the 1945 Attlee Government of a welfare state based on the Report written by New-Left economist William Beveridge that created the National Health Service to ensure free medical care for every citizen and support for people who had lost their jobs or were too infirm to work. The Government also brought into public ownership several major privately owned industrial, energy and transport organisations to create a mixed economy comprising both state owned and private capital. Similar developments had also emerged in other Western European nations creating a mix of affordable health and education facilities and a strong state owned industrial sector. In the United States the 'New Deal' programmes of President Franklin D. Roosevelt also ensured that the public agencies would have greater control of welfare and economic developments.

Social democracy has, however, been at all times a potentially unstable set of beliefs, sandwiched as a well-meaning compromise between more messianic and extreme values on the left and right of the political spectrum. Theoretically it is exposed to the danger that the compromises necessary for democratically establishing socialism in societies based on highly inequitable wealth based on a free capitalist economy, are never likely to satisfy the interests of the wealthy in society who must bear some reduction in their living standards. On the other side of the coin those who look for radical policies to enhance their living standards are quickly disillusioned by the slow rate of change and inevitably see the standard bearers of their hopes all too often absorbed into the life style of the wealthy.

Liberalism acting through social democracy despite its problems has become the bedrock of populist thought both within the democracies themselves and in the thoughts of many repressed subjects of autocracies. The assumptions on the benefits of what is termed liberal democracy have consequently permeated much of the writing on public policy in the United States and, to a lesser extent, in Europe, as will be discussed in later chapters. It is, however, based on what many theorists, such as Habermas and Bourdieu or Fox and Miller (2007), show to be hope rather than experience.

Rational choice theory

Within the United States and to a lesser degree Britain, the development of social democracy did not push *laissez faire* liberalism into total eclipse. Since the 1970s social democracy in Western states has increasingly given way to a number of theories founded on a restatement of capitalist liberal ideology. The terms given to these ideas such as neo-liberalism, public choice theory or the New Right all signify different nuances in how this ideological development emerged in the 1930s in reaction to the growth of both social democracy and fascism. I have used in explaining this ideological genre the term New Right as it has arguably become the most used term and also conveys the trend in practical politics for conservative parties to evolve from a paternalist to more competitive modes of production and allocation of resources.

Despite the development of policy theory stemming from Herbert Simon's critique of the possibilities of developing a predictive science of policy that arguably has its current manifestation in the form of complexity theory, there remains a highly influential stream of thought, rational choice or, in terms of political systems, public choice theory, that popularised an approach to social action founded on the view that human action can in general be predictable. Rational choice theory claims that human nature can be modelled on the assumption that individuals are predominantly self-interested beings who wish to maximise our access to material resources and that this is an essentially moral stance since everyone in a free society will benefit from the pursuit of enlightened self-interest. Thomas Hobbes had in the seventeenth century maintained that people were motivated solely by self-interest and in the late eighteenth century Utilitarian philosophy as developed by Bentham similarly argued that people sought their personal happiness. Economic theory based on a, not always accurate, reading of the works of Adam Smith, added grist to the mill.

> In Victorian Britain many economists and popular social commentators such as Samuel Smiles defended what may now be seen as rather crude but effective versions of rational choice theory. A predominant ideological position among the governing elites argued that those with wealth had a right to their fortune, in part because God had smiled upon their entrepreneurship and their efforts were justly rewarded. The unemployed poor by and large had no one to blame but their indolence in not finding work in an economically expanding society and should be assigned to work houses which would provide them with a living standard worse than anyone in employment in return for forced menial labour (Fraser 1984; Checkland and Checkland 1974).

Rational choice theory argues that individuals normally seek the best outcome for themselves when making economic or social choices. In the sphere of economics this is usually related to securing value for money and the accumulation of capital. In the social sphere gains are more difficult to quantify but broadly it is argued that rational individuals seek to gain utility, a broad term covering the trade-off between acquiring wealth and spending our resources on leisure and pleasure. A central premise of New Right theory argues that, given freedom from state control, individuals will strive to gain greater economic and social resources for themselves and their family and the most able will, as a consequence, dominate the economic if not the political system. Nevertheless, the least well off in such a system may also be richer, in terms of absolute wealth, than in an egalitarian socialist society, since the capacity of entrepreneurs to spend the money that they create in a free society fuels invention, productivity and employment. The wealth created by private entrepreneurial practice will then trickle down to all levels of society through higher employment and wages and cheaper and more technologically effective commodities and services. In contrast to a free society, a welfare state that subsidises the poor through state provided social services simply builds up a class of people who see it as in their interest to live on state benefits rather than to work in the private economy. Such a policy, argued Friedrich von Hayek (1944) in the title of his pioneering work in this genre *The Road to Serfdom*, blunts, through distributive taxation, the incentives of entrepreneurs to develop wealth and creates a class of more indolent individuals who feel they have no need to work and simply accept unearned hand-outs from the welfare state.

A further development of this line of thought led a group of United States economists to argue that in a social democratic state resources are not only unnecessarily wasted on keeping the poor in a situation of dependency on state hand-outs but the system creates a class of state employees who become predatory on private capital. A prominent member of this Virginia School of theorists, William Niskanen (1971) argued that self-interest leads politicians and civil servants to expand the size and complexity of their public empires in order to obtain greater chances of promotion and higher salaries. Niskanen, following some rigorous econometric calculations, argues that bureaucracies in the public sector are at least a third larger than is needed to fulfil their functions. The practical method of resolving this state of affairs is privatisation of state run enterprise and, under the broad title of New Public Management, schemes to ensure that private firms compete to implement public sector contracts, and that the output of bureaucracies is carefully evaluated and monitored in order to weed out those organisations and individuals that are acting inefficiently. Taken to its extreme by, for example, Robert Nozick (1974), public choice theory argues that government should be given minimal responsibilities to ensure the protection of individuals' property from theft or foreign invasion. Under this vision, there would be few public services as individuals should use their resources to provide for their own welfare with the freedom to choose the type of services that they felt they required and could afford. The state would, to use Rhodes' (1994) phrase, be 'hollowed out'. Society would in such a system be highly unequal in the distribution of wealth but it is better to protect individual freedom from the taxation and inefficiency of the state rather than subsidise the workshy and unproductive public bureaucrats who undermine economic progress.

There is much that can be criticised in the extreme versions of such a theory. The view of Niskanen and the Virginia School of public choice theorists that public sector monopolies become grossly inefficient in an uncompetitive environment has been challenged by Patrick Dunleavy's (1991) bureau shaping model that suggests that senior public bureaucrats may not be concerned to enrich themselves but to enjoy power and hence may wish to create small streamlined bureaucracies where decision making is restricted to a small coterie of players. It is also questionable whether a minimalist state creates the trickledown effect that may give the poorest and least physically or mentally capable in society a better standard of living than a system that provides a degree of welfare. The capacity for the rich to simply hand on by inheritance their wealth to their children may create an unproductive wealthy class that simply squanders the assets of their forebears. The poor but capable citizens willing to help create wealth may not, on the other hand, be able to afford to educate themselves to the level that they need to make the most of their potential. Moreover, substantive inequality between rich and poor in a society, as Lipset (1981: 47–8) and others have argued, may give rise to social unrest and instability within society.

Despite the many shortcomings in New Right theory, it has since the 1980s become a dominant ideology within Anglo-Saxon liberal democracies and most liberal democracies have indulged in policies that derived from these ideas, such as the sale of public assets and services such as gas and electricity supplies, transport systems, banks and insurance schemes, and health and social security services, on the premise, that is often not fulfilled, that the resultant private companies will be more efficient. Taxation has in Britain and the United States been progressively increased for the poor and cut for the wealthy (Piketty 2014: 493–515), leading to an increasing gap between the wealth of a small elite in society and those in positions of poverty. There is much debate on whether these changes have led to a more prosperous or more just world but, for every success claimed by New Right theorists of public choice, there are also many examples of the failure of the theory.

The application of public choice theory to private sector financial institutions in the United States and Britain under the Reagan and Thatcher Governments through freeing banks from many of the restraints imposed by governments initially led to an unprecedented boom in economic growth but was followed, following the 2008 banking crisis, by an historically longer period of economic depression, and uncovered evidence of financial corruption among senior bankers as extensive as any recent examples of corrupt practice by civil servants in liberal democratic states.

Partial ideologies

The political and economic developments that promoted liberalism also emphasised an underlying ideological concern for nationalism. As small communities became more integrated with the development of more advanced means of communication and extensive patterns of trade, loyalty to a small community, be it a village or rural community, expanded to greater support for a nation. The interests who gained wealth through trade needed to dominate potential rivals in other substantial communities and impose their own terms for undertaking business and raid poorly defended regions of the globe to amass greater resources to fuel their nation's economy. For the dominant nations of the world a standing army and, for maritime states, a navy were essential requirements and to fund and use these resources required not only taxation but also strong loyalty to the institutions of the state. Nationalism thus emerges as an often unquestioned ideological fixture within the minds of most subjects and policy advocates and formers in major nations.

In spite, as in Germany, France and Britain, of the attraction of socialism as an ideology, the large numbers of committed socialist leaders in these nations sprang to the defence of their nation at the outbreak of the First World War, rather than seeking any brotherly fraternity to their fellow socialist thinkers in opposing belligerent states (Hobsbawm 1987, 163–4).

Nationalism is however for most proponents of this stance one of the many sets of convictions that cannot easily be appreciated as a standalone ideology rather than an attitude that informs a set of values within the context of other beliefs. Thus a nationalist with a preference for elite rather than democratic values may be seen as a Fascist, as opposed to a Stalinist who would wish to establish socialism in a specific country with a view to its exportation by conquest of other nationalities. It may also be suggested that racialism should, within the broad framework of nationalism, be seen as an all too important if for many unwelcome organisation of political attitudes. The unpalatable aspects of this systemisation of beliefs have led few writers to identify it, Heywood (2012) perhaps excepted, as an ideology, but racist beliefs were a major determinant of colonial policies since the 16th century, and in the twentieth century were a defining characteristic of the German National Socialists led by Hitler and post-1945 determined the all-encompassing apartheid policy of South Africa.

Wholly different and in this century more respected partial ideologies concern the growing realisation for a need to change human behaviour in terms of consumption of the planet's resources. These concerns are embedded in green, or better named, ecological political movements which draw attention to the dangers and ethical problems associated with an assumption that the human species can ignore its impact on future generations for the functioning climate and biological system that makes the planet a habitable harbour for life. As a partial ideology, however, supporters of ecological ideologies tend to be divided in terms of how to orientate their central concern to fit other central ideological interests in respect to personal liberty and equality or the ethics of regulating population size. Thus, green movements can be divided into what are seen as deep green values where the ecological concerns override other ideological factors to light green where proponents will strive for 'saving the planet' within the framework of other widespread beliefs concerning freedom and equality.

Feminism similarly is a significant and important political movement but like green politics is divided between enthusiasts who demand radical and even violent means to secure the dominance or, at least equality, of women in society, whilst other feminists wish to see the equality of women in society but within the context of liberal or new-right capitalism or in contrasting socialist values. The feminist may to a lesser extent be echoed by campaigns for any form of sexual practise to be a dominant element in ideological content.

The limits to ideological explanations of policy decisions

Ideology is far from being the only motivating factor in policy development. Personal self-interest of policy entrepreneurs and self-interest within public opinion is a further major influence in making public decisions. Moreover, within a purely ideological world policy makers may frequently be faced with serious dilemmas as to how far to push forward their ideological ideas through a consistent programme. Many ideologies appear to be less than perfect in the real world and create a climate in which policy advocates find themselves faced with contradictions that cannot easily be resolved from a purely ideological base. Politicians frequently confront moral dilemmas as to their conduct as a public representative and their personal duties to those close to them. Should a politician ignore the personal interests of their close family in order to pursue an ideological ideal that they have little chance of immediately bringing to fruition? A further problem with a purely ideological explanation of policy content and its evolution is the frequent inconsistencies within a policy framework. Classically, enthusiasts for democracy are always faced with the problem of how far you can permit the rise of political interests within civil society that campaign for the overthrow of a democratic system in support of an autocratic regime.

The democratic Weimar Republic established in Germany following the First World War enabled Hitler to have the freedom to campaign for its replacement by the highly autocratic and xenophobic ideology he succeeded in imposing on the nation (Lipset 1981: 127–152).

It may be argued that ideology is far from static and that an effective ideology as a system of ideas must examine the contradictions that might be entailed by its principles and synthesise these into a more complex system of beliefs. However, embroidering a consistent set of beliefs in order to overcome moral or practical doubts about some of the implications of the theory frequently sets up further problems of inconsistency. Inevitably any ideology is riven with contradictions that are left unresolved and so political blueprints are fractionated into rival interpretations, each an often inconsistent variant on an initial theme. Behind the many interpretations of basic ideological positions are political factions engaged in the struggle to make their policy views dominate national policies.

Conclusion

As shall be discussed in the next chapter, few individuals are dogmatic ideologists and most political actors will distort how ideas are practised from the point of view of their individual self-interest as applied to a more abstract ideological formula. It is, nevertheless, unwise to dismiss ideology as a significant factor in determining choice in policy dilemmas, despite the tendency of policy practitioners to distort the central core of their values in established ideological positions, or to retreat from ideological discussion under a smokescreen of the end ideology. Ideological perspectives shape the trends in much of our political and economic thought and consequently are a background reference that shapes much of the direction of policy. Whilst ideology for many is not fully consistent or even absorbed as part of an individual's or group's unconscious assumptions, it may be a central guide to how they will determine both the content of policy and also the processes for determining, refining and implementing policies.

5   Self-interest

Even if you do not accept the cynical belief that politicians and the senior managers of either public, private or charitable organisations are solely 'in it for themselves' rather than the common good, you will be living a rather sheltered life if you have not come across popular assumptions that self-interest motivates political leaders as much as an altruistic desire to benefit all of humanity. Ideological ideas are held by political activists with different degrees of understanding and commitment and are often 'more honoured in the breach than the observance'. This chapter considers the extent to which self-interest may both reinforce ideological and ethical commitment but also destroy any earnest pretensions to ideological and moral correctness. In this chapter the term 'self-interest' is attached to that aspect of human behaviour that is concerned with the advancement of an individual's personal development or that of their family members or close friends, rather than the good of society in general. This is a definition that needs some explanation.

Schools of psychology view motivation from differing perspectives. Positivist paradigms championed by some experimental psychologists argue that there are intrinsic needs and desires that are wired into the genetic make-up of the human brain that will react in differing ways when faced with similar environmental conditions. These behaviourists believe that they can get some idea of how the machinery of a normal brain will operate by observing the reactions of individuals when placed in similar situations. In contrast, it is argued that human motivation is subjective and we must understand what this may be through statements from an individual as to what they feel and perceive. Phenomenological thought suggests that our desires and fears are personal to ourselves and it is difficult if not impossible to understand whether the concept of, for example, ambition, has the same meaning for each person (Ashworth 2000: 105–8). The subjective approach to human psychology creates a problem of classifying motives. Recognised motives and emotions such as a desire for power or love may be a consequence of very different feelings and result from the impact of differing unconscious motives and behavioural impulses. For example, it is frequently argued that many politicians are motivated by a determination to gain power, but what may be the source of that attitude? How far is the desire to wield power a consequence of a concern to satisfy further personal motives such as to ensure our security or to gain the praise of others or to altruistically establish humane policies?

During the twentieth century many social psychologists have attempted to classify and, also, morally order the sources of motivation. Among the early proponents of policy studies, Harold Lasswell (1948) was particularly interested in this issue and in his earlier works suggested that politicians frequently seek power as a consequence of the suppression of their ego in their childhood. Maslow's (1970) pyramid of social well-being that culminated at its apex in the notion of self-actualisation is probably the most well known of these theoretical models. More empirically based understanding of the growth of human behaviour is based on Piaget's (1977) studies of child development, which identified stages from an infant's early self-absorption and egocentric motivation to the later dawning in childhood of a realisation that others have similar concerns and wishes as themselves. Lawrence Kohlberg (1973) developed a more complex theoretical model of motivation and moral consciousness arguing that at a higher, and more adult, level of moral interaction the individual accepts that their ego must come to terms with the well-being of others. This structuring of self-interest has considerable resonance within the discursive democratic theories of Jürgen Habermas (1990: 2001).

Self-interest as defined in this analysis is attached to motives that satisfy the ego, that is the self, and does not extend to concerns for community or humanity as a whole. This should not, however, imply that self-interested actors are wholly uninterested in ideological views. The ubiquity of self-interest as the basis of human motivation prompts many critics of this position, such as Frank Fischer (2003: 21–7), to spend some time defending ideology as a motivation that cuts across the assumption that we are all self-interested and have no sense of genuine altruism. Many individuals will be attracted to ideological positions that reinforce their own self-interested inclinations and hence the two forms of motivation can often be complementary. Individuals who are wealthy are, for example, more likely to support right wing values opposing the redistribution of wealth, whilst those who feel that they are unjustly treated in terms of their share of wealth will be attracted to redistributive socialist policies. In a global society based on self-governing states, self-interest tends, for example, to be linked with ideological support for nationalism and the political structuring of the national constitution and the national interpretations of that country's history.

Alienation from the policy process

Before advancing further into a discussion of how public policy content and processes may be affected by political self-interest, it is important to show that for the majority of people self-interest is not directed towards participation in the networks that determine public policy and that, in a negative sense, they make their presence felt by their alienation from the political game. Public policy activists stand out in most regimes as a powerful minority, because of the apparent lack of interest of most citizens in understanding or influencing the demands made on them by that system. As Table 5.1 shows, from an authoritative survey conducted in the United Kingdom, over half the population appear to have made no contribution to the policy process and those that have are operating at a very low level of influence with only two per cent of respondents being members of a political party. In other liberal democracies, for example in Scandinavian countries, participation is probably slightly higher but by no means to the extent that this suggests widespread time and effort is devoted to campaigning on policy issues.

There are many predominantly self-interested factors that ensure that only a minority of individuals are extensively active in promoting and advancing policy and even during the stage of implementation many active in such a process are socialised into following what is expected of them rather than making any profound acknowledgement of the value and importance of their actions. Several reasons for the lack of engagement in the policy making process can be cited but perhaps the most compelling

Table 5.1 Political engagement in the United Kingdom

In the last 12 months have you done any of the following to influence decisions, laws or policies?	%
Contacted a local councillor or MP/MSP or Welsh Assembly Member	12
Contacted the media	3
Taken an active part in a campaign	7
Created or signed an e-petition	15
Created or signed a paper petition	16
Donated or paid a membership fee to a charity or campaigning organisation	20
Boycotted certain products for political or environmental reasons	10
Attended political meetings	3
Donated money or paid a membership fee to a political party	2
Taken part in a demonstration, picket or march	2
Voted in an election	18
Contributed to a discussion or campaign on line or on social media	6
Taken part in a public consultation	6
None of the above	52

Source: Adapted from Hansard Society Audit of Political Engagement 11: The 2014 Report, Table 3 p. 90 (accessed 29 July 2015 at www.hansardsociety.org.uk/wp-content/uploads/2014/04/Audit-of-Political-Engagem ent-11-2014-pdf).

is that the more numerous the population that is the target for policy ideas the more diluted will be the possibilities for any citizen to have a significant role in developing and sustaining policy initiatives. The institutional structuring of public policy making systems allow but a few individuals to have a major role in setting or resolving policy problems. It would be rational for most individuals in terms of their need for gaining resources of money or expertise to seek them in other avenues than involvement in the political system and resign themselves to what they hope will be a quieter life by avoiding the stresses of seeking office in social organisations. Holding down a paid job or seeking work or managing a household is time consuming and a more important fruitful employment than involvement at a low level in policy formation. A further and very different rationale for opting out of involvement in the public policy process will be reflected in non-pluralist autocracies. In the most draconian tyrannies and totalitarian regimes that require a positive rather than passive support for the regime, citizens may accept their roles within the state through fear rather than from any ideological motives. Even within less oppressive autocratic regimes it can be more advisable to refrain from political activity to sustain whatever standard of livelihood the regime permits.

Self-interest in policy making

The problem of demonstrating through the use of positivist methodology how personal interest and motivation may substantially affect the development and implementation of policy is complicated by the universal tendency, not only demonstrated by politicians, that whilst we are eager to chronicle our deeds and praiseworthy motivations we rarely wish to reveal those characteristics that appear self-interested let alone those that may be unethical and corrupt. Politicians in their memoirs are far more concerned to discuss how they have sought to secure what they claim to be in the interests of the common good of society, such as the creation of wealth or the security of citizens, rather than how they satisfied, for example, an urge to wield power over others. It is impossible to know the exact objectives of every policy actor. Issues of self-interest often cloud the possibility of ascertaining the many objectives that lie behind the construction and implementation of policy. The issue of political self-interest is the elephant in the room that many of the 'classical' rationally orientated essays in policy studies choose to ignore.

Some attempts have however been made to quantify the extent to which policy decisions are based on ideological or more self-interested motives or longer-term political strategies. The studies, however, tend to reach very different and often incompatible conclusions. In a review of a number of studies on the motives of private and public sector workers in the provision of welfare in Britain, Julian Le Grand (2003: 35) concludes that 'Overall, it is hard to dispute the view that altruistic motivations are prevalent among the providers of public services'. Sears and Funk (1990) using survey data conducted in California show that voters in the state were not greatly influenced by their own self-interest in a referendum on taxation. However, a study using Canadian data by Danish researcher Mads Jaeger (2006: 332–3) finds that poorer citizens are far more likely to support state welfare schemes than individuals in secure employment. Among studies of policy implementers there is similar evidence of differing attitudes to self-interested or ideological values depending on what is subject to analysis and the methods of investigation. As discussed in the previous chapter, public choice theorists such as Niskanen (1971) argue that they can demonstrate that the majority of public bureaucrats are motivated to expand the size and wealth of their departments in order to benefit themselves and their coterie of fellow public servants, whilst Patrick Dunleavy (1991: 200–2) shows that senior public administrators seek to gain power and influence largely for their wish to influence policy and to work within a politicised environment. In a review of these approaches based on the analysis of voting behaviour in United States legislatures, Jackson and Kingdon (1992: 816) concluded that:

> In the end, actual legislative voting is driven by a complex mix of factors – ideology, the motivation to select 'good' public policies, a desire for re-election, party loyalty, career advancement, the pursuit of power within the legislature, and probably several others. Most of the time, various considerations that legislators weigh point them in the same direction. When those considerations conflict, we need to understand which of them receive greater weight, under what conditions and with what frequencies. Beyond understanding the positions of legislators, constituencies and parties, we need to understand the intensities of those positions and the impacts of intensities.

They point out that 'There is no single ideal design for studying these issues' (Jackson and Kingdon 1992: 816) and despite their hopes that better techniques may make such divination more plausible, there seems little advance on this score in more recent positivist literature. For some party politicians and bureaucrats with a somewhat shallow grasp on ideology there can also be the personal interest in simply getting a task handed down to them by their superiors completed successfully to their satisfaction. It may generally be concluded that most if not all policy decisions involve both policy entrepreneurs, office seekers, policy implementers and the general public in a balancing of both ideological, altruistic and self-seeking motives and that this balance is related to specific social, political and economic characteristics of whichever groups or individuals are in question. Thus, the self-interested motives of individual policy entrepreneurs even when tied up with more altruistic ideological motives can, as is suggested above, have an important influence on the birth, development and death of policy proposals.

Office holding or ideological commitment

Whilst it is impossible to quantify the motives of politicians when confronted with policy decisions, almost all commentators recognise that some element of self-interest, alongside more ideological and altruistic values, help determine political choices. For most ambitious politicians the capacity to gain office or major influence over public opinion is a necessity if they are to have any chance of developing policy. In many cases there can be serious conflict between relatively like-minded politicians who are struggling to attain high office.

> The differences between Obama and Hillary Clinton in their struggle to become the Democratic Party candidate for President in 1998 did not revolve around differing ideological or policy perspectives given their later capacity to work together in government. As Williams (2013: 12) observed 'Once-bitter rivals Barack Obama and Hillary Clinton made doubly sure that the hatchet was firmly shoved into the earth during an interview love-in yesterday … Asked why they had agreed to the rare joint interview, she responded: "A few years ago it would have been seen as improbable because we had that very long, hard primary campaign. But, you know, I've gone around the world on behalf of the President and our country, and one of the things I say to people … in politics and in democracy, sometimes you win elections and sometimes you lose elections"'.

In practice almost any political institution or bureaucracy encapsulates a complex and constantly changing network of relationships that vary from strong friendship and loyalty through indifference to hostility and destructive rivalry. Differences may often be based on ideological grounds but this may be further complicated by personal motives as policy actors seek to gain status within their organisation at the expense of others. In order to out-manoeuvre a potential rival or to destabilise the position of a party leader, politicians may often attack a colleague with whom they share common ground in the quest for power within their organisation.

> It may be questioned why in 2016 the out-going mayor of London, Boris Johnson, decided, despite declaring in the previous year his support for Britain remaining within the European Union, to change his mind and canvassed for British withdrawal when it became apparent that David Cameron was staking his reputation and continuation in the office of Prime Minister on staying in.

Ambition for power or esteem may also motivate policy activists to reject policies put forward by their rivals in order to create space for their own ideas in the crowded agenda for political reforms. Within parliamentary systems there are frequently behind the scenes battles between leading politicians to get their particular interests onto the active political agenda and this may require them to set about opposing the interests of their rivals. The development of policy is often ground out through the day-to-day battles between ministers or secretaries of state, which hinge on both ideological and rational considerations mixed with personal and institutional concerns. A particular battlefield within governments is the struggle for financial resources to be able to launch a policy. A brilliant idea for a policy advocate may not, as the following example illustrates, be acceptable to a finance minister.

> The rivalry between Gordon Brown and Tony Blair dominated the later years of the Labour Governments from 2000 onwards. For many commentators and senior members of the Party at the time the conflict was more about the quest for power and a feeling on Brown's part that promises had been broken on the agreements said to have been made to him by Blair on when he would step down as Prime Minister and allow Brown to succeed him as opposed to any ideological issue. Chris Mullin (2009: 370) records in his Diary comments made to him by Cabinet member Alan Milburn, 'Gordon is the source of all sorts of problems – briefing against the Public Finance Initiative, top up fees and goodness knows what else ...' 'So what is it all about then?' 'Goodness knows but Gordon never does anything for ideological reasons ...'

Whilst the internal political battles within most organisations may have an ideological element or are a dispute over strategy, such battles will have a strong admixture of personal interest. The capacity of a politician to make their way within their party will in part rest on their capacity to wrest time from a crowded policy agenda to get their ideas discussed or to battle successfully with a treasury to gain the financial resources to fund their proposals. Failure to achieve these goals will frequently suggest that a politician is being sidelined and lacks the esteem, status and power needed to progress within the political hierarchy.

> In 2012 a significant cabinet battle emerged between the Secretary of State for Work and Pensions, Iain Duncan Smith, and the Chancellor of the Exchequer on the introduction of a simplified system for welfare benefits to the unemployed. The system was established to encourage more unemployed people to come off benefits and obtain work by ensuring that they would not immediately lose most of their benefits if they took on a low-paid job. However, the Chancellor of the Exchequer, George Osborne, attempted to block important aspects of the reform because of the immediate costs of the proposal. As the dispute developed Duncan Smith was offered but refused a different cabinet posting and continued in office to press for his reforms. Whilst the division reflected dilemmas over welfare and costs, it was also an issue in which both senior members of the Conservative Party had to invest considerable personal interest in ensuring they retained their political esteem (Easton 2013).

The continuation or death of policy is also composed of the fluid intermingling of both ideological and personal motivations. The personal motives for supporting and developing a policy can lead policy entrepreneurs to nurture ideas far more intensively and for longer than rationality would suggest is acceptable. A politician may embark on a policy campaign and soon become so identified with their ideas that failure to develop the policy will be seen as a personal failure for that politician. In these instances political activists may irrationally ignore sound advice as to the problem their policy may face and may even attempt to unfairly discredit their critics in order to avoid the loss of face and authority by having to abandon a policy initiative to which they are publicly attached. As Shakespeare's henpecked Macbeth communes to his inner self:

> I am in blood
> Stepped in so far that, should I wade no more,
> Returning were as tedious as go'er.
> (*Macbeth* 3, 4: 136–8)

There are many examples in recent Western politics of leaders who have unwisely pursued a policy against gathering opposition for so long that they have lost much of their store of trust as a consequence. The following examples may suffice.

In the United States the capacity for leading politicians to become remote from the electorate by embarking on badly thought through policy and trying to wriggle out of taking blame for the consequences is apparent in President Nixon's initiation of the bungled Watergate break-in and his frantic efforts to cover up his involvement in the attempt to eavesdrop on his electoral opponents. Similarly, both Tony Blair and George W. Bush appear to have been convinced that Saddam Hussein as dictator of Iraq held 'weapons of mass destruction' that could be used against the West and continued to use this argument to justify their invasion of Iraq even when no such weapons were ever found.

Margaret Thatcher had since the early years of her leadership of the Conservative Party come to the conclusion that every citizen rather than only home owners should be liable to contribute through taxation directly to local authorities. She, thus, reasoned that, given that local income tax was not thought to be a sound option, the community charge, popularly known as the poll tax, levied on all mature citizens would be the most viable means of securing her aims. Against substantive opposition from within her Cabinet let alone public opinion she persevered with her idea, first in legislation that applied to Scotland that immediately met with active opposition from a substantive group of citizens who refused to pay the tax. Despite the setbacks in Scotland she still continued to promote and implement the poll tax in England and Wales. The result was public defiance and serious rioting in England that was a major factor in her downfall as Party leader and Prime Minister. Her successor John Major immediately set about enquiries that resulted in a repeal of the poll tax (Butler, Adonis and Travers 1994; King and Crewe 2013).

Policy advocates may exaggerate their fund of trust and support and may believe their position is unassailable. Experience along with genetic temperament may have taught the politician that attack is better than compromise and believe such a formula will always serve their interests. Surrounded by a small circle of sycophantic aides certain politicians become so remote from other sources of interest in the core executive that they lose touch with reality. Many policy entrepreneurs achieve their status having sufficient confidence in their own abilities that they are willing to take calculated risks in order to gain what can be an important goal of achieving fame and honour. A successful policy maker must therefore both believe in their own abilities and run the risk of losing the esteem of others if they are to fully achieve a sense of complete personal and external self-esteem. In certain cases this may also create a sense within political leaders that they are above the masses and need only listen to their own values and not the concerns of the multitude. Blair's pledge of British support for the United States in the second Gulf War may be cited as an example of such an attitude:

> I had discovered long ago the first lesson of political courage, to think anew. I had then learned the second: to be prepared to lead and to decide. I was now studying the third: how to take the calculated risk. I was going to alienate some people, like it or not. The moment you decide you divide. However, I would calculate the upset, calibrate it, understand its dimensions, assess its magnitude and ameliorate its consequences. And so I got over the surprise of the onslaught and became used to the derision, began to develop the carapace of near indifference to dispute that is so dangerous in a leader yet so necessary for survival.
>
> (Blair 2010: 28)

An essential element of successful politicians' equipment is 'a thick skin' composed of a deep conviction as to their own ability and value to the outside world and a resultant strong conviction that those who oppose their ideas must be defeated. It is also a common human trait to convince oneself of the virtues of the rational and altruistic merits of policy decisions that will have emerged, at least in part from strongly self-interested motives.

> Chris Mullin (2010: 411) a junior Minister in governments formed by Tony Blair observed in his Diaries that 'Palmerston said of Gladstone "He has the ability to persuade himself of any view that he chooses to hold". Of whom does that remind one?' He meant of course Tony Blair.

At its worst self-esteem may be in certain individuals a belief in their own abilities coupled with a total disregard for the opinions of others. An absence of empathy for other individuals is widely recognised as a characteristic of some of the most violent criminals and has in the realm of policy makers been ascribed to dictators such as Joseph Stalin (Service 2004: 336–45). Such moods may also be built on a sense of personal self-esteem that rests on the knowledge that as a political autocrat you may be hated by others but also so deeply feared by those you lead that they will not dare to turn against you.

> The police states of the communist world under the control of Stalin, Hitler's Germany or Saddam Hussein's Iraq sought with considerable success to cement the powers of their leaders through ensuring that any potential opponents to their rule would be summarily eliminated by secret police who could, as in Stalin's paranoid world, be in turn eliminated in case they may be emboldened sufficiently to turn their knowledge against their political master (see for example Chase 2007).

The struggle for office and its consequent baggage of esteem and wealth must not, however, be viewed solely in the context of bitter struggles between politicians but is as likely to be the source of continuity and support for policy development and legitimation. Many of the apprentice or middle ranking members of political parties or bureaucracies will hitch themselves to factions in their party or a civil service in the hope of securing preferment and promotion. Many a rising political hopeful will cast around for ideas consonant with the belief systems of their organisation that will advance their progress.

> Soon after becoming an MP Margaret Thatcher came second in the annual ballot for backbench MPs to present a Private Member's Bill to Parliament. 'I had only given the most general consideration to the topic I would choose, but had just a week to make up my mind' (Thatcher 1995: 109). She pursued seriously two ideas before alighting on a proposal to ensure local authorities could not hold council meetings without the press having a right to be present by decreeing that the whole council could meet as a committee of the council (Thatcher 1995: 109–12).

Middle ranking politicians will in many cases be likely in public to support rather than oppose the ideas of their leaders, even when they harbour serious reservations concerning their policies, in order to retain favour from those who will determine their promotion or retention of office in the organisational hierarchy. Hugo Young (1989: 522) in his biography of Margaret Thatcher observes in relation to her insistence on pursuing the poll tax that:

> This was one issue on which the Conservative backbenchers, sensitive to intense local feeling in their constituencies, did produce a small rebellion. It was seen off with contemptuous ease, many of its supporters scuttling for cover when they contemplated the trade off between pleasing marginal constituents and not displeasing the person who exerted absolute control over their political careers.

Politicians often face a difficult dilemma when showing support for their political party, faction or leader even though they seriously disagree with some of their organisation's or leaders' policies. Members of legislatures are usually highly sensitive to the problems that may emerge if they publicly oppose policies supported by their leaders. Intransigence and rebellion will, at least in the short term, not only damage a politician's chances of promotion within the organisation's hierarchy but in liberal democratic systems erode public confidence in that party and could precipitate their fall from power and possible loss of their seat in Parliament.

The institutional consequences of personal motivation

The impact of self-interested motives in driving, at least in part, the actions of most politicians and policy makers should not be viewed solely as a factor in determining the biographical details of individuals but becomes, from the point of view of a study of public policy, a significant force in the structuring of policy making institutions and behaviour. The institutional basis of any political organisation is built, not only on ideological grounds, but on self-interested motives such as belonging and being loved by others and perhaps more prosaically to have an aim and goal in life. As implied by Maslow (1970: 20–1) the desire for love is to have close contact with a partner and family and a circle of friends but the sense of belonging that is allied to this motive could be extended to the values that bind us to a particular nationality, political party, clan or ethnic group. From a political perspective it may also be argued that these motives are more fundamental in the beginning of a political career and form the platform for the acquisition of security, esteem and power within the policy arena. The motivation to collaborate with others is a basic instinct that underlines the capacity of human beings to be so successful as an animal species since we collectively can work together to strive for common goals. As Adam Smith (1999: 110–126) realised, collaboration is essential for efficient production of goods and, we can also infer, for the effective implementation of policy. Assigning to ourselves and partners different but complementary roles that engage people with different skills is the key to successfully completing complex projects. The desire to belong to social groups ensures that many policy makers are not only loyal to their immediate family but to wider social groups, be they a political party, a clan or a nation. For many political activists, particularly in the rank and file of their political party or interest group, membership of their organisation can determine their circle of friends and create mutual loyalties that, despite inevitable strains, may be difficult to dissolve.

Partisanship may also be built, especially in autocratic regimes, on the contrasting motives of a concern for self-preservation. A substantive tranche of support for authoritarian and totalitarian regimes may be based on fear concerning the consequences of rebellion against the values espoused by the state ideology and self-interested concerns of its policy makers. Self-interest can also be an agent of change as policy activists will often seek to impose their own ideas on their organisation in order to advance their political ambitions. Such behaviour inevitably leads within organisations to tensions over policy as adversaries group themselves into factions that become a more potent vehicle for their loyalty than the organisation as a whole. For many aspiring politicians the path to success is to develop policy or, more negatively, oppose policy suggestions made by rivals to high office in order to further their political career. It is in such circumstances that the many examples of apparent reversals of professed ideological values and policy sponsorships cut across any semblance of disinterested rationality that normatively is often seen as the touchstone of ethical policy development. McMenamin and Gwiazda (2011) demonstrate that in the national legislature of Poland representatives are more likely to switch parties if they fear that their party may lose seats in the next election rather than any concerns over policy differences or their capacity to gain office in government. A combination of ideological and self-interested motives, often reacting to social changes in their environment, can eventually lead to the development of rapid policy change within a political structure.

The vote winning slogan 'New Labour' that accompanied Blair's leadership to move the Party closer to the centre ground was in part based on a determination to create more popular policies than had characterised the years in opposition in the 1980s and 1990s but also required personal determination of the new leader to press forward the idea. 'Alastair (Campbell) invented the phrase "New Labour, New Britain". He said we should put it up in the hall as the strapline for the (Labour Party Annual) conference. Looking back now, it seems obvious that we should have done, but at the time there was a serious dispute … Finally I thought, Let's go for it. There was indeed a reaction but it was containable, and the impact was massive, an emphatic signal that this was not going to be a minor refurbishment but a wholesale renovation' (Blair 2010: 85).

Pluralism and the cadre party

Within liberal democratic regimes where there is a tendency, not necessarily towards an end of ideology, but for the domination of a specific form of social capitalism in which the policy direction of parties that are competing for power, may within this broad ideological envelope, be largely determined by self-interested values. An increasingly important avenue towards the development of policy for the largely self-interested values of party leaders is the creation of political parties that seek to maximise their vote in states where there is, rather than an end of ideology, the domination of a broad, hegemonic, ideological consensus. In social democratic states this trend was argued by Otto Kirchheimer (1966) to be the basis for creating 'catch-all' parties that competed with each other to secure the greatest number of votes even though they scarcely differed in their fundamental aims. The parties, therefore, attract ambitious politicians who were largely interested in seeking power within the consensual political system for their own interest rather than any specific ideological aim. This view has been further developed using the term 'cadre party' by Katz and Mair (1995) to refer to organisations close to the state whose policy entrepreneurs act as professional policy makers seeking a role as the intermediaries between the state and civil society. Within such a framework the political leaders of these mass parties have a deep-seated career interest in developing policies that ensure their survival in power. Indeed for some the self-interest in making a career out of politics and ensuring the self-satisfaction of securing positions of leadership and power is an essential glue that helps keep the cadre party together. A frequent consequence of the cadre party systems in Western liberal democracies is the creation of patterns of coalition politics that, as the result of increasingly convergent ideological positions, appear to be highly flexible in relationship to their partnerships.

The institutional role of political parties and many interest groups to gain power in these circumstances is a product of the aggregation of the ambitions of their active members who will be concerned to secure their own individual interests through the medium of institutions and networks. The conflicts between rival political parties will also be reflected in the intra-party conflicts and alliances among policy activists within almost any institution. Similarly, within bureaucratic agencies, conflicts emerge between ambitious public servants who seek to reach the highest positions within their organisation. Individual politicians will in catch-all party systems seek out the most popular policy option rather than the most ideologically rational views, they will denigrate the views of their rivals from higher office and will be as much, or more, concerned with the skills of presenting their ideas rather than developing a disinterested judgement of the policy problems facing their nation. Bureaucrats will be asked, or be driven, to implement policies that will best appeal to those who will further promote them in their political career and, rather than disinterestedly evaluate their policies, will seek to validate for the public their actions to suit their own professional political interests.

Such an analysis of cadre party systems may first appear to present a serious critique of such systems. They can appear to be based on systematic amoral behaviour concerned with individuals and their institutions seeking to gain power by pandering to popular interest rather than developing among themselves reasoned arguments to ensure the good of the citizens whom they govern. However, it must be remembered that democracy is based on the idea that those who govern must be sensitive to popular opinion. It is a system that can puncture the pretensions of idealist ideologically driven demagogues and corrupt dictators. If the cadre parties of liberal democracies fail to develop fair and effective policy, it is arguably as much the fault of mass society given the aphorism that in such systems 'we get the government that we deserve'. Certain pluralist and participative theories of democracy may argue that the core executive should forget their own interests and simply seek to forward what they consider to be majoritarian policies. However, as John Stuart Mill pointed out, the role of the executive should be to forward policies that are based on ethical principles founded on sound intellectual reasoning that will give them a superior idea of the effectiveness of a potential policy than could be developed through reference to the beliefs of a much less educated electorate. Within liberal democracies members of core executives who seek power as a personal goal and lack substantive ideological aims or ethical beliefs may lend support to a mix of populist but irrational policies that have little bearing on the strategic development of their society.

Corruption

Self-interest not only is a factor determining the structuring and cohesion of parties and party systems but at a deeper level also in the ordering of the political and civic culture of many regimes. Popularly it is seen, especially in Western liberal democracies, to lead to the accusation that certain regimes harbour political practices favouring their powerful elites and even trickling down to invade mass society with immoral practices that are consequently seen as corrupt. The issue of what may be seen as immoral corruption will be visited in the following chapter on ethics. There are many views of what constitutes moral and immoral action and differing political systems may have differing views on what actions are immoral. There is a complex debate on the circumstances in which self-interest is promoted by deception or domination, often through fear or bribery, and when this crosses a line between moral and immoral action and becomes corruption. Exactly where such a line lies is a problem considered in more detail in the following chapter. The pursuit of self-interest allied with a concern to benefit the general welfare of society is often regarded as acceptable, and for adherents to New Right theory is a mainspring for social advancement. There are, however, circumstances where the content of policy, or even more seriously the structure of the policy process, is established so as to benefit solely the personal interests of the individuals who make and implement policy rather than any concern for the good of society. Such behaviour may be termed corruption. The term is subject to many interpretations but can be usefully defined as 'behaviour which deviates from the normal duties of a public rule because of private-regarding (personal, close family, private clique) pecuniary or status gains; or violates rules against the exercise of certain types of private-regarding influence' (Nye 1967: 419).

For some individuals the acquisition of personal wealth over and above the means to simply meet physiological needs becomes an important lifelong motive. Some policy shapers enter their political and bureaucratic careers as an avenue towards obtaining well rewarded positions and, when circumstances allow, corruptly raid the public purse.

The scandals that surfaced in 2009 concerning expenses of MPs in the British Parliament demonstrate that many politicians will, if given the opportunity, seek to feather their own nest. The temptation to corruption stemmed from the establishment of a rather broad set of rules concerning the reimbursement of expenses as a trade-off for below inflation increases in MPs' salaries. Considerable numbers of MPs not only claimed the maximum for legitimate expenses but also stretched the limit of legitimacy to demands never envisaged by their original rules, such as claiming for the construction of a duck-house in a pleasure garden. Many MPs were subsequently obliged to pay back expenses received for exaggerated claims and a handful of MPs faced prosecution for making fraudulent claims.

In states in which the rule of law is not backed by a strong civic culture, public policy making can be suffused with an interest within the government to develop schemes that allow extensive corruption. Policy implementation can in many countries be seriously distorted by endemic requirements by bureaucrats to receive bribes in order to overlook a citizen's need to conform to the law or induce them to undertake their duties. In underdeveloped nations such a tendency is sharpened by the low salaries that are available to rank and file civil servants or police officers who may feel obliged for the security of income to take bribes. Whilst corruption of this form is most frequently associated with underdeveloped states it must be remembered that a capacity for most governments to be able to implement policy on an equitable basis is a relatively recent phenomenon. Moreover what is corruption is in the final analysis as much a subjective as a legal judgement. In many European countries such as Britain, prior to full democratisation of the political system, politics was a career that required politicians to undertake what would now be seen as corruption as a normal requirement.

A post in government or the membership of the House of Commons or Lords was not a salaried position and civil servants did not until the eighteenth century receive a substantial wage. It was expected that an up and coming bureaucrat or politician who had not made or inherited a fortune would use positions of power to feather their own nest by unlawful means in order to pay for the costs of getting elected to Parliament and to be able to live the standard of life necessary to gain influence in powerful circles (Hennessy 1989: 1–51).

Corruption may also involve not just a concern for money but a quest for personal esteem or security that can frequently be a significant component of a desire for personal power. This may involve distortion of truth or concealment of unethical behaviour to develop policy in the personal interest of a policy leader.

Lloyd George, British Prime Minister from 1916 to 1922, sold peerages to leading industrialists in order to use the funds to establish a break away party, the National Liberals, from the Liberal Party following his displacement of Herbert Asquith as Prime Minister but not as leader of the Liberal Party. 'All prime ministers, then as now, nominate individuals for honours in return for political support or financial contributions to party coffers, and there was more than a touch of hypocrisy in the objections to Lloyd George's use of this patronage. However, as a Welsh outsider, untroubled by the respect for the aristocracy, Lloyd George had encouraged a larger traffic in these baubles, particularly after the war. Lacking any other substantial resources, he traded on the vanity of the rich to build up a tidy little fund (some 3 million by 1922) for his own political use. Knighthoods were flogged off for around £10,000, a hereditary peerage for at least £50,000' (Constantine 1992: 65–6).

Whilst the issue of corruption is clearly seen as a propensity to pursue interests that break the law or established rules of conduct, there is also an equally corrosive form of corruption where those in power distort the customarily accepted rules of that society to create legal means to benefit themselves. It is for obvious reasons difficult to ascertain how widespread this concern may be as individuals will normally wish to avoid the accusation of corruption by clothing their actions in a veneer of rationality.

In Italy during the political dominance of Berlusconi the ruling coalition established as policy that the Prime Minister would be immune from prosecution during his or her term of office. Given the numerous accusations of corruption being levelled against Berlusconi his acquiescence to such a policy might well be regarded as a self-interested concern.

The need for security can also promote even darker sides of political intrigue and, at its worst, violence. The successful politician is frequently concerned to retain and enhance their position of power by destroying their enemies who are rivals for the existing position or for their potential promotion, or are opponents of their policy aspirations. History is littered with essentially insecure autocrats who have wreaked vengeance on any real or imagined impediments to their capacity to make policy.

Stalin has been regarded by most of his biographers as racked by insecurity but as Robert Service (2004: 238) argues 'Stalin was willing to pay any price in lives to attain his objectives. In all lives but his own. For Stalin the supreme criterion of political judgment was the need to enhance and protect his political power'.

Conclusion

This chapter has shown that policy decisions and implementation can be greatly affected by the personal interests of political activists as much as ideological concerns to benefit society as a whole. Similarly, the political choices of voters are influenced by the extent to which policies may affect themselves as individuals rather than a more dispassionate concern for justice and fairness. In many regimes, including liberal democracies, socialisation of citizens based on the view that only a few can profit from political engagement ensures a majority in the population are largely alienated from taking action on forming public policy. How far personal or wider ideological interests predominate in such choices is, however, difficult if not impossible to quantify, either at the level of the individual or wider society. Not only is measurement of attitudes a problematic task but also the capacity to clearly delineate what is personal and what may be altruistic interests. Nevertheless, the presence of private interest in the determination of policy outcomes cannot be brushed aside and such an interest seriously undermines any pretensions towards developing rational value-free policy based on an appeal solely to evidence. An analytical framework to public policy must show an awareness of the impact of personal as well as ideological interest and serious consideration of how far societies should accept policy ambition stemming from personal interest to be an ethical basis for political decision making. Moreover, the motive of self-interest is not simply shown in terms of personal corruption of policy activists which in many wealthy and well regulated states is kept to a low level, but more significantly serves as a motive in keeping political groups such as bureaucracies and political parties acting in the interests of their powerful paymasters and mentors for their career advancement.

6   Ethics and public policy

Ethics, as the study and practice of moral beliefs, by its very nature ought to be a major consideration in any process of policy development. Morality concerns how an individual's behaviour to others and themselves may be justified. It is impossible to process public policy that has no moral implications. Any workable society is dependent on moral rules as to how we should behave towards one another and, as Thomas Hobbes observed, without such rules there can be no society. Robinson Crusoe when alone on his desert island was morally free to do whatever he pleased, but one man alone does not of course constitute a society. As with any statement of preference moral claims are not issues that can be judged by any scientific positivist thought to be either right or wrong. Morality whilst subjective is, however, as discussed in Chapter 3 subject to rational thought, as the study of ethics which can, from basic principles concerning the value of human life, construct theories that can guide how we ought to behave towards others.

Ideologies normally claim to have an ethical dimension and the two often are complementary and closely intertwined but are best considered in studies of social analysis or theory as separate elements of study. Ideological analysis largely describes and seeks to understand systems of social ideas but is not always concerned to justify whether the ideology has a rational foundation that ought to be accepted by all of humanity. Ideology is also generally less prescriptive as to how everyone should behave and is wider in scope as it concerns how political and economic institutions should be constructed to conform to its precepts. Few ideologies are wholly constructed on the basis of ethical thought given that they must incorporate consideration of how society can be built given the physical and social realities of human behaviour. Moral analysis concerns itself less with the reality of human behaviour but how the human race ought to behave.

The impact of moral considerations on policy content

Politicians, especially in pluralist liberal democratic societies, are frequently hesitant about providing well reasoned moral justifications for their policy preferences even though numerous policy possibilities are instantly rejected by politicians because their sense of ethics and morality makes particular actions unthinkable.

> Chris Mullin writing when undersecretary of state at the Foreign Office records in his Diary that 'On Serbia I don't have a problem. We cannot allow the return of ethnic cleansing in Europe. Any doubts I had were clarified by the slaughter at Srebrenica' (Mullin 2010: 132).

In certain policy areas some engagement with moral issues is unavoidable as the process of digging into complex ethical debate becomes essential if progress towards consensus can ever be obtained. Within the United States and Britain arguments on abortion, homosexuality or animal rights have been important political flashpoints that are based on moral argument. These controversies may fall into the category of 'wicked issues' that are difficult to resolve with clear policy directives, not because resolution and implementation of these policies are problematic, but because there is deep disagreement on whether a particular policy is morally acceptable. Among the most difficult decisions for many political leaders is whether to become involved in military action that could lead to death, injury and the destruction of homes, commerce and the natural environment.

One of the most profound moral dilemmas faced by any politician confronted President Kennedy and his closest advisors during the Cuban missile crisis. As President of the United States, Kennedy had a duty to his nation to ensure their safety against the possibility of attack with nuclear weapons by foreign and ideologically opposing nations. However, to oppose the Soviet Union's placement of nuclear missiles in neighbouring Cuba he would have to confront Soviet warships supplying the weapons which would risk the possibility of a nuclear confrontation that could have untold consequences for human life and civilisation.

Douglas Amy (1984: 587) has observed that 'Ethical analysis is shunned because it frequently threatens the professional and political interests of both analysts and policymakers. The administrator, the legislator, and policy analyst all shy away from the risks involved in ethical inquiry.' Frank Fischer (1983: 5) similarly observes that 'In political and social theory generally, the neglect of ethics and normative discourse in modern organizational life has been an enduring theme'.

Although morality is a major issue in determining how we ought to live and, consequently, the policies that we create, it is often not discussed as a concern that needs to be addressed as an essential filter that should determine the outcome of policy deliberation and implementation. Few politicians set out their stall by arguing they are adopting a specifically ethical approach to their policy decisions. The first Foreign Secretary appointed in 1997 by Tony Blair was Robin Cook, a voluble and capable left wing Labour MP. Cook startled the electorate and initially gained plaudits by announcing he would establish his foreign policy on ethical grounds. The attempt was difficult to implement in practice and whilst never renouncing his stance Cook was moved to a different cabinet post and later resigned from the government over his opposition to Blair's decision to join with President George W. Bush in the invasion of Iraq.

Although explicit discussion of moral values is often avoided in political debate and academic analysis of policy issues, this is not a result of a lack of any well accepted guidelines as to what may constitute moral practice. However, the complex issues of determining what is acceptable ethical behaviour may often be avoided as they could unnecessarily unearth serious differences of opinion among citizens. The complexity of ethical debate and the impossibility of showing that certain moral codes are logically right or wrong can plunge analysts into an inextricable morass of argument and debate. Many policy makers, often without success, would prefer to kick such issues into the long grass by avoiding debate or legislation on such issues.

Christopher Mullin (2010: 414–15) reports in his Diary a conversation with former Foreign Secretary Robin Cook concerning the revelation following the second Gulf War, that was ostensibly pursued to counter Saddam Hussein's use of Weapons of Mass Destruction (WMD), that in fact no WMDs existed in Iraq:

'I think we are in trouble' he (Robin Cook) said. 'The news over the next month or so will be dominated by the American Congressional hearings. The problem is that the Americans never wanted to use WMD as the reason for going to war. They only went along with it to keep us happy and now that war is over, they no longer see the need to keep up the pretence.' The Man (Tony Blair) says Robin will 'probably be acquitted of lying but he will be very damaged'. He will want to talk about anything but Iraq, but it won't go away. The one thing he will not face up to is that to focus on WMD was a mistake. 'All he keeps saying is, "This is what the intelligence said at the time."'

A further issue that may blunt the extent of moral discourse is the broad issue of corruption. The demands of moral theory even when almost universally accepted are by no means obeyed within most societies. The problem of corruption is particularly prevalent in the relationship of citizens to the public sector as discussed in the previous chapter. There is even in the most developed societies a tension between self-interest and the demands of the state on issues such as taxation or business regulations on health and safety or disclosure of information. Those who are tempted to break moral codes for their own personal self-interest or the interests of private sector organisations will be concerned to conceal their behaviour and undermine policies that are designed to create a safe and fair society. Given that ethical codes and moral values are seen as essential, if rarely made explicit, components of both the subject matter of most policy statements, as well as the means through which policy is processed, it is useful to outline as briefly as possible some of the key moral codes that have global prevalence in today's world.

Morality derived from religion

Until the eighteenth century religious texts as interpreted by scholarly clerics tended to be regarded as the fount of ethical behaviour. In Western Europe until the reformation and enlightenment, ethical precepts were derived largely from edicts of Christianity and Jewish faiths that had over the centuries also incorporated a strong element of classical Greek thought and particularly the rather conflicting views of Plato and Aristotle. In the Far East, a similar mixture of religious precepts and more secular ideas tended to codify moral value as in Buddhist and Confucian thought. For many policy advocates religious justifications provide the moral basis of their policy actions and within some cultures and sub-cultures, such as the 'Tea Party' factions in the United States or the Muslim fundamentalists leading the ISIS incursions in the Middle East, the word of God as they interpret it is the sole fount of their policy aims and objectives. However, reference solely to a specific religious text is unlikely to result in a rationale that can create peace and harmony throughout the world. Zealots for one specific interpretation of the word of God or of Gods must reflect that in the case of most religious texts different people have widely differing interpretations as to what the text may mean, as is illustrated by the many divisions within the world's major religions. Moreover mature reflection may lead to the thought that if the God or Gods may praise and punish us for our deeds in an afterlife, they have given the duty to us to work with the whole of humanity to determine how we should live peacefully and well together.

The development of scientific methodology and religious scepticism has, therefore, led to the emergence of more secular ideas and the creation of several schools of ethical thought based on rational humanist grounds. Rationality is meant here not, of course, in terms of absolute logical proof but relates to the objective of ensuring humanity lives in harmony rather than in a state of constant conflict. An important development in the creation of modern Western ethical thought was that individuals were born with basic natural rights. These ideas were established by John Locke (1924) and are now extensively placed on a worldwide level through the United Nations charter on human rights. The claim for rights is, however, not on its own a strong philosophical position as one person's claim to have a right may be to remove rights from others. If, as Locke and Nozick claim, we all have an absolute right to our property, can there be a moral duty for us to pay taxes without our individual consent, and, if we claim an absolute right to freedom, can we imprison those who break the law?

Utilitarianism

An important stream of ethical and essentially secular thought that tried to avoid a simplistic appeal to human rights emerged in the late eighteenth century through the work of Jeremy Bentham (1748–1832).

> Bentham died in the year of the Great Electoral Reform Act, 1832 that he did much to promote in terms of political theory. However, he is still to be seen today at University College London where he sits each year at the dinner table for a celebration of his role as one of the founding creators of the University of London. When he died he wanted his brain and body used for science. They were preserved and remain in the University.

Bentham argued on similar grounds to Hume that there was no scientifically provable justification for moral beliefs and that we must found these ideas on our personal preferences (Parekh 1973: 45–50). He also broadly accepted the view of the English philosopher Thomas Hobbes (1588–1679) that we were primarily self-interested beings concerned with satisfying our own desires and that the claim that we have natural rights was 'nonsense on stilts' (Parekh 1973: 269). At root individuals preferred whatever made them happy, or, to be more precise, gave them the most utility, by which Bentham meant the greatest pleasure for the least effort or pain. In the absence of any other possible guide we should, therefore, pursue whatever makes us happy and reject as wrong whatever makes us unhappy. However, in the real world, since some people's idea of happiness is likely to make others very unhappy, we have to compromise on this position. As it is impossible to secure a society in which everyone is totally happy, we must at least try to attain a position in which we secure for the sum of individuals in the world as much happiness as is possible. For Bentham, 'it is the greatest happiness of the greatest number that is the measure of right and wrong' (Bentham 1779: 3). Utilitarianism is often classified as a consequentialist argument in that it is the consequences of an act that determines its morality. The implication of the Utilitarian philosophy is that morality is not a universal code but is relative to the individual's situation at any particular moment. It may, for example, in certain circumstances be right to harm someone if by such an action a larger number of individuals' lives are made happier. However, this should not be interpreted as suggesting Utilitarianism allows us to undertake any act that immediately produced happiness. Bentham was aware that habitual lying might damage the trust that binds society together and, therefore, eventually erode human relationships to a point where everyone would suffer. He similarly did not think it acceptable to imprison an innocent person in order to deter others from committing crimes.

Utilitarianism for all its apparent logic nevertheless presents some serious problems for establishing a clear and equitable theory of ethics. It is firstly difficult to operationalise since it is impossible to determine how much one person's happiness or pain may be greater than another's. Bentham believed pleasure and pain could be quantified through what he termed a felicific calculus but this seems a highly dubious proposition in practice. Critics of Utilitarianism also pointed out that certain pleasures could not be argued to be of equal value. Is the pleasure of a student who indolently repairs to the pub with the prospect of getting drunk to be valued more than that of a student who painstakingly struggles with understanding a mathematical problem? John Stuart Mill (1863: 260) attempted to answer this question by arguing that:

> It is better to be a human being satisfied than a pig satisfied; better to be Socrates dissatisfied than a fool satisfied. And if the fool or the pig are of different opinion, it is because they only know their own side of the question. The other party to the question knows both sides.

A further problem is whether we can accept some of the consequence of Utilitarian thought that suggests that it is permissible to harm an individual if this increases the general happiness of the population.

Following the attack of 9/11 on the Twin Towers, the government of the United States embarked with allied countries on a policy of rendition in which alleged terrorists who were suspected of aiding attacks on Western nations were secretly captured and removed to states favouring the Western powers who would be likely to use torture to obtain information or concessions from the prisoners. Such action was to be kept secret and under a Utilitarian view could be justified if it was clear that the unhappiness meted out on the prisoners was mitigated by preventing far worse unhappiness to those who might be killed or injured by terrorist atrocities that might be committed or supported by the detainees. Many ethical codes such as that of Immanuel Kant would, however, dispute whether such action was at all moral.

Some Utilitarians argue that this problem can be resolved if we argue that it is essential for everyone's happiness to keep to rules that guarantee general well-being. Rule Utilitarians maintain that we should calculate the happiness derived from everyone following a particular rule rather than the happiness derived from each individual act. Thus, if telling the truth generally ensures a happier society this should be the rule to be followed even on occasions where the truth may in this instance cause more unhappiness than happiness. The basis of this view lies in the point that if everyone told lies believing this would make everyone happier, then sooner or later trust would disappear as people's deceit was discovered and the happiness of society would suffer. However, if the basis of morality is still the calculation as to whether an act increases the sum of human happiness, then how can rule utilitarianism be justified in cases where the rules are broken but it is certain no one will find this out and no one is made less happy as a consequence?

Kantian ethics

Whilst Utilitarian ethics had an important influence on Anglo-American political and social culture it has throughout the twentieth century been contrasted with ideas developed in continental Europe and particularly centred on the ideas of Immanuel Kant and later theorists such as Hegel and more currently the ideas of the Frankfurt school of critical theory and the United States ethical analyst John Rawls.

Immanuel Kant was born in 1724 in Königsberg in what was then Prussia but is now a Russian enclave between the Baltic States and Poland. Kant spent his entire life as a professor at the University of his home town although his earlier career was devoted to the sciences and only in mid-life did he turn to writing philosophy. Despite the relative obscurity of Königsberg his writings and lectures rapidly gained a wide audience and reflected the high minded and pious values of the intellectual classes of that time. It was necessary for students to arrive an hour early for his lectures in order to get a place in the lecture hall (Scruton 2001b: 5). His work, though not easy to read even in translation, has been a cornerstone of much Continental European thought and covers a huge range from ethics to epistemology and metaphysics.

Kantian ethics is now widely seen as a major critique of the more flexible justification of moral values in Utilitarian thought. Kant accepted to some degree Hume's idea that moral values could never be absolutely proven and were matters of preference. As in the currently fashionable theory of critical realism, there is perhaps absolute truth but, through the distortions of our personal thoughts and perceptions, we can never be certain of it. However, we develop ideas and beliefs that both work to build a functioning society that instinctively seem to be right and are accepted in the realms of practical reason. Morality lies in this arena. Kant argued in relation to these moral views that mature individuals knew what was morally correct 'a priori', that is innately and without the need for further justification. This in-built understanding formed the basis of an acceptable ethical code which he refined into three statements that he referred to as categorical imperatives. Roger Scruton (2001b: 85–7) translates these as:

1   Act only according to that maxim which I can at the same time will as universal law.
2   Act so as to treat humanity, whether in my own self or in that of another, always as an end, and never as a means only.
3   Every rational being must so act as if he were by his maxims in every case a legislating member of the universal kingdom of ends.

Moral beliefs are for Kant statements of universally accepted actions. We must, argued Kant, ensure that what we do is what is good for everyone and should therefore as the first imperative commands only act in a way that we would expect others to behave towards ourselves. Thus, we must not kill or steal from others or lie in order to deceive people since a world in which everyone acted in this way would disintegrate into chaos. We intuitively know, argued Kant, that killing or hurting one another is wrong and we would not want anyone to kill or hurt us. This is argued in the first and reinforced in the third strand of the categorical imperatives that require us to accept the universality of moral rules. Moral actions, Kant argued, relate to each individual and cannot be distributed and alleviated by membership of a group. Central to this view was that human beings were to be treated as 'ends' in themselves and not, as could be the case in Utilitarian thought, 'means' to an end.

> The decision of the United States government to imprison without trial in their base on Guantanamo Bay in Cuba captured Taliban or Al-Qaida fighters who were suspected of being key commanders opposing Western interests in Afghanistan may arguably be justified by Utilitarian theory but could find no justification on any Kantian interpretation of moral conduct.

Thus, as the second element of the categorical imperative says, moral imperatives are not arranged to establish the best actions for the totality of human beings but are directed equally to each individual and related to each particular individual. We must also pursue these actions not because it is expedient and will simply be beneficial to us but from a sense of a 'good will'. We have, in contradiction to the Utilitarian view, a duty to act selflessly.

Kantian ethics can be criticised as it suggests that there should be greater consensus as regards what is morally correct than appears to be the case. It does not, moreover, tolerate the view that moral beliefs are relative and that one action may be right for one person but wrong for another. This creates difficulties in explaining moral dilemmas. If moral beliefs are universal how can they sometimes appear to contradict one another? In such circumstances a Kantian may resolve the problem by asking how would any reasonable person act in the case of the dilemma to resolve the difficulty but such a response presupposes that there are obvious answers to all difficulties. The argument is often illustrated in relation to Kant's insistence that we must always tell the truth by the absurdity of telling the truth when by lying to someone who was intending to commit a murder we might save an individual's life. Few sensible individuals would not say that in the case of this clash of moral imperatives, lying or murder, it is better to lie. However, many moral dilemmas, such as Kennedy's gamble regarding the Cuban missile crisis, are not so easily resolved:

The nature of politics is to exaggerate success, to oversell, to deny failure, to spin – or as the public interpret it, to lie. Even the giants of the past, Roosevelt and Churchill lied. On occasion they had no choice in order to serve their nations' interests.

(Flynn 2012: 250)

Kantian values became more fashionable in Britain in the late nineteenth century as theorists sought to reconcile idealist ethics with the liberal values of the century. Prominent among such thinkers was Thomas Hill Green who began to lay the foundation of the idea of the welfare state, arguing that for a fair society it was essential that the state provided the essential facilities such as education and public health amenities that were needed for every person in a society to have the means to make the best of life chances. Thomas Hobhouse later developed from Green's ideas much of the moral ground for the later foundation of the welfare state.

John Rawls and justice as fairness

A development of Kantian values by the American philosopher John Rawls (1971) has done much to establish a clearer version of how to secure in policy making a system of freedom with a fair distribution of resources and power. He argues that the concept of justice translates to the issue of fairness. If we know nothing about two individuals, common sense, equivalent to the Kantian view that we know what is basically morally right as self-evident, would suggest that we treat each person equally. He gives the example of how two people marooned on a desert island would divide the resources available to them assuming they had no prior knowledge of one another. The presumption in such circumstances is to divide the resources equally. If, however, one of the individuals is disadvantaged compared with the other we would be inclined to compensate the less advantaged person and would certainly not add to the advantages of the better-off person. However, such compensation can only be made if, by rewarding the disadvantaged person, that reward is to their material benefit. Thus, it is nonsense to allow a student with no mathematical ability to take a degree in the subject but it might be reasonable to compensate a student who has potential to be excellent at maths but is disadvantaged because she has not had the adequate preparation to be at a level equivalent to other students of the same ability. Rawls develops a principle that:

1   each person has an equal right to the most extensive basic liberty compatible with a similar equality for others
2   social and economic liberties are to be arranged so that they are both a) reasonably expected to be to everyone's advantage and b) attached to positions and offices open to all.

(Rawls 1971: 60–1)

Among social democrats the ideas of Rawls have been widely praised as a means to reconcile the values of fair distribution of resources and opportunities in a society that welcomes regulated competition in which the unfair inequalities that result from a strategy of the survival of the fittest are evened out by an ethical policy of redistribution through networks of public democratic agencies (Hattersley 1987). The theory has however been subject to much criticism both of a constructive character and more destructively, as in the work of New Right theorists such as Nozick (1974). The more constructive developments of Rawls' theory relate to issues such as encompassing diversity and differing needs of separate communities or the necessity for global justice rather than differing judicial principles within individual states (Hutchings 2010).

Realist politics

None of these arguments concerning the foundation of morality, religious revelation, Kantianism, Utilitarianism or Rawls' concept of fairness, are without flaws. However, despite their problems these are powerful arguments that can and do have strong practical application. As it is impossible to conceive of a world that is wholly without moral values such reasoning must present some of the basic groundwork for guiding our ideas in the debates and controversies to be encountered in this study and this may be illustrated by considering some of the more familiar ethical dilemmas faced by those who develop and implement public policy. It may be argued that theories underlying ethical behaviour based on religious, or secular argument are too fundamentalist to be operated within the real world. All such theories have serious flaws and if carried forward with slavish and unflinching zeal can result in serious injustice and unwarranted violence. A pragmatic school of thought popularised by the American theorist John Dewey (1998) maintained that whilst many moral theories provide useful practical insights into how we should determine our decisions, it is unwise to always accept a single theoretical viewpoint in all circumstances. Policy should on these grounds be made with reference to moral values that appear to be most suited to the complex circumstances in which they have arisen and to which they may be applied.

It is argued by many pragmatists that policy decisions must be made in the real world within a framework of what is termed realpolitik. This does not entail that policy makers are necessarily amoral but that they are guided by moral views that are appropriate for specific environments and in the interests of those obligations placed upon them, by the nature of their office as a policy entrepreneur and gate-keeper.

> It would be difficult to justify the assassination of Osama Bin Laden on the grounds of Kantian ethics, New Testament Christian beliefs or many aspects of rule utilitarian theory. The decision made by President Obama to send United States troops to uni-laterally invade Pakistan territory, storm Bin Laden's home and kill him without any serious attempt to capture him, let alone hold him to trial, seems difficult to accept in terms of the moral guidelines through which he appears to justify most of his decisions.

One of the first and best known proponents of this pragmatic view was the Renaissance Florentine politician, Niccolò Machiavelli (1950), who maintained that, since the world was populated by individuals of ill will and little virtue, any leaders who seek to act with scrupulous honour will be outwitted and deceived by their enemies both within and external to the state. The leader of a state, whom Machiavelli referred to as the Prince, should lie, cheat and, if necessary, physically attack the country's enemies by assuming a virtuous stance when in reality they have none. Thus, it is argued by realists that in a world of competing states, conventional morality must be left to one side. International peace and prosperity cannot be ensured by using the morally acceptable judgements that apply to individuals in civil society. Realist theory remains a central tenet of approaches to international theory as developed in the twentieth century by E. H. Carr (1939) and Hans Morgenthau (1948). More latterly Kenneth Waltz (1979) argues that in the absence of any superior regulatory world power national leaders will always seek to act to benefit the interests of their country and that the potential of a state to operate at this level depends upon the economic and military resources at their disposal. There is an expectation that the political leaders in any community and particularly those who are the nation's leaders will promote what they see as the well-being of their subjects. In liberal democracies this imperative is reinforced by the theory that the government should be based on the will of the majority of citizens. Policy gatekeepers are consequently often faced with the moral dilemma of whether they should favour the interests of their country against the more encompassing moral claims to defend the interest of humanity in general.

> The Cuban Government had a right to defend their state, which had already been invaded by an American funded force of irregulars in the Bay of Pigs incident. Fortunately for the world the choices made by President Kennedy during the Cuban missile crisis paid off but it is questionable whether he morally should have gambled United States' security from potential missile attack against the threat of nuclear war.

Moral dilemmas and domestic politics

The issue of 'real politics' is generally applied to policy concerning international relations but at root the moral dilemmas inherent in the dictum 'my country right or wrong' also are intertwined with domestic politics. Within liberal democratic regimes political leaders are expected to pursue policies that they believe are in the wider moral interest of their citizens. This expectation inevitably creates a number of difficult moral dilemmas for many policy advocates and also those who are required to implement policy. The problem they may often face is how far they can compromise one set of values in order to secure other ethical imperatives in both their public and private life.

In terms of public morality an issue that frequently generates considerable media comment but is rarely considered in rational ethical terms is the moral dilemmas inherent in membership or employment within a close-knit bureaucratic organisation and hence within a political party. How far should a politician lend their public support to a policy on which they privately are in disagreement or even believe to be morally wrong? Should a public sector employee resign their post if they feel they are required to implement a policy that they believe to be immoral?

> Tony Benn, a former Minister and long serving MP on the left of the Labour Party, confided in his Diary his dislike of the recently established 'New Labour' direction of Tony Blair: 'I don't want to be thrown out of the Party. I will be quite candid in my diary. I do want to be in the next Parliament and that is a factor to be taken into account, but after the next election I shall vote according to my conscience, and between now and then I shall speak my mind. But I also have in mind that I don't want to embarrass Hilary' (Benn 2002: 339). Hilary was Benn's son and also a Labour MP who became a Minister in later Labour Governments and foreign secretary in Jeremy Corbyn's first shadow cabinet.

Within most liberal democracies politicians are elected to support the manifesto policies of their party rather than their own independent platform. Independent candidates rarely attract sufficient votes to place them in a position to influence public policy. The expectation of those who support a politician is that they carry forward the policies of the party leaders for whom they voted rather than the individual candidate. Defection from the senior ranks of politicians elected to a legislature is, however, in Europe, a relatively rare phenomenon. The disaffected politician usually must weigh up in moral terms whether their disagreement with the policy direction of their party on specific issues outweighs their general support for the ideological and moral direction of their party in comparison with opposing political parties, especially if by publicly opposing a major plank of the party's policies, the government they support is seriously weakened.

Behind, however, the moral dilemmas over supporting a specific policy against the wishes of their political colleagues, there is, for many an ambitious politician, a decision to be made between their moral values and their quest for securing positions of greater influence within their party. The dilemma may often for the politician take on a more moral tone than for more distant observers in circumstances in which someone must choose to either resign a powerful position or submit to the weight of opinion of their ministerial colleagues. Frequently the politician may believe that staying in the inner policy making circle of their colleagues will be the better long-term option for them to pursue their personal policy ideas which they are likely to persuade themselves are more reasonable than those of their colleagues. As observed in the previous chapter self-interest and self-belief is a powerful motivating force in policy making and can often shape the ethical views of an activist to coincide with what is also likely to secure their ambition for power.

The juxtaposition between public good and personal duty may also create ethical dilemmas for politicians at a rather different level of the pursuit of their ideals as opposed to the reality of undertaking their duties to their close dependents. British politicians on the left may strongly support the ethical principles behind equality of opportunity but as relatively privileged members of an unequal society should they deny their dependants better health care or education by using private hospitals or schools?

Prominent left wing Labour MP Diane Abbott was widely criticised at the time of the 2010 election for sending her child to a private fee paying school rather than the local school in her constituency of Hackney which had a poor record of achievement. How far should she have put her long-term ideals to create schools in poor areas that had high standards of achievement against the parent's duty to ensure that their child had the best education available to them?

It is, especially from a Utilitarian perspective, difficult to provide rational prescriptions for circumstances in which there are clashes between a duty to close dependants and to ideals that are not practised in the activist's society. Each situation needs to be examined in relation to the consequences of whatever action the politician or bureaucrat decides to take to resolve the ethical dilemma. The case of whether a left wing campaigner against private education should send their children to a poor state school when they can afford to provide them with a better private education partly depends upon making judgements about how an individual child will cope with the state school in terms of social as well as educational factors. The solution is arguably a matter of Utilitarian fine judgement on the character of the child that is best left to the informed parent and should also reflect the view that children, who are people in their own right, should not be disadvantaged because of their parents' ambitions. From a Kantian perspective it appears even more problematic to resolve the ethical dilemma between obedience to the state and duty to one's dependants. However, it may be argued that it is right to publicly campaign for policies that an actor believes to be beneficial for society, but in the absence of that policy being implemented, they must undertake their duty to their dependants in the world that exists in practice.

Self-interest and a fair society

Perhaps the most important task of moral philosophy for policy studies is to provide the rationale that untangles the issues of self-interest and the wider concerns of ideology. The issue that should concern any individual is how these interlocking motives can be coordinated on the foundation of a disinterested ethical set of values that works for the good of all within our wider environment. The issue within this tangle concerns how to act in the given world in a manner that is just and fair both to ourselves, our immediate dependants and humanity and the living environment in general.

In the sphere of policy making one of the major areas of controversy concerns the issue of reconciling personal freedom with social justice or fairness. As outlined in the chapter on ideology there has within developed Western nations been, since the second half of the twentieth century, a tension between libertarian New Right policy and social democratic theory with its emphasis on establishing a more egalitarian society without unjustly diminishing personal freedom. The philosophy behind New Right theory is based on a view of human nature not dissimilar to Hobbes' and Machiavelli's in that human beings are essentially self-interested creatures who seek to maximise their own interest in securing power, and hence liberty, through the acquisition of wealth and influence. The power that flows from the acquisition of wealth will therefore be far from evenly distributed in society but those who are less inclined or lack the capacity to be at the cutting edge of economic and political development will nevertheless receive benefits from the efforts of the entrepreneurs who through competition ensure consumer goods are increasingly made more cheaply and efficiently so that the advantages that accrue to the wealthiest in society can over time trickle down to all strata of society. This may be unfair to the less able but Hayek (1960: 93–4) argues there is no such thing as social justice. Society cannot be composed of individuals of equal ability. Should those with the intellectual and entrepreneurial capacity to develop a better world not be rewarded for their efforts? As self-interested individuals, they will have no incentive to use their ability and perseverance to labour towards creating innovations for which they will receive little benefit. If New Right theory has merit it is in its critique of socialist practice as demonstrated in the Soviet Union or Mao's China in which liberty is removed from citizens in the name of an egalitarian theory which, in practice, is never followed by the political leaders who are the beneficiaries of state power.

New Right ideology as founded on an appeal to natural rights to liberty and ownership of property finds little appeal in terms of later Utilitarian or Kantian ethics. The concept of natural rights even in its modern translation as human rights has serious problems. The right to property is difficult to sustain in any absolute sense in societies that require cooperation between individuals. The indifference to any concept of fairness does not appear to make the theory as acceptable in an integrated society as the Kantian view that requires individuals to act in a way that takes others into account.

> Should individuals who work hard in honest toil for the benefit of themselves but also society in general, receive less reward than an idle socialite who has the luck to inherit a fortune?

New Right theory becomes effectively an expression of self-interest that is supported not surprisingly by the rich and fortunate rather than a theory that could provide the greatest happiness for the greatest number, let alone the Kantian ideal of mutual concern for our own interest alongside the interest of others.

The environment and morality

Failure to openly state a rational moral case and to live up to its implications can for certain key issues create a serious threat to humanity in an increasingly globalised world. Perhaps the most daunting and politically difficult issue that haunts public policy leaders is to face up to the ethical dilemmas that may seriously damage the life chances of future generations but require what many would argue to be sacrifices and erosion of personal liberty for present generations. This can be illustrated with reference to the debate on the dangers of climate change due to human over-consumption of the world's limited fossil based resources of oil and coal. The increasing weight of scientific evidence suggests that there is a strong possibility of serious consequences for many human populations in the next century, due to the thinning of ice sheets, changes in sea currents and wind patterns, and increasing possibilities of drought in some areas and too much rain and tropical storms in others. The exact consequences of such changes can still be disputed but those who ignore such warnings and refuse to act to help secure the future are making serious ethical decisions. Few of the answers to the Earth's environmental questions are likely to be readily acceptable to the wealthy within Western democracies, let alone in the developing democracies of Latin America or Asia. In terms of scientific practicalities there are answers to many of the problems facing future generations. Possibilities can include, as has been practised in China, enforced birth control to decrease or even reverse population increases. Limiting the consumption of meat and requiring citizens to survive on a vegetarian diet or limiting the use of private transport and hence the use of cars are further solutions to help master climate change. However, relatively few citizens can contemplate agreeing to such measures and most are unlikely to vote for governments that would advocate such policies. This problem was clearly illustrated in the failure of the 2012 United Nations Conference on Sustainable Development in Doha to develop the initiatives raised twenty years previously:

> Rio+20 proved to be a squandered opportunity. Although the attendance at Rio+20 was more than double that of the 1992 Earth Summit there were fewer heads of state. Notable absences included Barak Obama, Angela Merkel and David

Cameron and it failed to produce the same level of political commitment and institutional innovation.

(Christoff and Eckersley 2013: 200)

As a result of the slow pace of international climate negotiations and the difficulties in imposing the implementation of the policies that have been agreed in such symposiums, we are left with policies that unrealistically simply hope that either scientific breakthroughs will resolve problems such as global warming with no reduction in current living standards in Western nations or that this is a matter for future generations to resolve when the chickens harboured in our present age come home to roost.

It is tempting to suggest that democracy cannot seriously deal with these longer-term ethical challenges. However, few would argue that autocracies can in themselves be an ethical form of governance given that by their very nature they undermine, as J. S. Mill (1861: 179–98) observed, the human value for self-determination and no one person can be so well informed and of such ubiquity and energy and ethically sound in thought to manage a complex society. As Stuart Wilks-Heeg (2015: 57) points out:

> The tendency for democratic politics to focus on the short-term interests of electors within a nation-state framework is clearly at odds with the development of long-term solutions for global ecological problems. Similarly, the priority given to political and economic considerations ahead of scientific evidence reflects the difficulty of achieving a broad societal consensus in a democracy about the need to take tough policy choices. Nonetheless, there is scant evidence to suggest that non-democratic approaches provide any kinds of alternative. There are very strong theoretical, pragmatic and empirical reasons to support the view that democratic decision-making constitutes 'the only game in town' when it comes to adapting to the challenges of sustainability.

Conclusion

The chapter is intended to show how moral questions are often at the root of the political juncture between self-interest and ideology. It is shown that there are serious moral dilemmas that face politicians between, for example, their private life and duties and their public life, their support for a broad ideological position as opposed to contrary pressures from the party that best encapsulates their ideological influences. This chapter will have raised more questions than answers. It does not attempt any definitive answers, in as much as these can ever be discerned, as to whether truth and honesty should always be at the root of political action or whether there is a clear criterion for ensuring the policy decisions are always fair and just. Its purpose is to demonstrate the extent to which questions of morality lie at the heart of many policy decisions. Frequently policy makers may attempt to hide this dimension of policy making and its implementation, even though to avoid discussion of such issues is a moral issue in itself. There are, however, issues of policy that unavoidably turn on moral debate and must be decided by the capacity of certain groups to insist that their moral views must be imposed on others. A more acceptable way forward may be to adopt whenever possible tolerance of the views of others and a moral pluralism provided that the moral positions in question do not seriously harm others. Any policy entrepreneur will also face moral dilemmas during their careers whether it is between the interests of society at large and their own duty to party, organisation and family. The choice taken by any politicians when faced with a dilemma can never be logically proved to be correct but is also best made with informed, rational and, whenever possible, open debate on the alternatives. The questions raised by ethical standards will be an underlying issue in the following chapters on the use and misuse of political power and will also be more explicitly relevant to the penultimate chapters in this study that enquire whether and how through greater discourse within a globalising world it is possible to ensure a rational approach to the subjective issues that underlie public policy solutions and outcomes.

7 Policy and power

This chapter begins to shift the focus towards analysis of how public policy is processed in today's world with reference to the emotions and motives that have been discussed in Chapters 4 to 6. A central question to be discussed in the following chapters is how the many policy ideas that are churning around the social environment of political systems, that is civil society, are filtered to become issues that form part of a government's agenda and may then become so embedded in the social fabric of the state that they enter the arena of the largely non-conscious assumptions within the social environment. This chapter, therefore, begins with a broad and largely theoretical discussion on the nature of power within civil society as a basis for framing answers to the question of who, if any, are the beneficiaries and the excluded in the struggles to develop and implement public policy within what may be termed civil society.

The concept of 'civil society' has a variety of definitions but is often used to denote 'the sphere of private interests, associations and material needs, independent of the state' (Gamble 1988: 255). Thus, the term pertains to the actions and motives of individuals and collectively social groups. As such civil society is clearly made of many opinions and values that because of their subjective nature cannot be fully understood or appreciated by anyone but the individual holding that particular set of ideas at any particular time. Civil society is, in a world divided by nationalities, and social and economic groups, a complex and differentiated phenomenon. Its manifestations on the one hand can in totalitarian states appear on the surface to be highly uniform as the state attempts to control civil society. In contrast in liberal society the values inherent in the freely determined thoughts of citizens are often expressions of a desire to shape and control the state and may appear to be highly diverse. Few theorists of civil society, however, argue that civil society is such an anarchic and undifferentiated concept that it lacks any form of organisation and structure. The ideas of individuals do not emerge as some form of spontaneous creation but through experience and interaction with the physical and social environment in which we live. Association with and dependence on others create structures within society that in turn may promote and maintain common sources of ideas and action as policy. Frequently the concept of civil society is used, following the ideas of the German nineteenth century philosopher George Hegel, to designate social and political values in society as distinct from the values harboured within the sphere of those who govern. However, it is in liberal democracies and even in the most autocratic of states difficult to clearly separate those who govern from the society over which they may have at least a measure of influence. Thus, an important question that can be raised within any state is how the relationship between civil society and the state determines what policy ideas emerge as serious issues that require further development by governments to become matters controlled by public policy edicts.

The nature of power

In terms of the creation of public policy perhaps the most important structuring element is the concept of power, that is, the capacity in an individual or collectively a group or institution to ensure that others will accept and abide by their policies. Political power is widely defined as the capacity for an individual or group to ensure that others will accept their demands and requests (Finer 1970: 11–12; Kingdom 2014: 5–6). Since public policy concerns the establishment of rules or an agreement to act in a political way, those who are instrumental in forging public policy are also those with power. However, as will be discussed throughout this study, a central question concerning the development and evolution of public policy is the extent to which power is widely distributed in specific societies or is concentrated in the will of a few. The nature of power has been widely debated in the literature of social sciences and viewed as being exerted in a variety of distinct paths that are crucial in the depiction of human relationships. An all too obvious and felt aspect of power is the use of violence. Violence may be seen as the use of physical restraint by the strongest in a community over the physically less adept. At its most extreme it may involve killing opponents as in times of war, but also it may be exerted through the capacity to threaten serious harm to an individual or their property if they do not accede to the orders of another. In many states the capacity of the state to compel obedience can be secured by the use of violence to restrain the actions of those who rebel, by removing them by assassination or through enforced imprisonment to prevent them from acting freely in civil society. The threat of violence by the state also lies behind the capacity to financially impoverish through fines individuals who disobey its edicts or to ensure they are disqualified from positions of power or employment within that society.

Max Weber (Gerth and Wright-Mills 1948: 77) argued that the definition of a state is that it is the one organisation in any nation with a legitimate monopoly on the use of violence to compel compliance with its demands, although many private institutions can also have the power under the auspices of the state to use the threat of violence to secure their interests. Organisations such as privately owned businesses can expect to guard their physical and intellectual property with the use of security guards and also have powers, ultimately backed by the use of violence on their behalf by the state, to enforce compliant behaviour from their employees. All states and many informal organisations within civil society regularly use violence as a means to secure a measure of power but many only do so as a last resort. More extensively in civil society power is exerted through the use of persuasion. The importance of persuasion as a means of power can be centred on rationality. Simply put this is the power vested in us to use argument often backed by evidence and theory but also by stimulating the imagination and aesthetic sense of others. At the level of debate on the development of public policy this aspect of power pertains to the ability to provide reasons that may, to use Herbert Simon's term, 'satisfice' the concerns of others on the feasibility of a course of action. As shall be discussed later in this book, the capacity to have power is in this context intrinsic to debate and argument between individuals and groups who are not knowingly constrained in developing and expressing their opinions. Subjectivists analyse the structure and uses of such debate under the term of discourse although this may be not necessarily through face to face conversation but developed by critical reading and theorising through a wide range of media outlets. In a wider context power through persuasion can be secured through the dissemination of moral and ideological values. Policy is in this instance the outcome of rational argument debated among equals on purely intellectual terms to secure a common view point for all concerned.

Perhaps the most extensive use of the power of persuasion lies in the capacity of individuals to work together for mutual self-interest but not necessarily because intellectually they are convinced by the final outcome of discourse and debate with other contrary interests. Much of human action is based on contracts, often not formally written down or even perceived as such by the parties to a debate. Nevertheless, they take the form that actor A will agree to conditions laid down by actor B in return for the provision of resources from actor A.

> Within this context, most people at various points in their lives agree to pay taxes in the expectation that they will receive protection from the state in the form of social welfare and, through the police and courts, protection from violence to themselves and their property. Similarly the contracts of employment between private businesses and their employees are based on supplying the mutual need for income for the employee in return for their labour within the enterprise as required by policies set out by the employer.

This form of persuasion through contract differs in an important respect from discursive persuasion in that, whereas intellectual agreement or compromise with another actor can be based on a level playing field in terms of equality of material resources, this is not necessarily the case for agreements based on a contract. In discursive argument the most powerful player is usually the person with the capacity to make the most rationally powerful arguments that convince all parties to a debate that they should follow his or her suggestions. Contractual agreements are often not forged on a basis of inequalities of intellect but on the inequalities in material needs.

> An unemployed and impecunious student may, for example, be a brilliant debater in his university seminars but when it comes to securing a job to help pay his or her way through college will have to take employment under policy conditions that intellectually they may feel are stupid, unfair and degrading.

Power is also exerted in a less visible form through habitual and at times unconscious states of mind. This is often seen in terms of the capacity of the state and its agents to exert authority over people's behaviour. 'Authority' is usually regarded as the belief or assumption that certain others have a moral right to expect your compliance with their edicts and policies. It may of course be the case that the belief in the authority of others is a consequence of moral or ideological persuasion and discourse but for many it may be a consequence of unconsciously held habitual forms of behaviour based on a belief that those in power ought to obeyed or simply that we feel safest following the instincts of our human herd. Whilst there are many opinions that form a civil society, political stability also requires a strong measure of consensus on the structure and routines of the political system. Such values can form in stable societies a reserve of what Robert

Putnam (1994) has described as social capital, a reservoir of social belief such as the need to cooperate with others, to pay taxes, to volunteer to help others, to care for dependants and to obey the laws of a legitimately formed government, that enable society to function in a reasonably harmonious and cooperative manner. This view often re-emerges under the banner of citizenship or, using David Cameron's buzz word, the 'big society'. Without such social capital, the interactions and habits of respecting the property and security of friends or strangers, and hence the capacity to amass capital and indulge our consumerist reflexes, would not be possible.

The sources of power

Power is a capacity that permeates society but few argue that it is a capacity that is evenly distributed. For some ideological and moral codes, for example those professed by the New Right, power is always unevenly distributed by the very nature of differing skills and ability among people and any attempts to resolve this situation will inevitably fail with disastrous consequences. In developed societies the power to influence and drive public policy is even in the most democratic states not given in equal measure to all citizens. There are many factors within civil society let alone in government that contribute to the ability to have power over others. As a consequence the capacity to wield power is held by some individuals, groups and institutions with far more potency than by others. Power is a capacity that may be used by individuals but it is in most complex societies located not just within the hands of individuals but also within their role in institutions. The President of the United States comes into office with a much increased capacity to wield power not so much on account of his or her abilities but through the authority, wealth and capacity to use violence that are attached to the constitutional powers of the office. Outside the confines of the state considerable power can also accrue to businesses and, in particular, corporate business given the huge resources of capital and potential revenue they command which they can use to buy the most capable managers within their field or specialist expertise from the professions through hiring accountants and lawyers or establishing themselves with a measure of authority in their field through their capacity to purchase the most skilled in persuasion and marketing. Thus gaining substantive political power for an individual usually requires gaining positions of authority in an institutionalised society. This can be achieved through possession of personal resources such as intelligence, charisma, capacity for hard work, but such capacities are arguably widely distributed in society. In many cases power is secured by good luck through being in the right place at the right time and with the right associates. Fortune is however a factor that does not in itself favour any people, class or grouping in society.

Often in periods of conflict it is the luck of having survived. General Franco, who commanded the Fascist forces for most of the Spanish Civil War and from 1939 to 1975 the dictator of Spain, was as a junior officer commanding units of a Spanish foreign legion during a colonial war in North Africa. He was fortunate to have survived given the high death rate among officers in the field. Some of the officers who were killed in action rivaled Franco in terms of prestige among right wing enthusiasts in Spain and may well have become leaders of the military coup that initiated the Spanish civil war. Moreover, the more senior officer who was to have led the coup was killed in an air crash on his way to take command of the nationalist army (Preston 1995).

However, one crucial differential that creates a society of uneven capacity in terms of power is the extent to which individuals have had access to resources, first to gain knowledge and skills through first rate education usually bought by their privileged and wealthy parents in private, as opposed to state, schools that lead to access to elite universities. Through such upbringing, connections are made with similar privileged individuals that are of value in acquiring promotion in state organisations, the professions or corporate business. As a consequence positions of power are passed on from one generation of the powerful to the next, perpetuating what can broadly be described as class or life world distinctions within society.

Models that seek to differentiate and define the sources and forms of power are legion but elements in the development of network theory derived from a model established by R. A. W. Rhodes (1981) may usefully set out a workable framework to begin this discussion. The basic model provided a theoretical grounding for a major research initiative on inter-governmental relations in Britain but it has since been much more widely developed and applied. Rhodes argued that the relationship between what he terms the core executive of central governments and external agencies of government and powerful interest groups, was not based on either partnership working or using them as agents of the state but through a more complex set of interactions between central and local governments in which each political institution bargained with each other to achieve their favoured interests through an exchange of what Rhodes termed resources. These resources were effectively the means through which each institution in the bargaining process could exert influence over the others. In the context of central–local relations these were identified as:

- Their constitutional and legal position
- Their political legitimacy and capacity to mobilise public opinion
- Their resources of money and finance
- Their organisational capacity and control over staff, property and services
- Their information, knowledge and access to data.

(Rhodes 1999: 80–1)

Thus, policy emerged in respect to the powers, structuring and financing of local government as a result of the ability of central government and local authorities to use the resources of power at their disposal to ensure that compromises were reached when differences arose between them. Rhodes, however, pointed out that central governments had a further and substantial resource, the capacity to change 'the rules of the game' by which is meant their ability to develop legislation or government orders that set the rules of how the network should operate. This can in some circumstances be a trump card in ensuring that the core executive can determine policy decisions in its favour.

The capacity of Trade Unions to be a major player in British business and economic policy development has been seriously downgraded since the 1970s by a series of legislative measures brought in by the Thatcher Governments and retained by later Administrations. These include requiring Trade Unions to ballot their members before they can declare a strike. This resource it is suggested by the Conservative Party under Cameron requires further weakening by demanding that any such ballot must receive over 50 per cent of potential voters to be operative (Lewis Silkin Journal, 2014).

The state as an instrument of capital and hence power

As outlined in the chapter on ideology, the uneven distribution of power has for at least two hundred years been seen, by socialist commentators, and in particular followers of Marxist economics, as a function of differences in the control of economic policy between capitalists who own the means of production and those who supply by hand or brain the labour force needed to manufacture goods and services. The use of resources of capital to ensure that the capacity for some individuals to receive an upbringing and an inheritance of property to provide them with substantially greater resources of power than the majority of citizens, when translated and multiplied within the context of the organisation of groups and institutions, becomes a highly potent force in also organising the content of contractual agreements and also the authority relationships within society. The financial resources that can be commanded by corporate business and central governments are such that they can be the most significant influences in setting the ideological values and moral compass of developed societies. Through their control over financial resources such organisations can acquire through contracts the expertise of the best professionals, such as lawyers, accountants, scientists and marketing experts. In an open pluralist society these interests can, through control of printed and visual media, persuade consumers to accept as essential for their well-being what is in the professional or business person's interests rather than what is for the public benefit.

There are many more recent theorists who broadly accept Marxist ideas but argue that the influence of capital is far more subtle and less confrontational and less likely to eventually break down in a confrontation between classes that will usher in a socialist era. A particular issue are theories that discuss how in developed societies many citizens are unaware of the extent to which their social and economic position in society is shaped, not usually to their advantage, by the elites who control the system. The Italian communist Antonio Gramsci (1971) observed how elites seek to create a hegemony over society, that is they attempt to use the means of communication and education to imprint their ideological views over the society they govern. Thus, the exploited in society are denied the capacity to consider their own interests as opposed to the interests of the elite. Typically, they may be led to believe that they do not have the capacity to develop different ideas on equality and governance from those of the elite and believe that they should defer to those in positions of authority. This attitude, prevalent in Victorian times, is encapsulated in the less carolled lines from the well-known hymn 'All Things Bright and Beautiful':

> The rich man in his castle
> The poor man at his gate
> He made them high and lowly
> He ordered their estate.

Post-war, neo-Marxists such as Poulantzes (1968) or Ralph Miliband (1968) explained from somewhat differing perspectives how the development of welfare states in capitalist economies created the means through which capital could create a more educated and healthier workforce that would ensure greater and longer productivity from the exploited. Social democracy, through the development of public services to alleviate ill health, homelessness and periods of chronic unemployment within the state, creates the means that enables the elite holders of capital and power to ensure the proletariat who supply through hand or brain the productivity to amass capital are sufficiently educated, healthy and willing to be exploited for their efforts so that the capital required to establish an exploitable workforce can be recouped by the elite with interest.

From a different perspective Peter Bachrach and Morton Baratz (1962) argued that the power to make decisions must be balanced against the power of organisations and politicians to keep potential concerns off the political agenda and, thus, make 'non-decisions'. They outlined three avenues where an individual or an organisation may decide not to press an adversary to change their policies. This creates the tendency in liberal democracies to concentrate power in a few hands by alienating the majority from having a serious interest, as observed in Chapter 5 on politics and policy. The aggrieved organisation seeking a policy change may:

a   Not press their cause because they fear they will be seen as disloyal to the organisation.
b   Realise without having to process their case that they hold a minority view and therefore it is not worth wasting time or their reputation in pursuing their policy interest.
c   The political structures in which the policy advocate is operating are such that they realise that their ideas would be pigeon holed by their opponents who control the policy making system.

(Bachrach and Baratz 1962: 949)

Stephen Lukes (2005) in his study *Power: A Radical View* took this critique further by arguing that the earlier non-decision making viewpoint misses out a further dimension of power.

What one may have here is a latent conflict, which consists of a contradiction between the interests of those exercising power and the *real interests* of those they exclude. These latter may not express or even be conscious of their interests ...

(Lukes 2005: 28)

The most influential theoreticians of the divisions between capital and labour within capitalist societies provide further understanding of how the economic orthodoxy of the capitalist state maintains and perpetuates division in both wealth and power. Habermas (2001) holds out the possibility of a discursive democracy in which those with understanding on matters crucial for the maintenance of a developed society could communicate with others within the civic culture. In what he describes as 'the life world', the social sphere in which we perceive the world and create social links and practices that enable us to understand one another, it is possible to create in local societies common understandings and the unwritten rules of acceptable conduct. This capacity is, however, being colonised in capitalist society by more globalised forms of communication by systems that measure their success in terms of money and power. Thus, our capacity to become grounded as individuals in society is increasingly domi-nated by the values of capital. In practice, political values within liberal democracies derive increasingly from interpretations of values and explanations by communities of businesses and professional thinkers that are often attributed to professional scientists and sociologists. These policy advocates alongside the politicians who refined and legitimised policy tended to be self-referential and consequently cut themselves off from civil society. Networks existed among the elite in specific fields but these interests could impose their superior understanding on the less privileged in society. Liberal democracies as established in Western nations are far from providing equal power and opportunities to their citizens. Strong democracy, to use a term established by the American writer Benjamin Barber (1984), could only be secured through systems that allowed serious discourse that promoted understanding and the exchange of ideas between the policy makers and citizens (Davies 2011: 65).

The position taken by Habermas is also reflected from a rather different angle in the works of the French anthropologist turned sociologist Pierre Bourdieu. As with other critical theorists and post-modernist thinkers Bourdieu considers that the use of language has a crucial role in shaping societies and can in an age of mass communication be turned to reflect the interests of elites. His generally more accessible writing presents a rather clearer picture than Habermas of the means by which capitalist elites can insidiously infiltrate civic society to create a society concerned with consumption. A key concept in Bourdieu's writing is the term 'habitus' to denote the lifestyle and understandings of individuals and classes of individuals:

> Habitus are generative principles of distinct and distinctive practices – what the worker eats and especially the way he eats it, the sport he practices and the way he practices it, his political opinions and the way he expresses them are systematically different from the industrial owner's corresponding activities.
>
> (Bourdieu 1998: 8)

The habitus of an individual is replicated within a child's upbringing and with the aid of the state in differing forms of schooling. Society divides to produce on the one hand elites who govern through the resources reflected in their habitus. This background can ensure a more effective and distributive form of opinion, plus other more material resources such as economic capital. In contrast a governed class has a much diminished capacity to bargain for power, trading on a less distributable habitus and fewer resources. Classes for Bourdieu are however states of mind rather than real phenomena and they are inter-penetratable and divided. He perceived for example differences among the more elite groups between intellectuals with a high capital in terms of understanding as opposed to wealth, in contrast to industrialists with generally a less resourceful intellectual habitus but greater economic capital. For Bourdieu (1998: 45–6) the state not only monopolises the legal means of coercion through the military, police and the legal system, but also imposes a cultural monopoly on its subjects. States frequently codify the accepted language to be used within the state, determine the transmission of knowledge and understanding through the educational system and develop the myths of what sustains the values cherished and rewarded by the state. Individuals who wish to collaborate with the state are obliged to adopt its language and beliefs. This tendency Bourdieu characterises as symbolic capital (Bourdieu 1998: 102–3) that provides power for those who dominate the system to ensure that those whom they dominate do not recognise they are aiding the very means by which they are dominated. The capacity of the state to dominate the policy process is not primarily due to its ability to coerce its subjects but through the deployment of cultural capital. We accept policy and hence rules made by the state and generally implement its rules out of habit, termed 'doxa' by Bourdieu, and because we have no idea of any alternative but to follow these rules:

> State injunctions owe their obviousness, and thus their potency, to the fact that
> the state has imposed the very cognitive structures through which it is perceived
> (one should rethink along those lines the conditions that make possible the
> supreme sacrifice: *pro patria mori*).
>
> (Bourdieu 1998: 55)

Cultural post-modernists such as Frederic Jameson (1991) similarly argue that
during the twentieth century capitalism has extended its role from industrialisation to
the sphere of communication and aesthetics. Art and literature have become commo-
dified and rather than being a source of protest and criticism of the social system have
become in terms of mass appeal a means of replicating consent if not enthusiasm for
consumption. Thus, the arts of marketing and the measurement of works of art in
terms of price and volume of sales increasingly shape popular culture to accept with
little reflection an increasingly divided society between the dominant and exploited
groups (Drolet 2004: 32–4).

Power as a capacity and as a relationship

The Marxist, neo-Marxist and critical realist conclusions on the inequity of power relationships in liberal democratic, let alone autocratic, states are extensively and widely condemned by theorists placed not only on the far right of the political spectrum but by
liberal and many social democrats. Conservative theory following Tory precepts maintains that those who are educated socially to rule, or through self-education rise up the
social ladder to elite positions, have the understanding and wisdom to ensure that society
grows in wealth through social paternalism to the benefit of the lower orders. This
paternalist view even in Britain let alone the United States, as discussed in Chapter 4, is
increasingly giving way to new-right and neo-liberal theory that maintains that the
unequal division of resources in society is a major condition of the driving force for the
positive evolution of all in society as it rewards hard work and ingenuity among individuals who will in consequence of their entrepreneurship use their skill to benefit not
just themselves but many others not as gifted or fortunate as themselves. Even Rawls from
a social democratic perspective whilst establishing his precepts on the equality of all
people, then qualifies the position through principles that allow inequality in situations
that create universal benefit. These objections are not, however, normally directed towards
a denial that the life chances of individuals and groups in the world are inequitable and
at times grossly unfair but argue that such a situation cannot and for some ethically
should not be remedied through the intervention of the state. Indeed such ideas value
inequality but see this as a morally beneficial characteristic of any society.

Perhaps in Foucault's thought there is some reconciliation of the view of whether the
state should protect inequality or foster or even impose equality. Power, Foucault
reminds us, is not something that individuals possess but is a capacity that they can
exercise. Moreover, it is exercised at many levels in society not only by those in institutionalised authority, but by numerous people exerting their understanding of their
world and their relation to it. 'Power must be analysed as something which circulates,
or as something which only functions in the form of a chain ... Power is employed and
exercised through a network like organisation' (Foucault 1980: 80, quoted in Mills
2003: 35). In his earlier work Foucault was critical of an objectified, positivist, view of
the state as a collective body that monopolises power in society.

As Fischer (2003: 40) points out, power for Foucault cannot:

> be identified as the privilege of a dominant elite class actively deploying it against a passive, dominated class. Disciplinary power in this sense does not exist in the sense of class power. Instead it exists in an infinitely complex system of 'micro powers' that permeate all aspects of social life.

Foucault rejects the Marxist belief that the state operates on behalf of a ruling class to dominate civil society for the interest, in this epoch, of capital. The concept of the state he argues is too diverse to have much meaning and cannot be described, as is often the case, as some super-human entity that has specific aims and capacity. The 'state' is rather a term describing an entity with unclear boundaries that is made up of numerous networks that are as much in rebellion as in agreement with each other:

> But the state, no more probably at any other time in its history, does not have this unity, this individuality, this rigorous functionality, nor to speak frankly this importance; maybe after all the state is no more than a composite reality and a mythicised abstraction, whose importance is a lot more limited than many of us think.
>
> (Foucault 1991: 103, quoted in Mills 2003: 48)

Policy from this perspective is not usefully seen as an aim and creation of the state but as the response of numerous agencies that choose to exert both their capacity for power and means for resistance over others. Foucault argues that 'power relations are rooted in the social nexus, not reconstituted "above society" as a supplementary structure whose radical effacement one could perhaps dream of ... a society without power relations can only be an abstraction' (Foucault 1982: 791). The resultant maelstrom of pressures and wills results in a concatenation of forces whose objective meaning and consequences, in so far as this ever appears to be interpreted as the same entity by all individuals or collective of individuals, is too complex to analyse. By rejecting the idea of a structured state oppressing with force a subordinate governed class, Foucault suggests that political activists at all levels of society are concerned to reach consensus on matters that concern them and develop therefore values and ideas that facilitate the governability of society. However, some final goal of, for example, the Marxist socialist state where politics withers away and society is only concerned with the management of fulfilling our needs, is wholly illusory. Governability requires some form of control and Foucault himself cannot in later writings escape acknowledging that 'power relations have been progressively governmentalized, that is to say, elaborated, rationalised and centralized in the form, or under the auspices, of state institutions' (Foucault 1982: 793, quoted in Davies 2011: 72).

Foucault is right to suggest that the system has fuzzy unclear edges between the state and society but even he reluctantly admits power in society is more ordered than his earlier work may suggest. We are left with a view in his later works that the state for Foucault and his followers is important for the policy process but the capacity of the state, or maybe better said, a core executive of a state, to establish policy needs to be viewed as a function of many views and interests in the wider civil society. This position is also suggested by Habermas (2001) as a consequence of globalisation, which is currently undermining the capacity of nation states to act independently from, as he terms it, the post-national constellation, of institutions for global governance and the growing dominance of transnational corporations.

Conclusion

This chapter has discussed theories of how civil society can be viewed from several perspectives as being a highly diverse background to the creation of public policy. There are many views given the complexity of social systems and the many subjective elements that may determine individuals' attitudes that characterise the social environment of policy issues and outcomes. As a consequence, what may be an issue that has sufficient importance to require widespread attention, such as Britain's exit from the European Union, will have many often impressionistic solutions competing for public approval. Within this web one person's opportunity may be a problem or a non-issue for others, and one person's problem may be of no concern or even be seen as an advantage to others. However, society is viewed by most sociologists as an arena of conflict as concerns public policy in which there are substantive inequalities among individuals, conceptualised by some as the 'habitus' or 'life worlds' that they inhabit. These inequalities ensure that the power to push many specific issues into the consciousness of a wide swathe of individuals and interests and then create the possibility that they may be taken up by governments as an issue, is located predominantly in educated and well-resourced elites in terms of wealth and, hence, the capacity to communicate their ideas to a wide audience. The following three chapters will discuss in more detail how differing approaches and theories can explain the differences and similarities in the relationship of civil societies with, what may be rather crudely termed, the policy making elites.

8   Public policy in autocracies

Most studies on public policies are written with reference to the complex arrangements established by liberal democratic states. However, it must be kept in mind that by no means all nations are liberal democracies and many are governed as oligarchies or dictatorships. The following chapter outlines the subjective values such as self-interest, ideology and, in some countries, a cavalier concern for ethical principles that determine the content and policy processes within the many non-liberal democratic regimes and organisations. This discussion is not, however, to demonstrate how far policy making is a wholly different process in such regimes from the practices of liberal democracy. It is made from the point of view that within Western liberal democracies many of the institutions, public and private, are also autocratic in structure and attitudes. Liberal democracies through their electoral systems build a further dynamic and greater element of complexity into the processing of public policy. They do so, however, through the operation of elements of the state that has autocratic institutional and procedural arrangements that are influenced by many independent and often highly autocratic private interests such as corporate businesses and much of the media and particularly the printed media. In most regimes, for example, whether autocratic or democratic, civil services, the military and police, some political parties, almost all newspapers and many private sector companies operate hierarchic, top down leadership styles. Consequently, the following discussion on policy making in autocracies, whilst being of interest in its own right, can be used also to illustrate some of the less than open and responsive elements of the state in liberal democratic regimes.

The autocratic state

A frequently used but somewhat misleading differentiation made between autocratic regimes is to divide them into dictatorships, systems dominated by a single ruler, and oligarchies which are systems ruled by a small elite. As discussed earlier only the smallest forms of society can in any sense be governed by a single individual without recourse to advice and help in implementing their wishes. The role of the dictator in autocratic societies and even more the prime ministers and executive presidents of liberal democracies is not so much to act as policy advocates and policy makers but as policy gate-keepers. In this context they survey a range of options that are put forward to take advantage of an opportunity or resolve a problem and have the capacity to decide which options should be chosen and which ideas should be excluded. This is not to say that gate-keepers cannot at times be passionate policy advocates on particular issues but that they are unlikely to be capable of promoting and working through the details of all but a few of the policy issues on which they must make decisions.

The perfect dictator cannot exist and, whilst there are examples of individuals who have a dominant role in relation to the policies of a state who are usually referred to as a dictator, there is some degree in which they are but first among equals in an oligarchy. An abstracted autocracy would be a polity in which one person makes policy and ensures it is accepted and obeyed by all other members of that system. In practice such a system is rarely if ever encountered. This is largely a function of the interconnectedness of social groups and their relationship to a changing physical environment. An autocrat can only make policy decisions with reference to the social and physical world he or she inhabits. First, a dictator is circumscribed, like King Canute, by physical and natural forces that they cannot control. Secondly, no autocrat in any but the smallest political system can by themselves alone control the inner dimensions of the political system. Any community that is larger than a small village cannot be wholly under the control of one unassisted autocrat. Dictators must rely on a number of lieutenants to assist in their governance of a society. As communities become more complex with differing groups within the society undertaking discrete specialised functions, such as farming, metal working or serving as soldiers, an autocrat cannot themselves be master of all the functions needed in the polity and must rely on professional advice from specialists to help understand the problems that they and the community face and the range of options open to them to meet any challenge they may bring.

As a generalisation, the larger a community the more its autocrat will have to rely on a greater number of trusted lieutenants to report to him or her what they see as the problems that their subjects face and the extent to which they support and follow their policies. Translated to a modern nation state, individuals commonly depicted as archetypal dictators such as Stalin, Saddam Hussein, or Robert Mugabe are reliant on the support of government ministers and below them a substantive bureaucracy for information and advice on policy decisions of which an important component may be how they may be able to retain their position of apparent dominance. Any major state whether a liberal democracy or a dictatorship must also be reliant for policy development on the specialised activities of bureaucrats who are formed into agencies as civil servants or more autonomous bodies such as the military. These bureaucracies are also interwoven with interlinked networks of professional organisations that are regarded as the fount of expertise on specific technical subjects such as the law, health, accountancy or engineering. Professional groups exert influence in both private and public sectors and, where most potent, dominate values within their area of expertise by training entrants to the profession, determining who is qualified to practise and give advice in that sector, and disciplining those who forward ideas contrary to the profession's ethos (Fischer 2009).

Policy roles

Policy outcomes in autocracies are popularly seen to emanate from a dictator whether this be the president, a prime minister, monarch or some other title giving the impression of the central character as both the personification and absolute ruler of a state. As indicated above no autocrat can have the time or will to determine all policy initiatives and ensure they are effectively refined and implemented. Policy gate-keepers have the less arduous but crucial role of being able to decide which policy initiatives are to be accepted and implemented within their regime and in many cases which issues are seen to be major policy problems or are new initiatives to grasp and what are the means by which others should be commanded to work out solutions. They may similarly determine which policies are unworkable and need to be abandoned. The gate-keeping role is not, however, necessarily focused on one person. In oligarchies, the few, small elite groups of senior politicians with not necessarily similar ideological views let alone compatible self-interested ambitions may quarrel among themselves as to the outcome of the gate-keeping role.

Stalin made sure he was the sole gate-keeper in the USSR by eliminating any pretenders for some piece of this role but his successors were never as able to ensure total domination of this key function. Nikita Khrushchev had during his early reign as Secretary of the Communist Party shared some of his power with Prime Minister Bulganin. His successor Leonid Brezhnev similarly shared power with Prime Minister Leonid Kosygin.

Gate-keepers often bring around themselves a coterie of powerful policy advisors, either in a formal capacity as leading Ministers of State or frequently in a less formal position as personal appointees as policy advisors. Such roles may resemble the structures in presidential systems as in the United States where the Head of State appoints his close supporters as leading members of the White House staff who will keep the President advised on policy issues sometimes in opposition to ideas being formulated and implemented by appointed Secretaries of State. Such men are the Thomas Cromwells to Henry VIII in England or Cardinal Richelieu to Louis XIV in France who, whilst powerful, may however be highly vulnerable to the whims of their gate-keeping sovereign or party leaders and can be jettisoned or, as in Thomas Cromwell's case, beheaded when they fail in their advice.

Policy may be proposed and vetoed at this level by gate-keepers and their close advisors in dictatorships and oligarchies but it will rarely be made and refined in detail. Policy determination in larger states will usually be divided in accord with specific functions to established ministerial departments headed usually by politicians favoured for that role by the gate-keeping autocrat. Ministers may then be given a relatively free hand in the policy determination relating to a specific technical area of policy if the dictator has little interest in the matter and may, provided they give support to their patron and ensure they do not make embarrassing mistakes, act as a subsidiary gate-keeper for policies in the specific areas covered by the department. However, many a wary dictator may wish to shuffle the pack of his ministers to ensure none become so entrenched or popularly successful in their post that they may be able to challenge him or her for power.

General Franco, the dictator of Spain from 1939 to 1975, was careful to ensure that those whom he appointed to sit in his cabinet were balanced between leaning to the left or right of his views and were also balanced between military and civilian backgrounds (Medhurst 1973).

The ministerial teams in many dictatorships, especially for example in military regimes, are in most roles unlikely to be specialists in the policy field and, rather like the most senior autocrats, will be reliant on information relevant to their departmental activities that may point to a problem or an opportunity and a possible solution and strategy for dealing with the issue from both interests in civil society and professional policy advisors. The role of the professional advisor is just as crucial in most autocratic regimes although in the most centrally controlled totalitarian states membership and education of professionals may be rigorously controlled to conform to the gate-keeper's ideological sensitivities and personal ambition.

Gate-keepers must also be sensitive to the ideas of movements critical of the ruling elite and judge whether sections of civil society need to be silenced or appeased or indeed have in their opinion a worthwhile initiative they can follow. Broadly these groups may be described, to use John Kingdon's term, as policy entrepreneurs, that is the individuals and, collectively, the institutions that analyse and develop policy solutions. These roles can be centred in a wide number of organisations including political parties whether in government or opposition, think tanks, or, in their areas of specialism, interest groups such as large businesses, the military or major non-governmental charities. Within many but by no means all autocracies, where those in power are tolerant of individual freedom and enterprise, they will seek within such groups support for the political system. However, whilst wealthy lawyers or bankers may in many autocratic regimes operate at this level provided they do not rock the political elite's boat, such groups in the most totalitarian of regimes will like professional groups also be brought into the bureaucratic arm of the state. In this context the agencies concerned with communication whether in print or broadcast or accessible through information technologies may be dependent on the compatibility between the ideological and ethical values of the ruling elite and the mass of civil society and as such be either an instrument important for policy change within the state or persecuted and subject to government control.

Often further down the pecking order of power within a state, but nevertheless important to ensure a regime is stable, are the street level bureaucrats who are given the task of implementing in practice the policy decisions that have been accepted and ratified by the gate-keepers.

The institutions of the autocratic state

Although autocratic regimes may be founded on differing ideological values, there are, as in liberal democracies, a number of institutions that must support and reinforce their leaders. Common to both liberal democracies and autocracies is the adoption of bureaucratic organisation. As classically theorised by Max Weber (1948) bureaucracy, as an ideal type, comprises a system in which its personnel are:

- permanent salaried officials
- organised in a hierarchy
- given specific areas of authority and discretion
- politically neutral
- technically trained and hence qualified in their field and
- selected and promoted by ability within the organisation.

As such, bureaucratic organisation, any more than military organisation, is not in itself democratic, even though from the more comprehensive point of view of liberal democratic theory this can be argued to ensure that the unelected bureaucracy or military does not subvert the policy decisions of the elected representatives who form the government. Within an autocracy, however, the limited discretion given by a dictator can ensure a disciplined framework within the bureaucracy for developing and implementing the policies. In both autocratic regimes whether under military or civilian control and also liberal democratic regimes, much of the detailed work of the state is conducted by a bureaucracy of civil servants who are required to work to the orders of their political masters. Within civilian or military-led autocracies there is often no clearly definable division between political and bureaucratic posts. A dictator may select as his or her closest lieutenants individuals who are given power over government departments and within each department the minister, with the autocrat's approval, will in turn select a hierarchy of advisors to help refine and oversee policy and administrators to ensure policy implementation. It would generally be expected in such a system that, as in military organisations, lower tier officers and workers will be provided a sphere of discretion to fulfil the tasks set for them by their superior officers and potentially through the hierarchy be subject to the head of government.

In contrast to democracies most civilian-based and some military-led autocracies also seek to establish a measure of ideological control and authority over their populations by establishing leadership through a single political party which is similarly organised largely on bureaucratic lines. The role of such a party may in some states be of relatively little consequence in terms of policy formation for the state, as the organisation is maintained solely to provide a vehicle to spread the ideological values of the nation's oligarchies and also to provide a means by which fellow travellers with the regime can be recruited, trained and made ready to spread these values the best they can into the wider public sphere.

> During Franco's dictatorship on Spain, a small fascist Party, the Falange, was picked out as the only official State Political Party, partly because its founder had been conveniently killed during the Spanish Civil War and given the support received from Germany and Italy during that War it was a means for the Spanish army to suggest it had Fascist credentials. After the defeat of the Axis powers in 1945, Franco found it expedient to relegate the Falange to a minor bureaucratic role within the country (Carr and Fusi 1981: 24–8).

Within regimes established through a revolution based on strong ideological principles the party may in contrast be the major centre of power and its central leadership serves as a central institutional base through which gate-keeping autocrats review and pass or reject policy suggestions. These systems are associated in the twentieth century with the arrangements of totalitarian regimes such as Fascist Italy and National Socialist Germany and the Marxist–Leninist ideologically driven communist party systems of the USSR and China under Chairman Mao. In the twenty-first century China retains more than any other major state the trappings of domination of policy development and initiation through the framework of a single party system.

A further resource sought by would-be autocrats is control over the media. The media, that is, organisations such as the press, television, radio and increasingly the internet, have a substantial influence on both the government and the public but also must, to be influential, reflect the views of their readers and viewers. Collectively the media gathers their strength in the policy process by publicising widely what their editors and owners perceive to be in the public and very often their own interest. Governments will have close contacts with the most popular elements of the media as both institutions need one another (McNair 2003: 47–73). The press requires information on the latest government policy in order to have material of interest to publish whilst the government seeks favourable comments on its accomplishments. Public opinion is to a considerable extent formed by reference to how the media reports this mutual exchange of information and analysis between the policy makers and the media editors. Within the most totalitarian states the media are agencies of the state and wholly under government control.

It is sometimes argued that new technology is substantially democratising the flow of information and exchange of opinions. Currently the importance of the press to shape public opinion is beginning to be attenuated by the growth of information technology that allows members of the public to create their own websites or express their concerns on platforms such as Twitter. Certainly in repressive autocracies such as Syria in 2012 and more broadly in China, the use of information technology has had an important role in spreading alternative views on the policies and politics of these nations. However, enthusiasm for the democratisation of information has its limits as, with a few exceptions as in the case of Wiki-leaks, governments can keep state secrets close to them and the information spread widely on the internet is as likely to have emanated from the conventional media (Freedman 2012: 103).

Large scale social systems such as a nation state not only rely on the activities of complex public bureaucracy but are also unable to function effectively without support and compliance of the private sector and in particular the centre of productive action in which sufficient wealth is accumulated. Organisations such as multi-national corporations are like public sector bureaucracies, whether operating in autocracies or liberal democracies, and are, with only a few exceptions, organised for their internal policy making processes as autocracies. The freedom of the private sector to have a measure of independence from the state varies greatly between forms of autocratic state as shall be detailed below. Within communist totalitarian command economies the private sector was predominantly owned and operated as part of the central state apparatus. Thus, the senior managers of industries or public services are relatively little differentiated from other sectors of the bureaucracy. Similarly professional bodies are largely incorporated within the bureaucratic or party structures of the state. In more attenuated forms of autocracy such as in China there can be greater freedom for a civil sector concerned with productive services provided they do not use their resources to undermine the power and ideological outlook of the ruling elite.

Ideology, self-interest and autocracy

Autocratic states are founded on a wide range of ideological and ethical values which are, of course, more diverse in these respects than liberal democratic states which for all their differences are bound by a more coherent ideologically driven civic culture. Autocracies differ greatly as a consequence of the subjective motives harboured by their policy elites. These may be driven by strong ideological convictions or by individual or group self-interest. These motives will also influence the extent to which a state may adopt totalitarian features in which the ruling elites believe that they should control all aspects of civil society, be they economic or social, and expect positive demonstrations of support for their regime from their population. In contrast, in some autocracies where self-interest and corruption are central motivations within ruling oligarchies, civil society may be allowed to develop as it will, provided that it does not turn against the political arrangements of the state. Whilst it is possible to make some generalisations concerning the source of public policy decisions in autocratic states within a close circle of co-opted activists bound together in patron–client relationships, there are major differences in the ways in which the policy makers relate to civil society. Largely as a consequence of the motives of autocrats, the institutional structures and the frameworks through which public policy originates and is processed can also differ. There are, therefore, significant differences between the totalitarian autocracies of the Soviet Union and the corrupt regime of Saddam Hussein in Iraq or the military regime of Myanmar.

Totalitarianism

The most extreme systems of autocracy are totalitarian regimes in terms of the extent to which the oligarchs in power seek to dominate all aspects of the social life of their subjects. These regimes predominantly, at least in their formative years, are founded on strong ideological beliefs whether these be secular or religious in their character and are brought into being following a revolutionary overthrow of a preceding regime strongly opposed to their views, either through civil war or international conquest. An aspect of such regimes is their tendency to expect their citizens to do more than simply avoid showing any interest in the politics of the state but to demonstrate publicly their political support for the state. At its fictionally most graphic this was a central theme of George Orwell's (1949) novel *1984*.

The classic academic popularisation of the term totalitarianism by Hannah Arendt (1967) or Carl Friedrich and Zbigniew Brzezinski (1965) was concerned after 1945 to show that there was little difference in the practice of government between Stalin's control of the Soviet Union and Hitler's control of Nazi Germany. They point out how the state was controlled by a monolithic political party led by a small oligarchy of leaders who required a mass membership selected by its leadership to extol the virtues of their political movement in all elements of social and economic life. In the context of service to the state most younger citizens would be expected to be conscripted into military service. The state especially in the Communist and Fascist regimes ensured that it dominated economic production in society to the extent of nationalising the means of production. The media was similarly completely dominated by the state and any writing or broadcast material contrary to the state's wishes was censored and banned. Policy in such regimes therefore emerges largely from within the higher reaches of the bureaucratic or party system of the state, although sometimes both agencies are effectively fused organisations. In the heroic early stages of a political revolution, policy is informed by ideological views of professional political activists who may believe that those over whom they expect to rule do not fully understand their leaders' ideological position and need to be educated by the revolutionary state to accept what its leaders see as their common good. Hence, the genesis of policy must lie within the conclaves of those that are seen to be fully immersed in the favoured ideology and can as a consequence be brought into the party of potential organisers of the state and also be recruited into official bureaucratic positions in government. Within such regimes the views of the less ideological fellow travellers will, of course, be canvassed, but if their ideas cannot be easily accommodated into the ideology of the state, they will, at best, be ignored and at their worst the perpetrators of what the party leadership regard as heretical views will be eliminated. Tyrants will seek the views of their subjects as much to guard themselves against compromise as to learn and profit from the views of others.

A major problem with the totalitarian state is that the concern to guard its ideological commitments against opposition can quickly generate a conservative outlook among its ruling elite in the sense that they are often highly reluctant to embrace change. In consequence the ideological principles of the state become an ossified religion that over time cannot build the basis to ensure policy can evolve to meet new global circumstances. The system is also likely to quickly deteriorate through the operationalisation of self-interest within its dominant policy making elites who seek to hold on to their positions of power and the associated privileges of wealth and prestige. They may go further and, as in North Korea, seek to ensure that they are succeeded by family members and thus form a ruling dynasty. Frequently under these circumstances the official ideology of the state evolves as required by its leaders or leader and then may become a vehicle largely to forward the leaders' self-interest rather than the greater good.

Totalitarianism is normally defined as civilian government and within such systems the military is firmly subordinated to the rule of the dominant party. It is also possible in relatively complex oligarchies based on strong and widely popular ideologies to ensure the military remain subordinate to the government by the capacity of the civilians in power to place themselves in the position of being head of the armed forces with sufficient authority to remove from power any rebellious generals or admirals. This may often be the consequence of an ideologically based revolution removing the army of the preceding regime and populating it with their own supporters.

> The military in the USSR remained loyal to the oligarchy within the central Politburo and Secretariat of the Communist Party, partly because the institution of the Red Army was created by Lenin and Trotsky to defend their revolution against the Tsarist Army, and during Stalin's assumption to supreme power by his capacity to purge the army and navy of its senior generals from time to time and to have their activities constantly surveyed by Party commissars (Deutscher 1966: 375–7).

Successful autocrats will attempt to create around them a cult of personality by developing the myths and legends that may suggest they are the irreplaceable leader of their nation, without whose firm hand at the helm of the state its society would collapse in ruins. Such ability is in part aided by the capacity to remove any criticism of their actions by substantive if not total control of the media. However, such a capacity is also enhanced by widespread attitudes within civil society that seek to identify with and follow the guidance of leaders. Developing authority through the creation of the myth of the great leader can be a dangerous practice that is difficult to secure following the lifetime of the autocrat.

> The more longer lasting autocracies, as within the People's Republic of China or the USSR, whilst using violence and the cult of personality as an established policy of their state, also sought to gain authority that would secure their right to rule through cultivation of ideologies. Lenin and Stalin in the USSR or Mao Tze Tung in China

maintained their superiority with reference to the need for strong leadership in order to defend the revolution against its capitalist enemies. In Nazi Germany and Fascist Italy an ideology of elitism and a concept plagiarised but not fully understood from the writings of Darwin, Spencer, Nietzsche and Wagner developed ideas based on a cult of nationalism, racism and personality.

It is, however, rarely possible to continue the myth of the strong benevolent leader after their death. Perhaps North Korea is the only regime that appears to have managed to retain a specific family in power for over three generations aided by a cult of personality. In China after the death of Chairman Mao, the cult of the great leader was not extended to his successors but modified to a position in which the Communist Party is the defender of the revolution, and thus the less than democratically selected leaders should hold sway over the policy system of the nation acting largely as gate-keepers ensuring the filtering of policy proposals to what they, in their discussions and bargaining in closed oligarchies, found most acceptable (Moise 2008: 206–8).

Personality cults may be on occasion a successful device for ensuring gate-keepers can over their remaining lifetime reinforce their authority, but whilst it is a substantive feat for an ambitious politician to gain autocratic power within a political system, it is quite another and more difficult matter to build any form of permanent dynastic control of the polity following their death. Lasting autocracy where power is handed from one dictator or monarch to an accepted successor without an interlude of violence and usurpation of power is far from common, as in North Korea, but needs greater support than simply a structuring of patron–client relationships. The lasting dynastic autocracies have been able to build up ideological constructions of the moral authority of the state and those who have been chosen to succeed to positions of power. In pre-industrial states ideologies such as the divine right of kings, that argued that God had ordained that a particular family should always inherit the crown, ensured periods in which there were relatively smooth transitions from one ruler to another. Despite John Locke's (1924) powerful arguments in the seventeenth century presented to demolish the idea that kings had a divine right to rule, there is still in some Middle Eastern States such as Jordan or Saudi Arabia a widely held acceptance that the powerful families that founded these states in the early twentieth century should continue to provide their gate-keepers. Even in liberal democratic Europe several nations such as the United Kingdom choose their head of state following the tradition of vesting the position in the most senior member of a particular family.

Liberal autocracies

Totalitarianism does appear, however, to be more of a twentieth century rather than a twenty-first century phenomenon. The communist regimes of the Soviet Union and the People's Republic of China have evolved as much by policies determined by the ruling communist elites into less pervasive authoritarian regimes or rather shaky democratic systems that in the economic sphere rely on capitalist individual freedom to generate wealth and hence make little pretence to control all aspects of civil society. It may be argued that globalisation of world trade ensures that any state that refuses to allow multi-national corporations access to their societies can only survive, as does North Korea, as predominantly underdeveloped and isolated nations.

In the late twentieth century the isolation of the major totalitarian regimes of the USSR and the People's Republic of China along with the demise of an ageing oligarchy of leaders and pressure from well-resourced discontents in the lower reaches of bureaucracy and commerce, led to dramatic shifts in the policies of these regimes. In the Soviet Union the institutions as well as the ideological underpinning of the state collapsed and were replaced by a capitalist orientated system based on ostensibly democratic principles but increasingly led by newly wealthy oligarchs commanding political parties built around personalities as much as ideological values. In the People's Republic of China following the death of its founding leader Mao Tze Tung, his closest relations and lieutenants failed to sustain a personalised totalitarian dynasty. The resultant regime retains its autocratic tendency to co-opt ideologically like-minded politicians to its inner circles of policy makers and retains a totalitarian grip on education and capacity for innovative social thought and also on social relationships. However, it has greatly eased controls over economic life allowing rapid growth through promoting entrepreneurial capacity and rather light touch regulation of labour relations. The greater if highly unequal spread of capital in such regimes ensures there is a more substantial counter elite to challenge any return to a wholly totalitarian form of government.

Military regimes

A specific variety of autocratic government is based on government by the military that usually comes into being as a result of a *coup d'état* against a preceding regime. As quintessentially hierarchical social systems, military rule is based at best on an oligarchic arrangement of senior generals but more often than not determines one of their number to be the senior gate-keeping autocrat of the state. The capacity to seize and keep power is in many cases focused on the military's monopoly on the means of violence within the state. However, such a regime is also open to division among its leaders and many a military dictatorship has been overthrown by counter coups by disaffected elements of the military. Military governments are also in the most complex states usually short lived as the generals may soon realise that without the help of professional civilian advice their resource base may lack the expertise to control the economy and social welfare systems of the state. The more advanced a state in terms of its economic capacity the more likely it is that the military will become less dominant within the policy making process and eventually relinquish power to more civilian leadership.

Following the Spanish civil war Spain was an authoritarian right wing military state firmly under the control of General Franco and governed at the centre by a Cabinet composed predominantly by Generals. The regime attempted to generate a single party structure, the Falange, to attract a measure of civilian support but the organisation was always subservient to the military and gradually faded into insignificance. By the 1960s the military had defeated any possible left wing civilian counter-revolution but remained in comparison with much of Western Europe far less developed than the neighbouring powers that had been devastated by the Second World War. With the acquiescence of most of the military, internal policy changes were spearheaded by a number of right wing senior civilian bureaucrats who had been appointed to deal with specialised professional interests within economic and industrial Ministries and fashioned strategies to develop a more vibrant industrial and commercial private sector. With the growth of tourism and successful attempts to gain alliances with the

United States as a base for stationing defence systems against the Soviet Union, Spain began to shed its pariah image as a Fascist state within Western democracies. As the economy of Spain began to accelerate due to these strategies the military were increasingly marginalised from day to day policy making. On the death of General Franco in 1975 King Juan Carlos was able, with the support of the civilian techno-cratic civil service who had forged the economic renaissance of the state, to establish Spain as a liberal democracy and remove the last vestiges of rule by the military (Carr and Fusi 1981).

Those military regimes that have been able to subsist for decades, such as Myanmar or, despite its supposedly civilian dictator, North Korea, only continue through the most severe measures to cut the nation from engagement with the rest of the world and usually do this at the cost of substantial relative poverty within the state in comparison with the natural resources that can be used to develop their economies. Within such states attention is directed largely to ensuring the continued dominance of the military fuelled as much by group self-interest as by any deeply entrenched ideological, let alone moral, concerns.

In Myanmar in the absence of any substantive civilian professional input to govern-ance, the welfare of the society outside the military elite is principally characterised by neglect. The regime has under most international comparisons among the worst health or education services and, despite considerable potential, remains a largely underdeveloped state (Wilson and Skidmore 2008: 1–9).

Ethnically divided oligarchies

A form of autocratic dominance can be based on a capacity for leaders of specific racial or religious factions within a divided state to ensure that those who affiliate to the values of the lead faction are given disproportional advantages compared with those factions who are less enamoured by their treatment within the state. In these circumstances the oligarchic framework of the regime may survive for some time if the supporters of the dominant faction are sufficiently numerous to provide the controlling majority of the police, military and bureaucracy of the state and means are imposed to create public policy that ensures far fewer resources, such as the means to gain a high level education, health and welfare care or a capacity to operate profitable businesses, flow to the oppressed classes within the state. Such systems do not exhibit the totalitarian tendency to demand that all citizens show positive support for the state and many seek to isolate large sections of the population from any forms of political activity or economic entrepreneurship save small-scale services to their subservient communities.

Examples of this form of autocratic regime abounded in the twentieth century. The apartheid regime of South Africa between the 1940s and the 1990s was based on domination by Dutch and British white settlers who arranged among their racial group liberal democrat institutions that provided public policies to exclude the majority non-white African and Asian population from access to positions of authority in the government or access to social welfare (Nolutshungu 1983). Similar divisive structuring of state public policy to favour specific ethnic or religious groups at the expense of others contributes greatly to the tensions in the twenty-first century afflicting Middle-Eastern regimes, be they Syria, Israel or Iraq.

The acquisitive dictatorships

Not all autocracies are, at least in their initial phases, driven by strong ideological or racial or religious convictions that establish a strong party or military bureaucracy to dominate the polity. In some cases ideologically driven revolutions become little more than dictatorships dominated, as was the case with the USSR under Stalin, by an individual concerned above all to retain power against his real or imagined opponents. Many a military coup is similarly the product of the adventurism of a commanding officer to use the forces at their disposal to supplant whosoever may be in power and exert their tyranny with the central conviction of serving their own self-interest. Parties, often led by a dominant autocratic leader, may also emerge in civil societies through corrupt manipulation of the electoral system. Such demagogues corruptly, though given they control public policy, usually legally, are most interested in using the resources of the state to increase their own wealth and reward their client followers.

Idi Amin, who controlled Uganda from 1971, amassed a considerable fortune and was able when overthrown in 1979 to live the rest of his life in comfortable retirement in Saudi Arabia. Nigeria, following a cycle of imperfect elections interspersed by military coups and serious regional conflicts, has for many years been regarded as one of the most corrupt nations in Africa (Hill 2012: 59–62).

Within such systems, public policy, such as it is, may reflect the whims of the tyrant who will show little interest in the popular welfare of society and surround themselves with similarly minded individuals lacking in empathy who are empowered through violence and are rewarded by extortion. Through fear and superstition the dictator and his family are kept in power.

Conclusion

However policy emerges within any complex society, it does so through the activists who serve as gate-keepers of policy within predominantly autocratic systems. Policy development within a liberal democracy as shall be discussed in the following chapter is, in most situations, a process in which policy demands are forged from within the internal predominantly autocratic unelected political structures of government. What may also be concluded from this rough and ready classification of public policy making in autocracies is that what often drives the direction of the institutions and process of their policy making is, at root, the values and traditions that the gate-keepers wish to maintain or establish through their position of power. The next chapter considers how political power vested in the autocratic policy structures of any state may in liberal democracies be compromised and reconciled by their pluralist structuring.

9   Liberal democracy

Most of the academic debate and analysis that specifically turns its attention to public policy is written from the perspective of governance within liberal democratic states whose ideological foundations were briefly outlined in the profiles of ideas systems at the end of Chapter 4. In this chapter and *passim* throughout the rest of this study liberal democracies are a central focus. This chapter provides a detailed discussion of the development of this ideological position and its associated ethical values, from its largely eighteenth century re-discovery to its embedding into Western political culture as the candidate for becoming the source of 'an end of ideology' or in reality a triumph of a single ideology. In much of Europe the ideological grounding of liberal democracies was until the early twentieth century struggling to be put into practice and it was not until after the Second World War and perhaps even the fall of the Berlin Wall that the doctrine was accepted in Eastern Europe and, at least in theory, in Russia. Subsequently, the ideology has been widely maintained, to the extent that many autocracies will claim they have a democratic foundation. It can, nevertheless, be questioned how far the democratic as opposed to the liberal element of the doctrine has been seriously realised in such regimes. Liberal democracies are not, in many of their policy making structures, that dissimilar from many developed autocracies. As observed in the previous chapter, the bureaucracy and the military are in both systems hierarchical structures. In all but the most totalitarian of states, businesses are largely organised as autocratic states with strong bureaucratic controls over their employees and policy gate-keeping reserved to a single managing director or a board of shareholders with power given in relation to the extent of ownership of each shareholder. Professional agencies are generally closed democracies open only to their members, as opposed to their clients.

The democratic element of liberal democracy is premised on the argument that a capacity for every citizen to have a voice in determining public policy within their state is assured, should they choose to exercise this right. This is guaranteed if the state allows them liberty in the form of freedom of speech, communication, assembly, provided this is not to harm the well-being or property of others, and collectively a right to choose the representatives in governments both at state and local level who will forward and implement the policy decisions that affect their society. This chapter will critically assess these arguments on the belief that liberal values allowing such freedoms can ensure the right of an individual to have some influence over determining the issues in the context of the development and evolution of public policy.

The emergence of liberal democratic theory

The ideologies that broadly comprise the liberal democratic framework as established in developed West European and North American nations emerged in various and not wholly compatible forms in the eighteenth century in France, Britain and the United States with an emphasis more on liberalism than democracy. A liberal society, as noted in Chapter 6, in its original formulation, is a society that limits the power of governments to ensure that they respect the fundamental rights of man. Drawing from the writings of English philosopher John Locke (1924: 117–40) these fundamental human rights were seen as a right to life, liberty, freedom of speech and the ownership of property. These ideas were developed in the constitutional ideas of Montesquieu who suggested that the powers of governments could best be confined, so that liberty could be respected, by which he meant the capacity to obey and be protected by just laws. Government, in what he took to be the best regulated nations such as England, was divided into separate compartments for legislation, implementation and justice, as institutions that would balance the potential of the other sectors of government, and especially a monarch, to dominate individual rights (Jones 1947: 226–47). The juxtaposition of these ideas formed the central core of the first essay into liberal democracy within a modern substantive political system with the development of the Constitution of the United States. Alexander Hamilton, James Madison and John Jay collected together within *The Federalist* in 1788 a set of recently published papers that argued the merits of a constitution and the emerging federation of North American states. These ideas influenced the creation of the present Constitution based on a balance of powers between an elected bi-cameral Congress, the separately elected President and a Supreme Court that could arbitrate on the interpretation of the Constitution. In addition, power was further divided between the national federal government with highly restricted powers and state governments that could take charge of most domestic issues. Effectively, the capacity to legitimise policy had to be determined by compromise between the various horizontal as well as vertical layers within the public sector. Not only was power divided, it was also limited. The Constitution in 1791 was amended to incorporate what is now referred to as a Bill of Rights that could not, without overwhelming agreement, be overridden by either federal or state governments:

> Nine of the amendments were concerned with the rights of the individual. They guaranteed freedom of religion, of speech, of assembly, and of the press, the right to bear arms, and immunity against arbitrary search and arrest. They also prohibited excessive bail, cruel and unusual punishments and quartering of troops in private houses. The tenth amendment reserved to states all power except those specifically delegated to the federal government.
>
> (Jones 1995: 77)

The theory underlying the Constitution focused on the liberty of the individual. Political equality to ensure that all citizens had equal opportunities to influence policy was less of a concern for the Federalists. Whilst United States citizens were allowed a vote to select national, state and local representatives, the idea that all established residents in the polity should be considered as citizens was far from being secured. As in ancient Athens, the classical model for democracy in the United States would not now pass muster as a democracy given that, in both regimes, the right to stand for office or vote for policies and representatives, did not extend to women, slaves and in America the persecuted original residents of the country and procedures in each state determined when a resident could qualify as a citizen.

A rather different approach to democracy emerged in Britain within the intellectual circles of the utilitarian thinkers such as Jeremy Bentham and James Mill. Both sages rejected the idea of natural rights. Their adherence to liberal democracy around the ethical framework, as discussed in Chapter 6, was built on their utilitarian theory that individuals were concerned to maximise their happiness with the least possible cost to themselves and that each person was the best judge of how this was to be achieved. Since one person's happiness may be at the cost of unhappiness for others, an ethical society must have a rational means of resolving disputes. This could only be secured if each person could vote in a specific geographical area for the rules that may govern their conduct and the majority vote must prevail to secure the greatest sum total of happiness. Bentham argued that a large state in which all individuals could vote directly on all public policies was impractical and advocated a representative system in which all citizens were able to vote for whomsoever best represented their views in a national parliament. The majority opinion of members of that parliament should then be the sovereign body that determined law and the content of policy for the nation (Peardon 1974: 132). Bentham's ideal, unlike those of the American Federalists, implied that parliament should be sovereign over society and hence its powers could not be limited. Governments, as in Britain, in the form of a prime minister and his cabinet and all local governments should, as a consequence, also be subordinate to the representative central parliament and might assist but not determine the process of establishing national policy. The idea of a division of power was an anathema to Bentham and James Mill but they believed that majority opinion in society, especially within a wealthy economy, would not tolerate laws that substantially eroded personal freedom. The views of Bentham and James Mill were for many an overly logical but impractical prescription for developing effective and efficient public policy, but, when amended by John Stuart Mill, formed in Britain the most successful radical interpretation of Britain as a liberal democracy.

John Stuart Mill (1806–1873) was the son of Bentham's confidant and collaborator James Mill and as a child educated at home by these mentors. 'By the age of six Mill had written a history of Rome; by seven was reading Plato in Greek; at eight soaking up Sophocles, Thucydides and Demosthenes' (Reeves 2007: 12) but by the age of twenty he entered a period of depression as he was unable to accept the ideas inculcated in his younger years by Bentham and James Mill. He recovered by developing a more practical approach to utilitarianism and his political and economic writing frames much of the character of liberal democratic institutions and practice in the early twentieth century. His liberal values supported by his partner Harriet Taylor provided some of the strongest arguments in favour of the political emancipation of women (Mill 1869).

J. S. Mill, like many critics of his time, argued that in the practical world of politics governments representing large populations needed to make quick decisions on matters of considerable technical and moral complexity, and had, therefore, to be given the capacity to govern. Workable policy could not be made by either direct participation or even at times by a representative assembly but must be developed and implemented by a disciplined government:

There is a radical distinction between controlling the business of government and actually doing it. ... The commander of an army could not direct its movements effectually if he himself fought in the ranks or led an assault. It is the same with bodies of men. Some things cannot be done except by bodies; other things cannot be well done by them. It is one question, therefore, what a popular assembly should control, another what it should itself do ... in order to determine through what channel this general control may most expediently be exercised, and what portion of the business of government the representative body should hold in its own hands, it is necessary to consider what kinds of business a numerous body is competent to perform properly.

(Mill 1861: 214)

Mill also had sympathy with a widespread elitist view in Victorian Britain of what he termed the potential for a 'tyranny of the majority' in which the ill-informed could override the more rational and moral judgements of the most intelligent and best educated citizens. Although Mill accepted that many less informed voters would defer to the greater wisdom of the well educated, as a safeguard he also thought that those who were illiterate or dependent on public support through the poor law should not have the vote (Mill 1861: 277–83). Mill, thus, advocated the structuring of a more limited representative democracy in which citizens could vote for representatives who would then support a government led by the prime minister and his or her chosen ministers. Governments would have to present policies requiring legislation to parliament for approval and at regular intervals submit themselves with all other parliamentary representatives for re-election. Such a system would be founded on the principle that there should be freedom of speech that stopped short of advocating violence against fellow citizens but also the obligation on each citizen to obey the laws sanctioned by parliament.

Egalitarian theories of democracy

Whilst the United States Federalists emphasised liberalism as freedom from governmental oppression, in France the philosophy of Jean Jacques Rousseau placed far greater emphasis on direct democracy as a means of ensuring liberty through equality.

Rousseau (1712–1778) was born in Geneva but was of French protestant extraction and lived much of life in France. In his earlier life he lived a rather dissolute life often dependent on his various female partners but at the age of thirty-seven had a sudden conversion to a more productive life in publicising his thoughts on education, freedom and government.

Rousseau's ideas permeated democratic thought in revolutionary France and, in part, derived from a rather rosier view of democracy in ancient Athens than was warranted by reality. He argued that in societies where one person's action may differ from another, policy should only be determined if each citizen was able to directly participate in debate and argument. Policy decisions for the good of society and the good of all should be reached through compromise or mutual conviction as to the strength of an argument. It was, Rousseau pointed out, essential for societies to cooperate together to reach workable agreements with one another and hence if a consensus is reached following free deliberation then that decision was binding on its members. Anyone who subsequently dissented from the community view, for the good of themselves and their society, would be 'forced to be free' by being obliged to conform to the common consensus (Hampsher-Monk 1992: 185–6). Rousseau himself advocated the development of a polity, like the city states of ancient Greece or his place of birth, Geneva, that was small enough to allow all the citizens to gather in an appropriately constructed forum or market place to argue over policy until consensus emerged.

An obvious problem with such a theory, which will be discussed later in this book, was the practicality of allowing what is now seen as deliberative democracy within a large community. The population size and complexity of most national liberal democracies ensured that the ideas of Rousseau did not carry great practical weight in their policy processes. However, it must be borne in mind that at the more micro level of decision making within small groups, as in a family or professionals who are seen as corporate partners in law, accountancy or architectural firms, participatory democracy may well be the normal method of reaching decisions. In such small circles decisions are rarely arrived at by voting but through intensive discussion by all concerned until a consensus is reached on the way forward.

In modern times the idea of direct democracy in relation to public governments is still upheld in certain parts of the United States and especially in New England where town governments are still based on local assemblies of all citizens who elect their officers such as a mayor or their head of police and on a regular basis determine policy through debate and discussion in meetings open to all citizens of the township.

The liberal democracies that emerged in the late nineteenth century were never designed to accommodate Rousseau's ideas of participatory democracy. The Madisonian view of limited government based on checks and balances alongside Bentham's and J. S. Mill's ideas of representative democracy took centre stage. The developing strands of democratic theory in the 18th and 19th centuries were used to justify differing institutional structures of policy making in the United States and most Western European nations. The United States tradition favours limited powers for the public sector through an emphasis on the liberty of the individual and policy making structures in which there is a balance of powers between local and central institutions and within such institutions a balance between executive, legislative and judicial arms of governance. Although the ideas of Rousseau had some influence, particularly in the writing of De Tocqueville for local community governance in the United States, it could not be translated easily into issues of policy making at state or federal government level. In contrast the European tradition is more directly concerned with establishing a more powerful central government that is required to determine and implement the majority views within civil society whilst allowing minority opinion to be expressed in the hope that they may eventually garner majority support.

The elitist challenge

It did not take long for these systems to be subject to serious criticism of their pretensions to be democratic as opposed to being in practice oligarchic systems of government favouring the wealthiest citizens of such states. The classical interpreters of this elitist doctrine were the Italian intellectuals Gaetano Mosca (1939) and Vilfredo Pareto (1966) who both despaired at the democratic pretensions of the Italian Republic following its formation in the 1860s. Both used arguments based on their rather pessimistic reading of human psychology to argue that a small organised political elite could control power against the interests of the much larger but less organised masses. Mosca also founded his ideas on an appeal to the elitist nature of bureaucratic organisation in technologically advanced society (Dryzek and Dunleavy 2009: 58–60). His pupil Roberto Michels more firmly spelt out the mechanics of elite dominance arguing 'who says organization says oligarchy' (Parry 1969: 42). A successful political party with the capacity to secure election to government will become an organisation led by professional full-time party bureaucrats as opposed to the more amateur rank and file party members, let alone its electoral supporters. Given their professional and technical expertise the party leaders will be better placed and more adept in developing party policies and have the capacity to communicate their interests, including their policy proposals, to party supporters and the electorate. They will also have the power to determine the internal rules for their party to suit their own interest, determine who could stand for office within the party leadership, and expel those who threaten their policy decisions. Finally, the need to create vote-winning policies ensures that a party leadership that is professionally committed to gaining power will moderate its values to suit the views of the electorate rather than its rank and file members. Thus power and policies in democracies are dominated by self-selecting party elites rather than their mass membership (Parry 1969: 43–4).

Pareto based his ideas on a wealth of Western European thought on the importance of power and leadership reflecting, like Niccolò Machiavelli three centuries earlier, that power required leaders who could act like lions by using force and violence to retain authority or like foxes who could beguile and fool the masses into following their ideas. These basic psychological tendencies were difficult to reconcile in one person and hence, Pareto argued, regimes circulate between those led by foxes, who through the sham of democracy gave the masses the idea that their interests were being carefully nurtured by their leaders. When the masses realise their mistake there is a reversion to rule by men of coercion, the lions, who in turn would eventually fail to retain their dominance and be outwitted by the foxy wing of the elite.

Corporatism, iron triangles and professionalism

The classical 18th and nineteenth century theories of democracy were also undermined by initially little noticed community power studies conducted within the United States. These were largely behaviouralist influenced empirical studies of the distribution of power in small political systems such as town and city governments. In 1929 Robert and Helen Lynd published a study of the industrial city of Indianapolis, which they saw as typical of United States cities. They concluded that politics within the city was largely controlled by its leading businessmen. Floyd Hunter (1953) gained even greater attention and notoriety in a study of the city of Atlanta and its region that similarly concluded that a powerful business elite controlled local politics. Later community power studies in Britain from the 1950s to the 1980s further emphasised the view that power within local government systems was predominantly dominated by a small elite of professional or semi-professional local political leaders and the leading members of their local government bureaucracies (Birch 1959, Newton 1976, Green 1981).

Paralleling the elitist orientated community studies, in Britain the importance of group politics was popularised in Samuel Finer's (1958) study, *Anonymous Empire*, that considered the influence of, the now rather archaically named, lobby groups on parliament and government. Further development of this theme in Richardson and Jordan's (1979) influential *Governing under Pressure* analysed the formation of public policy in Britain through the lens of party interaction with interest groups. Such studies emphasised, in apparent contradiction to the pluralist model, how in liberal democracies close connections between the core executive and wealthy interest groups allowed powerful interests to influence the development and implementation of economic or welfare policies. A more theoretical critique of pluralism in left wing circles in the United States centred on a concept of the iron triangle said to be a foundation of policy development that existed in the close relationship between members of the powerful policy committees in Congress that look in detail at policy and legislative proposals. Congressional committees were seen to be greatly influenced by groups representing major industrial and commercial interests, and the federal bureaucrats who relied on these interests for information. The close working between lobbyists, congressmen and bureaucrats created a durable and hence iron clad policy making machine that was difficult to oppose.

In the 1970s a revival of elitist theory emerged in European ideas, using the term, borrowed from studies of Fascism, of 'corporatism' to describe the close relationships between the core executives of European governments and the leading business sectors. The views developed by J. T. Winkler (1976) and then more substantively by Phillippe Lembruch and Gerhard Schmitter (1982) were strongly influenced by the apparently stable political structures then in place in West Germany and Scandinavia. The governments of these areas were closely intermeshed with favoured national interest groups on policy development. Corporatist theory suggests a model of policy making in which the serious players in determining policy are a close and generally small circle of political leaders working with senior leaders of major businesses or the representative groups for small and medium sized enterprises. The representative organisations may also include in some regimes the employees' representatives in the form of large professional bodies or major trade unions.

The long-term dominance in Sweden of the Social Democratic Party between the 1920s and the 1970s led to the creation of a system of consultation concerning legislation and policy change through royal commissions with trade unions and employers' groups or, relevant professional associations for specialised policy areas such as health care. Implementation of policy was similarly conducted through government agencies on which national interest groups concerned directly with the boards' role were represented. Thus the government recruited into its policy making circle the leaders of the major representative bodies of organisations concerned with policy change or policy retention.

A concern for some Swedish citizens in the 1970s was that whilst the political system was one of the most open and democratic among states, power was in the hands of a small coterie of party leaders and heads of interest groups who had similar views and values (Hancock 1972).

The problem with these elitist theories was that they fitted certain regimes rather more successfully than others. In Britain, for example, during the 1970s attempts to create a system of economic planning or control over industrial relations were never successful as a consequence of differences both within and between interest groups and also the emergence of strong populist movements pushing for greater militancy within the trade unions. By the 1980s the arrival of a New Right government concerned to roll back the frontier of the state further diminished any possibility that employers and the trade unions would be able to co-operate on equal terms with the government. States like Britain could however be better characterised as veering from corporatism benefiting the right of the political spectrum rather than, as in the then more stable Scandinavian regimes, the centre left.

The power of the elected politician was seen as being further confined by the dominance of unelected bureaucrats. Max Weber (1948), who was generally sympathetic to liberal government, had raised the spectre of the professional by arguing that the expertise and organisational skills of modern bureaucracy were such that they would become dominant centres of power and be the source of policy development that could be dangerously detached from mass opinion. American theorists picked up on this theme. James Burnham (1941) argued that the organisational skills of professionals in both the private and public sector would increasingly transfer decision making powers away from the owners of businesses or voters to the public and private sector managers (Burnham 1942; Parry 1969: 50–2). C. Wright-Mills (1959) later developed this view, arguing that policy making in industrialised capitalist economies would be dominated by a 'power elite' composed of overlapping bureaucracies including the managers of corporate private sector businesses, military leaders and core executive public sector politicians and civil servants. The most powerful policy makers are the individuals who have a foot in all three camps (Wright-Mills 1959: 287–92). Further commentaries on this pattern of institutionalised elitism argued that an iron triangle dominated United States politics, composed of the interaction and mutual self-interest between members of Congress, their powerful supporters within interest groups and the federal bureaucracy.

President Eisenhower (1961), general and politician as he was, warned Americans of the potential power of an industrial military elite in which private business interests joined forces with the military to develop an arms race that empowered the state both nationally and internationally.

The socialist critique

In the longer term the most pertinent critiques of the representative democratic system were the socialist theories that by the early twentieth century became dominated by the writings of Marx and Engels, which implied that liberal democracy enables a wealthy capitalist class to contest elections by controlling the media and means of populist education so that the working classes believe they are being governed by parties concerned with and sensitive to their interests. These ideas are discussed in Chapter 4 and need only a summary here. Should sufficient numbers of voters realise their subjugation by an elite and begin to protest against their lot, their leaders may be forcibly repressed or bought off by the capitalist class by allowing a few of their more malleable leaders to enter the ranks of the bourgeoisie provided they mitigated their objections to the system of capitalist government. Later, neo-Marxist thought as outlined in Chapter 7 argues that concessions to the proletariat are the source of the development of welfare states. Nicos Poulantzes (1978) and the earlier writing of Manuel Castells (1977) maintained that the generation of capital is better secured if the exploited proletariat are kept throughout their working lives relatively healthy, well housed and given sufficient education to be useful tools for exploitation in an increasingly complex, knowledge based society.

Rescuing democracy

By the 1940s the rise of totalitarian governments required a serious reconsideration of democratic theory given the many critiques of the existing theory. One of the most influential attempts to revise democratic theory was the work of economist Joseph Schumpeter (2010, first published 1943) who suggested a measure of reconciliation between democracy and the position that political parties were elitist organisations by arguing that free elections obliged the party elites to show some sensitivity to their electorate by favouring popular currents of opinion rather than the more ideological views of their rank and file party members. Schumpeter thus built a platform for later pluralist thought by defining democracy as:

> That institutional arrangement for arriving at political decisions in which individuals acquire the power to decide by means of a competitive struggle for the people's vote.

> (Schumpeter 2010: 241)

Schumpeter argued that, whilst public policy is generally made by the elites, an open electoral system would ensure that the politicians that are on balance most acceptable to the electorate would, at least until the next election, have the power to determine public policy. Schumpeter's view did not for many political theorists effectively undermine the arguments of elite theorists, let alone the contrasting views of Marx or Weber, but provided a theory that gave at least two but hardly three cheers for the image of liberal democracy as a system permitting freedom of expression and association. The political-economic orientated ideas of Schumpeter were reinforced by the beginnings of what may be termed a public choice calculus on how policy activists and gate-keepers must react in an environment where votes determine power. Antony Downs (1957) argued that, given that the large number of voters in stable democracies occupied centrist rather than extreme values, it was inevitable that successful political parties would seek to occupy the middle ground in politics and thus be responsive to the mainstream of political and social values of public opinion.

Studies of voting behaviour such as Butler and Stokes' (1969) survey of the British electorate indicated that there was little evidence of strong partisanship between left and right wing parties and that class was increasingly less likely to define party preferences. A number of American writers began to gnaw away at the iron triangles approach to show that policy was influenced in many areas by more diverse populist interests than those of the professional politicians or leaders of corporate business. Congressmen, for example, had to take on board the issue of responding to social groups campaigning for specific objectives within their constituencies or to be aware of strongly felt currents of opinion on issues like the cost of oil and hence private transport (John 1998: 80). It also began to be fashionable to argue that in developed democracies there was rapidly becoming, to use Daniel Bell's overused phrase, 'an end of ideology', which more realistically could be interpreted that there was a decline in ideological conflict in such states. Gabriel Almond and Sidney Verba's (1963) survey of civic values suggested that trust between citizens and those in power was a founding feature of stable democratic government. Seymour Martin Lipset (1981: 469–90) tried to show empirically that the wealthier and more prosperous states tended to be stable democracies. There was, therefore, a strong current of academic and popular ideology that maintained that, whilst power may be unevenly distributed between major political actors and society, it was essential for those in positions of authority to ensure that their decisions reflected the core values of the majority in civic society and that liberal democracies operated on the platform of public trust that the core executants ruled in the interests of their subjects rather than their specific class or the power elite.

The pluralist response

In addition to the behaviouralist and public choice theories of Schumpeter, a further response to the elitist critique of liberal democracy was gaining greater attention through studies of interest group politics. In the earlier twentieth century little thought had been given to the importance of interest groups in forging policy. This activity had been recognised by the pioneering behaviouralist Arthur Bentley (1908) in his study *The Political Process*, which argued that organised groups were the driving force in the United States. The study initially received little attention. George Catlin in 1927 re-emphasised the role of group competition in the American polity and in 1951 David Truman re-discovered Bentley's pioneering work and, in the influential study, *The Governmental Process*, put group interaction firmly on the map of American political science, despite the critique of democracy based on interest group domination in the work of the community studies of Lynd and Lynd (1929) and Hunter (1953):

> The total pattern of government over a period of time thus presents a protean complex of crisscrossing relationships that change in strength and direction with alterations in the power and standing of interests, organized and unorganized.
>
> (Truman 1951: 508)

Following this line of enquiry, the most influential of democratic community studies supporting a more favourable democratic approach was Robert Dahl's (1961) *Who Governs?* which analysed policy making in New Haven, Connecticut, the home town of Yale University. Dahl was concerned to refute the conclusions of earlier elitist orientated community studies by considering the power of interest groups developing what became known as pluralist theory. Pluralist theory argues that civil society in industrial democracy is composed of a complex web of interests that are open to all members of a society. The social organisations developed by citizens are a response to political and social problems and interests and have a major role in determining how citizens will support or oppose policy and political activists.

In his study of New Haven, Dahl (1961) argues that the core executive of a city government, in this case an elected executive mayor, is constantly bombarded with demands from groups of citizens for and against suggested policy change. Individual citizens may be linked in various ways, from, for example, work, family or financial interests to a range of political interests and demands. If mayors are to retain authority by continuing to win elections they must retain a high level of rapport within their community by constructing a set of policies that can maximise popular support. The mayor will select among the many demands made by an array of interests on the city government those that on balance secure the greatest support from their potential electors. The successful politician will, therefore, support policies that are not necessarily of their own choosing but those most favoured by the electorate. Dahl improved on Schumpeter's ideas by showing how demands on politicians do not just surface during an election and are then set in stone without addition or subtraction in their electoral manifesto. Politicians are continually consulting with their citizens and reacting to new demands and events in society. The sources of pressure for change or reform are, moreover, dispersed among a wide number of organisations. Specialist political institutions usually have power and authority in specific policy arenas. Banks and financial regulators may concern themselves with public finance but will not be party to, for example, disputes over family law. Demands on the core executive will also come from more populist interests that are widely dispersed in civil society such as opposition to higher taxation or demands for better transport or health care facilities. The elitist theorists' assumption that power is concentrated in a small coterie of institutions by an unrepresentative group of dominant politicians is, in a liberal democracy, argued to be wide of the mark. Even within a complex set of governmental institutions differing specialist centres of power are dealing with differing groups of interests. A new generation of community power studies also supported this pluralist reading of policy development in contrast to the earlier largely corporatist finding of Hunter.

Sayre and Kaufman (1960: 712) in a study on the governance of New York city concluded that 'No single group of participants in the city's political contest is self-sufficient in its power to make decisions or require decisions of others. Every decision of importance is consequently the product of mutual accommodation. Building temporary or lasting alliances, working out immediate or enduring settlements between allies or competitors, and bargaining for an improved position in the decision centres are the continuing preoccupations of all leaders.'

The free and fair vote that for Schumpeter formed the basis of liberal democracy, does not simply determine who has the power to determine policy following an election but is a constant pressure on the core executives who must be constantly reacting to a wide range of citizens' preferences, if they are to remain in power.

It may be argued that the forces of self-interest among many opinion formers both in the United States and through diffusion of the pluralist case to most liberal democracies have ensured that by the twenty-first century many of the doubts concerning the efficacy of liberal democracy as the best form of practical governance have disappeared within centrist party systems in such states. Miller and Fox (2007: 4–5) observe under the heading of 'the Loop model of Democracy' that:

It is widely assumed that in the United States *the people* are sovereign. Policy reflects their wishes. The majoritarian model of democracy is supposed to work like this:

1   The people are aware of what they want or need.
2   Competing candidates (or parties) for electoral office – political entrepreneurs – offer alternative packages of wants or needs that can be satisfied by particular methods.
3   People choose a representative by voting for which alternative package seems to best match their preferences.
4   Coalitions of winning entrepreneurs pass laws reflecting the people's choice.
5   A vigilant populace pays enough attention to the process and the results to judge the elected representatives as either successful or wanting.
6   If satisfied with the results, people will reward incumbents with their votes; if unsatisfied they will vote for alternative entrepreneurs offering alternative packages.

This characterisation of the liberal democratic process is, argue Miller and Fox, seriously flawed in terms of its capacity to ensure effective democracy given that 'subjects are constructed and created through discourses – and yet they are not necessarily the author of their own construction' (Miller and Fox 2007: 128). This radical critique through the caricature of the liberal democratic loop is expressive of some apologists for the system but should not, however, be stretched to include much modern day academic analysis of democratic practice and the making of public policy in pluralist societies. As will be shown in the following chapter, this conclusion does not, as later critics including Dahl or Lindblom realised, entail that the capacity to influence policy decisions was evenly distributed in liberal democracies. Since the 1980s many mainstream positivist, let alone more subjectivist, theories of public policy making suggest that liberal democracies may deliver on liberalism but not in any strong sense on democracy.

Conclusion

This chapter has raised the question of the extent to which liberal democracies provide a more ethical ideological foundation for systems to develop public policy based on the evolution of what may be termed classic conceptions of liberal democracy as they developed in the 19th and 20th centuries in response to its critics from both right and left wing perspectives. The question remains whether liberal democracy may give the appearance but not the reality of democracy and is but the evolution in advanced society of policy systems to secure power in the hands of elites with the consent or at least acquiescence of the majority. The following chapter advances this discussion to show how more recent theory and empirical research on policy development in liberal democracies that is based on the role of interest groups within the policy process creates a more balanced view of the extent to which liberal democracies secure a capacity to democratise the policy making process over and above the accusation of critics that liberal democracy is but elitism with a human face.

10 Networks and the Advocacy Coalitions Framework

Whilst many of the supporters of pluralism, such as Dahl (1989) or Lindblom and Woodhouse (1993), were prepared to admit that in practice democracy did not distribute power evenly or even give equal opportunities to forge policy, such concessions did not amount to a rejection of the merits of the pluralist ideal. It could still be claimed on the basis of economic theories of democracy, as developed by Schumpeter (2010) and Downs (1957), or, empirically, through community studies, that however imperfectly liberal democracies distributed power, citizens enjoyed considerably greater political freedom than if they lived in autocracies. The tension between elitist and pluralist views of liberal democratic regimes required not so much a restatement of opposing paradigms but theoretical frameworks that could reconcile the two positions to present a more balanced view of liberal democracy as a system that facilitated mass participation and communication and also ensured substantive opportunities for debate within civil society that allowed politically engaged citizens to attempt to influence the policy process. Reconciliation of these tensions in the liberal democratic state has since the 1980s developed through the policy network theories that have led to a fashionable depiction of policy making as a result of governance, as opposed to top down government, and a parallel, and more ideas-led, depiction of the policy process by Paul Sabatier and Jenkins Smith in a recasting of network theory through their Advocacy Coalitions Framework (ACF), which in many studies appears as the most favoured explanation of policy development and evolution within pluralist liberal democracies (see, for example, Cairney 2012).

Network theory

Network theory evolves from studies of liberal democracies that perceive the system as built on the pluralism that results from freedom of communication and assembly, and facilitates the emergence of interest groups as associations of citizens seeking a common objective. As indicated in earlier chapters, the role of interest groups has had an important bearing on twentieth century theories underlying evaluations of the moral status of liberal democracies as either central to ensuring democratic government or for corporatists, rather sinister coalitions of self-interest with the resources to undermine popular representation or the general welfare and the good of society. Network theory attempted to support the ideas of Truman (1951) and the earlier writings of Dahl (1961) that coalitions of interests competing to influence governments formed themselves into networks of sufficient breadth in terms of representation of popular interest to diffuse power widely within a liberal democratic polity. An important stimulus to the development of network theory was the study by American scholars Hugh Heclo and Aaron Wildavsky of policy making in the British Treasury, *The Private Government of Public Money* (Heclo and Wildavsky 1974) which unfolded a view on the inner workings at the centre of the British political system as based on the cultivation of close relationships and trust. They argued that:

> the distinguishing feature of Treasury men who deal with public spending is not their intellect or ideas but their emotions. Their supreme skill lies in personal relations. We have therefore interpreted our subject matter, not in the usual terms of relative power and division of responsibility, but in terms of community and policy. Community refers to the personal relationships between major political and administrative actors, sometimes in conflict, often in agreement, but always in touch and operating within a shared framework. Treasury influence rests not on a hard nosed interpretation of formal powers but in personal networks, sensitive bargaining and up to date information.
>
> (Heclo and Wildavsky 1974: xiv, xv, 380)

The term 'policy community' was later broadened out by Heclo (1978) to describe on a rather wider scale the relationship between individuals and organisations engaged in policy making in the United States that emerged from the development of social welfare programmes following the Kennedy and Johnson Administrations:

> Looking for the few who are powerful we tend to overlook the many whose webs of influence provide and guide the exercise of power. The web, or what I will call 'issue networks' are particularly relevant to the highly intricate and confusing welfare policies that have been undertaken in recent years.
>
> (Heclo 1978: 102)

The term 'networks' has been defined by the United States theorist J. K. Benson (1975, 1982: 148) taking the idea from C. Wright Mills as a 'complex of organizations connected to each other by resource dependencies and distinguished from other ... complexes by breaks in the structure of resource dependencies'. The idea was subsequently elaborated by R. A. W. Rhodes who with David Marsh (Rhodes and Marsh 1992: 14) further developed the network theory by classifying specific types of networks which are, in the main, categories that have been identified by earlier theorists. The Rhodes and Marsh framework is, however, only one of many possible formulations of networks. I have in Table 10.1 provided a classification which may better fit the arrangement of this study. This may of course be criticised as containing overlapping boundaries. Many interest groups are active in more than one functional category. It is difficult, for example, in relation to an organisation for trade unions, to determine how far it should be characterised as a producer, supplier or even a professional network, or that more realistically it would have characteristics of all these categories. However, the formulation provides some guide to forms of inter-active policy groups in regard to policy making and may easily be reformulated to suit differing areas of enquiry.

Rhodes linked the extent to which particular networks could achieve their goals through his power dependence theory, discussed in Chapter 7. The network approach attempts to reconcile the earlier debates between pluralist and elitist theory. It has particular value in demonstrating how policy is made in a pluralist society as a

Table 10.1 Policy communities and networks

Type of network	Characteristics	Examples
Inter-governmental	Ideological Discursive within a highly restricted elite membership	United Nations World Bank European Union
Political interests with an open agenda of goals	Ideological and harbouring self-interested motives Generally autocratic	Conservative Party of Britain United States Democratic Party
Sub-governmental	Ideological and self-interested Autocratic or discursive within a restricted membership	Public–Private Partnerships Local Authority Associations
Professional	Self-interested Discursive within a restricted membership	British Medical Association American Bar Association
Producer	Self-interested Generally autocratic	Confederation of British Industry General Motors
Consumer and supplier	Self-interested and often ideological Tend to be discursive and democratic	Trade Unions OXFAM
Issue	Often ideological or ethical and self-interested Tend to be discursive and democratic	Campaign for Nuclear Disarmament Amnesty International

consequence of the interplay of relationships between groups. At its most basic level a policy network approach can be a valuable means of establishing the major players in any policy decision or in the development of policy issues. By identifying the groups most concerned with a particular issue and how they may relate to each other a researcher can demonstrate that they are covering the important actors within the study.

Network theory should be seen largely as a meso-theory that does not attempt a comprehensive explanation of policy making as it gives little help in explaining the micro level of detail needed to explore a specific policy area. As a discerning reader can appreciate in reviewing the diagram of how a policy network may be illustrated, questions arise as to where to stop the spread of institutional webs. It does however give an important indication of the need to examine the widespread linkages that might influence any attempt at an explanation of policy development. In a complex society each policy institution, which can be seen as a reasonably stable community of interests in its own right, may be connected to further institutions which have their layer of interconnections that may not directly impinge on the central policy making networks but can exert considerable influence on the policy decision through more indirect means. It must also be kept in mind that, as Rhodes later asserts in partnership with Mark Bevir, institutions are in reality collections of individuals and that networks are often bound together by ties of self-interest and ideological concerns between key players within an institution (Bevir and Rhodes 2003; Rhodes 2006: 438).

A further problem of network theory is its static framework, in that it does not provide an explanation of how networks come into being and how they evolve over time. As Jeremy Richardson (2000) has pointed out, as governments change their ideological direction or encounter new environmental factors the connections between interests and government may strengthen or fall apart. Network theory is, however, Rhodes argues, not meant to be a theory of everything (Rhodes 2006: 441–2) and networks will differ in respect to their cohesion. Certain forms of networks such as issue communities are generally seen as loose collections of interests that may reinforce each other to press for change or delay on policies which are being actively considered by government. In some cases these networks may be temporary alliances of interests which are on other matters seriously opposed to one another.

> In an attempt to stave off a 'yes' vote for independence in Scotland in 2014 the leaders of the three major parties in Britain, Conservative, Labour and Liberal Democrat, agreed that they would work together to create a constitutional framework for increasing the power of the Scottish Parliament within the United Kingdom.

Even in the case of policy communities that are seen as long-term, closely interrelated networks, external events may substantively distort the ties that join them. A change of government may, for example, restructure the policy communities.

> In Britain, the arrival of the New Right Thatcher Government broke up the tri-partite policy community between the Government, the trade unions and employers' organisation that had in the previous two decades been viewed as the central entity that determined the nation's financial policy. The antipathy of the Thatcher Government to the trade unions, demonstrated through legislation, and sustained campaigns from the predominantly right wing press, ensured that the trade unions were within five years ostracised as an influential force in the development of industrial policy (Kingdom 2014: 598–600).

Policy networks can be vulnerable organisations that can split apart as a result of ideological change or the capacity of policy activists to play the one group off against the others. It requires additional theories to explain how coalitions of interest on specific subjects evolve over time.

Governance

If policy networks are to serve as a useful framework for analysing the development of public policy they must also be linked to theories of power that can give some guidance as to why a particular network may be more effective than another. This was given some substance by relating the capacity of networks to forward their ideas to the power dependence models developed by Rhodes and Marsh that have been discussed in Chapter 7. Thus, policy networks within liberal democracies exert their influence through the resources of authority and capital that they can command and a corollary of ascribing power to networks must be to diminish the extent of power under direct control by the state. Governance theory argues that within liberal democratic societies centralised governments are ceasing to exert any substantive authority over civil society independently from powerful, well-resourced interest groups both within and external to their geographical boundaries. Governments can only govern with the support of a substantive network of interest groups. These include, within the private sector, large multi-national companies in both the manufacturing and service sectors and also, in welfare provision, major third sector non-profit making agencies. Government itself is also divided into devolved layers of regional and local governance and also national public agencies operating at arm's length from central government. Adherence to New Right and New Public Management theory motivates politicians and senior civil servants to contract out the operation of many public services to private or third sector organisations. Hence, according to Rhodes, central governments are being hollowed out, generally with the support of the majority in their electorate. Under these circumstances policy making is in almost all sectors of government subject to regulation by central government rather than being under their direct control. Frequently such regulation is regarded as a 'light touch' framework of controls that facilitates major economic and welfare providers' considerable influence in the determination of what may be regarded as a policy problem and how it may be resolved and implemented.

In both the United Kingdom and the United States light touch regulation of the banks that was increasingly the norm following the introduction of New Right policies in the 1980s under the Thatcher and Reagan administrations paved the way for the 2008 economic crisis. In the absence of any strong restraints from central governments or regulatory agencies such as the Bank of England and, in the United States, the Federal Reserve, private sector financial business interests worked as a network relatively independent from government control. This led to a complex web of borrowing between banks to insure themselves against losses that may occur from high risk investments. The consequence was that the financial sector was generating money that was unsupported by the real value of the economy, leading to the collapse of the system like a pack of cards. It was then left to central governments to establish a regime of austerity through higher taxation and lower central government spending to pay for the continuation of the private banking system that was now too substantial an element in the economic policy making of these pluralist states to be allowed to fail (Hutton 2015: 73–9).

Whilst the 2008 economic crash may be regarded as the most dramatic manifestation of the hollowing out of the state, central governments on the right of the political spectrum continue as a matter of policy to hive off many of their services in the financial and welfare sectors to private sector or third sector agencies.

The decline in the power of central government claimed by some enthusiasts for governance theory has been translated into a view that liberal democratic societies subject to New Right values that have hollowed out the state create a wider circle of organisations influencing the public policy process. Most commentators on governance are careful not to suggest that governance is a step towards a democratisation of society rather than widening of the circles of those with some influence within the public policy process. Typically Moran, Rein and Goodin (2006: 12) observe that:

The argument that, increasingly, government is giving way to 'governance' suggests something more interesting and something peculiarly relevant to our 'persuasive' conception of policy studies: that governing is less and less a matter of ruling through hierarchical authority structures and more and more a matter of negotiating through a decentralized series of floating alliances. The dominant image is that of 'networked governance' (Heclo 1978; Rhodes 1997; Castells 2000). Some actors are more central, others more peripheral, in those networks. But even those actors at the central nodes of networks are not in a position to dictate to the others. Broad cooperation from a great many effectively independent actors is required in order for any of them to accomplish their goals.

The Advocacy Coalitions Framework

Paralleling network theory a model devised by Paul Sabatier and Hank Jenkins-Smith, which they term the Advocacy Coalitions Framework (ACF), has overcome some of the criticisms levelled network theory's rather static, non-evolutionary stance. Initially the aim of Sabatier and Jenkins-Smith was to rescue policy studies from debating the topic through the chronological identification of policy stages, and bottom-up or top-down approaches to policy implementation by concentrating on the role of scientific and technical information in understanding the policy process. However, their approach still retains a rather positivist categorisation of pressures that combine to create policy outcomes. Jenkins-Smith and Sabatier (1994: 180) maintain that:

> The ACF assumed that actors can be aggregated into a number of advocacy coalitions composed of people from various governmental and private organizations who share a set of normative and causal beliefs and who often act in concert. In the United States automotive air pollution control, for example, one can distinguish an environmental coalition (composed of environmental and public health groups, most officials in federal and state air pollution agencies, some legislators at all level of government, and specific researchers and journalists), as distinct from an economic efficiency coalition composed of most automobile manufacturers and petroleum companies and their allies in legislatures, research enterprises and the mass media.

Sabatier and his collaborators develop this approach by placing at the forefront of their theory the impact of ideas as the glue that brings together coalitions of interest that can use their resources of power to push for policy change or on occasion oppose new policies. Ideas can be classified as deep core beliefs of actors that are rarely subject to change and may be seen as equivalent to the moral and ideological beliefs as laid out in the earlier chapters of this book. Distinct from these deep core beliefs are core policy beliefs such as the extent to which government may be engaged within the economic framework of the state (Cairney 2012: 205; Sabatier 1993: 31; 1998: 110) and thirdly there are what are seen as the more minor secondary operational issues such as the means of funding a policy initiative. Common shared attitudes towards these core beliefs create the glue that establishes a common bond between a wide range of groups, and thus an advocacy coalition that can drive forward new policy or ensure the continuation of established ideas. The actors within the advocacy coalition are argued to be wider than simply a group of governmental actors and external professionals but may include elements within the media and business and commerce. Their chances of success are largely built on the extent to which they can coordinate their various sources of power to create the necessary following within government to secure the desired policy outcome. Predominantly the essential power is the ability of a successful coalition to present evidence and theory that will convince influential sections of the public and participants in government. Many demands for policy change by an advocacy coalition will meet resistance from those opposed to the ideas forwarded by a coalition and governments may be not simply one element of an advocacy coalition but also serve as brokers between contending interests, given that a government will often regard stability of the policy system as a crucial goal that requires their intervention between contending parties. Thus the governmental system is often involved in creating and nurturing compromises between policy coalitions to retain an ordered evolution of the social system.

One value of the theory of advocacy coalitions is that its protagonists can place the policy making system in a framework of change. Policy may take many years to mature and during this time an advocacy coalition will itself evolve. Change may be through what theory describes as exogenous shocks to the coalition's sub-system, such as the election of a new government with fundamentally different core or system beliefs than its predecessor or some unexpected change in the physical or social environment of society. Coalitions will also change gradually from their experiences in seeking to forward or develop policies as they learn how to evolve new insights into the issues under discussion and through research learn how other countries resolve a problem. Sabatier and his colleagues illustrate this model by extending the parameters within the Easton systems framework of external support and pressures on the 'black box' of internal political interaction within government. Coalitions within the system of governance therefore compete to gain their policy objectives, with a central government on occasion acting as arbiter between conflicting issues. The pressures and support external to the policy sub-system that influence advocacy coalitions are characterised by stable patterns of social relationships and circumstances that promote change and adjustment to new conditions. The relationship between these variables and capacities is simplified in Figure 10.1 using terminology that more closely fits with the terminology used in this book.

What is left for democracy?

The advocacy coalition theories, like network and governance theories, do not suggest that even in liberal democracies policy making is a democratic process. As Weible et al. (2011: 17) observe:

> There are no guarantees for influencing the policy process. The best individuals can do is to place themselves in a position to have a chance to make a difference, which includes developing the following strategies: (1) developing deep knowledge, (2) investing in networks and (3) participating for long periods of time.

Although Weible et al. (2009: 123) suggest that more needs to be done to clarify the relationship between what they label as the policy sub-system, that is those groups that are central to the policy process, and the external world, the framework in no way can suggest that policy making is a substantively democratic process but rather is one in which specialist and longstanding professional groups hold sway.

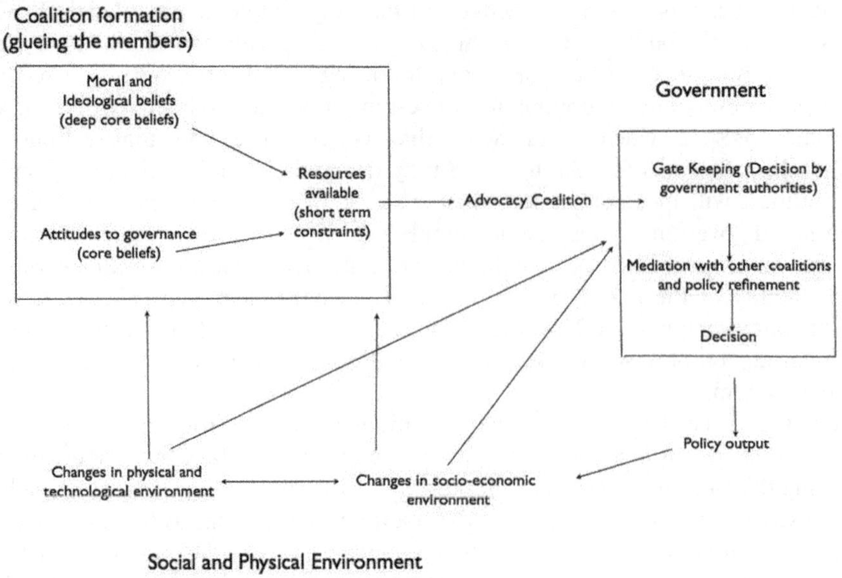

Coalition formation
(glueing the members)

Figure 10.1 AFC restructured
(Simplified and adapted from Jenkins-Smith, Weible and Sabatier, 2014.)

The limitations of network and policy advocacy approaches

Network theory, the advocacy coalitions framework and governance theory all contribute to a now established view that in liberal democracies, central governments are not the only or even the major policy determinants in town. It is, however, questioned by Michael Moran (2010: 32) whether these theories in practice say much that was not known to earlier writers such as Easton, let alone Pressman and Wildavsky.

In the nineteenth century, both in Britain and the United States, many policy issues gained national prominence with a mass following that integrated into their cause politicians and other sympathetic policy interests favouring their ideas. Central conflicts that attracted substantive coalitions of interest either for or against an issue are, in both the United States and Britain, the issue of the abolition of slavery or, in Britain, the Chartist demands for democracy and the Anti-Corn Law League that battled for free trade.

Whether or not the recent literature on networks, governance or the ACF is discussing a recent phenomenon in a wholly novel way, there are a number of issues on which questions can be raised concerning the central themes of these models. These arise from the institutional restructuring of government in relation to society inferred within these theories. How far is the power of central governments being hollowed out and more crucially how far does this trend, such as it exists, suggest that in liberal democracies the policy process is further democratised? Within this framework network and ACF theories appear to be contrary to the ideas of critical realist thought on the motives of policy entrepreneurs and hence the content of policy aims. The contention within ACF that ideology is the glue that keeps the contending networks together, never ventures into the arena of personal self-interest that may often be a further and at times contrary force to ideological and ethical interests that can both join individuals and groups into coalitions and also determine their fragmentation. A coalition may be held together by consensus among its members over ideological beliefs but it also may have within it many adherents who are largely seeking their own self-interest and will destabilise the coalition when circumstances suggest that they personally have little to gain by pursuing further a particular goal.

The refusal of many Labour Party MPs, and the former leader Tony Blair, to endorse Jeremy Corbyn as the left wing candidate for leader of the Party on the grounds that his ideological values are, they believe, unlikely to ensure that Labour may win future elections, suggests that winning power seems much more important than achieving the goals of a more equitable society, which appears from the grass roots support for Corbyn from Party members to be the wish of the majority of its members.

Historically, Benjamin Disraeli, the Prime Minister who was a major influence in transforming the Tory Party into the Conservative Party, came to prominence by campaigning against the repeal of the Corn Laws that protected smaller and predominantly Tory-voting farmers from competition from imported wheat from the United States and Europe. However, when it was clear this issue was not widely supported throughout the country he reversed his position and began to rally around the cause of free trade and, in consequence, helped to undermine and destroy the old Tory Party (Blake 1970).

The glue, such as it exists, that forms coalition must be regarded as a highly fragile force. For some, membership of a coalition may be simply a means to gain favour among those of influence in order to ascend the greasy pole of the political system for their self-esteem and financial rewards. In contrast, some individuals may cling on to ideological beliefs long after they have been seriously undermined, out of loyalty or fear that by changing their position they may weaken their capacity to control others, as was perhaps the case with Margaret Thatcher and the poll tax.

Both network theory and the ACF assume that policy in liberal democracies is largely initiated within civil society and thus, is the expression of opinions expressed outside the Easton 'black box' of policy resolution rather than within the core executives of the state. However, in many liberal democracies policy may be pushed forward by the belligerence and resources of power held by key gate-keepers and policy advocates such as a prime minister, president or entrenched member of their executive. Policies can emerge on a political agenda as a consequence of the thoughts, and for some, the whims, of specific policy actors rather than through concerted pressure from specific interacting groups. Powerful politicians can foster widespread concern that one specific issue is a problem or an opportunity, whilst other, possibly more pressing, issues are ignored. Frequently the politicians, along with their close advisors, are the advocates of the solution to the proposed problem and they are in a position to create the circumstances in which their views have a window of opportunity to emerge from policy idea to agreed policy decisions. The capacity of a single powerful politician to push forward policies that have never been seriously entertained by professional policy advocates is illustrated by Mrs Thatcher's support for the poll tax.

What was popularly known as the poll tax was a flat rate tax for local authority services that replaced the rates, a property tax that ensured families living in the most expensive properties paid the most tax. As a flat rate tax the new provision, with a few exceptions, was levied uniformly on each adult member of every household in Britain. The issue of property rates was a problem looking for a solution. There were long-running debates on local authority taxation that included a major government commissioned enquiry published as the Layfield Report, in which the idea of a non-progressive tax that ensured that a millionaire would pay as much tax for local services as a person reliant on state benefits, had never seriously been entertained. Few of Mrs Thatcher's advisors supported the idea but her standing in the Party following her third election victory in 1987 gave her the capacity to brook no dissent from her cabinet. She plunged into pushing through a policy that led to some of the most serious riots in central London during the twentieth century and widespread civil disobedience as many poll tax payers refused to pay the tax (Butler, Adonis and Travers 1994).

Major policy changes can not only be vetoed by policy gate-keepers but may be pushed through on the whims of an individual minister, not through any meeting of ideological values between political activists or as a result of strong interest group pressures outside the core executive of the state, but as a result of some unholy alliance of senior politicians seeking power with differing agendas and motives. The following example illustrates a situation where an individual Minister, Richard Crossman then Secretary of State for Housing and Local Government, created a chain of events that led to a significant sea change in the institutional organisation of the state, largely on his own initiative. The success of his ideas was greatly aided by the support of Prime Minister Harold Wilson, who, though uninterested in the actual issue, saw within it the means to favour the electoral position of his party and his own interest to remain in power.

'The day of my speech to the A.M.C. (Association of Municipal Councils) annual conference at Torquay ... I had previously agreed with the Department (Ministry of Housing and Local Government) that I would speak on two topics; local government press relations; and the ethics of the councillor. However, yesterday I suddenly decided that I would add a third topic, the reform of local government; and that I would announce that the situation was getting unworkable and I was thinking of winding up the Local Government Boundary Commission. ... I called in J.D. Jones (Deputy permanent secretary in the Ministry), who was very good indeed, and with his advice I came to the conclusion that I should propose a committee of enquiry with very great authority and with terms of reference that instructed it to lay down the principles of local government reform ... I rang up Harold Wilson (the Prime Minister) to tip him off that I was going to do this and he liked the idea.'

(Crossman 1975: 331)

Richard Crossman's speech initiated a process that led to the Redcliffe-Maud Royal Commission on local government that obliged both the Labour Government and after 1970 the incoming Conservative Governments led by Edward Heath to embark on a wholesale reconstruction of the local government system in Britain. Although, for some years prior to Crossman's intervention, there had been concerns about the structure of local government in Britain, politicians thought a major restructuring of the system might be a contested and lengthy operation that would please few voters. The issue was not part of the Labour Party manifesto or the Parliamentary agenda under Harold

Wilson's leadership until Crossman's sudden mid-term conversion to the cause. The central factor that enthused Wilson and several other cabinet ministers to support Crossman's initiative was not any pressure to reform local government structure but to delay a restructuring of Parliamentary constituency boundaries that would have lost the Labour Party seats at the next general election. As constituency boundaries had to fit the boundaries of local authorities an enquiry into their structure would delay the implementation of the proposed constituency boundaries at least until after the next election (Crossman 1975: 339–41; Chandler 1988: 146–148).

Not all policy coalitions are effectively the result of a number of forces coming together but, in autocracies and some liberal democracies those in elite, gate-keeping positions within the policy hierarchy may be able to initiate and carry to fruition policies that they have thought up on their own and, on occasion, for purposes that are not made known to the general public or even to their would-be fellow travelling colleagues. Such examples illustrate the capacity of members of a core executive to forward policy without reference either to the policy entrepreneurs or to the support of public opinion. In the Crossman example it may be argued there was a clear opportunity to force through an enquiry into local government restructuring because he realised, unlike some of his advisors, that the public was generally indifferent to such a change and that there were no stalwart supporters of the local government system in the cabinet.

Harold Wilson whilst agreeing to a Commission to restructure local government observed to him 'You have got nobody like Herbert Morrison, Chuter Ede or Nye Bevan ... who really is an authority on local government. In this Cabinet there isn't a single person of that quality and that's why you have been getting away with murder' (Crossman 1975: 440).

The extent to which policy can be generated within the closed confines of cabinet governments, the leading inner core of a political party or, in civil society, the board-room of a multi-national company, is in part a function of how much a policy is seen as a salient issue within the organisation's core executive and as such may, as in the Crossman case, be a matter of luck that within a relatively small group of Ministers no one was particularly concerned to challenge his ideas.

The capacities of policy gate-keepers also to be highly successful policy entrepreneurs should they wish needs to be emphasised. The extent to which policies can be pushed through by a determined and single-minded individual must also be analysed in the context of the reaction of individuals within civil society to the policy. In a pluralist society while any member of a core executive may ride roughshod over extensive opposition based in public opinion, this can in the longer term frequently end in failure, as was the case with Mrs Thatcher who did not survive in office for long after serious riots against the poll tax.

Democracy and hegemony

A central criticism that is levelled against network and governance theories is the tendency of the studies to suggest that 'hollowing out the state' by transferring public services to the private sector through privatisation or partnership arrangements will, necessarily, facilitate more extensive citizens' control within the policy making process. Jonathan Davies (2011) argues on the basis of Gramscian and Bourdieu's thought that the idea of governability that is currently strongly embedded in Anglo-American positivist literature on liberal democracies is seriously limited. The idea that policy in liberal democracies emanates from the bargaining between numerous networks of interests does not effectively model the realities of the distribution of power. Whilst there can be, as Foucault suggests, many networks of power and corresponding conflicts, the networks that matter occupy, to use Bourdieu's term, the same habitus. These act, as Habermas suggests, as agencies greatly removed from the 'life world' of the majority of citizens but nevertheless can through the commodification of relationships and culture colonise the life world. Thus, the dominant networks create a hegemonic control over civil society which broadly is discerned as the values of the liberal democratic state imbued increasingly with the values of New Right economics and ethics.

Habermas' view of the 'life world' of most citizens or Bourdieu's concept of habitus do not suggest that debates between organisations with the resources to influence policy decisions frequently lead to substantial democratisation of decision making. Partnerships, even at the local level that supposedly involve the general public, are effectively controlled by the technocratic elites who can understand the language of science or sociology and as a consequence can dominate debate within a partnership and convey their views to its governing mentors.

> The 'New Labour' governments of Blair and Brown sought to revive areas of social deprivation through establishing local area partnerships involving substantial funding to these areas managed by professional bureaucrats who were, in theory, responsible to boards of local political activists. In reality most commentators on the programme suggest that the senior managers dominated the partnerships and delivered policies as required by central government. John Diamond (2001: 282) quotes one manager as saying 'I need to make sure my staff work effectively and implement what has been decided. We don't have the space or to be honest, the motivation just now. I am more concerned with making sure we deliver what we are signed up to – or otherwise I will have the Government Office on me and then I will have failed.'

Davies argues that the development of governance is a trend for capital to ensure hegemony over policy within the liberal democratic state. Rather than distributing power throughout the political system, influential networks bring together the interests of the dominant groups in society and also exclude involvement of organisations that do not ascribe to the ideological values and habitus of elites. These are, as Habermas reminds us, increasingly global rather than national networks. There are a number of mechanisms that develop widespread consensus within civic culture that favours the dominant liberal democratic model but the main component of dominance is in the capacity of the ruling elite to create, through the system of state and private education and control by the dominant capitalist elite over the media, public consent towards the political and socio-economic system that determines public policy. Following the arguments of Bachrach and Baratz and Steven Lukes in Chapter 7 it must be kept in mind that many citizens never become seriously involved in the public policy process, partly because of the costs in doing so, the impossibility to master the many technical languages and intellectual demands that place barriers against informed intervention except by professionals and especially in the more autocratic regimes, fear of coercion and violence. In totalitarian regimes state controlled systems of education can from early childhood be brought to bear on the political values of citizens who will receive clear instruction on the need to dutifully obey and acknowledge the authority of the leaders of the state and their agents. If the regime has the capacity to isolate the public from communication from dissident groups it is small wonder that citizens will tend to be passive recipients of elite values. However, it must be questioned whether in liberal democracies, despite an appearance of more open government, a small elite can have a hegemonic influence over all elements in society and ensure that policy demands are predominantly initiated and pushed forward to their implementation by a small political class.

Many of those citizens who manage despite the costs to involve themselves to some degree in the process of policy formation are then subject to attaining their understanding of a social issue through the filter of their educational experience and the media. The education systems in liberal democracies can take a rather varied range of approaches to shaping the ideological and policy values of their citizens. In some pluralist nations such as the United States there is a substantive and rather conservative, if not even totalitarian, tendency to inculcate deference and obedience to the state through ceremonies like saluting the flag and singing the national anthem. In other regimes such as the United Kingdom little attempt is made in state schools to inculcate in any formal way an interest in civic education, politics or sociology.

A curriculum for civic education in Britain was introduced in 2002 but was hedged with concerns not to be prescriptive on ideological lines. This initiative has been given little support by Conservative-led governments since 2010 leaving the political values of children, in their earlier years, to be influenced by their family and by their peer groups and also the political media.

How far the media, especially the press and radio and television, influence citizens' attitudes is open to question (Wilks-Heeg, Blick and Crone 2016). It can be argued that newspapers have a relatively small influence on people's individual beliefs, as most citizens connect to the channels of communication that best frame their views. Readers of the press tend to seek confirmation of their ideas through the media, rather than to further develop their basic values. It is also accepted that most people are not so enthralled by political discussion as opposed to issues such as gossip about celebrities, sport or entertainment, and choose newspapers that relate to their lifestyle interests or continue with the familiar style they inherit from their parents. As a consequence, many voters with little interest or understanding of public policy issues will, if they are obliged to make a decision in an election or referendum, make their choice with reference to the media they have chosen largely for entertainment value rather than its political content. Thus, the political values of news media may become subconsciously a significant factor shaping their attitudes to public policy. Moreover as Amber Boydstun (2013: 6) argues:

> Political agendas, including the media agenda are disproportionate information-processing systems meaning that agendas do not process real-world events in real time or in proportion to the 'size' of those events, instead agendas lurch from one

hot event (and its related policy issue) to the next at the exclusion of many other important issues.

What is much more certain is that in most pluralist states the trend is always for the majority of media outlets in terms of the printed and commercial televisual and radio media, to defend values that tend to promote inequality and 'free' market values. This may be explained by the need for newspapers and commercial television to generate profit by advertising and, because ownership of a newspaper requires access to capital, the majority of those who control the press are beneficiaries of, and thus likely to be strong supporters of, inegalitarian society and Conservative or New Right values (Kingdom 2014: 240–4).

It can therefore be argued that political opinions, and of course the lack of them for many citizens, are generated, as are their voting choices, by reference in their early adult years, to their parents and peer group influence and through the broad tenor of the dominant social mores that are necessary to survive within the market economy. Hence, as Ulrich Beck (1992: 100–101) maintains, in an individualised society citizens are increasingly disinclined to place themselves in any class group and establish their ideological and moral views on a utilitarian basis on policies on which they have a strong opinion without establishing any consistency between their values.

It is impossible to dogmatically answer the question of whether large sections of civil society are manipulated by a power elite who establish a hegemonic control of the culture of a society, or whether a pluralist society is based on many conflicting values which are formed and cherished independently of the systems of socialisation controlled by the state. On certain issues there can be near but very rarely complete unanimity that a particular policy would be morally wrong, ideologically unsound and opposed to the self-interest of a majority. The poll tax perhaps was moving to the further reaches of achieving such a status. On the other hand there are issues which are highly technical and not widely understood in society that allow power elites not so much to dominate public opinion on the issue but, for example, on issues such as quantitative easing, bore it to death to the extent that many are not aware or really concerned about the issue and its consequences. The core executive may also succeed in suggesting that policies in the interest of an elite are in fact in the interest of all.

Conclusion

Network and governance theories and more especially the ACF framework have much to recommend them and there can be little dispute that in pluralist societies many public policies are advanced or blocked as a consequence of pressure from coalitions of ideologically similar individuals. However, these theories have serious shortcomings in that they over-emphasise how much policy is a consequence of coalitions of interest joined around fundamental agreements, when in many cases coalitions are at one level much more shaky constructions often based on wholly differing appreciation of what a policy is intended to achieve and often they contain very differing motives as to what it will achieve for each participant. It is therefore rather too high minded as to the motivations of many policy makers who are playing a much more self-interested game rather than an altruistic assessment of policy consequences.

However at a more over-arching level liberal democracies are basically unequal societies and given that those with most resources in terms of material capital and intellectual capital have a much greater capacity to dominate within their society, the motive of self-interest even when directed to the long-term stability of a society will nevertheless ensure there is little semblance of equality in that society. As such it may flourish and be better suited to the majority of citizens than an autocratic or totalitarian society. Liberal democracy at least provides a much greater degree of personal freedom and security to the community than the mirage of a more equitable society suggested by many seemingly far left autocrats that over time dissolves through their self-interested motives to retain wealth and status for themselves. It is, however, far from democratic in relation to the ideas of the participative Rousseau and exponents of strong democracy.

11 Getting policy on the agenda

Chapters 11 to 15 discuss in more detail and in the context of the chapters on subjective values and the distribution of power in society, the stages in the process of policy development. In the formative years of writing on the policy process a starting point was to identify a number of interlinking stages that were involved in determining the policy development, as critically outlined in Chapter 2. It can be conceded that for the sake of clarity policy activists must be involved in ensuring a number of functions. These include in this chapter how policy problems may arise, and how they become part of a government's agenda. Chapter 12 considers how these policy issues are evaluated and then subject to validation, that is, as opposed to objective rationalisation of policy in as much as this is possible, subjected to arguments for or against policy proposals that suit the government's interest. Chapter 13 considers how policy taken up by governments is refined and legitimated, whilst Chapter 14 analyses implementation and the following chapter how that policy may evolve.

The source of policy ideas

Society is awash with policy ideas. Within a pluralist society where citizens have little fear of expressing their opinions, there are numerous individuals who are willing to declaim their views as to how governments and public, voluntary or private agencies should arrange their ideas in relation to specific issues. Freedom of association facilitates the creation of interest groups and, as indicated in the preceding chapters, there are a huge number of such organisations dedicated to the promotion of a particular cause or concern. However, most policy ideas, such as perhaps the ideas you expressed in your usual watering hole about funding for students, are declaimed with no serious hope that they will be entertained by governments, political parties or interest groups. A question to be unravelled is not so much how policies emerge, given the tendency for many people to have views on what they feel would be a sound policy solution to many specific social problems, but how, from the many interests expressed by individuals and organisations, some have importance and receive serious consideration by policy gatekeepers and may actually develop into policies that can be imposed on society. The translation of demands for new policies from widespread and unfocused debate within civil society to an issue that is seriously being considered by a government is often termed as the process of setting the policy agenda.

As a shorthand term to differentiate the boundary between privately articulated policy and the discussion of authoritative action by governments, the agenda metaphor makes some sense, but it is also a rather simplistic view if it is taken to mean there is some clearly definable point when policy emerges onto a public agenda. A policy initiative cannot be said to be on a government's agenda only when it has formally been announced as a forthcoming matter for legislation or an official enquiry. Months or often years of internal evaluation and wrangling occur in government circles and between a government and interest groups before policy proposals can be formally placed on the Parliamentary table. Some important policy decisions such as changes in a country's attitude to other states may not require legislation and may not even be openly acknowledged concerns let alone widely debated issues.

> In the United States many changes in attitudes to foreign policy events such as their shifting responses to the civil war in Syria and their changes in attitude following the use of chemical weapons were never the subject of legislation but developed by discussions between the President, the Secretary of State and their senior foreign policy advisors.

Policy can similarly not be said to have originated within the manifestos of political parties. Parties may announce a proposed agenda usually before forthcoming elections, but they do not necessarily follow these proposals to the letter even if they are able to govern with an overall majority in their legislature. Many a party harbours policy aims in the minds of its leaders that it has no wish to announce to the public.

> The Conservative Party led by David Cameron announced in its Manifesto for the 2010 election that it will overhaul the structure of the National Health Services to ensure greater efficiency and effectiveness of the Service. However, some commentators argue that within this policy is embedded a desire to privatise many aspects of health care, a policy that was not favoured by the majority of voters (Jones 2014: 197–8).

In order to secure election within a pluralist society political parties undertake considerable research and deliberation among their leaders before they announce formally any of their policy ideas. They must take the temperature of the electorate's views and values and compromise their thoughts with the demands of interest groups that support and finance the party and also take heed, as was emphasised in the chapters on democracy and networks, of certain political groups that are more influential than others on particular questions.

Whose problem?

Many studies of political policy discuss the accretion of policy ideas into concrete proposals as responses to policy problems (see Hogwood and Gunn 1984: 7 or Kingdon 2006: 197–8). Issues that are widely agreed to be problems that need to be resolved through public policy are not infrequent.

> The tsunami that devastated much of the Indonesian archipelago in December 2004 clearly created obvious policy problems of rehousing the living, burying the dead and in the longer term establishing systems that can give better warning of such a disaster.

However, the use of the term 'problem' can, as stated earlier, be rather misleading. For many policy advocates a policy suggestion may not be aimed at solving some serious difficulty but to grasp an opportunity by forwarding a novel idea to increase social and economic well-being.

> The rapid development of information technology since the 1960s to ensure that extensive data on the background and habits of individuals can be collected by electronic readers and stored so that they can be accessed by private or public sector agencies has created many opportunities for both private and public sector interests to be able to identify individuals with particular tendencies to favour certain forms of consumption and hence be targeted by advertisers. In the public sector new technologies have enabled states to undertake surveillance of individuals who those in government believe may create threats to citizens in general or to themselves in particular.

However, for most policy opportunities there are corresponding problems that will emerge, as the example inset below demonstrates. It is perhaps not particularly useful to see the majority of policies as being responses to either problems or opportunities for society in general. A problem or opportunity for some people may very often be a non-issue for others, and, what is from some points of view an opportunistic policy, may for others create a serious policy problem. Whether a problem exists in society is a subjective rather than concrete issue and is often a statement of the concerns of often specific interest groups in a political system rather than a majority of citizens. In some cases opportunities in the opinion of certain individuals and groups in society may in themselves be seen as a serious problems for others.

> For socialists inequality is a moral problem but for the New Right it is an inevitable and acceptable element of a prosperous society. Thus, policies in the United States under Republican governance or Britain by Conservative Governments have, following New Right ideology, cut back the role of the state and decreased taxation for the rich on the grounds that the inequality this may create is of little concern given their belief such action will raise living standards for every income group within their societies.

It is pointed out by Michael Cohen, James March and Johan Olsen (1972) that rather than problems preceding solutions, in many political systems solutions exist awaiting problems to which they may be attached. They argue that most institutions are not based around a defined set of values and practices but 'can be described better as a loose collection of ideas than as a coherent structure' (Cohen, March and Olsen 1972: 1). They cite as their exemplar for such a fuzzy organisation a university where many of the professors and managers have differing roles and interests and will have formed divergent attitudes on how they would safeguard or improve their interests and the values they cherish within the organisation. Collectively no one set of actors has a clear oversight of the whole of the organisation. Vice-chancellors or prime ministers may have a powerful coordinating role but do not have a view of the organisation that is held by subordinate actors. In such organisations there are many policy advocates with very differing views on what they feel are the problems and opportunities that they face. Core executives of complex institutions will also have little knowledge of the concerns of specific specialists in their multitudinous departments. Having a solution to their problems the many policy entrepreneurs at each level and department of the organisation need to search for the means to get them enacted. Potential solutions to fulfilling the interests of actors within the organisation are dumped in what Cohen et al., rather confusingly, refer to as garbage cans from which they may be fished out as the answer to a problem or opportunity that must be considered by the organisation or eventually be carried away to the rubbish dump of unfulfilled hopes and dreams. Solutions may in this sense, therefore, exist prior to a wider society recognising whether a problem exists.

From the author's point of view as subject leader for the study of public administration within the Business School of my university, I had strong ideas and policy designs on developing this subject area but within a Faculty dominated by the private sector interests of most business studies academics who had their own interests to defend, there was little chance of gaining an opportunity to ensure my ideas became Faculty policy, for a subject recruiting relatively low numbers of students and often harbouring different ethical and political values than is current in the private business sector. Not only are there often very sharp differences in what may be perceived as a problem or opportunity between members of any society, but these differences may be based on differing forms of perception and motivation concerning the structuring of that society.

What may be for some individuals a common sense scientific approach to, for example, avoiding unwanted pregnancies through using contraception, may be, as in Ireland, for others an immoral offence against the will of God that should be prevented by law.

In other cases, especially within the darker reaches of politics, a policy may be advanced by a powerful politician, not primarily to resolve some problem that concerns his or her moral or ideological sensibilities, but simply to address a problem of advancing their career, wealth or personal esteem. As Philippe Zittoun (2014: 41) observes:

> Analysing the definitional process that actors use to critique society by making the reality unacceptable and the action of the State necessary therefore makes it possible to grasp this agenda setting process. It gives account of how the actors politicise a problem by making it the symbol of a society in disorder.

Social problems and opportunities are in other words made by those with power to determine what is a problem or an opportunity.

From ideas in civil society to a government's agenda

The classical stages approaches to policy development usually begins with a consideration of how policy ideas emerge from interests articulated with sufficient clarity and concern in civil society to then present themselves as a policy problem from the core executive of a government. This is, for several reasons, a misleading depiction of how policy initiatives evolve into a matter that requires further governmental attention. Many policy developments never actually leave the attention of the political establishment but are issues that may be constantly subject to review to ascertain whether they require further attention to deal with changes in the economic or social tenor of their society.

> Policy change in the economic sphere, for example on the setting of the bank rate at a particular level, can have a very significant effect on a nation's economic development but is a decision that is constantly subject to review in the light of changes to variables such as inflation, balance of payments and economic output.
>
> Similarly, policy on health care or crime is within developed states subject to constant monitoring with a view towards ascertaining whether policy needs to be changed if trends in these areas do not appear to be favourable for a government and its citizens.

Many new entrants onto the policy agenda of governments are in practice demands stemming from a perceived need to change in some way an existing arrangement, as for example the restructuring of health insurance policy by the Obama Administration. Occasionally unforeseen events may arise to require a reappraisal of policies but in most regimes within the governance of the state the permanent bureaucracy has established strategies for dealing with the unexpected but possible emergencies, ranging from issues such as nuclear war, terrorist attacks, to natural disasters such as earthquakes, floods or even meteorite strikes. Where more innovation may be required is the need to place some controls over the consequences of rapid technological change. The development of information technology and especially the World Wide Web has, for example, required many governments to develop policies on the extent to which the opportunities and dangers posed by such technology can be either realised or curbed. However, following from Cohen et al.'s garbage can model of policy solutions awaiting policy problems, it may be suggested that governments are the prime source of developing policy solutions which can be adapted to fit many unexpected occurrences that may affect society. It has also been shown in Chapter 9 that in many cases policy ideas are not forced onto the government's agenda because of strong external pressures but as the consequence of the interests and whims of powerful individuals within the core executive of government. The reform of local government structure in Britain has been given as an example.

Policy transfers and diffusion

Many policy initiatives are plagiarised from the decisions implemented in other states. These are based on ideas that have been around within the chattering classes of the world for some time and many are ideas whose exact origins are obscured by time. Few policy ideas are wholly original but are, it could be said, plagiarised or copied, from other organisations. Most policies advocated by governments can now variously be said to be the result of policy transfers and diffusion of policy (Kingdon 2006: 197–8). In earlier writing, policy transfers may have been signalled through terms such as 'issue search' as a stage in the policy process (Hogwood and Gunn 1984: 7). This process was developed through the term 'lesson drawing' by Richard Rose (1993). The now more widely used concept of policy transfer has been defined as 'a process by which knowledge of policies, administrative arrangements, institutions and ideas in one political

system (past or present) is used in the development of similar features in another'
(Dolowitz 2000: 3). This has become the term now most widely applied to the phenomenon of the spread of policy adoptions on a globalised scale (Benson and Jordan
2011: 366–378) as the following examples illustrate.

'The (Labour) Party is also likely to support a US-style requirement on foreign banks to
inform UK tax authorities of its UK account holders. The move is based on the US
Foreign Accounts Tax Compliance Act which aims to crack down on tax avoidance by
requiring foreign banks to report US account holders to the Inland Revenue Service'
(*The Guardian*, 2 April 2013: 6).
   The widespread adoption of privatisation of state assets which in Europe was largely seen as a policy of the British Governments under Thatcher is an example of
policy transfer. The idea was arguably always practised in the United States where the
Federal and state governments were generally ideologically averse to public ownership
and was also fortified by the return to popularity of New Right economists such as
Hayek and Friedman who had for many decades been advocating such a
development.

Although policy transfer is often the consequence of voluntary adoption of policies
advocated by others, there is a growing tendency for governments and public agencies
to directly or indirectly be coerced to accept policies demanded by external forces
(Dolowitz and Marsh 1996: 347–9). The global development of transnational agencies such as the International Monetary Fund and regional cooperation as in the case
of the European Union not only ensures policy advocates and entrepreneurs may be
more familiar with policy making in other states but obliges them to follow their
proposals if they wish to be beneficiaries of these agencies.

The financial crisis faced after 2008 by the European Union over the capacity of
Greece, Spain and Italy to continue to service their debts has forced on such countries
demands that they must radically change many of their economic policies concerning
pension rights or job security in the public sector if they are to receive long-term loans
from the European Bank that may stabilise their capacity to pay their short-term debts.

At the sub-national level many units of governance are, similarly, required to accept
policies formulated by the national, or in federal systems, state governments. In Britain
a highly centralised system of local governance has increasingly given very limited discretion to local authorities on expenditure or the type and standard of services they can
provide (Chandler 2009).
   It is of course almost impossible to draw a clear line between the borders of coercion
and voluntary acceptance of new policies. Most sovereign states may, as sovereignty
implies, be free to choose their policies but in practice those requiring support from
international agencies or other states can often be left with no choice but to accept aid
with attached demands from donor countries, which may undermine their preferred
policies for social welfare or economic growth. The extent to which any country will
slavishly copy policies adopted by other regimes must also be limited by the need to
take account of differing systems of governance and political culture. Ideological and

ethical differences may for some regimes be a formidable barrier to copying widely practised policies in other regimes.

> Saudi Arabian attitudes to the role of women in society have so far made it difficult to sanction what is standard policy in most nations to countenance the right of women to vote or even to hold a driver's licence.

Rarely can a policy practised in one regime be simply dropped into another political system without a measure of adaptation to suit differing political conditions.

> Within the European Union implementation of policies developed by the Commission is left to the member states that, within limits of European Law, adapt the policy to suit local circumstances. Thus, England, which until the Blair administrations had not established regional governments, was allowed to group together local authorities in *ad hoc* consortia to bid for regional development grants (Chandler 2009: 27).

Many policy transfers are not the result of a conscious and deliberate copying of policy but a result of diffusion of ideas as governments start adopting successful policy initiatives by other political regimes in order to keep up with the development of globalised attitudes towards governance (Graham, Shipan and Volden 2012). Acceptance in civil society of established practices in other countries can create strong pressures for reformist governments to adopt new political and policy strategies.

> Internal pressures within Middle Eastern nations led to governments coming to power, at least temporarily, adopting democratic structures in what has been popularly termed 'the Arab Spring'. A major driver of these policy revolutions was the result of policy diffusion as many members of these societies realised that continued autocratic government may not lead to personal freedom or long-term economic success.

Pressure for change in respect to more specific activities of government may similarly emerge from a popular realisation that policy adopted in other countries or organisations, such as privatisation, appears to show greater success in terms of either ethical or more material welfare. Such pressure may come from a number of sources. Graham, Shipan and Volden (2012) suggest that these may be from members of a government, pressure from external non-governmental interests or from organisations, such as the European Union or the IMF that try to bridge conflicting interests among member states. Whilst wholly original ideas are rare, there are developments in any socioeconomic environment such as the creation of new technologies that are important factors in determining innovation as policy entrepreneurs realise the opportunities that emerge from new ideas.

> The emergence of a globalising world based on internet technology creates new opportunities for governments to communicate with society, to cut costs for certain services and to build more readily accessible data bases about each and every one of us. New technologies also create problems. The relatively recent invention of the

petrol and diesel engine created the need for policy to regulate mass transportation by ensuring that road travel does not descend into chaos.

On occasion policy makers can also make breakthroughs in the social sciences. The economic theories of John Maynard Keynes for example radically revised the fiscal policies of nations and these were further modified with the advent of the counter theories of monetarism.

Although technological and social innovation may create the need for new policy, these developments usually emerge from earlier incremental change. As Isaac Newton observed, 'If I have seen further it is by standing on the shoulders of giants'.

The development of policies on motor transport is in part based on extending rules and regulations for handling horse drawn transportation to the new faster mode of travel.

The development of Keynesian economic policies was not a complete break from the past but had to be established through institutions, such as the Bank of England or the United States Federal Reserve that regulated the pre-Keynesian economic practice.

The view that governments make policy by a rational process of learning from practice used in other countries or private and third sector organisations is, however, a too simplistic rationalisation of the policy process. It suggests that most organisations are so integrated they can have a clear aim and a coherent method of resolving problems or grasping opportunities. However, as each organisation is in some way unique, a policy effective in one institution needs some adaptation to fit the properties and environment outside the boundaries of the polity, as both Lindblom (1965) and Etzioni (1967) pointed out. More significantly policy transfer or diffusion is limited on many issues to copying practices between nations with similar ethical and ideological cultures or, in autocratic states, the culture of the ruling elite. The characterisation presented by these models is most pertinent to developed liberal democracies rather than non-liberal autocratic regimes.

The policy soup and policy streams

A further modelling of policy formation and diffusion developed by John Kingdon (1995) endorses many of the ideas within the garbage can model of Cohen et al. that suggests that policy solutions await the arrival of problems to which they can be coupled in order to gain a place on a government's agenda. In what Kingdon refers to as the policy streams model, he makes more sense of the multi-layered aspect of both agenda setting and the capacity to attach solutions to opportunities. He observes that policy emerges from what he terms a 'primeval soup' of ideas within society. The soup is composed of the mess of often contradictory attitudes and solutions to policy issues. It is from this maelstrom of ideas that a few proposals gain widespread attention and emerge as possible contenders for new policy initiatives.

The ideas that gain sufficient strength to be taken seriously gain this position through the coming together of different supports for the proposal. He depicts these as the following three streams:

- Demands for policy change to solve problems such as an economic recession or some natural disaster.
- The thoughts and ideas being put forward by those whom Kingdon (1995) refers to as policy entrepreneurs. These may be the professional individuals and groups, campaigning journalists and politicians enthusiastic to take up a particular cause or academics. It is from these sources that solutions to problems are developed and publicised.
- The presence of an appropriate political climate for pursuing particular ideas such as the attitude of the media or whether an election has returned a government with an ideology that might facilitate new paths for policy development.

(Kingdon 1995: 146–162)

Kingdon's model like some earlier theorists uses the language of problem solving as a basis for policy development and the model might have been better expressed without the metaphor of streams, which are in essence normally visualised as composed of similar material that can merge together to create a stronger river of ideas.

Kingdon, nevertheless, usefully illustrates that several differing conditions must be present for policy to emerge and that the process is complex and often unpredictable. There are, Kingdon reminds us, constant pressures on governments for the need to develop or renew and evolve existing policies. Harold Macmillan, British Prime Minister in the late 1950s, is said to have responded to an interviewer seeking to discover what factors blew a government off course with 'Events dear boy, events'. By 'events' Macmillan referred to the unexpected changes in the national and world environment that required an immediate response by government and, even more troubling, those that undermine established policy. These events may be natural disasters, or financial problems such as the collapse of Lehmann Brothers that initiated the 2008–9 banking crisis and the subsequent downturn in world economic growth. Issues may also arise from the data gathering activities of governments, their agencies and certain trusted private sector forecasters. The material they amass, especially on the economy, such as the growth of the trade balances or levels of unemployment constantly require governments to make economic adjustments when the prognostication provides a gloomy outlook. Whilst economic policy is perhaps of greatest concern in more pluralist economies, data on social issues such as rates of crime or of illnesses may similarly create demands for policy change. Finally, there can be the issue of feedback on the effectiveness of established policies. Policy change is also often forced on a government by the unforeseen events or the actions of other countries. Often reaction to one problem, such as a natural disaster, can prompt further difficulties in, for example, foreign relations.

The outbreak of a cattle disease in Britain that was believed to be easily transmitted to humans, BSE, more popularly called 'mad cow disease', created a scare in the 1990s and the consequent ban on the export of British beef by the European Union (EU). Prime Minister John Major observed that 'the reaction across the European Union to our initial announcement on BSE was hysterical ... No EU official believed that British beef was dangerous following the measures already in place. They were responding to fear among their consumers after the hysterical press coverage' (Major 2000: 651). 'I was as infuriated by this outcome as any Euro sceptic. I had played by the club rules and the club had changed them. It persuaded me to take action I disliked, and subsequently regretted ... I decided that Britain would not cooperate with our partners if they would not cooperate with us' (Major 2000: 653).

Governments may frequently be beset by problems but churning in the policy soup is the second stream contributing to policy development, potential solutions. These may be, as Kingdon (1995) points out, solutions to some groups in society, but from a government's perspective unwarranted demands. These ideas may enter the policy stream from interest groups with sufficient resources to require that action is taken to either accept or fight against the organisation. Government must in liberal democracies respond to a strike for better pay or working conditions by trade unions representing workers in an industry such as energy supply that has an immediate impact on the economy. In a pluralist society the role of the media is also crucial in pushing some issues onto a government's agenda. A newspaper may take up the cause for policy change on a specific issue to the extent that the issue is publicly debated in society and, if ignored, could lose popular support for the ruling party. These are solutions which, observes Kingdon, building on the garbage can model, are answers seeking to attach themselves to a problem.

The development of solutions to policy issues, Kingdon points out, requires the presence of policy entrepreneurs. Thus, at a time of fiscal crisis, the ideas of economic experts, be they academics, journalists, civil servants or politicians, will be sought and often widely publicised in the press. These sources can create a climate of informed opinion as to how to deal with a crisis or develop the capacity to take advantage of an opportunity. The policy entrepreneurs will not, however, all be singing the same tune and in most cases, especially when they have substantive ideological or ethical differences, will forward differing solutions to the perceived problems or argue at times that no problem exists.

Within a developed pluralist society it is arguably Kingdon's third political stream that is most crucial in determining the timing of policy developments. The emergence of policy is dependent on which of many policy advocates can secure a window of opportunity to forward their ideas. In this context changes in governments or their key personnel can have an important bearing on whether a window of opportunity opens up to favour a particular policy solution. The support of an authoritative interest group may also be crucial, as will a strong current of support from the media. Kingdon (1995: 5–9, 217–222) illustrated his ideas with a number of case studies such as the failures during the Carter and Clinton Presidencies to develop a more universal national health insurance scheme in the United States.

Problems of inequality in health provision could clearly be identified in the *laissez faire* attitudes of preceding administrations. There were also during both Presidencies many policy entrepreneurs forwarding possible policies to resolve the situation but in the absence of a strong advocacy coalition supporting a resolution to the inequality problem neither the Clinton nor Carter administration could overcome the right wing opposition that any change would increase Federal spending and lead to higher taxation. The window of opportunity never arose that could create sufficient impetus to forward substantive reform in this area. The comparatively more successful attempt to restructure health policy in the United States by Barack Obama is a consequence of a swing of public opinion away from the new-right values of the Presidency of George W. Bush that helped to nurture the conditions that led to the banking crisis of 2008. It could be argued that the earlier creation of the British National Health Service to create a more equitable provision for health care faced the same challenges but, following the country's experiences in the Second World War, a much stronger sense of social support.

Power and hegemony in establishing a policy problem

The emergence of a social issue to the status of a policy problem recognised by government as advanced by Kingdon suggests, like many discussions on the public process, that at least within liberal democracies, policy tends to be made in the interests of the majority. However, reference to the preceding discussion on the distribution of power and also to the discussion in Chapter 7 on the critique of subjectivist theorists such as Foucault, Habermas or Miller and Fox (2007) and on how problems are defined by capital, must suggest that some caution is advised on the extent to which policy problems emerge from the democratic will of individual citizens.

Whilst stable liberal democracies based on a strong civic culture can allow numerous ideas to circulate within the polity, models concerning the setting of the authoritative government agenda, such as Cohen et al.'s garbage cans and Kingdon's policy streams, tend like network and governance theories to exaggerate the impact of civil society as opposed to that of the core executives of governments. It is the decisions of powerful actors within government that make the choices and take the risks involved in determining which issues affecting societies are to be thought of as problems or opportunities of sufficient importance to require the take-up of solutions that may ameliorate the problem. As noted above, the demands on governments to deal with natural or financial disasters may usually be self-evident and in many cases those in power will look to the solutions that the government has stored in its library of contingencies.

Where policy solutions emerge from strong public pressure for change, it is the policy gate-keepers, that is, prime ministers, executive presidents and, dependent on the importance and specialised subject area, senior ministers, who will make a decision based on their moral, ideological and self-interested preferences as to whether to take on board a specific issue or bat it into the long grass. The decision will, therefore, require balancing a number of variables subject to their importance in the minds of politicians in their role of policy gate-keepers. On occasion there may be no question that the policy could be ignored by policy gate-keepers should they wish to retain their positions. It can be the case that the pressures from civic society, or from individuals within government are in agreement with the ideological, moral and self-interested values of the policy gate-keepers. A further, but arguably less crucial, issue that may confront policy gate-keepers is the extent to which the government agenda may already be determined and perhaps overloaded with even greater and more pressing demands. A fashionable 'overload' thesis developed in the 1970s by, among others, Anthony King (1975), argued that, in complex pluralist regimes, governments were failing to develop appropriate and effective policies because of the sheer number of demands for change that they were expected to resolve. Governments in this situation either failed to develop effective policies as they lacked sufficient resources for refining their ideas, including time to reflect on legislation, or had to seriously limit the number of initiatives they could pursue despite the constant demands they faced. However, in an emergency, time can usually be found to make required policy adjustment, and where the policy is not a matter of urgency, arrangements can be made to research the issue through commissions of enquiry before at a later date placing the matter on the route to legitimation through the legislature.

However, if the popular demand is one that is opposed by gate-keepers and their party supporters, they will need to consider their position through a variety of options. In a liberal democracy and many an unstable autocracy this may require policy gate-keepers to balance a number of conflicting issues. To a large extent this can be broken down into a decision first on the extent to which they will not countenance on ideological or moral grounds a populist policy. Leaders with strong views will in such circumstances seek the means to weaken their policy opponents through appeals to their citizens stating reasons for their opposition. Such behaviour is likely to use information or misinformation that is only authoritatively known by the government and, being the government, can be widely communicated. These strategies may often be weighed alongside the desire of gate-keepers to retain their position and resources of power. They will consider whether any popular support they lose by following policies different from those that may be widely advocated by their electorate or, in autocracies potential rebels within civil society, will seriously damage their standing or that of their party. Calculations will be made by gate-keepers in liberal democracies with an interest in remaining in power concerning when the next election may be due, or the fragility of a coalition government, and the time they may have available to them to rebuild popular or inter-party support by rejecting a well supported proposal for policy change.

Conclusion

This chapter has considered how policy becomes a live issue on the agenda of core executives within a political system such that the gate-keepers must either reject the pressures for change or continuity or set about preparing policy change or innovation to ensure that through legislation or executive orders they have a strategy to deal with the policy issue. Policy emerges from the thoughts and desires of a multitude of individuals acting alone or as part of an organisation and few of these atomised interests receive widespread attention. In order to receive serious consideration by policy gate-keepers, an issue must become a widespread concern that is usually given prominence by policy entrepreneurs with expertise in the subject area that is either recognised by the policy gate-keepers or of sufficient strength that it poses a threat to their public support.

A further factor that is crucial to the advance of policy proposals is changes in the political and social environment that ensure a policy solution is widely perceived as relevant to the concerns of that time. This may be the result of political change, the election of a new government for instance, or social or economic change such as the slide into economic recession. Such changes also may bring forward rapid change and then tail off later into periods of relative stagnation in the evolution of policy. Such an evolutionary account in much of the literature is however driven by a pluralist perspective and takes insufficient account of the power of institutions both within government and through interested groups in a capitalist state. The political strength of members of the core executive places prime ministers, executive presidents and their leading advisors in a key position to advance their own policy concerns on their policy agenda. Power, as shown in earlier chapters, is far from evenly divided in liberal democracies and as argued in this chapter, policy can emerge on the political agenda largely through the ideology or the self-interest of elite politicians or groups.

12 Evaluation and validation

Evaluation is an intrinsic element informing all elements of the process of policy making. Few individuals have ever set about formulating a policy that will guide their future conduct without having some reason, however absurd it may be, that has not been based on at least a subjective evaluation of what the policy might achieve. This is even more certain when the policy is a decision affecting a group of individuals, let alone the conduct required of the citizens of a town or nation. Evaluation takes place in the minds of activists from the moment a suggestion for change enters their heads. Often these formative ideas are rejected immediately as cursory evaluation reveals it to be either impractical or morally unacceptable. If an idea does initially seem to be a possible course for action within the mind of a policy activist, it must be communicated to others who will also subject it to further cursory evaluation as it begins to advance towards a publicly recognised proposal. Through these initial stages the policy idea will be combined with similar notions from other activists and will be further refined and reshaped and then further re-evaluated. These iterative procedures can on occasion lead to the development of new initiatives and the continuation of a policy cycle. Once the policy is implemented it is, of course subject to evaluation especially from those who experience the effects of the policy, if not always by those who championed the policy.

Much of what may be termed evaluation in earlier policy studies, however, tends to be post implementation evaluation which is not always undertaken by governments and their agencies and, when it is, will often be an impressionistic rather than a grounded or scientific approach. Policy evaluation in older studies tends, therefore, to be positioned as a chapter following the consideration of policy implementation. Public policy is by no means always fully evaluated by the governments that have enacted the innovation. Moreover any enquiries and evaluations are far from being dispassionate reviews of the potential or actual effectiveness of policy ideas. The more a policy is refined within the working of a government or, for that matter, opposing political interests, the more evaluation ceases to be a meaningful title for what may be being practised in relation to the refinement and legitimation of the policy ideas. As policy advocates and gate-keepers become more and more ideologically infused with particular ideas and are increasingly seen as identified with a specific approach to a policy problem, the more their self and public esteem is identified with that issue. It is at this point that the dispassionate evaluation may tend to drop by the wayside and the interest of the policy advocates is not to evaluate but to validate by seeking and proselytising arguments and evidence that support the case for their preferred policy solution and by attempting to undermine rival arguments supporting other policy solutions. This chapter will, therefore, first review more conventional positivist views on evaluation and then the views of Pawson et al. on realistic evaluation, before turning to the *realpolitik* of validation.

The development of evaluation

As illustrated by William the Conqueror's creation of the Doomsday Book, among the earliest bureaucratised systems of evaluation of public policy on a national scale is the need to establish auditing procedures to ascertain what resources are held by the state and especially those that can provide money from taxation or manpower through conscription. It is also essential that a government can ascertain whether money allocated for public expenditure by a central treasury is spent as decreed by the state. By the late nineteenth century wealthier industrialising states started collecting a wide range of statistics to monitor the changing conditions of their societies. Collection of data is so essential to planning policy that currently almost all governments assemble volumes of largely quantitative data on areas of public concern such as demographic change, public finance, educational attainment, housing and health.

> In the United States the first Federal Census was carried out in 1790 and in 1902 Congress made the United States Census Bureau into a permanent institution for collecting statistical data for the Federal Government under the umbrella of the Department of Commerce.
>
> In Britain, a national census of population was initiated in 1801 and carried forward on a ten yearly basis from 1841. The task of collecting and publishing such data is in the hands in Britain of the Office for National Statistics which typically in June 2012 released over 200 differing sets of statistical data.

It was not until the nineteenth century in most European and North American states that systems of audit were sufficiently robust to prevent what are now seen as corrupt practices that allowed local bureaucrats to pocket much of the funds they received for their own rather than citizens' consumption. In the twentieth century more forensic auditing attempted to ensure that public funding was being used efficiently and effectively. This form of evaluation was particularly crucial in assessing the effectiveness of government fiscal policy. As governments began to take on a role in dealing with the welfare of the unemployed and destitute or the provision of education, states needed to determine not only whether funds were being spent as required but also whether the funding was being used to provide services as Parliament and its executive had intended. Governments began to appoint inspectors to check whether an agency entrusted with undertaking policy had actually complied with the wishes of the policy gate-keepers. This form of inspection was extended throughout the century to encompass areas such as education, prisons and policing and essential services in the private sector such as the safety of railways or coal mines.

> The 1834 Poor Law Act, which was a landmark in bureaucratic development in Britain, established teams of inspectors working to the orders of the central Poor Law Commissioners who would report back to their principal agents the extent to which local poor law unions were complying with their regulations so that effective action could be taken to try to prevent policy drifting away from the central principles of the Act (Chandler 2007: 39–42).

The development of private sector techniques to evaluate established business strategies led to a concern in the public sector to adopt means that could more rationally, if not scientifically, measure the extent to which public sector agencies were efficiently securing their objectives. Henry Drucker (1954) popularised the idea of management by objectives that required senior executives to set clear goals for their subordinates and systems by which both senior and junior management could measure how far their activities were achieving their objectives. The Federal Government of the United States developed in 1961 a framework for evaluation entitled Planning, Programme and Budgeting Systems (PPBS) for the spend-thrift Department of Defence that was adopted throughout the Federal Government in 1965. PPBS required departments to define their major policy objectives and to analyse whether their expenditure and use of resources secured the proposed aims at the lowest possible cost (Carter, Klein and Day 1992: 7). The attempt to make PPBS a universal system did not outlive the Johnson Presidency but the strategy became engrained both in academic and bureaucratic circles with the realisation that policy programmes of both the Federal and state governments should be subject to evaluation. In 1974 a division was established in the General Accounting Office to undertake non-financial evaluations of the effectiveness of policy programmes (Palumbo 1988: 124–7). The efficiency and evaluation drives in the United States began, a decade later, to be adopted in Britain, largely through the processes of policy diffusion. Wollmann (2003: 2–3) classifies these trends into three phases. In the 1960s and 1970s, at a time of raised welfare spending, attempts were made to systematically link policy making with the stages of implementation and evaluation which would feed back into further policy refinement. This strategy was aimed at securing greater efficiency and economy in meeting policy objectives. During the 1980s a second phase of evaluation emerged as a greater concern to decrease public spending through a reduction in policy initiatives and finally in the 1990s a third phase of evaluation was introduced by the adoption of New Public Management (NPM) techniques, which have among their essential characteristics, as defined by Hood (1991: 4), 'Explicit standards and measures of performance' and by Rhodes (1991: 548) 'focusing on management not policy, and on performance appraisal and efficiency'.

This trend towards smaller more streamlined policy reviews rather than more thorough but cumbersome and independent royal and ministerial commissions continued within the New Labour Governments led by Tony Blair. The 1999 white paper *Modernising Government* emphasised the need for better systems of policy making that should rest on the use of evidence-based policy orientated towards identifying and following best practice. The strategy allowed greater autonomy to street level bureaucrats working through arm's length agencies, although innovation at the point of service delivery was to be monitored through stringent targets and those who were found to provide the most effective and efficient services were to be awarded a beacon status and be encouraged to teach less effective delivery units how to learn from their success (Pawson 2002; Richards 2008: 133–4).

Monitoring and assessing performance of public agencies was further enhanced through elaborate systems of target development and complex multi-tiered assessment structures by the Conservative Governments of Mrs Thatcher and John Major and the Labour Governments of Blair and Brown. These agencies such as the Office for Standards in Education (OFSTED) and the Audit Commission became not just instruments for evaluation but agencies to assist the government in controlling the effectiveness of policy output. OFSTED reports on their school inspections are made public and if a school is deemed unsatisfactory and not capable of improvement it may be closed down or reassigned to new management systems. The Audit Commission rated the performance of local authorities on a wide range of their activities and publicly reported their findings. The complexity and the cost of the assessment procedures led the Conservative–Liberal Democrat coalition of 2010 to abandon the Audit Commission and much of the complex system of assessment largely on the grounds of its expense, although this policy was sold publicly as a means of freeing local administration from unnecessary central government interference.

Rationality and evaluation

The quest that began in the mid-twentieth century for scientific techniques to establish rational policy decisions was inevitably related to attempts to develop strategies that could evaluate the effectiveness of policy ideas and the effects of policy outputs. Peter Rossi and Howard Freeman (1993: 65) argue that:

> Evaluation research is the systematic application of social research methods to the assessment of social intervention programs. It draws upon the techniques and concepts of several disciplines and is useful at every stage in the conceptualization, design planning and implementation of programmes.

Sound policy needs evidence, both theoretical and empirical, that suggests how a problem may be resolved and also, once a policy is implemented, how far that idea may be meeting the objectives of its authors. Amitai Etzioni (1964: 6) influentially argues that the evaluation of output must be a reflection of:

- the effectiveness with which an organisation realises its goals;
- the efficiency of an organisation measured by the amount of resources used to provide one unit of output.

There are, as will be discussed later in this chapter, serious limits to the extent that this positivistic approach to evaluation can be stretched but, assuming that a policy proposal has a clear and widely agreed objective, there are well established means to evaluate whether that policy might achieve, and, with more certainty, following implementation, has achieved its goals.

Positivist public policy evaluation is based on a wide range of techniques that cannot be fully studied in this volume but are the subject of the many textbooks on social science methodology. Many are founded on the application of statistical information archived by authoritative institutions for data gathering. The bulk of official government statistics rely on evidence that can with reasonable objectivity be given a quantitative dimension. Thus, it is possible to measure with some degree of accuracy, given the methods of data collection, how representative the findings are in relation to reality through calculations of the probabilities of error. Whilst statistics may clarify that a specific indicator is going up or down, what has caused any trend is still far from clear in a complex social environment. Sophisticated statistical techniques such as factor analysis have been established to give greater clarity as to whether two or more statistical data streams seem to be related, although the truism that correlation does not necessarily entail causation requires researchers to advance further theoretical or empirical evidence to develop more certainty as to whether two correlated factors are directly involved in causing change. Connected with the gathering of statistical data are the findings of public opinion surveys that enumerate public attitudes to proposed or enacted policy developments. It is also possible to evaluate opinion on the effectiveness of a public service with reference to the number of unsolicited complaints or enthusiasm for a service. Such evaluation has considerable added resonance to politicians since widespread dissatisfaction with a policy initiative may in a liberal democracy spill over into criticism of the general tenor of government activity. There are, however, further difficulties connected with reliance on opinion survey data. Questions need to be drafted with care to ensure that all respondents have similar understandings concerning what a particular question may mean. Individuals will also differ on the extent to which a preference will be ranked on a Likert scale especially where questions require a normative answer.

It is also possible for evidence on the potential success of a policy to be drawn from comparative observations of similar activities being tried within other political systems. Such activity is, as discussed in the preceding chapters, the foundation of policy development through policy transfer and diffusion. There has also been in recent years greater enthusiasm for social experimentation by establishing potentially well supported policy proposals on a relatively small scale before, following evaluation, widening the idea to become a national policy initiative (Breckon 2015). In some policy arenas, such as the treatment of health problems or the means of getting the unemployed back into work, it is possible to set up experimental methods of incentivising individuals and assessing the extent to which the chosen methods reach their goals.

A widely published long-term experiment conducted in the United States by the RAND Corporation between 1974 and 1982 based on a random selection of individuals and institutions attempted to evaluate the use of medical services and the health outcomes for people who used pre-paid systems to secure support as opposed to those who had to pay fees for services at the point of treatment. The RAND Corporation were also involved in experimentation to show whether welfare to work programmes providing training for the unemployed improved their earnings and reduced overall the burden of taxation, which had an important influence on later social care services (Greenberg, Linkz and Mandell 2003; Weiss and Birckmayer 2006).

Within Britain since the Blair Governments there have been a considerable number of tentative rolling out of policies within specific regions.

One of the most disastrous failures in the context of social experimentation was the rolling out of the poll tax firstly in Scotland before it was imposed on the rest of the United Kingdom. The Thatcher Government, goaded on by the Iron Lady, refused to read the evidence of Scottish experience where many citizens refused to pay the tax.

Subsequently the New Labour attempt after 2000 to establish directly elected executive mayors in most city authorities was approached with much greater caution and has been rolled out on a piecemeal basis subject to favourable referenda by the local electorate (Copus 2006). Nevertheless the Blair Governments made considerable play of their intention to generally improve policy making in Britain by founding their ideas on 'evidence-based policy'.

What can be evaluated?

The brief survey of institutions for policy evaluation, as outlined above, suggests that practitioners frequently believe that rational methods of evaluating policy can be implemented and used as a guide for evolving policy to meet their required objectives. Nevertheless, despite the industry of government advisors, lobbyists and policy research institutes, the goal of a systematic science of policy evaluation has yet to be perfected and there are strong arguments that such a goal can at best only partially be realised. There is first the problem of determining exactly what the aims of some policies are. Many policy initiatives may be supported for reasons that are not implicit in the stated aims of some or all of their advocates. No doubt private conclaves of those supporting a policy for some secretive aim will evaluate in their fashion whether their goals have been met. This is not, of course, an objection to all forms of evaluation but simply one of many limitations on its scope. Evaluation in practice is usually focused on the publically stated aims of those who advocate a policy rather than any ulterior political motives that may have lent support to the idea. Policies are also often established by politicians with a view to assuaging popular unrest rather than securing what may be an impossible goal such as the New Labour attempt to ban fox hunting or legislation to remove dangerous dogs.

A further problem of assessing policy success is that one person's carefully crafted policy may be another's act of folly or even of immorality. In this context the complex issue of assessing normative and moral beliefs can seriously complicate the evaluation process. Whilst there are evaluation techniques that can reveal the nature and sometimes the degree of concern or support for a particular ethical standpoint, such as the value of equality, normative debate cannot necessarily be reduced simply to a utilitarian formula that sums up and weighs the contented against the uncontented. This is again a limitation on the scope of evaluation and not an argument to say that such an exercise is impossible or unnecessary. The views of those who disagree with the policy can, technically at least, be put to one side if the evaluator is simply concerned with whether the policy advocates and gate-keepers secured their aims. However, this stipulation begins to further narrow the range and utility of the evaluation process.

An argument that policy can be evaluated against criteria based on whether it achieves specifically stated aims presents a very restricted view of the consequences of policy decisions. The success of policy is dependent also on the broader consequences for its social and physical environment and how far this may result in often unforeseen and unexpected results. The issue of unexpected consequences creates a problem that may, after policy has been implemented, be subject to evaluation by a wider review of the effect of the policy than simply the extent to which it fulfilled its stated aims and the efficiency with which this was secured. Frequently, policy advocates are obliged to re-assess policy in this context.

Mrs Thatcher's Government claimed considerable success in creating urban development zones in which run down areas of a city were revived by removing many of the regulations that affected planning in the area and by creating tax incentives to attract new businesses into the area. The redevelopment of London's dockland in the 1980s was the flagship of these schemes, and superficially the policy to redevelop the area led to the creation of a vibrant centre for commercial developments, especially in the area of banking. However, it may be that the policy moved existing business from one area of the City to another so as to benefit from expensive subsidies and be freer of regulation, rather than attracting new business into the zone. The knock-on effect of such innovation for those living in the docklands area was that they were forced by the development to move elsewhere, which creates a further but unintended consequence of the policy. How far the policy was an efficient method of developing the city is still a matter of contention (Parkinson and Evans 1990: 70–77).

A further problem is that the repetition of similar observations that is the basis of inferential logic of the natural sciences is difficult to achieve either through experimentation or through observation. Both social scientists and physical scientists must be aware that correlation does not itself mean that 'A' directly causes 'B'. Correlations are in the social sciences as opposed to the physical sciences more likely to be an issue of unforeseen circumstances and small fields of evidence that can be collected. In this context, attempts to develop policy ideas through policy transfers create difficulties given individual differences within human cultures and behaviour, let alone the physical and geographical differences of states. Within each society there are also minority and individual traits that add further variables that require assessment. The ideal that social experimentation can mirror research in many of the physical and chemical sciences is also undermined by the difficulties in repeating social experiments, given that many variables associated with an earlier research activity will have changed over time. Ethical considerations may also limit any exercise in policy experimentation, for example in establishing a control group of communities that may be denied financial help or other essential resources.

Similar problems also limit the capacity to evaluate in the real world the extent to which a policy achieves its goals by the most efficient means possible. Etzioni's formula, that the ideal situation is to achieve an intended outcome by the most efficient means possible, creates a seriously intractable problem as different, independent criteria are used to measure these goals. As Jan-Erik Lane (1993: 191–3) observes, an efficient organisation achieving worthless objectives is hardly an acceptable criterion for success. Moreover there is controversy about what efficiency may entail since many of the goals of public policy relate to normative values.

How is the privacy of an individual to be evaluated in the context of the financial costs involved with operating an internet service that guarantees that an individual's health records can only be accessed by those, such as doctors, who are authorised by patients?

Thus, often the criteria of meeting policy goals and of efficiency are measured separately and it is left to the policy reviewer's impressionistic judgement how much emphasis to put on success in one category or the other.

The problem of evaluating the wider consequences of a policy within a highly inter-connected and complex society presents an even more problematic issue in evaluating policy consequences before they are implemented. A solution to the problem of revealing possible unintended consequences of a policy proposal is to establish pilot studies, seeking to parallel from a scientific point of view experimentation that will evaluate on a small scale the impact of new techniques and strategies. The problem limiting any attempts to evaluate through experimentation is that most public policy initiatives apply to complex social institutions that may differ from one another to the extent that they are individual rather than similar and comparable organisations.

> The largely successful efforts to revive the economy of the London docklands through creating an Urban Development Corporation which had powers outside the remit of the local government in London, was as much a result of the proximity of this area to the expanding Financial Districts of the City of London just across the river. Not sur-prisingly the creation of Urban Development Corporations was not in many cases as successful in the industrial cities which had a far less vibrant economy (Parkinson and Evans 1990: 79–82).

The issue of experimentation as an activity that can be replicated at any time by others is a hallmark of the physical sciences but creates a serious problem for the social sciences. Many scientific certainties are founded on inductive logic, based on the argu-ment that the more frequently a set of events correlate with one another the greater the likelihood that there is some necessary connection between the events. Social science experiments are usually impossible to replicate due to the difficulty of holding without change all factors as they existed in earlier investigations. It would, following the example of creating Urban Development Zones, be difficult to determine with a strong degree of certainty whether creating low tax zones within a deprived community may in itself create further economic development in that area. There are too many vari-ables in such situations including the types of industry in areas surrounding the enter-prise zones, differing transport facilities in each area and educational attainment and skills of the local workforce. To an extent multi-variant statistical techniques can help to give some sense of the impact of a number of factors but, given the difficulties of accurately measuring variables such as the skills of a local workforce, modelling the possible interaction of variables and the build up of possibilities of variation around the statistical estimates, the results rarely provide a strong measure of certainty.

Realistic evaluation

Whilst policy evaluation is fraught with difficulties it is, nevertheless, unrealistic not to evaluate whether a particular policy alternative is the best that can be chosen or, once a policy has been implemented, fulfils its advocates' expectations. A completely random selection of a policy would not be likely to satisfy any rational individual. Indeed, it would be virtually impossible to select a policy alternative at random given that most social problems will require not just one decision but the interaction of numerous small solutions that have to be combined to create and implement a policy strategy. There are therefore numerous possible potential policy solutions each requiring coordinated sub-decisions. Similarly, it is clearly unreasonable once a policy is put into practice not to attempt to evaluate whether the policy has secured the objectives of its advocates let alone the extent to which the policy has created further unexpected consequences.

Whilst there are many factors that are bound up with the difficulties, touched on in the preceding discussion, social scientists and policy advocates must undertake what Ray Pawson and Nick Tilley (1997) have termed 'realistic evaluation'. This they see as the use of strategy that cannot always claim to give a cast iron proof as to the value of a policy but at least seeks the most plausible methods to find a solution to a puzzle. They, first, argue that any policy proposal needs an underpinning theory that seeks to understand the mechanism of why a particular change may lead to a required result. Theories, especially in the social sciences are, however, fragile and need to be held with caution and the expectation that they may be found wanting. Inductive theories based on the observation of consistent outcomes over time are subject to change as attitudes and value change over time. In practice, argues Pawson (2006, 167–82), understanding develops by a gradual iterative process of challenging and communicating ideas among and within policy networks. Through such challenges, certain ideas are found to be unsustainable in different circumstances but communication also allows theorists to amend policy ideas and seek new paths of development for new circumstances. Over time a body of experience allows the policy analyst, using Lindblom's phrase, to 'muddle through' towards a reasonably informed decision:

> (Karl) Popper was fond of saying that science is informed guesswork. Well so too is policy making. It is created out of educated hunches, it is familiar with creating both winners and losers, it is rooted in the art of compromise and it is thrashed out of the expectation that there will be some truth in what most stakeholders have to say and thus some truth in every programme theory.
>
> (Pawson 2013: 192)

Pawson suggests that it is only through experience of using analytical techniques that the advantages and also the pitfalls of policy evaluation methods become increasingly brought into focus. In this context Pawson's ideas link well with the views of complexity theory, arguing that most effective developments of policy come through learning in a process of trial and error.

The argument concerning realistic evaluation has considerable merit, but it does not describe how in practice public policy is often justified in a politicised world. Pawson rightly suggests that evaluation can never be perfect but with a rational system of trial and error can lead to better solutions than assessing policy on unsubstantiated evidence or on the whims and fancies of policy advocates and opponents. In this context Pawson tends to see politics more as a distortion of any attempt to use evidence and theory to construct a more rational world:

> As one ascends the intervention hierarchy from practitioners to managers, to the bureaucrats to the political classes, the capacity to absorb complex information dwindles by the bullet point. Evidence can inform policy but it can also be used as a tool to park policy in much the same way as indecision is disguised by the need to await review committee reports. It can, of course, also be used to misinform policy through sifting, selection and simplification.
>
> (Pawson 2006: 175)

Whilst the predominantly positivist methodologies for policy evaluation provide what Frank Fischer (1995: 1) describes as a 'cook book' description on how to evaluate policy decisions following their implementation, such a process is not to be dismissed as it is essential in providing more concrete and informed discussion on the merits of policy than no attempt to provide some rational justification for its merits, either before or after its implementation. Well founded inference that rests on the best available evidence may not necessarily be an absolutely certain fount of truth but it will nevertheless be the best guide to the realities and consequences of policy. Simply making up stories on the effectiveness of policies without supporting evidence will not in a rational society be a viable alternative.

However as Fischer (1995: 172–4) points out, the value of a policy is for most people also contingent on subjective values and in many cases their worth differs from one person to another according to their personal and ideological values.

Following its inception President Obama's health care policies were, initially, criticised as being ineffective in terms of their implementation but, whilst this can be positively verified by reference, for example to the take up of the new insurance schemes, the central critique was not about the scheme's practicability but the normative issue of whether citizens should pay more in taxes to enable the poor to access better standards of health care.

It has been emphasised, particularly in Chapters 2 and 6 of this study, that evaluation is to some degree possible in relation to subjective issues through the development of rational arguments that flow from the acceptance of basic precepts that are overwhelmingly accepted within civil society. Thus, for example, in the potential conflict for claims for personal freedom and the value of equality in the life chances for all humans, as illustrated above in the debate on funding health care, it is important that conflicting views are clarified and then debated with the hope of achieving reconciliation through a discourse based on an appreciation of basic ethical theories.

Validating policies

As hinted by Pawson in the world of realpolitik, in many circumstances, little attempt is made by governments and political leaders to realistically evaluate policy as opposed to the more realistic tendency to seek to validate policy in the opinion of as many in society as possible. Given the complexities of evaluating policy, policy advocates and gate-keepers in the real world frequently attempt to validate claims that their ideas have successfully resolved a policy problem or grasped an opportunity rather than dispassionately evaluate as far as possible the consequences of a policy proposal or the impact flowing from its implementation. Policy advocates will more often than not skew the debate on the consequences of their action into channels whereby they seek to validate their actions in the minds of citizens, that is ensure that as many of their potential supporters agree that their policy proposals are likely to be effective and rational and, once they have been implemented, that they are successful in achieving their aims. The capacity to ensure policy validation is facilitated by the uncertainties that bedevil any positivist let alone normative evaluation of policy ideas and their outcomes. In a climate of uncertainty concerning the causes of social change political activists will frequently be able to find theories or facts that appear to validate their actions even though these theories and facts can be countered by different points of view. Policy advocates therefore emphasise and, in many cases, come to sincerely believe in facts that support their case despite the absence of any compelling supporting evidence.

President G. W. Bush and Prime Minister Tony Blair continued to maintain that they were justified in attacking Iraq in the second Gulf War as President Saddam Hussein was building or had already developed weapons of mass destruction despite no substantive evidence ever emerging to support their case.

They will also usually support and communicate only data that appears to give some support to their case with theories that are consonant with their preferred choice of factual evidence, whilst ignoring evidence that may counter their beliefs. The legalist style of Anglo-American adversary debate is particularly slanted to such confrontational and often unprogressive failures to resolve policy problems. At its worst the process of evaluation simply results in proponents and opponents of a particular policy throwing their own ideas at one another with little or no concern over creating a discourse to resolve the dispute.

Skilled political leaders who have as a central motivation an interest in keeping themselves in power are adept at taking huge leaps in the dark over policy with the confidence that they may be able to validate their decisions either because they were lucky enough to make the right guesses or that, if faced with failure, they can find others to carry the blame. In the following case study on responses to the economic crash of 2008 canny opposition politicians could develop policies to suit the interests of their party faithful and be confident that they can achieve power by blaming the governing party at the time of the slump.

A central plank of a governing party's electoral manifesto is to show how their economic policies have been more successful than those forwarded by the opposition. It can be seriously questioned how far any government within a liberal democracy can on its own engineer even in the medium term of a four or five year term in office favourable economic growth. Economic performance is in itself not a single issue but composed of many indicators, such as growth in per capita GNP or the rate of inflation, but also more normative issues such as the distribution of wealth. Most party leaders nail their policies to the mast of some but not all of these often incompatible indicators. The capacity to control a range of more measurable indicators, let alone those with more normative consequences, is in an increasingly globalised world, limited. Inflation and levels of employment are affected not only by national policies but worldwide economic changes. The over-heating of the global economy fuelled by interlocking webs of borrowing and underwriting of loans that staved off for over a decade the time that would precipitate the worldwide economic crash in 2007/8 was never an aspect of policy intention. Similarly the recovery from the economic crash may be seen as the result of economic policies but also as a consequence of economic cycles that have been historically present and so far unavoidable since the development of capitalist society in which economic progress is a consequence of the decisions of numerous independently minded centres of financial decision making each trying to outbid their rivals.

In the United States President Obama and in Britain David Cameron were both in the fortunate position in the second decade of the twenty-first century to assert their economic policies were working and well judged in contrast to the economic failures that were associated with the Bush Administration or in Britain the government led by Gordon Brown. However, whilst the Obama Administration argued for increased injection of cash into the United States' economy to solve the effects in the United States of a global problem, the Coalition Government in Britain also claimed success for its contrasting policy of cutting public spending. In reality they have been propelled into government at a fortuitous time when the economic worldwide slump had reached its lowest ebb and the tide of economic forces could be exploited to create greater economic growth.

Policy validation is in practice a procedure that drives policy evaluation, rather than, as positivist theory entails, that validation is the consequence of evaluation. On many issues, such as debates on the success of macro-economic policy, contending political parties will choose theoretical grounds, such as public choice theory or Keynesianism as a proven theory and then apply whatever data and facts there are at hand to support their case and dismiss opposing evidence as either biased or theoretically unsound. Frequently, the consequences of a policy can be validated simply by claiming that the strategy worked, even though countervailing strategies, as illustrated in the above case, might argue that this was either through luck or the result of global trends that will be little affected by the individual policies of specific nations.

At an institutional level validation is further secured by establishing institutions to give the appearance of being politically neutral founts of rational expertise to evaluate policy developments and outcomes. Governments frequently set up research bureaus or boards of enquiry whose memberships are known to reflect the interests of those in government.

The Redcliffe-Maud Commission which laid the basis of creating fewer local authorities in England that had been a strongly entrenched goal of civil servants was appointed predominantly on the recommendation of such officials. The Commission was composed of a strong representation from larger upper tier local authorities but had no representatives from smaller rural and urban districts. Expert opinion from outside local government was drawn from former civil servants, party loyalists and journalists who had advocated local government reforms based on much larger units of government. As Richard Crossman, who had initiated the evaluation, expected, the Commission proposed the wholesale remodelling of English local government into large sub-regional units based on large urban centres that incorporated their surrounding rural hinterland and proposed the abolition of lower tier district councils (Chandler 2007: 197).

As the above example illustrates, enquiries may be set up on an *ad hoc* basis to review a specific area of policy but evaluation is also conducted or influenced within governments by numerous departments and agencies established on a more permanent basis. These may include regulatory agencies whose membership is often manipulated by governments to suit their ideological position or may be organisations more embedded close to the core executive of a government that similarly can be established to reflect the ideology and the factual outlook supported by the policy gate-keepers.

> Following the economic crash of 1929 as part of the New Deal programme President Roosevelt persuaded Congress to establish in 1934 a Securities and Exchange Commission to regulate the central agent in the crisis, the American stock exchanges. However, as Michael Moran (2009: 34) observes, 'the leadership of the Commission was drawn from the very markets where scandal had originated: its first chairman Joseph Kennedy, founded the fortune of the Kennedy political dynasty by financial speculation in the 1920s. More important still, the Commission worked through a kind of franchising system: it delegated responsibility for regulation to the stock exchanges themselves, restricting itself to authorizing and supervising these self regulatory bodies' (Seligman 2003: 103–23).

The development in the United States of agencies that were often protective self-referential debating chambers between business and capitalist politicians led, as has been discussed in the chapters on networks, to less than democratic elitist sub-systems of governance that paved the way to the 2008 economic crash. Whilst there have over the years been efforts to modify these corporate structures to allow a stronger consumer voice in their proceedings, government regulatory agencies concerned with the private business sectors have continued to structure the direction of evaluation in both the United States and Britain through such light touch regulation that contributed greatly to the causes of the post-2008 financial crash and consequent worldwide slump.

Validation of policy institutionally requires agencies that will report the findings that support the standpoint of a political regime. In autocracies this is normally a state controlled media informed by the civil service. In liberal democracies governments can communicate through an ideologically neutral media in terms of support for major political interests such as, in the United Kingdom, the British Broadcasting Corporation who are expected to provide authoritative reports on both government and opposition actions and policy. Successful political parties will rarely have achieved such eminence if they are also not supported by substantial elements of the media, particularly the press, that are broadly sympathetic to their ideological direction. The civil service may also express their doubts about the spin that politicians may wish to place on the value of policies but if unsuccessful in convincing their political masters, are usually obliged to support as best they can their masters' account. As Sir Henry Wotton, a diplomat in the Court of James I, observed 'An ambassador is an honest gentleman sent abroad to lie for the good of his country'.

Whilst liberal democracies, by definition, allow some capacity for critics of governments' evaluation of policy, there can be a much more entrenched system of deception through validation of the official opinion on policy within many autocracies and especially where a ruling elite has a totalitarian grip over communication in the polity. Frequently the uncertainties that cloud social science debate give considerable scope to political advocates to maintain their position without heed to opposing points of view. The effectiveness of attempts by political agencies to validate their views is further facilitated or undermined by the civic culture that has evolved within a polity. At the extreme, the dominant political classes within a state may have steered a community towards acceptance of its moral authority to govern and the validity of its values. Such a position has been discussed in relation to Gramsci's phrase, of a hegemony of the ruling elite over the members of a polity. In such circumstances, as in North Korea, citizens may be predisposed to believe in the authoritative pronouncement of the state. Even in stable liberal democracies there is a tendency for certain problematic issues to be given little critical attention, such as the capacity of the state to favour its nationalist interests above those of rival political regimes. Such a position is rarely if ever wholly achieved even in the most repressive totalitarian regimes. Nevertheless, as Almond and Powell (1966), Lipset (1981) and Fukuyama (1995) suggest, the most stable liberal democracies tend to be those where there is a high level of trust between government and the population and such an attitude normally requires a substantive measure of freedom of speech and a strong level of social science literacy within civic society if citizens are not to be fobbed off with rationally weak and challengeable statements on the efficacy and effectiveness of policy proposals.

Conclusion

Evaluation is a process that is intrinsic to all elements of the policy process. Policy advocates must form their ideas from the impressionistic evaluation of problems or opportunities in the world as they see it. Placing the policy on the political agenda and refining it into a legitimate command of the state that is subject to implementation similarly requires constant evaluation and re-evaluation of policy as it stands at any particular point within the policy cycle. It is, however, also possible to identify for some policies a particular point after implementation when policy evaluation assumes a more formal retrospective analysis by, often but by no means always, neutral and dis-interested observers. There are numerous techniques that must be used within these forms and stages of evaluation that must be designed to relate to the context of the policy and the varied concerns about its potential or actual impact. Whilst many of these techniques can provide some understanding of the consequences of a policy, few evaluations can chart the totality of the consequences of a policy and frequently have not the time to explore the long-term impact of decisions, let alone in comparison with the consequences of policy options concerning an issue that has been shelved.

However, often within the framework labelled as evaluation is the concern of policy advocates and gate-keepers, not so much to evaluate their chosen policies, but to seek some arguments that may validate their actions, in order to place as favourable a gloss on those actions as is possible to catch the interests of voters or powerful interests. In practice on most policy issues politicians accept, in accord with their ideological views or through self-interested motives, a particular enthusiasm for, or strong opposition against, a policy initiative and will work, often with the help of their close advisors, to gather material that will convince the public that their policy should be pursued whe-ther or not a detailed and comprehensive evaluation of the subject area can bear out their version.

13 Refining policy towards legitimation

It is a recurring theme in this study that liberal democracies are far more liberal than they are truly democratic. Whilst they allow freedom of speech and assembly such that citizens can join permanent well-resourced groups such as political parties, businesses or interest groups, the capacity of each individual to have a strong personal voice in the making of policy that affects their interests is seriously, and as shall be argued later, unnecessarily limited. Within each liberal democracy there is, as discussed in Chapters 7 and 8, a bureaucratic structuring of institutions and values that operates largely through autocratic channels. This theme can be further observed in those elements of the policy making process occurring largely between the time that policy issues are taken up by government and the legitimation of policy. This may be depicted as a period of policy refinement in which a government, having agreed in principle that a change in policy may be necessary, then sets about determining in greater detail how this is to be codified in legislation or decrees prior to legitimising the decisions in some form of ceremony communicable to the wider domestic and international societies. By no means all policies follow such a path, as some policy changes may lie outside this more complex pattern, such as changes in attitudes of a ruling elite to other nations or interests that will colour their future behaviour toward these organisations. Similarly, the many elements within policies based on self-interest and the struggle for power within a state are rarely communicated to the wider public.

Policy refinement in an autocracy

In order to simplify the process of policy refinement we may first imagine how policy may be refined by an idealised autocracy in which the interests of civil society are disregarded by a controlling oligarchy of similarly minded gate-keepers. Some writers have suggested that autocratic governments have a much greater capacity to forward policy proposals from inception to implementation. In respect to the environment, Stuart Wilks-Heeg (2015: 44–6) has coined the term 'green authoritarianism' to typify this attitude towards policy making in the context of global warming issues. In such a system it is likely that many policies can be developed from the internal discourse within the oligarchy that may be driven by both self-interest and ideological and ethical considerations. In the most basic societies discourse is reinforced by demonstrations of power and authority backed by the threat of violence to establish who has the capacity or right to impose their policy as legitimate practice. In more complex autocratic polities the contending interests can better promote their ideas by using arguments based on the opinions of professionally educated specialists in the many aspects of an issue that concern them.

However, self-interest and related professional interest is likely to create a bureaucracy in which not all professions or activists will work together towards a common interest. In particular the senior cadre in the military will have not only authority over their special interests but direct command over the means of violence within the regime which can be used to coerce the political oligarchy to accept demands that favour their values and interests. In some cases failure of the political leadership to recognise the concerns of the military leads to a *coup de d'état* and the replacement of the civil autocracies by a military autocracy.

Civilian bureaucracy in an autocracy is also likely to be riven by factionalism as members of a government will attempt to increase their capacity to steer government policy by appointing to more senior positions in the political and bureaucratic hierarchies individuals who will act as their obedient clients. Rarely is it likely that within an autocracy the civil service, military or the judiciary incorporate the best available founts of technical expertise given that their positions will be tenanted by the political factionalism that beneath the surface divides a regime and through power struggles that determine the output of its policies. As Gilley (2012) observes, theories that autocracy can be more effective in ensuring policy development and implementation need to be questioned given that in large bureaucracies such as in the People's Republic of China the complex chain of command and devolution of policy making to cities and regions can create very different results on, for example, climate change, than intended by central government.

Policy refinement and legitimation in pluralist societies

There are major differences between pluralist liberal democratic regimes and autocracies especially in the capacity of citizens to freely form associations to forward their interests and to collectively have an opportunity through discourse among citizens, and the possibility, through elections, to remove or sustain a government. As discussed in Chapters 9 and 10, the pressure of public opinion and the open electoral process can have a significant effect on the extent to which party leaders in government can ignore pressures developed within civil society. Nevertheless, certain attributes of public policies may significantly lessen the extent to which public concerns may be a factor in determining the content of policy outputs. At the heart of the policy development machinery in liberal democracies, as is argued in Chapter 9, are sub-systems of government that may not differ substantially from the inner ranks of some autocratic regimes. Policy decisions in many liberal democracies are, as in autocracies, processed by relatively small groups of senior politicians within oligarchic party systems and are advised by hierarchic Weberian ideal type bureaucracies and similarly structured private corporations and professional organisations favoured by the ruling party elites. Policy refinement in liberal democracies is likely to be shaped by the same social interests and forces that affect the framing and agenda setting issues that have been analysed in preceding chapters. The policy entrepreneurs chosen by gate-keepers to bring their policy issues onto the agenda of the core executive of a government will also be likely to continue to be the interests that further refine the policy until it becomes legitimated. Policy is refined in liberal democracies as much as in autocracies such as the People's Republic of China through discourse within predominantly unreported meetings, many over the internet or by phone, between government ministers and secretaries of state, civil servants and representatives of professional networks that are ideologically largely of the same mind as the government. Although the core executives in liberal democracies are more likely to make decisions in the interest of majority values within civil society than are the leaders of autocracies, it must be stressed that the power to make decisions that follow public opinion or to take the risks contingent on ignoring popularly held values, lies with the core decision makers. Gate-keepers such as an executive president or a prime minister have the power of an autocrat to determine whether they believe they have the resources to change such opinions and whether they have a sufficient reservoir of support to tide them over any unpopularity for their stance on a specific policy.

Whilst the autocratic sub-systems of governance have a major role in liberal democracies, this should not, however, lead necessarily to a view that liberal democracies are simply autocracies in disguise. There are many variations in the institutional structuring of liberal democracies that may heighten or lessen the extent to which core executives may be exposed or sensitive to majority opinions within their electorate. Moreover, the pattern of cleavages around ideological values and the attitudes to the pursuit of self-interest as opposed to more altruistic moral values will also shape the extent to which policy gate-keepers will be able to establish more autocratic policies. The impact of such differences on policy refinement will be unique to each system of governance but can be to some extent clarified, which is the task of the remainder of this chapter.

As argued in earlier chapters, the most important of the pressures that may limit the capacity of groups in civil society to influence the governing parties are related to the extent that a large number of citizens are seriously concerned about policy proposals, such that it can change their opinion in favour of the parties in power. The greater the public concern that is created in favour of or in opposition to solutions concerning a perceived policy problem, the more the capacity of the core executive to quietly and secretively shape the policy details will be compromised. The lower the popular interest is in a policy issue the more decisions will be made, as in an autocracy, through closed deliberations between the political elites, the bureaucracy and external interests closely networked into the central decision making process. Governments also have means to exploit the issue of public interest. Some policy areas fail to attract popular interest but others, which may have a substantive impact on public well-being, can be kept firmly under wraps. As indicated in previous chapters, policy that is made to appear complex and difficult to understand without substantive education may be left to debates involving a small number of professional interests. Policies that require bargaining between states or between states and multi-national companies may be kept away from public scrutiny on the grounds that they are formative deliberations that need to be conducted by professionals or are too delicate for individual parties in the debate to be made public. Governments frequently prefer to discuss policy development with powerful well-resourced organisations in private, to avoid, often for both sides in such discussions, courting an upsurge of popular hostility to the ideas being hatched.

At the time of writing negotiations are being held between the United States and the European Union within the framework of the Transatlantic Trade and Investment Partnership. The negotiations are largely held in secret and have yet to become headline news in the press or the broadcast media. Nevertheless, the deals that could be forthcoming attempt to develop greater commonality in trading between Europe and North America and it is feared are influenced by large corporations seeking to avoid public sector regulation. The negotiations could, for example, open up public health services in Europe to competition by the privatised health services in the United States. Demands are being tabled to remove barriers in Europe on the use of genetically modified foods and many pesticides. There is also pressure to allow, as is the practice in some nations, large companies to successfully sue governments if they can claim public policy decisions have lowered their expectations of generating private profit (see for example Williams 2014).

Institutional factors

The legislative route that characterises most mature liberal democratic political systems in Europe is based on checks and balances usually between an executive, legislature and judiciary but also in empowering other territorial units of government, such as federal states or national agencies with a measure of authority to make decisions without the consent of the core executive of the state. However, this institutionally ordered separation of power exists in many forms and may in some liberal democracies be almost non-existent. The extent of any separation of powers and therefore policy developed by compromises forged between the executive and the legislature is dependent on the cohesion within the political party or parties that gain a sufficient majority of seats in the legislature to enable its leaders to form the government and hence hold all the senior posts in the executive and command the majority of votes in the legislature. In a large part due to the use of a first-past-the-post electoral system, in Britain and some of its former dependencies such as Australia, Ireland or Canada, a single party frequently gains an overall majority of seats in a dominant lower house of the legislature and hence can establish its leaders as members of the government to the exclusion of its competitors. In many European states using systems of proportional representation one party is rarely able to enjoy a majority in the legislature and hence coalition government is more the norm.

This framework is most clearly established within what was termed the Westminster pattern of government as established in the United Kingdom. Public policy in such a system is dominated by Secretaries of State appointed by the Prime Minister who, as the leading members of the dominant party, also command the loyalty of lower status lieutenants not in government but serving as backbench members of Parliament. In such an arrangement the gate-keepers of public policy are, effectively, the leaders of the dominant party or parties and are able to filter out which issues, current within the wider political environment, require their attention and determine how they should be dealt with. The legislative committees which have the role of considering the details of proposed legislation will through the gate-keepers have command over party discipline to ensure that problems relating to legislation can be amended in its formative stage, if this is clearly in the interest of the dominant party, but can also be easily rejected if they are contrary to the core executive's wishes.

Paul Flynn, a British Member of Parliament since 1987, observes in his book *How to be an MP*, that 'The chore of Public Bills Committees is a hideous shock to novice members. Their current operation demeans Parliament and can lead to the creation of bad laws ... Government backbenchers are the winners. All that is required of them by the whips is their constant attendance and dutiful voting. Speaking is a time wasting obstacle to the speedy passage of Government bills, the main task of Public Bill Committees. Government MPs learn how to fill their time productively by opening the mail and writing replies. With slackening rules on electronic devices, dealing with the e-mails is a productive time-filler. Opposition MPs are lectured that their only influence is the ability to delay Government bills. They are urged to fill time spaces with words whose main purpose is to gum up the works. Improvements are attempted to bills, but rarely are they accepted by the elective dictatorships of governments' (Flynn 2012: 80–1).

In contrast to Westminster style constitutions, the institutional arrangement of Presidential systems based on the United States model facilitates a more open and pluralist conflict between the executive and legislative arms of government in relation to policy decisions requiring legislative support and legitimation. Policy that requires legislation, even if it is proposed by the executive, must be introduced through Congressional committees of either the House of Representatives or the Senate where they are subject to considerable detailed debate and often never allowed to proceed. If the policy proposal is to proceed it emerges as amended by the committee and is then debated and voted on by the chamber in which it was introduced. If the amended document is agreed by the majority vote of this assembly it is then sent to the other chamber for further debate and refinement before passing to the President. The President has the power to veto the proposal, although this sanction can be overridden by a two-thirds majority in both Houses of Congress in its favour. Whilst most Congress members tend to vote in line with the wishes of the majority within their party, cross voting within a party is much more likely than in the more disciplined Westminster model, in part because there is far less threat to members of Congress that their ideologically fellow minded members of the executive will lose power if they choose to vote against their party leaders. This legislative framework applies even to bills drawn up and favoured by the President of the United States who is often obliged to make deals with key members of Congress to ensure his or, at the time of writing potentially, her initiatives are passed into law more or less as he or she intended.

Since facing a Congress with a Republican majority the Democratic President Obama has faced each year a struggle to ensure that Congress will accept his budget proposals. Bargaining between the parties in October 2013 reached a state of 'shutdown' in Federal financial operations as the budget was not resolved by the date necessary to allow the provision of further spending by the Federal Government, leading to several days of administrative impasse until both sides reached a workable agreement.

The examples given based on United States and United Kingdom experience demonstrate two extremes within liberal democracies in how the legislative process may or may not override the intentions of the policy advocates and gate-keepers who are seeking to implement policy through changes in law. Each political system tends to have variations on these patterns. France for example has a more hybrid structure with a President as leader of a Party expecting unity within the Party during committee stages in the legislature but who will depend for ensuring the passage of a bill on the approval of the Prime Minister who is appointed by the President but may not, if the majority in the Assembly is from a party different from that of the President, necessarily be of the same party as the President. Many European systems of legislative government are subject to wider discourse, at least among party leaders, if the electoral system or ideological divisions in civil society create coalition governments on a regular basis. A specific party leadership is consequently less able to forward its interests without making some compromises with its partners within government although it can in some instances not necessarily result in a widening of discourse within civil society.

On occasion, as in Italy from 1946 to the 1980s, central political parties can dominate the structuring of the coalition government by determining which parties to their immediate left or right they can call on to join them within government (Spence 2014: 105).

The structure of the internal bureaucracy of a state is also a factor that may disperse decision making within the core executive. In Britain a tradition of Weberian party political neutrality within the civil service and the military has been argued to create a powerful corrective to ideological zeal or self-interested motivation among the leading politicians (Richards 2008: 193–6). However, the idea of a civil service counselling policy decisions that stand above the quarrels of the politicians now wears rather thin. Since at least the 1980s, party interest has tended to ensure that senior members of the civil service are chosen to reflect the value of the party in power and, perhaps more to the point, the British civil service has tended through its recruitment and training practices to ensure its top echelons are imbued with a culture that is sensitive to the values of the left or right centrist views of the two dominant parties (Richards 2008). In contrast, France, Germany or the United States make little attempt to establish at the highest levels of their civil service a climate of impartiality but appoint as the senior advisors to politicians individuals known to be sympathetic to the government and the values it represents (Chandler 2014).

Governing by decree

Although public policy on many issues within liberal democracies must be submitted to refinement and legitimation as legislation, by no means are all governments obliged to put all public policies through such a framework. Core executives can have considerable discretion on some issues to by-pass complex legislative procedures and rule by some form of decree. In many regimes the executive arm of government is given, through the constitution or enabling legislation, a capacity to determine new policy directions without the need for legislative sanctions. In the United States these are termed executive orders and have been widely used by Presidents ever since the American Civil War.

Even without the formal power of executive discretion it is accepted at times of national emergency that the capacity to make decisions concerning foreign policy can be made without immediate recourse to the legislature.

The decisions made by President Kennedy during the crisis of 1962 to confront the Soviet Union's policy of establishing missiles in Cuba capable of striking United States cities were taken within an executive committee chaired by Kennedy that included key cabinet members and military commanders.

In a very different but crucial emergency in 2008 in most Western states the collapse of Lehmann Brothers created the possibility of a meltdown in the globalised banking system that required many states to take immediate executive action without reference at the time to the legislature. In the United States policy decisions were made between President Bush and his economic advisors, the Treasury and importantly the Chair of the Federal Reserve Alan Greenspan. In Britain Prime Minister Brown and the Chancellor of the Exchequer in consultation with the Bank of England arranged meetings with the major banks under pressure to bail them out with sufficient guarantees to resolve the economic crisis, paving the way to major changes in public policy on austerity and regulation of the financial industry.

Within this context timing remains a major factor in favouring core executive control over a policy making process. When events require or circumstances allow the executive to make quick decisions to resolve a policy issue there is unlikely to be substantive and exhaustive debate with external interests. In these circumstances the process of refining and amending policy is usually determined by the minister concerned who will consult with senior advisors and senior civil servants. Legislatures usually have the capacity to review and comment on foreign policy or commercial decisions after they have been enacted but rarely does this retrospective review require or result in a reversal of policy, even though on matters of serious national concern the consequences of adverse criticism may haunt the governing party for years to come.

Substantive shifts in ideological outlook may also occur within dominant parties in liberal democracies that will subsequently colour not only policies subject to legislative change but also those issues that are determined by powers granted to the executive. A government may, for example, replace the chair of an executive agency or regulatory body to ensure a different approach to its role from, for example, light touch regulation to more hands-on control. More substantively within the leadership of a ruling party decisions can be made outside the institutional framework of checks and balances to break off or renew alliances with particular interest groups or national governments. Such broad policy decisions which may affect the constitution of the advocacy networks that dominate a sub-system of informal governance may have profound knock-on effects for the pursuit of public policy.

Determining how to decide

An important and not always very visible power centred in core executives of many liberal democracies is the power to determine how policy demands may be processed. Legislatures may make demands on the executive as to whether an issue should be subject to the legislative process as laid down by the constitution or precedent or subject to government decree or enquiries, but where, as in Britain, the legislature is dominated by a party which forms the government, the balance of power between executive and government is sufficiently eroded to allow the governing party's core executive to determine how policy may be refined. This power may be illustrated by the capacity of core executives to influence policy making through enquiries or referenda. Rational theories of policy making would suggest that debate and discourse using evidence-based arguments may be the best method of creating effective policy solutions to complex issues. Refining ideas to create policy that may resolve widely agreed policy problems can in liberal democracies or on a world inter-governmental level be considered following extensive evaluative research through government-sponsored enquiries and commissions or inter-governmental congresses, such as the series of climate change conferences promoted under the auspices of the United Nations that have been supported by considerable preparation behind the scenes by the participating governments. However, policy refinement through open discursive inquiry is beset by many difficulties. Such inquiries will normally entail considerable resources in terms of expertise and finance and several years to complete and scan the most fruitful areas for research. More problematically they are likely to involve what are often termed political issues, that is, they concern issues that raise differing ideological, moral or self-interested positions on which the contending parties can find little agreement. These will often undermine any positivist conclusions on developing clear policy outcomes to resolve these differences.

> One of the major issues affecting planet Earth is the repercussions of climate change as a result of over-reliance on the use of fossil fuels leading to a build-up of greenhouse gases. Despite a substantial if not wholly universal acceptance of the likelihood of damaging and irreversible climate change during the latter part of the twenty-first century many short-term and self-interested values have distorted any sustained attempts to sufficiently reduce the output of greenhouse gases. Many countries cannot develop the technology required to create power or fuel transport in order to raise their economic status in the world and few of the wealthier nations are prepared to use their resources to aid such countries to become serious competitors themselves. Governments and the multi-national companies that support them see their ability to strengthen the economy of the state as the means to achieve re-election to positions of power and states are self-interestedly reluctant to make the decisions that will be damaging to themselves in the short term in order to avoid possible global catastrophe that may happen to later generations.

In practice many government inquiries are also the consequence of a concern to kick an issue into the long grass of protracted debate without any serious intention of gaining an immediate answer to the problem. A core executive may also subsequently ignore the conclusions of the inquiry.

> The Leveson Inquiry into illegal activities by the British press in obtaining information may be such an example. The Inquiry, lasting some twelve months, eventually made recommendations which were largely ignored by the Government that had little interest in curbing the transgressions of newspapers which largely defended the actions and values of the dominant Conservative Party (Jones 2014: 118).

In many cases governments will also establish inquiries that will provide answers that are favourable to their interests, as in the Redcliffe-Maud Royal Commission on local-government outlined in Chapter 4, through the appointment of a chairperson and other members of the inquiry who will be supportive of their interest to the exclusion of their serious critics.

It is similarly within the power of core executives to determine whether policy decisions are transferred from a small political elite to a much wider constituency through the use of referenda or other means of reflecting the opinions and ideas of civil society, such as think tanks or public opinion surveys. In the technologically developing world it is increasingly possible to move to far more direct forms of democracy. On many important issues it would be possible to subject demands for policy change to legitimation through a public referendum on the issue. The use of referenda is in many liberal democracies reserved for major legislative changes in the constitution of the nation or transfers of power to a super-national agency. The use of referenda is also avoided as it may tie a government into a long period of debate on a public issue to the detriment of other policy initiatives. In reality however these objections can carry little weight compared with the probability that most members of any core executive, including party leaders, have no wish to compromise the pursuit of their objectives by reference to a much wider arena for consultation, the electorate, as opposed to favoured policy interests and supportive government bureaucracy. The process of determining detailed policy from a broad policy intention is often determined through a trade-off between several concerns. The motives behind the policy, if at root self-interested, may lead policy advocates to seek if possible to ensure the refinement is conducted in private bureaucratic conclaves rather than through wide debate. Similarly policy that may be thought to be for the general good of society but nevertheless widely unpopular, such as raising greater taxation, is likely to be confined to the reclusive area of discourse between the party leaders and the civil service.

Policy refinement outside central government

The detailed arrangements of broad policy decisions are often assigned by legislation to public bodies that are given discretion as to how they will interpret the broad powers given to them by legislation or executive decree. In effect, it is difficult in such circumstances to make a clear distinction between actions that can be seen as policy refinement and those which may be seen as consequences of the process of policy implementation. In federal systems such as the United States, policy made in Washington can be shaped in its detail by the powers of implementation given to the state governments (Pressman and Wildavsky 1973). Whilst not technically a federal system, the United Kingdom has granted substantial powers to a Scottish Parliament and to a lesser extent the Welsh and the Northern Ireland Assemblies. Policy deliberation is also further decentralised within liberal democracies through devolution of powers to regional and local governments. Within the United States many of the federal states have adopted a system in which local governments have powers of general competence over issues that are not specifically reserved by the Constitution for the Federal Government or proscribed as matters to be dealt with at the state level by the federal units of government. Since 2011 similar powers of competence have been given to English local governments, although in both these cases the restrictions placed on the subordinate local government units are often so substantial they never amount to a serious devolution of power.

Policy may also be shaped in many pluralist regimes by judicial decisions. Within the United States the powers given to the Supreme Court to interpret the Constitution and the laws that flow from the constitutional power to make legislation can on occasion dramatically restructure policy in specific areas.

In the United States 'The black struggle for equality entered a new phase in May 1954 with the historic Supreme Court decision in *Brown v. Board of Education of Topeka* handed down by Chief Justice Earl Warren, whom Eisenhower had appointed the year before ... Speaking for a unanimous Court Chief Justice Warren reversed the 1896 decision in *Plessy v. Ferguson* that segregation did not violate the Fourteenth Amendment (of the Constitution) so long as equal facilities were provided for each race. Though in practice facilities for blacks were markedly inferior, the "separate but equal doctrine" had provided a legal sanction for segregation' (Jones 1995: 535).

In Britain public policy, woven into a measure of permanence through law, is built up not only by legislation but by historic judicial rulings that set precedents on how laws should be interpreted. As in the United States, senior judges can set aside precedent or the meaning of legislative rulings by providing new interpretations of policy decisions. The many independent agencies set up by legislation similarly have a role in refining policy within the envelope of their powers granted by law.

In 2009 the Labour Government in the United Kingdom established an agency, the Independent Parliamentary Standards Authority (IPSA), to monitor the expenses, and later, the salaries and pensions, paid to MPs, following a series of scandals concerning the abuse of the preceding system for checking MPs' claims. The legislation setting up the agency does not itself set out the exact policies that IPSA must determine on the matter of MPs' expenses but vests in the agency the power to determine exactly what an MP may claim in expenses.

Governments can, however, through executive action, re-shape the policy of an agency by appointing its senior policy makers with a view to securing a different policy direction in the organisation. Such action may often need only to be seen as a threat to ensure that such executive agencies take care to manage their powers in such a way that they do not ruffle the ideological or self-interested feathers of central government.

Privatisation

Whilst many states have developed frameworks for refining and legitimising policy, many, especially since the 1980s, have in effect passed this task to non-governmental organisations through the process of hollowing out the state. Particularly within New Right pluralist economies, much of the refinement of policy that affects the public, but is not usually perceived as public policy, is undertaken by governments that through privatisation and light touch regulation ensure that many services necessary for public well-being are determined and implemented by private corporations. In many Western liberal democracies issues such as determining the cost and distribution of fuel supplies or the provision of public communications by rail or road transport have been increasingly handed over to the private sector as a result of New Right ideology favouring privatisation. Such action may be seen as the transfer of power away from governments that may change their ideological direction to the more stable systems of elite capitalist or, some may argue, hegemonic control within the confines of the life-world or *habitus* of liberal democratic societies.

> The near collapse of the world economy in 2008 is widely attributed to the failure of the banking systems in the United States and the City of London that was a consequence of light touch regulation of the financial system brought into being by New Right government (Hutton 2015: 72–9). Despite the failures of the private sector in this context, right wing governments in Britain have not seen it as appropriate to retain ownership of the failed banks that had to be bought out by the state as a consequence of their unbridled greed but as soon as possible sold the banks at a discount back into the social networks that were the preeminent contributors to the financial crisis.

Legitimation

Many older and less critical studies of governments place considerable emphasis on the process by which policy ideas are refined and legitimated into public policy. Policy legitimation is here seen as the point in the policy process in which any organisation with some measure of permanence, be it a government or a private interest group, has reached a specific view on how to deal with a policy issue and intends that the collective conclusions will be put into practice. Legitimation does not necessarily mean that all members of a group agree with the decision but it is a statement that all members of the group, like it or not, will be expected to follow the requirements laid out in the policy. On many occasions in the case of public organisations, and especially governments, legitimation is accompanied by some form of widely published statement setting out the terms of the policy and this may on some issues be accompanied by ritual ceremonies.

> In Britain, policies that are framed into laws must be signed by the Queen as Head of State and witnessed by some members of the Privy Council. In the United States and France the document delineating the legislation has to receive the President's signature.

By no means all public policies need to be legitimated as laws and statutes that are binding on every citizen of the state. Many policy changes issued by government may not have legal status but are statements of attitudes that will be taken by those in government to guide their relationships with other states or private sector organisations. These statements of attitude may be framed in an official government publication or simply be expressed by a leading government minister and in some cases may be subject to legislative approval or simply be justified under existing laws that provide government with authority to rule on such matters. Policy may also be changed within governments through secret arrangements on, for example, military strategy or foreign relations, and much policy is also present as secret and at times corrupt deals benefiting core policy makers and their client supporters.

Conclusion

It would appear from this review of the process of refining policy decisions prior to their legitimation that whether a policy is to be changed through legislation or by the use of executive powers, the main players within the review process remain the gate-keepers at the centre of a core executive. Whilst the process of review may, especially in terms of legislation, be seen as a public process in which external groups to a government can publicly proclaim their support or criticisms of a policy and suggest amendments, the final decision to either amend or push through the policy as it originated still lies within the executive. Many of the more serious objections will, however, be provided outside the public gaze by civil servants or through unpublished meetings between key decision makers and key interests who have overall loyalty to a government and realise that they benefit from close consultation with government rather than staging public confrontations against its policy decisions.

Gate-keepers and policy advocates are often not averse to receiving criticism and suggested amendments to the details of policy prior to its implementation especially if these are given behind the scenes. Such discourse may help the policy advocates to develop more effective and watertight policy instruments as a consequence of professional advice seen publicly to be generally supportive of their proposals. The organisations that can exert such influence are, therefore, largely insider groups with a broadly common ideological perspective to those in power. Changes that are forced through as a result of widespread popular concern from interests that are generally unsupportive of the government's ideological stance are therefore much more noticeable but much rarer and normally will only be successful if they create widespread concern among voters or deal with an issue where there are deep ideological splits between the leadership or their parliamentary lieutenants in the ruling parties or coalition.

14 Implementation

Jeffery Pressman and Aaron Wildavsky's seminal work *Implementation* (1973) has the lengthy but graphic sub-title:

> How Great Expectations in Washington are Dashed in Oakland. Or why it's Amazing that Federal Programmes Work at All. This Being a Saga of the Economic Development Administration as Told by Two Sympathetic Observers who Seek to Build Morals on a Foundation of Ruined Hopes.

Their study showed how a policy, once handed to those who are supposed to put the policy into practice, evolves into a form that was never envisaged by the original policy champions. On many occasions policy advocates have in mind exactly how they wish to see their favoured policies implemented but this is far from being generally the case. Policy intentions can be subverted, as Pressman and Wildavsky found, to the interests of those who implement the policies. From another perspective, policy is often legitimated by core executives, without any expectation that their aims, as much as they have any clarity, will be fulfilled, to demonstrate to the public that the governing parties recognise a problem exists even though the policy makers have little idea on how to resolve the issue. On occasion policy advocates may simply hope that those with responsibility to make a policy work as intended will somehow find ways of adapting general ideas to fit the real world.

> The decision by several major states in 2014 and 2015 to bomb some of the insurgent groups involved in the complex civil wars in Syria is widely seen to be far from a decisive programme to end the war and can at best be seen as an expression of hostility towards some of the belligerent groups involved in the conflict, pending the possibility that some diplomatic action might create a coalition with a clear idea of how to end the conflict.

Definitions of policy implementation concern the enactment of policy after it has been legitimised by the government of a country but it is necessary to be cautious about what implementation might entail. Many policy decisions are never in themselves codified in law or even revealed explicitly to the public. Policy outputs can even be broad and ill-defined attempts to operationalise ideological or self-interested goals. They may also be motivated largely by the desire to show that the government or a political party is actively justifying its *raison d'être* within the political system by seeking to deal with problems that may not need their intervention save to calm social disquiet or demonstrate an attempt to deal with a matter that is beyond their capacity to remedy.

Policies appear as a set of concrete values but often enclose more multi-faceted intentions. A political party may be united only in the interest of gaining votes in order to ensure its leaders stay in power or more generally can remain in power in order to follow a specific ideological commitment which can then generate and inform any subsidiary policy aims that require some form of definition and legitimation. The result of these factors working jointly in the minds of political leaders is to create policies that are implemented with often differing and even conflicting aims.

One of the most dramatic policy failures in the United States was the eighteenth amendment to the Constitution, ratified in 1919, that prohibited the sale or manufacture of alcoholic drinks. The amendment was made as pressure from high-minded campaigners against insobriety was heightened by arguments that it would improve the efficiency of the armed forces in the Great War and divert cereal production to aid the war effort in more beneficial directions (Jones 1995: 426). 'The Prohibition experiment reflected a utopian faith that the alcohol problem could be eradicated by legislation ... but it proved impossible to enforce. Thousands of illicit stills were seized, millions of gallons of wine and spirits were destroyed and jail sentences for liquor offenses rose to 44,678 in 1932, by which time federal prisons were full to bursting. But because of Congressional parsimony there were never enough enforcement agents. Mostly political appointees, they were poorly paid and thus susceptible to bribery. A more fundamental difficulty was the extent of popular opposition ... In 1929 New York City possessed 3,000 speakeasies – twice the number of saloons before Prohibition began ... The worst consequence of Prohibition was to stimulate organized crime. Attracted by huge profits underworld gangs set out to control the illicit liquor business' (Jones 1995: 441–2). In 1933 following the landslide election of the Democrats to the White House under the Presidency of Franklin D. Roosevelt, the eighteenth amendment was repealed.

Discovering implementation

Descriptions of the governing process were in the nineteenth century largely premised on the Westminster model that incorporated the assumption that the essence of efficient and effective democratic government rested on the widespread acceptance of the 'rule of law'. This view maintained that policy was determined democratically by the core executive of a political system and was subsequently legitimised and refined through debate in the legislature. Once policy was legitimised the consequent demands had to be accepted and obeyed by the country's citizens. The philosophical underpinning of this idea is recognised in the writings of many late nineteenth century political theorists such as, in Britain, John Stuart Mill (1861) and Walter Bagehot (1867). Later enthusiasts for administrative science such as Graham Wallas (1934) and Oliver Sheldon (1925) insisted effective managers must clearly communicate to the lower orders of the bureaucracies concerned with policy implementation exactly what they must do and could assume that, if properly informed, orders would be carried out successfully

(Thomas 1978: 55–67). The fact that many policies were not implemented as their authors had intended was rarely explored until the second half of the twentieth century. An important step in the development of interest in policy implementation was Phillip Selznick's (1949) study of a major dam and irrigation project, guided by the Tennessee Valley Authority, which failed to fully measure up to the intentions of its policy makers. Later attention was directed to the failure of more radical social policies generated by President Johnson's 'War on Poverty' in the United States. Pressman and Wildavsky's (1973) study of implementation chronicles the difficulties faced by the programme as applied at the street level in the city of Oakland in California. They concluded that the failure to regenerate Oakland's economy was a consequence of the impossibility of ensuring coordination between the several non-federal, third sector and private agencies that were involved in the process. Many of the agencies had their own programmes for reviving the city and either disagreed with the Federal aim, or, whilst not opposing the Federal Government, had a preference for their own policies as they did not have the time and material resources to pursue their own ideas alongside those being pressed on them by other governments (Pressman and Wildavsky 1984: 98–102). Leaders in differing agencies also disagreed on who should take the lead in different elements of the project and often had diverse legal, financial and procedural methods of forwarding progress. A basic, and perhaps not surprising, view that emerges from their analysis is that the greater the number of organisations and individuals that are instrumental in the implementation of policy, the more likely it is that the policy will fail to be put into practice as its supporters intended. Writers such as Martha Derthick (1970; 1972), Helen Ingram (1977) and Hugh Heclo (1978) also underlined these conclusions by showing that without consultation between the various tiers of United States government it was difficult to develop any effective policy of regeneration at local level.

This prescriptive approach to implementation was given a more realistic treatment by James B. Rule (1973) and Christopher Hood (1976) who sensibly discussed the issue of policy implementation in terms of the limits of administration. Hood observed that there were firstly external factors outside the control of administrators such as a decline in financial resources or unanticipated consequences of a policy that may limit its effectiveness. There are further political limitations where groups who are the subject of policy change rebel against their restraints. A final group of limitations which Hood referred to as 'quasi-administrative limits' relate to the difficulties in laying down exact unambiguous rules to enable policy implementation and the consequent necessity for bureaucrats to be given some discretion in shaping policy edicts to suit differing social environments. Following the problems identified by Hood, Lewis Gunn (Gunn 1978; Hogwood and Gunn 1984: 200–206) typically laid down conditions that bureaucrats should attempt to achieve to ensure policy was implemented as its political authors intended. These conditions, which were suggested as goals for an ideal world, rather than aims that could in all cases be wholly achieved, are paraphrased as follows:

- Ensure that potential obstacles to perfect implementation are not outside the control of the administrators.
- Provide adequate time and sufficient resources for the programme.
- Ensure that the policy to be implemented is based upon a valid theory of cause and effect with few if any intervening links in the chain and that tasks are fully specified in correct sequence.

- Establish a single implementing agency that does not depend on other agencies for success.
- Ensure perfect communication and co-ordination and understanding and agreement on objectives.
- Ensure that those in authority can demand and obtain perfect compliance.

The various prescriptions on how government policy should be designed so as to ensure its successful implementation began to have an effect on the policy making process. Majone and Wildavsky (1984: 163–80) realised that there was considerable difficulty in defining implementation as a process that takes place after policy is determined and legitimised rather than as a process that may determine how policy is made in the first place. Most policy entrepreneurs are sufficiently rational to consider how their ideas can in practice be delivered at street level and will need to develop their ideas with the hope that their aims may not be distorted by those who deliver the policy or are affected by its demands. The view that the process of policy implementation was a top down process forged by governments laid to rest any search for a prescriptive recipe for perfect policy implementation. Andrew Dunsire (1978) depicted implementation as the continued interaction between authoritative government policy makers and interested public and private agencies. Barrett and Fudge (1981) developed a synthesis of a number of case studies of implementation which attempted to ascertain the factors that might create effective implementation between government and the actors with an interest in the process. They concluded that 'the relationship between policy and action could not be regarded as a simple transmission process but rather must be viewed as a complex assembly job involving the fitting together of different interests and priorities' (Barrett and Fudge 1981: 251). A fashionable variant of this theme during the Blair Government was an insistence that policy should be a product of joined-up governance (Chandler 2009: 67). The study points to issues that were reaffirmed in power dependence network theories in which organisations bargain with one another to secure policy initiatives that may be successfully implemented.

Top down or bottom up implementation?

By the 1970s theorists realised that it was very simplistic to look at failures of implementation as a consequence of the authoritative policy authors being unable to anticipate or communicate how their chosen policy will be dealt with by the agencies that are charged with putting the ideas into practice. Critics of what had been seen as essentially a top down model argued that in practice policy can often be developed through a bottom up process. One of the earliest essays in this genre was a study by Michael Lipsky (1971), who argued that policy implementation was dependent on the attitudes and behaviour of 'street level bureaucrats', as he termed the individuals on the ground who actually deliver the required outcomes for their policy principles. These anonymous faces in a crowd are, for example, the teachers who are required by a government or school board to adopt a different syllabus or punish unruly children using non-violent techniques or the soldier ordered on a suicidal mission to attack a well-fortified enemy trench. Faced with difficult or impossible requests the street level bureaucrat may adopt a number of strategies. If they confined themselves to Hirschman's (1970) celebrated formula of exit, voice or loyalty, they may simply leave their post, although professionals are rarely driven to the length of immediately taking such an option without at least voicing their concerns. In the longer term, recruitment to careers in which the practitioners face difficult or, for soldiers, dangerous demands is likely to be limited and the turnover of staff may be excessive, as in the example, cited later in this chapter, of the failure in the United Kingdom to recruit sufficient numbers of school teachers.

Within a liberal democracy, voice and loyalty may be complementary strategies rather alternatives. The loyal street level bureaucrat will follow their orders as best they can but may also make known, through their representative associations, their objections to the demands made upon them. In practice, most street level bureaucrats and professionals simply follow as far as they can what is reasonably feasible and make up their own provisions and amendments to circumvent the difficulties imposed by a new policy. Fudging, rather than exit, voice or loyalty is perhaps the most preferred option (Laws and Hajer 2008: 410–12). Michael Lipsky (1980) suggests that policy outputs are in the end what the street level bureaucrats make of the situation handed down to them by the core executives. Health workers or police routinely have to make decisions as to which of the many demands made upon them they can meet given the lack of funds and human resources at their disposal.

In the United Kingdom in 2016 Rotherham District Council social workers and South Yorkshire police failed to fulfil their duty to prevent the scandal of sexual grooming of children in their area. This may be due to misplaced judgements on the seriousness of such a problem, but also it is a reflection of cuts to resources from government to local and police authorities to carry out their many tasks.

The South Yorkshire Police Force was required to save nearly £50 million between 2011 and 2015 and the Local Authority faced cuts of £23 million in 2014. As a documentary on the South Yorkshire police revealed, at the divisional level the force was unable to effectively police two areas of Sheffield with problems concerning law and order with equal effectiveness as there were simply insufficient funds to keep a sufficient number of police patrolling the area and investigating local crimes (BBC 2014).

Fudging policy implementation is not necessarily confined to the street level bureaucrats but may be the result of rebellion from middle managers and indeed may be a reaction from any stratum in a managerial hierarchy that feels its interests or capacities are threatened by change.

Howard Elcock (1990) observed that the implementation of the 'Next Steps' initiatives proposed by the Thatcher Governments that attempted to restructure the British Civil Service was, in relation to its attempts to decentralise many central government tasks to arm's length agencies, more likely to be obstructed by 'people and groups further down the organisation's hierarchy who do not agree with their leaders' judgement that the balance between centralisation and decentralisation ought to be changed. "Street level bureaucrats", the staff directly responsible for the provision of services, are likely either to be, or to become enthusiasts for decentralisation. However, middle managers are almost bound to lose status and control to the decentralised units and will, therefore both oppose their establishment, and restrict their discretion' (Elcock 1990: 71).

The build-up of literature showing how supposedly subordinate individuals or levels of government could thwart the intentions of policy principles prompted Paul Mazmanian and Daniel Sabatier (1981; 1983) to develop a more sophisticated view of the implementation process that could reconcile the top down view of implementation with the studies that showed that there was a significant bottom up influence on the implementation of policy and hence its further evolution. They identified a number of variables that needed to be considered to secure implementation relating both to the difficulty and complexity of the policy in question and the resource dependency available to the implementing agencies and those organisations or individuals who are the target of their concern. They also identified the evolutionary character of policy, as shown in Figure 14.1.

Mazmanian and Sabatier's ideas remain in essence a top down model driven largely by policy making elites who are attuned to take into consideration the need to develop both structures and policy solutions that can be implemented in order to ensure that the street level bureaucrats undertake the activities that are expected from them. They emphasise, as does Gunn, that the goals of the policy initiative must be made clear and communicable to institutions that are to implement the policy objectives. However, they recognise that these are ideal aims that are not easily replicated in circumstances where compliance with non-statutory demands is involved. They must accept that such organisations will have

Stages of the dependent variables of the implementation process

1. Policy outputs of implementing agencies

    ↓

2. Compliance of target groups

    ↓

3. Actual impacts

    ↓

4. Perceived Impacts

    ↓

5. Changes in policy

Figure 14.1 Stages of the dependent variables of the implementation process (Adapted from Mazmanian and Sabatier 1983: 40)

the option of not accepting the government's demands. They also point out that the initial attempt to ensure implementation of the policy will be at best only partially successful. Sound policy implementation requires governments to evaluate the impact of their policy initiatives and if necessary understand why they may not have met their expectations, so that the policy may be reformed and matured to deal with the bottlenecks or intransigence that have stood in its path. Mazmanian and Sabatier (1983: 42, 278) also argue that the process of evolution is often analysed by commentators over too short a period, giving the impression that policies generally fail. It may take many years to perfect an initiative and success should be measured over, at least, a ten rather than five years' duration. In this context the long-lived Conservative Governments of Thatcher and Major were able to significantly restructure thinking on the welfare state, the private provision of public services and control of local government expenditure, despite many initial failures. Sabatier (1986) and later with Jenkins-Smith (Sabatier and Jenkins-Smith 1986) continued developing this model of the inter-dependency of policy formation and implementation in their Advocacy Coalition Framework. Policy, they maintain, is formulated by coalitions between elites in government and key agencies with views compatible with the government's ideology which form powerful policy communities that can steer through policy objectives, refine these when they appear to be moving off course, and consequently implement the policy interests following the accepted procedures of political society.

The power relationship

As in the emergence of a policy issue on a government's agenda and its subsequent refinement, the relationship between governments and the external interests concerning policy implementation depends on the distribution of power where there is conflict, and also the degree of common understanding and similarity of vision between the interests and elements in government that support an implementation strategy. Power rests with government through its constitutional authority and legal capacity to use violence to force compliance against those who seek to defy its authority. In failed states, where such capacity is non-existent, the implementation of uniform policy is largely undermined. In stable developed states implementation is much more centred in the capacity of a government to will the compliance of its directives. However, certain barriers may stand in the way of securing complete obedience to legitimised directives.

Governments must have the capacity to provide the resources to enable policy to be implemented by providing funding for any necessary capital investment and payments to those who must undertake or police the work. In underdeveloped regimes lack of finance and the resultant incapacity to train or buy in professional staff in areas such as health care or engineering can seriously damage a nation's technological capacity to provide much needed welfare and economic development. Usually the absence of resources means that poorer regimes advance many of the policies that are considered essential to public well-being in wealthier regimes but have few resources to enable such policies to be realised. However much a policy of free health care may be important to a nation's well-being, where the majority of the population live in comparative poverty, it is fiscally impossible for such nations to develop such a service that could be both comprehensive, effective and efficient.

Augustine Afari-Adomah (2009) in a study of the evolution of health insurance policy in Ghana shows how a policy advanced because insufficient government funding had undermined earlier policy to ensure free care in hospitals continues to be undermined as sufficient and regularly released government funds are not available to help the poorest and most geographically isolated in society.

In decentralised regimes, such as the United States, where a national government is obliged to respect the powers constitutionally allocated to regional states or local government, the central federal government may, in effect, have to bribe less wealthy state governments to accept centrally devised policies that, under the constitution, they are not obliged to accept.

'One of the most costly mandates passed by Congress over the past twenty five years is the requirement for state and local government to provide a "free and appropriate" education for all handicapped children. Traditions of local control of schools notwithstanding, this landmark piece of legislation imposed federal standards and protection on the entire field of special education with federal funds financing only a small portion of the costs of serving this new education target group' (Posner 2007: 126). Without, however, an element of federal funding pressure from educational interests, Congress would not have allowed the Bill to pass as an unfunded mandate on states and local governments (Posner 2007: 126–159).

The necessary resources to marshal professional help for advancing implementation of technical activities can create a further problem for wealthy advanced nations as well as poorer regimes. Without extensive investment in the training of doctors and nurses it would clearly be difficult to establish state-run health services. However, the development of professional expertise poses serious problems for the general public and most politicians, as many aspects of public concern, such as medical care, allow professional groups to dominate the policy making processes specific to their expertise. As Frank Fischer points out, 'It is increasingly recognized that as societies become more complex so does the importance of expert advice in matters relating to governance. But professional expertise is also seen as a barrier to meaningful citizen participation' (Fischer 2009: 17). This is the case in relation to policy implementation, not just in the role of professionals in administrating and interpreting policy, but in the specialist advice given by experts during the refining of policy in designing a policy that may work in practice.

However, it must be kept in mind that many governments have sufficient resources to enable them to try to ensure that specialist advisors will work in their interest rather than that of their profession. It is unlikely that the core executive of a governing party or coalition will be prepared to take on board the professional advice of an organisation which is ideologically far apart from its own values and that of the electorate. Within pluralist competitive democracies advice on, for example, health care, is largely taken from the leading advocates of the most popular scientific paradigms, rather than minority view points based on minority medical frameworks. This tendency raises the issue of whether public policy on many specialist interests is due to the capacity of a government to capture and develop experts from a particular ideological approach to issues such as economic stability, health care or crime prevention or whether those with expertise in such areas can capture the minds of the core executive of a party or government. As discussed by Foucault in his study of mental health, or argued in studies using the ACF framework, such changes in the mode of thinking within society are the result of long-term changes in which both technological, economic, moral and self-interested changes interact in complex webs of relationships.

It may turn out to be all right on the night

An assumption by earlier studies of implementation has been that once the format of a policy has been refined by the legislative process or as a decree through discourse between policy gate-keepers, policy advocates and the state bureaucracy, it is reasonably clear what is to be achieved. However, in many cases policies are not received as clear messages to subordinates as to what they should do and in some instances are never intended to be clear. Legitimated policy is often by no means a well-refined product but a statement of intent whose details are left to other agencies to put into practice. Policy encompasses not only a usually publicly stated aim but also a sub-text of the further motives held by its advocates that are never openly submitted to public gaze. These may include personal self-interest to outflank the aims of a political rival, or simply to bury a wicked issue by cobbling together a few ideas that are highly unlikely to be effective but may give the impression that the government is responding to public pressure.

Some element of deception, to suggest that there is a sound and well-meaning policy in place with little evidence that it is implemented, is understandable in some seriously underdeveloped nations. Having a strategy of regimes whose elites wish to appear more socially concerned than they are financially able to practise is to will into existence legislation without providing the resources to effectively implement the policy.

Such action was well entrenched as policy among the Conservative and Liberal Parties in pre-civil war Spain who boasted that they had advanced social welfare policies but never provided the resources for the inspectorates necessary to police these policies. It is less acceptable in the present age where the Conservative dominated governments in the United Kingdom have prided themselves on devolving powers to local government but at the same time greatly decrease the funding given to this area. In Britain the pressures placed on school teachers by the national curriculum and the creation of a far more invasive inspectorate, OFSTED, in the late 1980s, led to serious shortages of staff in the teaching professions due to many resignations and a lack of enthusiasm from graduate level job seekers to enter a highly pressured and yet relatively low paid profession. The problem had to be resolved through higher wages and ensuring greater discretion for teachers on how to implement the national curriculum (Dolton and Chung 2004: 89). A similar problem creating a shortage of teachers in 2015 is argued to be a product of financial austerity and further demands for teaching quality that undermine teachers' professional vocation (Weale 2015).

The development of policy that many who agree to its aims secretly hope may never be fully implemented is particularly marked in global politics. A succession of climate talks leading to widely, if not universally, accepted treaties has yet to be translated into firm policies that will ensure serious reductions in carbon dioxide emissions within most of its signatories.

Certain countries whose economy is strongly dependent on the exploitation of fossil fuels, such as Russia, China or Canada, have agreed to targets to decrease harmful greenhouse gases but show little sign of developing the consequent more detailed policies to secure the broad aims of the international treaties (Gilley 2012; Schreurs 2010). As Hugh Atkinson observes, 'Tackling climate change necessitates long-term strategies and commitments. Yet politicians invariably think in the short to medium term, governed by the exigencies of the electoral cycle. In short they want to get elected' (Atkinson 2015: 35–6).

The problems that beset common implementation of policies in the European Union similarly suggest that differing states with differing cultures, even when they are linked to a broad support for liberal democratic values, find it difficult to accept common policies. The Union was only able to form if premised on the agreement that European policy would be implemented by its members states. There are several countries that have opted out of certain policy frameworks, most notably those like Britain or Poland who have refused to adopt the Euro as their currency. Moreover the evidence of corruption within some members states concerning, for example, the distribution of funding to farmers under the Common Agricultural Policy, indicates the difficulties in establishing means to secure policy implementation across state boundaries (Jones 2001: 218–19).

Within most countries many policy initiatives that have been refined by state legislatures and central government bureaucracies and subsequently are legitimised in law are, at best, statements of intent rather than clear blueprints as to how the policies should be practised. In Western Europe as in the United States since the 1970s there has been genuine concern among successive governments that older industrial heartlands are failing to regenerate following the departure of many heavy industries to nations in the Far East and South America which have more plentiful supplies of raw materials and a more numerous and less expensive labour force. However, one government's policy succeeds another with little evidence of major change in the economic fortunes of these cities.

In Britain the issue of declining industrial cities led to broad policy proposals by the Conservative Governments, such as Urban Development Zones since the 1970s, but these do not appear to have effectively resolved the problem. The Conservative Government that came into office in 2015 is currently developing policy to create 'a Northern Power House' by rearranging powers in several major industrial areas in the north of England, such as Manchester, through the creation of new regional authorities to take over some of the strategic services such as transport and health care and placing them under the control of an elected executive mayor.

None of these policies to devolve power to these cities actually provide any substantive basis for resolving the problems of de-industrialisation, apart from suggesting that the government may be wise to appear concerned about the issue.

In practice such action can be read, as with attempts by previous governments to resolve the problem, as more an attempt to demonstrate that the party in power is dealing with the issue and therefore should continue to receive popular support, rather than that they have any serious ideas as to how to revive a local area, assuming they have a serious wish to do so. The advocates for the policy of devolution of power to these cities, whilst maintaining at national level a policy of economic austerity that prevents them from re-capitalising local infrastructure, suggest they are simply handing over responsibility for the problem to others given they have no wish to provide the resources to enable serious changes to be secured. Often in such circumstances policy advocates may hope that, with luck, others on the ground may implement policies within their broad statement of policy wishes to secure what their central administration cannot or will not achieve.

Gerry Stoker (2002: 417–34) has argued that the Blair Governments adopted what he termed government by lottery when seeking to change the role of local governments by developing a range of, on occasion, contradictory policies, for example some regional multi-level governments into unitary authorities but not immediately insisting that all local government systems were pushed into a unitary framework. In as much as some governments work on this principle, this behaviour is not so much a lottery but the cautious testing of a policy idea within differing environments steered by human agency of observation, evaluation and further decision making.

A further element that subverts the initial policy intentions of a government following implementation is that the passage of time and the appearance of new policy problems, either real or imagined, can erode serious interest in shaping earlier policies. Ideas put forward by governments as frameworks for creating popular support, such as President Johnson's 'War on Poverty' or the 'Big Society' initiative of the 2010 coalition government in Britain, may soon outlive their usefulness as a means of engaging public support and enthusiasm. There are a limited number of policy initiatives that a government may pursue at any one time and hence certain demands become largely forgotten within the core executive, when they lose their capacity to make media headlines. In such circumstances agencies may not pursue these forgotten issues with the same zeal and resources as in the past or may subvert the practice of that policy to satisfy their own interests rather than that of its original policy advocates.

Conclusion

It has been argued in earlier chapters that public policies are not always designed to be implemented in a uniform manner and that policy gatekeepers may sanction policy proposals without much idea as to how the initiative can be secured in practice but realise that they must be seen to be attempting to resolve a 'wicked issue'. Governments are often unclear as to the reception by the public of their policy proposals and will leave the details of implementation to other agencies and also expect that they may have to revisit a policy to ensure their central aims can more easily be accepted and implemented with fewer loopholes that may be used to circumvent the central policy objectives. Policy cannot be engineered with a degree of certainty to instantly enable perfect implementation. The process of policy implementation may take some time to reach its aims but through trial and error, aided by evaluation of results, the policy agent can often perfect the institutions, resources and rules necessary to ensure the policy is successful. However as, Massof Hyder (1984: 15) points out:

> A policy is only a tentative solution to a problem. That is all it can be in fact, however convinced its particular advocates might be of its effectiveness, for we cannot be certain of the policy's results in advance ... Policy is often a hypothesis bound up in uncertainties.

15 Policy evolution

A determined executive may often make initially unconsidered assumptions that agents and citizens will accept the policies they put forward or may develop underfunded or badly structured policies that allow agents to undermine the policy author's intentions. However, several treatises in the 1980s, such as Mazmanian and Sabatier (1983) or Barrett and Fudge (1981), pointed out that policy implementation is a longer-term game in which principals over time react to the difficulties encountered with implementation and amend their ideas accordingly.

The idea of evolution within the social sciences is far from a new development and in economics was certainly recognised by Joseph Schumpeter and further developed by Nelson and Winter (1982). An organisation will evolve by learning from its successes and mistakes, building up expertise and knowledge about what strategies and innovation may work. It is a process involving trial and error that may be built into a government's machinery for seeking effective policy change. Governments show an increasing awareness of chances of failure as much as success in their policies and create systems to guard against the possibility of rectifying mistakes before they have created too much damage. It is frequently the case that policies are borrowed from experience in other organisations or countries and tried in pilot studies and then subjected to long-term evaluation before becoming part of the accepted policy structures of the state. The argument that public policy is in a continuous state of flux through incremental change in both the form of policies but also how it is interpreted and implemented over time has strong resonance with Lindblom and Braybrooke's ideas on muddling through.

Later studies have further developed such ideas by arguing that the public policy process and its outputs must effectively be seen not as completed events but, as Peter John (1998) pointed out and the ACF framework shows, abstracted points in an evolving process. It is of value therefore to consider the social forces that determine such constant change and also the possibilities that have been suggested to manage and cope with such change. Peter John (1998: 182–8) suggests that the various elements within the policy process should be seen as the evolution of ideas and action:

> Single level approaches focus on one key principle as the foundation for the political system, and they often assume that political systems are stable as a result. What may be called evolutionary theory regards all these elements as continually interacting with each other over time. The institutions are sets of constraints upon actors that can sometimes be reshaped if actors so choose. Interests are important because they structure the sets of choices for other actors. Economic power structures similarly offer alternative choices. Individual self-interest drives the machine

and interacts with the constraints. But what drives policy is the continual interaction between these features. And evolution is the direction in which integrative accounts of public policy are heading.

(John 1998: 182–3)

The depiction of policy development as evolution is an analogy that should not, however, as John observes, be taken so far as to parallel the Darwinian view of natural selection, in which chance mutations in the DNA of living organisms occasion advantages for the organism that provide it with a greater chance of survival within its environment.

Policy as an evolutionary process

Although many policies evolve, it needs to be remembered as was pointed out in earlier chapters that citizens become accustomed to a policy initiative and, if it is continually pressed on them, accustomed to what they are required to do (Bowen 1982). Certain policies, such as compulsory attendance for children in state or privately run schools, become a fixture in the 'habitus' of most people's daily lives so that few will even recognise that such behaviour is the outcome of policy actions. Nevertheless, whilst the broad consensus on such principled policy stands may be habitual there are frequently debates as to how the basic standpoint may be achieved that lead to, as the example of compulsory education demonstrates, considerable conflict and evolution of how that policy is put into practice. Over time the development of new technologies, exposure to other societies and changing customs and beliefs will usually entail incremental and on occasion revolutionary changes in how fundamental beliefs are enshrined and enacted in public policy outputs at any specific time.

Policies will be subject to evolution as a response to changes in the social and political climate in which they were originally constructed. Frank Baumgartner and Bryan D. Jones (1991, 1993) observed that the policy agenda is neither a fixed nor a constantly changing process but one in which periods of stability can, to use their term, be subject to punctuated equilibrium. Answers to a particular problem can remain static for long periods, but as social values and environmental changes mount up, critics of once established solutions create a climate where policy is re-thought and re-fashioned.

Within both Britain and the United States the post-Second World War development of nuclear fission for peaceful purposes created huge optimism that harnessing this technology to produce electricity could provide boundless energy supplies for years to come and also develop material for atomic weapons. Accidents at Calder Hall in Britain and Three Mile Island in the United States plus concern over the disposal of nuclear waste and worries over the international spread of nuclear weapons by the 1980s had eroded enthusiasm for the development of further nuclear power generation within both Britain and the United States. However, due to later realisation that concentrating electricity generation on the burning of fossil fuels would accelerate global warming, there has been, especially in Britain, a return to developing new generations of nuclear power stations.

Policy ideas appear to be at their most potent when powerful interests establish a strong lobby to support a mutually beneficial course of action. However, circumstances may always over time break apart networks or advocacy coalitions and within liberal democratic and some autocratic regimes there can be limits to the extent to which powerful government interest networks can wholly act against the concerns of their civil society.

Baumgartner and Jones are happy to suggest that their idea of punctuated equilibrium can be seen as a theory (Baumgartner, Jones and Mortensen 2014: 59), but their claim, such that it is, misses the point that external to the rather narrowly interpreted world of policy studies is a vast field of theoretical and empirical analysis on social change that needs to be addressed if any understanding of the causes of change and evolution in policy outcomes and instruments is to be achieved. In order to understand the nature of policy change or stasis it is necessary to consider theories of policy revolt and revolution. Such an exercise would provide a further and important channel to link the study of public policy to the larger world of sociology and history.

Revolt and revolution

A distinction needs to be made between the various forms of social evolution. In many instances, as discussed in previous chapters, policy may, as Lindblom and Braybrooke suggested, be a process of muddling through, but eventually constant tinkering in the setting of the policy rules usually comes to an end in months and only rarely a few years. Further evolution may subsequently follow, as those who implement policy at street level revise their stance towards their task or judicial rulings reinterpret the original policy intentions, but usually on the smaller points of the policy. Within stable liberal democratic polities policy evolution is however a frequent process as governments decide that it is appropriate and expedient to radically change policies on particular issues. However, governments have only a limited capacity to research and reposition policies if they are not to risk the danger of overloading the political system. Thus most governments will at any one time set out a policy agenda for a year or, on occasion, for the term of their elected office, that will concentrate on one or two major reforms to the postponement of other desired goals.

President Obama concentrated during his first term in office on the restructuring of health care provision in the United States and his second term in office moved on to efforts to reform gun control but, given the pressure of external events such as foreign policy towards the Middle East and the ever present need to ensure economic growth, his administration had insufficient capacity to forward further highly contentious policy reforms.

Policy evolution is for most governments a decision about priorities and opportunities. The forces that may determine governments to revisit and restructure existing policies can emerge from a wide number of environmental variables. Technological change may create new opportunities, especially where this affects the economic capacity of the state. New threats from external movements such as hostile foreign governments or terrorist groups may raise issues of defence and security to a prominent position on the government's list of priorities. Change may also be spurred on by specific ideological or ethical interests of the major actors in any governing coalition. Radical policy change will also usually follow popular dissatisfaction with a particular area of policy, although often government gate-keepers may themselves create this mood rather than simply be following the general tenor of social values.

A rather different framework for piecemeal policy evolution may be expected within autocratic political systems as opposed to stable liberal democracies. Within auto-cracies policy change may be less concerned with developing new opportunities or steering through popular demands than with defensively controlling new innovations that may be damaging to the equilibrium of the state.

> The development of the I-phone and World Wide Web has created major restructuring of how we communicate with each other and also obtain our knowledge of the outside world. In autocracies such as North Korea or to a lesser extent the People's Republic of China, political elites have battled to control this technology whilst in more open pluralist societies the new methods of social interaction have been broadly welcomed even though there are serious policy problems on the margins of such changes such as the leaking of state secrets on a global scale, the opening up of new areas for fraud and the potential undermining of personal liberties that are still being worked out by governments.

In respect to policy itself a few basic pointers can be made beginning with the issue raised in earlier chapters that the more technical a policy and the less it involves unwanted change for its intended recipients the less likely will it be the trigger for a revolt. A major factor determining the pattern of revolt is also the nature of a regime. In a totalitarian regime it is less likely that subjects will collectively be made aware of common hostility to those who make and implement policy as control by the autocrats over the media and the use of surveillance and arrest of dissidents may make it difficult to form let alone oper-ationalise as outright rebellion. Nevertheless, continued failures of a ruling elite to tend to the needs and desires of their citizens may lead to the development of many individual acts of defiance that build up eventually into an endemic inclination within civil society to distrust their leaders which in turn may fuel the creation of sub-cultures of political and economic behaviour outside the policy framework laid down by the autocratic machine.

> In the Soviet Union it proved impossible to organise the agricultural system wholly under state control as many farmers and peasants illicitly hid food stocks from govern-ment inspectors and opened up an underground economy of trading produce outside the control of the state.

In such circumstances, when the capacity of the autocracy to create a reign of fear in their electorate breaks down, often due to divisions as in the USSR within the ruling elite, there develops a rebellion and an era of rapid policy change. Within less totali-tarian autocracies where a succession of rulers seek to dominate a poor and largely agrarian society, policy made at the centre is more likely to be ignored and subverted by the periphery.

In some acquisitive autocratic regimes the principal motive of the gate-keepers in the state will be highly conservative, seeking to retain a system which provides those in power with wealth and security against a wide range of disaffected groups which may be seeking fundamental change in the state but are just as likely to be wishing to sup-plant the existing corrupt government for their own self-interest. Military and political *coups d'état*, often violent in character, may be far from radical but simply, in terms of public policy, supplant like with like.

In states such as Nigeria there have since independence been governments with military regimes following on from a preceding military regime or periods of civilian rule supplanting government by Generals. However, many of these changes have in part been motivated by ethnic divisions and self-interest and had relatively little impact on domestic and foreign policy within the nation (Hill 2012).

Within a liberal democracy rebellion is far less likely to lead to breakdown of the policy making elites rather than the withdrawal or amendment of policies on which there is substantive and deeply felt opposition within the civic culture. Exactly when this point is reached will of course differ in relation to the confidence gate-keepers have in their own ability to override dissent and this will also be contingent on how they read their own situation and that of their party with respect to any impending election. As within autocracies, the unity of the gate-keeping elites on the advisability of the contentious policy will also be a factor that determines how far concessions will be made. This basic framework may be illustrated in Figure 15.1.

Such a diagram, however, does not go far in providing any explanation for the success or failure of rebellion. Numerous questions need to be asked about the political and social factors that may create disunity in government at any particular time for any particular policy. Successful dissent against a policy can emerge from the refusal of key specialised professions to accept the policy. Establishing new rules for doctors or

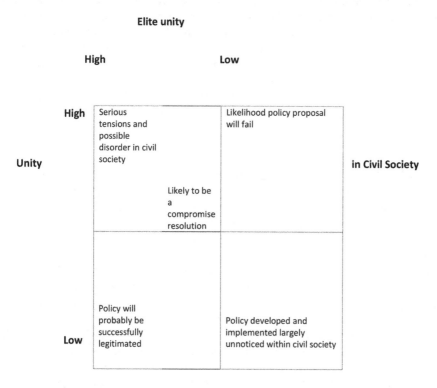

Figure 15.1 Tensions between governing elites and civil society

bankers is far harder to legitimate without the express consent of the profession than, for example, proposals to close libraries or sell local authority housing. There are also many potential scenarios that can lead to sufficient unity within civil society to challenge a government through rioting, civil disobedience or simply an obvious shift of votes from the governing to opposition parties. Most rebellions against policy or for that matter popular acceptance of major policy changes will have their own peculiarities and are arguably best understood through interpretive narratives.

Revolution

Rapid policy change can, however, occur on a more fundamental basis through revolutions, which are frequently seen as sudden and rapid breaks with the past but can also be used as, for example, in the phrase 'industrial revolution', to denote a longer period of change. Where such events take place few public policy arenas are unaffected and within either short or more lengthy periods little remains of previous practice. There are many definitions of what a revolution may entail but among the most concise, Michael Kimmel (1990: 6) suggests that 'Revolutions are attempts by subordinate groups to transform the social foundations of political power'. If we follow this description, within a revolution, groups of people who have been alienated from the policy process supplant groups that enjoy this status and bring forward new ideology and values of ethics and self-interest to replace the values that were rooted in the preceding system. Given the centrality of such values to the content of public policy, much will change should a revolution be successful. However, it is clear that many attempts at revolution fail and that there is much theoretical argument concerning the circumstances in which the ruling elite of a state may be sufficiently weakened so as to be unable to defend their interests. On many occasions a serious attempt by the oppressed and aggrieved of society may be undermined by what is often termed 'a counter-revolution' as threatened elite interests regroup to oppose change.

The bases of most revolutionary changes are complex and need to be explained as a process from the perspective of a range of pressures and events that lead up to attempts to restructure a society. Within this study the ideological background of such major events have been discussed in relation to Marxist theory and also the acceptance in the United States and Britain of New Right values since the 1980s. Few theorists would, however, fully except the Marxist theory of class struggle as the basis of revolution, although much can be said of Barrington-Moore's (1967) analysis of the differing interactions of social economic groups to technical change and the power of the state as a basis for explaining the nineteenth and twentieth centuries' breakdown of monarchic and aristocratic societies into liberal democracies, communist or fascist regimes. His arguments are based largely on an assessment of the extent to which the ruling elite within such states grasp the opportunities given by technological change or seek with disastrous consequences to retain the *status quo*. More firmly than Moore, Theda Skocpol (1979; 1985) sees the state as an autonomous structure standing for its own interests rather than being a representation of the interests of a specific economic class. Revolutions, she argues, come from pressures on the state from groups in society that are aware of successful revolutions in other regimes and wish to diffuse their cultures into the state that rules them. Thus, in her institutionalist model, revolutions only succeed if there is a serious weakness in the state. This may be a consequence of invasion or a breakdown in autonomy through the actions of foreign powers or through civil strife among the bureaucrats and politicians who control the state.

The position of the state as a central element within the context of revolution is developed in the works of Charles Tilly, who perceives the state as an entity that will constantly be seeking to expand its power over civil society within its boundaries and those outside it. However, Tilly recognises that any state will harbour subordinate and conflicting power blocks that for reasons of their own self-interest reject the power of the state. Tilly (1978: 216–17) sets out what he views as an idealised recipe for a revolutionary sequence as follows:

1 gradual mobilisation of contenders making exclusive claims to governmental control and/or unacceptable to the members of the polity;
2 rapid increase in the number of people accepting those claims and/or rapid expansion of the coalition including the unacceptable or exclusive contenders;
3 unsuccessful efforts by the government ... to suppress the alternative coalition and/ or the acceptance of its claims;
4 establishment by the alternative coalition of effective control over some portion of government – a territorial branch, a functional subdivision, a portion of its personnel;
5 struggles of the alternative coalition to maintain or expand that control;
6 reconstruction of a single polity through the victory of the alternative coalition, through its defeat, or through the establishment of a *modus vivendi* between the alternative coalition and some or all of the old members; fragmentation of the revolutionary coalition;
7 reimposition of routine governmental control throughout the subject population.

Tilly points out following this sequencing that many attempts at revolution fail and hence despite a period of social turbulence and violence in terms of policy little may change. However, where revolutions are wholly or in part successful there may be occasions when there is a substantive overhaul of many of the existing policies of the state and this may, due to the capacities of the state in terms of an overload of tasks, lead to a lengthy process of turbulence and change in public policy.

From a different perspective of revolutionary change brought about by the need to seize the advantages provided by new technologies, it can be suggested that many of the most potent revolutions occur largely without bloodshed in stable liberal democracies when governments are elected with new ideological and ethical values.

The victory of Mrs Thatcher in 1979 in the United Kingdom began a sustained, and arguably still, continuing revolution in the nation's public policy as she consolidated New Right as opposed to Disraelian Tory values within the Conservative Party and then within the country by the replacement of the mixed economy social democratic ideology that had been dominant within the political system following the 1945 Attlee government.

The factors that lead to revolution cannot for Tilly be understood in any basic economic class or interest group but through an historical analysis of the interactions of the groups that have the capacity to compete for power within the state. Such histories will in large measure be specific to that political system, although there will always be constants in terms of personal motivation of leaders of contending groups to gain their self-interest. As the revolutionary conflict proceeds, policy will be actively changed and then perhaps through counter-revolution be reassembled until a *status quo* arrives. On occasion, as a result of revolution, there may be many years before any new settlement emerges to structure public policy within a territory. It is also the case that in a few countries, as in Somalia, Libya or the interface between Iraq and Syria, the nation state may break down and fail and consequently it is difficult to perceive whether the rules, such as they may be, in these areas amount to anything that could be seen as public policy as opposed to rules that are intermittently and often violently imposed by warring factions.

Policy narratives

The frameworks for revolution as developed by Moore, Skocpol and Tilley may vary in emphasis on, for example, the role of the state as an independent variable, but they generally avoid class based theory for determining the framework of rebellion in favour of more narrative frameworks for understanding how many variables and circumstances can contribute to rapid change. Interpretive methodology as a means of explaining the subject elements of public policy within a framework that can accept positivist reality has highlighted the value of seeking to explain policy initiatives through creating plausible narratives, in effect stories, of how there is a need for and value in a policy. This tendency has been paralleled with an attempt to create a template for understanding public policy with strong links to the ACF, which has been labelled as the Narrative Policy Framework (NPF). This model provides a more formal template specifically relating to policy decisions that can classify each driver and element of the policy process set within micro, meso and macro levels of analysis, which correspond to the individual, group and institutional settings. Thus it requires attention to the social setting of the policy in question, the characters, that is the individuals involved in the policy process who may be seen both as heroes and villains, and a plot which denotes the relationship between the policy actors and a moral that is the policy outcome (McBeth, Jones and Shanahan 2014: 229–234). Specific elements of policy analysis can then be fitted into this framework of variables. Whilst the resultant checklist may provide a useful means of scoping the variables needed to understand policy development, it can however produce a rather cumbersome framework to assess issues which most earlier models have brought to researchers' attention. Moreover, the problem with this methodology, as with the ACF, is that the development of a narrative may cover all the variables such as ideas and context, but may still be challenged by other equally plausible narratives depending on the subjective emotions and values of each actor. Stories may be very credible for certain individuals or groups with similar backgrounds and characteristics but make little sense to others. In themselves, such approaches do not provide a template to seriously analyse the power relationships that determine who makes policy and the interests that the power elites and policy gate-keepers wish to pursue. Nevertheless the approach does introduce into policy analysis discussion of the role different subjective interests may play in the development of policy issues and in particular the fact that developing a plausible narrative to convince others of a particular solution to a policy problem or opportunity is, as discussed in Chapter 12, an important consideration in the question of how policy becomes accepted and diffused within social systems.

Engineering change

The evolution of policy is not simply the successful outcome of chance but is, to some extent, the result of agency rather than structure. Some decisions are also rather difficult to portray as the outcome of a process of successful policy evolution involving an insidious shift in public opinion, as opposed to being the outcome of a single or small group of agents.

> Crossman's weekend brainwave to set up an enquiry to restructure local government in Britain and Mrs Thatcher's insistence on the poll tax are examples illustrated in Chapter 6. In the United States, Nixon's concern 'by hook or by crook' to find information about his electoral rivals that led to the Watergate incident effectively dominated any of his attempts at policy initiation in his second term of office.

It may of course be argued that the examples of policy decisions that seem to stem from the decision of a powerful individual are part of an inescapable evolutionary change. One chance mutation in a bacterium may ensure that it is not susceptible to antibiotics such that it will proliferate and create serious infections throughout the world. However, the analogy of biological evolution cannot seriously fit an explanation of the evolution of societies in which reason and self-selected preferences determine the social and to some extent the environmental world in which we operate. The idea that President Obama or Margaret Thatcher came to power as a result of a lottery among the billions of atoms that made up both their person and their environment, let alone the arrangement of the thought processes in their brains, is no explanation of practical value to the issue of how we can understand the policy process.

An approach to dealing with the complexity of many policy problems is that they should be seen as a puzzle and solved through deliberation on how it may be resolved (Freeman 2008: 372–6; Winship 2006: 109–121).

> Christopher Winship (2006: 116–17) cites the resolution of a dispute chronicled by Wendy Espeland (1998) concerning planners who wished to build a large dam to supply water on land within a Native American reservation in Arizona. After years of conflict, the problem was resolved by newer more socially aware engineers who suggested building many smaller dams that did not entail flooding huge tracts of the reservation.

It can, however, be objected that whilst puzzle solving may be a useful metaphor concerning how policy dilemmas can be resolved, this does not take us very far in learning how to resolve policy problems. As should be clear throughout this book, there are numerous types of policy problems and opportunities and to some extent each policy puzzle requires different and unique means to resolve the issue. It is not possible in this study to itemise let alone critically evaluate the range of techniques that must be employed in a fully rounded grasp of the social sciences. Indeed few people can on their own master all elements of social sciences that may range from an understanding of psychology to economics. Moreover, few individuals have the capacity to be equally cognisant of the application of both quantitative techniques such as statistical evaluation of social preferences and the qualitative ability to, for example, evaluate the sincerity of a subject whom they have interviewed.

Complexity theory

A more valuable contribution to the question of how to engineer and direct policy change in a constantly evolving social and technological environment is presented by the late twentieth century advances in the natural sciences and mathematics broadly christened 'complexity theory', concerning the methods of prediction where numerous and apparently random variables had to be taken into account, which gave rise to the possibility of applying new techniques to renew interest in social science as a science. Complexity theories aimed at making sense of apparent chaos can be seen as applicable to policy studies, since the capacity of individuals to control the policy process is seriously limited given the number of variables, many unknown and unpredictable, that impinge on every process of policy development. The concept of complexity suggests that, whilst it is difficult to predict the results of policy change, it is possible through understanding this difficulty to at least develop strategies to minimise evolving dead end answers to social problems and to maximise the chances of establishing policy that is, at any specific time, fit for purpose.

Complexity theory suggests that policy making is not such a wholly chaotic and unpredictable procedure that it is outside the capacity of human beings to find strategies for its development. Policy does not happen without a measure of rationality. In the physical sciences the numerous atoms may be subject to a multitude of environmental forces but statistically there is sufficient probability that atoms and molecules will behave in specific conditions largely in the same way to enable the formation of scientific laws that are not wholly accurate but are sufficiently robust to enable mankind to create the numerous machines that make up the modern world. However, there are many cases where a social problem may be recognised and its potential effects understood, but there is much less certainty as to how the problem may be alleviated. It is clear from statistical studies that crime is likely to escalate in areas of relative poverty within a developed state but the means of alleviating this problem are much more complex. Is this problem to be resolved by, for example, assigning more police to such areas and imprisoning many offenders or by attempting to economically redevelop the community? Leaving aside for the moment the important issue of what would be a fair and just solution to criminal behaviour, the number of variables and interests concerned with economic regeneration of ill-favoured communities or saturating an area with police, are considerable and closely inter-related and hence make it extremely difficult to judge between alternative policies. At an even more problematic level situations arise in which the cause of a problem is not clearly understood, let alone any consensus as to how the issue may be resolved.

The civil divisions and strife in many Arab countries in 2011 created serious policy dilemmas for many Western nations as to whether they should intervene in the fractured nations, let alone which sides in the often multi-layered disputes should receive either political or military support. In such a situation many differing ideas can emerge as to how to deal with the situation and often politicians move towards a policy in a fog, as in the second invasion of Iraq by Bush and Blair, in which small moves may initiate, in the way that complex systems evolve, a path of action whose outcome is difficult to predict.

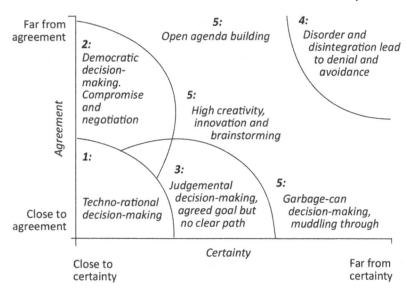

Figure 15.2 Stacey diagram of complex policy making
From Geyer, R. and Rihani, S. (2010): 67

The potential differences in understanding the causes of any problem and agreement on how to resolve the problem have been charted by Ralph Stacey (2000) as illustrated in Figure 15.2.

Position 1 is a situation of technical certainty and political agreement which is therefore potentially likely to be resolved. In contrast policy disputes positioned at point 4 where there is extreme division on how to resolve a problem and uncertainty about how this can technically be achieved is a situation where it is unlikely that contending parties will reach an accord on a way forward and, in many cases, the problem will not be resolved by debate and discussion rather than through force and violence. The most complex and difficult issues to resolve with any hope of a consensus lie in the point where there is little certainty on what solutions may best resolve a problem and also substantive disagreement among policy actors on the direction they should take. In reality most contentious policy problems do not align themselves at the extreme points but are aligned somewhere nearer the centre of the matrix. Within liberal democracies it is this area of problem resolution that may be most testing in terms of skills in debate and argument among policy advocates that will require the capacity to involve all sides in a discursive framework. Following on from the work of biological evolutionary scientists (Kauffman 1995; Coveney and Highfield 1995) on systems where there is little certainty as to the outcome on any action, complexity theorists developed a graphic suggestion of how preferred outcomes can best be managed through a process of trial and error (Geyer and Rihani 2010: 62–3). If over time policy makers seek a best solution they traverse a three dimensional landscape in which troughs symbolise degrees of unwanted outcomes and the hills preferred options, as depicted in Figure 15.3.

The innovator in such a landscape must be prepared to end up on occasion in valleys denoting failure and must accept failure as a normal outcome but be capable of

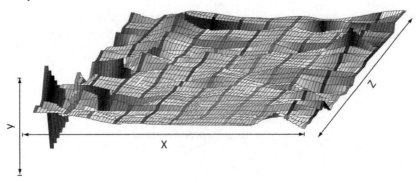

Figure 15.3 A fitness landscape
From: Geyer, R. and Rihani, S. (2010: 62)

changing strategy to climb out of a particular hole and engineering through trial and error a capacity to rise above the horizontal plane of indifference.

> In the realm of the applied sciences, such a procedure in practice leads pharmaceutical companies to develop new drugs from hundreds of chemicals that may have some bearing on the cure of a specific disease and begin a series of tests firstly on cell cultures, then on animals and then with human trials, in which most possible solutions fall by the wayside until with luck a product emerges that has substantive curative and saleable capacity. On occasion, as in the discovery of Viagra, the procedures to find a cure for a specific disorder may throw up a drug that has unrealised properties that are marketable to resolve an unrelated medical problem.

Similarly, it is argued the development of public policy to deal with complex chaotic problems must advance with experimentation, if possible on a small community, assessment of the results, followed by wider trials until some certainty is reached on the effectiveness of the cure but also on the unwanted and harmful side effects. As the British Labour Party statesman Denis Healey suggested 'First law on holes. When you are in one stop digging' (Labour List 2015).

The strategy of trial and error is further complicated by the constantly changing nature of the landscape since, using the evolutionary example, there are many environmental factors that can force a species into an evolutionary dead end valley, or ensure that some creatures evolve methods for their own security to ward off their predators. Thus, a strategy of making only small incremental changes in procedure or 'sticking to your knitting' as suggested by Peters and Waterman (1982) is, in the competitive marketplace or the complexity of the public sector, not in the long term an advisable option as new threats or opportunities in a changing landscape may create for the cautious a dead end and failure. The more innovatory policy makers can sometimes make mistakes but they can also engineer breakthroughs in design that may hoist them to the peaks of fitness.

If the complexity model is fitted to the question of who makes policy the inference must be that all humans stumble as best they can to maximise their advantages in a world that is beset by issues that are too complex to understand and subject to constant change owing to the behaviour of uncontrolled events. Prime ministers and presidents are equally at sea in how to steer in this climate as any student or old age pensioner. The theory has its limits for policy studies as it leaves almost without relevance the question of whether there are any central networks let alone individuals determining the direction of policy and as such cannot consider the normative issues of who ought to be able to determine policy or whether the policy outcomes were ethically justifiable.

Conclusion

Public policy is not in many cases a static set of rules and regulations but rather an evolving and frequently changing set of edicts and practices. Setting public policy in the context of social evolution opens up an avenue in policy studies that needs to embrace wider scale studies of stability, revolt and revolution. These issues are central to many of the great ideological visions of society and have been mentioned in earlier chapters of this study but also cover such a vast field of theory that they cannot adequately be covered or summarised in a single chapter. What has, however, been pointed out is that there is firstly a need to disentangle the form of evolution that may occur within a political system. In many cases policy as Baumgartner and Jones observe evolves in a stop–go format of punctuated equilibrium rather than any pattern of constant incremental change. In many political systems the pressure of demands for change can only enable gate-keepers to pursue change on a few major issues at a time.

There is, however, a step change from dealing with revolt concerning a specific policy area, such as education or gun control, to a revolutionary situation in which a government harbouring some consensus of ideology and ethical values is faced with a sustained and well resourced attack from interests that favour wholly different beliefs and are willing to overthrow the existing system and interests to implant their own values. Such conditions are infrequent but can usher in substantial periods of policy upheaval and unrest and even culminate in the destruction of a viable state.

As argued earlier, through reference to complexity theory and policy evolution, policy entrepreneurs can never with certainty engineer policy instruments that can enable them to predict the outcome of their activities but must stumble through a minefield of problems and make progress by evolving their approach to an issue so as to quickly climb out of dead ends and pursue lines of action that appear to approach their optimum outcomes. Instinctively most policy entrepreneurs are aware of these problems and design policies that are never as clear or as well worked through as they would like the electorate to believe. As has been argued in earlier chapters, policies are usually ambiguous multi-faceted decisions. On occasion a government may design a policy knowing that it might fail, as in the Blair Government's response to advocates of a ban on fox hunting outlined in Chapter 3 (Blair 2010: 304–6). More widely governments may mask the central issue behind a policy and seek to promote an interest that they know, if fully revealed, would be unpopular. These policies may be devised in such a form that the agent leaves the serious and usually unpopular policy decisions to subordinate agencies of government who, the agent hopes, will be the target of hostilities rather than themselves.

16 Success and failure

Early studies of the policy process, as initiated for example by Luther Gulick (1937) or Harold Lasswell (1951) may have hoped that such analysis might lead to a policy science. This could create a template for sound rational policy making that would obviate many of the serious blunders that have littered political disasters of previous centuries. As the preceding chapters have demonstrated, few policy theorists would now think a predictive science of policy is a realistic proposition given the complexity of human relationships and the unpredictability of the natural environment. Moreover, the central issue behind most policy instruments is what they are attempting to achieve. It must also be realised that many policies are constantly evolving through either human agency or environmental circumstances and hence it is unwise to condemn or praise policy outcomes based on a snapshot of its performance at one particular moment. Policy aims are, however, based on subjective motives such as policy advocates' ethical values, their ideological views and the extent to which their self-interest may overmaster their concern for more universalised values. Basically one observer's view concerning the overall success or failure of a policy may differ greatly from another's.

Prescribing means to secure good policies

There is, nevertheless, a literature that prescriptively attempts to provide 'do-it-yourself' guides for good policy making. This may be a consequence of the search for rationalism and a science of public policy that can guide policy makers to failsafe methods for securing failsafe policies. Lasswell (1971: 85–95) for example put forward over seventy prescriptions for improving policy outputs in his *A Pre-View of Policy Sciences*. These range from rational methods of obtaining intelligence on the problems to be addressed to criteria for applying, evaluating and terminating policy. Stuart Nagel (2000) argues that the best policies secure what he terms 'super optimum solutions' that ensure that there is a winning solution for all interests involved in policy change. He provides examples such as 'subsidies for business firms to move where there are pockets of unemployment' or 'better child care to allow mothers of pre-school children to work' (Nagel 2000: 238). Graham Room (2011: 312–18) has provided a template for what he terms an 'agile policy-making toolkit' for securing successful policies in a complex society. Decisions, he argues, need to be based on eight elements within the process which point to the need to allow others to become involved in the policy problem independently from the policy advocates' direction whilst allowing for the regulation of the probable conflicts between contending ideas and interests. It can also be claimed that complexity theory or puzzle solving, as discussed in the preceding chapter, provides a basic and perhaps over-simplistic pre-scription for more effective policy making.

General prescriptions as to how to ensure rational methods for securing optimum policy solutions have in practice a rather limited value. Frequently the ideal method of securing policy change may at one rather abstract level appear to be obvious, such as an entreaty to rival interests to get round a table and seek some optimum solution that would solve all their problems or to accept a compromise to resolve their differences. When cast into the real world of ideological and self-interested power struggles resolving differ-ences through debate and discussion is never so simple a process. The diverse nature of policies and the subjective nature of many of the underlying reasons behind policy advo-cates' attachment to their ideas ensure that specific policy templates will not be sufficient to generate optimal solutions to policy problems. In many cases policy conflicts are not win–win situations but zero-sum games in which the victors receive the spoils of conflict and the losers gain nothing, and in the worst cases lose everything, including their lives.

> When deeply engrained ideological values and also political self-interest clash, refer-ence is not made to some prescriptive template. The Cuban missile crisis pitched two ideological deeply opposed superpowers against each other and both the leaders of these regimes and those from whom they received support were fully aware their status depended on a favourable resolution of the crisis for their benefit. Not only was the ideological grounding of communist and liberal democratic capitalist values seen to be in the balance but, in terms of *realpolitik*, the United States' adherence to the Monroe doctrine of non-European interference in the affairs of the American continent and the concern of the Soviet Union that their leadership of the Communist movement should be recognised on a worldwide rather than just an Asian and European foun-dation were also important factors. It was clearly apparent during the Cuban missile crisis that the protagonists needed to reach some form of compromise but it was less clear how that compromise could be reached without the danger of sparking a nuclear conflict (Allison 1971). There were few easy templates to guide the conduct of the contending leaders.

In contrast to the relatively few prescriptive attempts to develop best practice in policy development, there is an extensive literature on the extent to which public poli-cies lead to failure. In the United States following the studies of Pressman and Wild-avsky (1973) on the difficulties of implementing Federal policies in communities, there has continued to be pessimism concerning the capacity of big governments to reach successful policy outcomes but, in comparison within European literature, less enthu-siasm for exposing public failures. In the context of post-1945 British politics there is a continuing industry charting and explaining how the political elites and the system of government create major blunders (Butler, Adonis and Travers 1994; Dunleavy 1995; Moran 2001; King and Crewe 2013). This interest diffused into a West European focus that similarly dissected specific examples of policy failure (Bovens and t'Hart 1996; Gray and t'Hart 1998; Bovens, t'Hart and Peters 2001). Much of this work is based on empirical studies and avoids serious subjective analysis of what may constitute policy success or failure by using versions of Etzioni's formula that policy failure occurs when policy advocates are unable to secure the objectives that they set out to achieve or do so by inefficient means. Allan McConnell (2010b: 351) brings in an element of subjectivity in that the policy must not only achieve its goals but also 'attracts no criticism of any significance and/or support is virtually universal'. King and Crewe (2013: 4) define a policy blunder more extensively as:

> An episode in which government adopts a specific course of action in order to achieve one or more objectives and, as a result either fails completely to achieve those objectives or does achieve some or all of them but at a totally dispropor- tionate cost or else does achieve some or all of them but contrives at the same time to cause a significant amount of 'collateral damage' in the form of unintended and undesired consequences.

They list a number of what they see as human failures and systems failures that have led to specific policy failures in post-1945 Britain but many of the issues that they highlight, such as a disconnect between the core executive of a government and their electorate, are more a complaint against a specific political system that needs to be viewed from a more comparative basis.

A rather smaller literature conversely attempts to identify successful policies and show their characteristics (McConnell 2010a: 3). As Michael Howlett (2012: 542) observes, many analysts view policy success as the avoidance of the characteristics that are positively defined as policy failure 'so that observers are not seen as creating their own interpretive or discursive universe in a purely subjective way, but rather are ren- dering judgements about an actually existing state of affairs'. Much of this work tends to be theoretically based rather than being founded on evidence gleaned from historical dissections of policy developments. This is in part a reflection of the more ephemeral nature of what can be argued to be a successful policy. Policy failure can in the short or medium term be clearly evident when a proposal by a government fails to reach the stage of being implemented or once implemented, as in the case of the poll tax, is within a few years abandoned. The really effective and long-lasting policies are fre- quently not viewed as policies but as established institutional or ideological pillars of a political system and its civic culture. As observed earlier, studies of policy success too frequently overlook examples of policies deeply embedded in political cultures and institutions. In many cases over time a policy may simply become an accepted and generally assumed feature of the political system despite its shortcomings. Moreover, there is a powerful mechanism largely deployed in the public media that will quickly relegate attention from older stories once the immediate political battles concerning their legitimation and implementation have been put into effect as the journalists take up newer and more hotly contested issues.

In Britain the education Acts from 1871 to the end of the nineteenth century that required all children up to the age of 14 to be educated free of charges to be paid by parents or guardians has never been seriously challenged. Similar public policies on education are implanted in almost all world states. The development of the British National Health Service can similarly be argued to be a policy that few dare to directly oppose.

Public policy may also be successfully implanted even on an international stage such as the eradication, much assisted by the World Health Organization, of deadly infectious diseases such as smallpox through mass immunisation or the stemming of the 2014/15 Ebola outbreak in West Africa.

It is clearly nonsense to suggest that policy solutions are never effective. An argument that public policies are always flawed and never achieve the goals for which they are designed is not only overly pessimistic but also occupies an unreal world in terms of what public policy represents in human experience. It is by definition impossible to conceive of an organised society and the benefits this brings without the requirement that its processes of governance are the result of policy decisions and their outcomes. Indeed, it may be said that the generally tolerable and civilised public provisions and public rules and regulations in society that have been the outcome of policy decisions have ensured that we are not living in an anarchic state of nature in which life as suggested by Thomas Hobbes is 'nasty brutish and short'. Few policies may immediately fully meet the aims and objectives of their advocates but over time there are many policies that can be regarded as being by and large effective. There was, perhaps, never a more golden age of civil society than the present age. The evidence of policy success is apparent in the development of most societies over the last two millennia from small claustrophobic, frequently violent, conformist and diseased societies, to the much larger, wealthier, pluralist and unprecedentedly long lived societies that in many parts of the world permit considerable freedom in terms of personal lifestyles.

Defining success and failure

There are several problems with the approaches so far discussed to evaluating policy success or failure. As Allan McConnell (2010a: 225; 2010b: 349–50) points out policy success must be evaluated from different perspectives. Few policies are unmitigated failures or wholly and completely successful. It should be clear from the preceding chapters that there are factors and procedures that seem more likely to ensure that, within a certain type of regime, policy can be devised successfully using the positivist formulas developed by Etzioni or King and Crewe. However, policy development is a product of many inter-related issues. Individual factors, such as the capacity within a political system to make quick decisions, may be a help or a hindrance to successful decision making, dependent on the subject matter of the policy and the political and social environment in which it is made. Simply relating a few generally obvious factors, such as whether policy advocates are out of touch with those whom they govern, does not advance debate very far since it is essential to understand the causes of such a breakdown and whether this relates to the policies themselves, the structure of the political system or the physical and social environment in which they are to be used. Together these considerations create too many varied and often unique narratives of the success or failure of a policy, even on the restricted question of whether that policy efficiently met the aims of its advocates. McConnell (2010a) abstracts three broad dimensions in which policy may succeed or fail. These are in relation to:

- The process of policy making in the sense that the government and the political machinery in which it is imbedded is able to operate to deliver and implement sound policy outcomes.
- Programme success which is meeting the objectives for those who make and support the policy.
- Political success through generating sufficient electoral support and goodwill as a consequence of the policy.

All three categories, McConnell argues, are essential for complete success. The policy process and support for a government may be in various ways soundly based but the policy can be a failure in terms of programme success if, for example, a government cannot deal with the technical challenges that are intrinsic to it. Success in these two arenas may be eroded if there are political dimensions in relation, for example, to the capacity of interests to support an idea without harming their prestige and support.

These broad categories can, as essayed by Howlett (2012: 550), be developed further by dividing each category into ways in which success or failure can occur within each of these broader dimensions. Howlett develops twelve potential means that can create policy failure. There are, however, serious problems with methodologies that attempt to describe social phenomena through listing the potential attributes that may lead to a measure of success or failure. The attempt results in the development of either broader categories that do little to establish detailed reasons why a policy may have succeeded or fallen off the rails or, on the other hand, dividing categories into sub-categories, and possibly, sub-sub-categories, that become too complex to easily apply to specific cases and make little sense of the unique contexts which differentiate political systems. The problem of establishing categories of behaviour within the social sciences is that the elements making up what are always unique social contexts are left out of the picture and even if these elements can be conveniently shoe-horned into separate boxes the proliferation of boxes would be too overwhelming to make any better sense of the complexity of reality. Under these conditions understanding is much more effectively portrayed using interpretive methodology.

It is also pointed out by McConnell (2010a: 104–11) that in justifying policy success, political activists use a wide range of measures for claiming policies have been a success or a failure. They may, for example, seek to demonstrate that they have succeeded in lowering unemployment or inflation in the economy through reference to comparative performance in other countries or from a different perspective with reference to the record of preceding governments in their own country. They can, especially in policy areas where there is no effective quantitative measure of success, such as foreign policy relations, claim that they are taking steps to improve the situation and, where relevant, add that their opponents did not successfully deal with the issue. As argued earlier, policy makers in practice do not so much evaluate policies but seek to validate their ideas by highlighting results that are favourable to their view point and burying or denying those which do not support their case.

The success of many policies is also intrinsically linked to its evolution and hence any evaluation may produce different results at different times. For example, the policy of *perestroika* as conceived by Gorbachev after 1985 is still being played out on the international stage. Many policies that were originally unpopular and seriously divided the policy making networks and coalitions that had supported a particular government over time have become so embedded in democratic political culture that they are never themselves viewed as a policy.

In the United States the conflict over the abolition of slavery and the break-up of the economic system founded on it was a policy that led to a Civil War even though today very few would consider returning to the human rights policies of Confederate States.

Most major constitutional reforms in Britain were at the time highly contested and in many cases seriously altered the framework of the politically dominant coalitions that had ruled the nation. These included the 1832, 1872 and 1884 electoral reform Acts that led to the break-up of the political dominance of the landowning Tory and Whig Parties, who ruled as elements in a plutocracy, and eventually to the period of liberal democracy based on one person one vote and the dominance of party stability since 1945 under the triumvirate of the Conservatives, Liberal/Liberal Democrats and Labour. Similarly within this process, despite the conflicts at the time of its development, the extension of the franchise to women is now in most regimes an almost universally unchallenged policy.

Whilst some policies are terminated and become effectively extinct, many develop over time and emerge as wholly different solutions from the original attempts to deal with a social problem. In part the driving force for such change can be external changes in technology or social beliefs and conditions.

The development of social security in Britain as a public policy that required state intervention involving legislation emerged in the reign of Elizabeth I as the first poor law act. The Acts entrusted local authorities, in the forms of towns and parishes, to raise the funds to support the destitute born within their communities. The policy endured with minor amendments until the early nineteenth century when as a result of greater social mobility through industrialisation and the growth of mechanised systems of transport, it became increasingly unrealistic for villagers to return to the parish of their birth to receive help. Changes in social and economic thought also saw the poor more as a burden on society rather than as victims of misfortune. There were several attempts to resolve the new situation within larger towns through the creation of workhouses to effectively imprison the destitute and force them to undertake menial and backbreaking labour. The 1834 Poor Law Act placed the workhouse system on a national footing but the restructured policy was never effectively implemented on a national basis due to strong opposition largely in the more industrialised northern cities (Prest 1990). By the early twentieth century the policies began to be reshaped towards the older system of out relief for the poor with, for example, the provision of old age pensions in 1906 and the development of Labour Exchanges. During the Second World War the Beveridge Review (1942) of the social security system further remodelled the system to create a system of national insurance payments to supersede the workhouse system to support the unemployed (Crosland 1964: 82). It was, however, later argued that the Beveridge Report findings based on the assumption of low levels of unemployment were not fit for purpose and by the 1980s the system of social security further evolved to again penalise those of able body who would not work.

The above example illustrates, as McConnell suggests, that policy on welfare in Britain cannot easily be termed a success or a total failure. The success of policy in this sector cannot be summed up by a simple 'yes' or 'no' response as it was more successful in some sectors, such as the mechanism for assessing and providing poor relief, than others, such as the costs to specific local communities or its capacity to redevelop the work ethic among the able bodied recipients of social security benefit. Moreover, the measure of success in various sectors differs over time and from different points of view that dominate at any one time the civic culture that informs observers' ideas. This tendency parallels the changing policies and attitudes to madness that were identified by Foucault, as observed in Chapter 3. Policy success or failure must, therefore, be evaluated over the long term and needs to bring in the context that policy evolves to fit new environmental, sociological or ideological circumstances on an irregular basis with periods of largely static or piecemeal incremental development punctuated, as argued by Baumgartner and Jones (1993), by more revolutionary periods of change.

The basis for failure as developed by McConnell, Howlett or King and Crewe are also misleading since failures in one extracted element of the political system, such as its environment which, among other factors, may include its political culture and the problems it is trying to resolve, are all inter-related. Any change in some elements will create repercussions throughout the system and may be attributed to political, programme or process failures.

> For example, the policies of the 2010 to 2015 Conservative Liberal Democrat Coalition to provide more affordable housing to meet population growth, using McConnell's categories, may be seen as a failure in terms of political, process and programme dimensions. However, behind the policy may also have been an unstated desire within the Government to secure the value of existing property values for their core voters.

Most importantly, the preceding definitions of what may determine policy success or failure, which are in the main positivist approaches, are generally limited by an assumption that the aims of any policy are the same for all of its advocates. It is often the case that policy advocates differ in regard to the policy aims and outcomes. Policies often harbour a number of aims, practical, ideological and personal.

> The failed public private partnership developed by the Blair Government for the London Underground was established not only with the aim of improving transport in the capital but also to ensure that the costs were not added to the Treasury's balance sheet. This aim of obscuring government capital costs was achieved only at considerable cost to the goal of improving the reliability of the service as it created problems for private companies that could not deal with the major undertaking of sustaining the London underground network (King and Crewe 2013: 201–221).

The consequences of any policy are, as shown above, often complex and may be successful in certain instances but disastrous in others. What complicates this fact, in relation to people's assessment of policy success or failure, is the likelihood that individuals from different backgrounds and holding different social roles and values will put a higher value on one factor rather than others.

> The rebuilding of London's dockland has revitalised, as the Thatcher Government intended, an area of the capital that was heavily industrialised and regarded as a centre of poverty, but the change has also had serious but far less visible consequences for the London poor who formerly worked and lived in this area, given that it did not concern itself with bringing industrial developments into the area or with providing subsidised housing (Lewis 1992: 31–6).

There are also many instances where it may be possible to argue that a failed policy can sow the seeds of a policy success. Given the complexity of many policy problems, effective answers are impossible to calculate prior to their implementation. If a potential solution appears to be a wrong turning, then, as long as this is realised and the policy strategy abandoned and replaced with new ideas, there is the success of at least rejecting one plausible but failed strategy in order to climb out of that hole in the landscape of satisfaction and develop possibly a better idea.

What factors may determine policy success?

The preceding analysis concludes that success or failure in terms of policy is a highly subjective process that cannot be determined by a simple 'yes' or 'no' answer. A policy success for certain individuals may well be a disaster for others. Many policies also encompass several differing and, on occasion, incompatible aims and frequently the publicly trailed reasons in support of a policy may not encompass all reasons why a government may have advanced a particular policy. Policy aims achieved in one publicly announced arena may also, due to unforeseen circumstances, create a policy disaster in a wholly unanticipated direction. Having made this point, it is nevertheless unwise to simply conclude that there is little point in analysing how far a policy may be successful and hence learning from the experience. Perhaps the most pressing need for some form of guidance is that it is unrealistic to argue that since there are so many factors that will determine policy outcomes we should never embark on policy development and simply let events happen as they will. As stated in the first chapter, a decision to abandon any social organisation within society is in itself a policy decision. Moreover, complete anarchy with no clear social rules will not create a more prosperous and equitable society for most if not all individuals. Governments form as a consequence of the development of human intellect such that most humans wish to work in cooperation with others rather than remain isolated and the expectation is that such governments will make policy for the general welfare of all.

There are clearly many general and common sense observations that can be put forward in relation to the construction of a policy and its relationship to its social and environmental environment that would make it more susceptible to being widely seen as a success or failure to meet either the publicly stated or more hidden aims of its advocates. Many of the issues that may develop a greater chance, provided all other issues were equal, have been discussed in the preceding chapters of this book and it would be repetitious to discuss them at any length here. These involve a need for policy advocates to fully understand as much as can be known of circumstances that may be the cause of a problem or create an opportunity to establish or reform an existing public policy. The understanding must be based if possible on sound research supported by widely agreed and tested theory. It must be recognised that the likelihood that a policy may be successful must be in part a reflection of the complexity of the issue in question and of the environment in which it is to operate. The most difficult issues will tend to be those where there is little clarity as to how a particular problem may arise within a complex environment, such as restoring economic growth within a national or the world economy following specific, and in many respects unprecedented, events, such as the banking crisis of 2008. Governments must also realise that to support many of their policies they need sufficient resources to operationalise their ideas. These may include diverting sufficient funds to the project, developing the necessary skills in the workforce to undertake the task or to police obedience to its requirements. Successful implementation is more likely to be achieved if a public organisation can convince the majority of those affected by the policy of the need for change and pro-vide assurances on how it may affect them for the better. Consideration must also be given to the time that can be devoted to an issue. Policy that has to be made rapidly, for example to defend a nation against an unexpected natural disaster or an attack by foreign forces, is less likely to succeed if plans have not been drawn up in anticipation of such circumstances.

Many of the basic and generally obvious principles that have been identified above are far from fool-proof given that by their very nature complex societies change in ways that are not easy to predict and that information available to even the wealthiest and most knowledgeable societies is not sufficient to predict the future impact of policy aims. It must be kept in mind by policy advocates and policy gate-keepers that what-ever actions they may take in such circumstances could fail for lack of understanding or capacity to implement their chosen policy and that they must be prepared to con-stantly review their decisions and be prepared, if necessary, to change course and climb out of holes they may have dug themselves into.

The subjective dimension

It is possible to suggest factors that through their interaction may make policies easier or more difficult to formulate and implement with some chance of success without generating disproportionate expenditure or serious popular opposition, but in the real world these are not the only criteria that determine the attitude of the public to any policy initiative. Policy success or failure is in many instances a subjective perception and may relate to both personal characteristics of particular individuals and also their habitus, rather than the result of the actual consequences, as much as this can be dis-cerned, of a policy. As Bovens and t'Hart (1996: 145–6) conclude, the question of what causes policy fiascos might more usefully be reframed as 'why have we become more inclined to understand policy events and policy episodes as fiascos?' Many policies secure limited success but in wealthy liberal democracies the media and the opposition parties gain greater public attention by sensationalising policy problems as complete failures. Moreover, the perception of policy failure or success is frequently attached to the capacity to blame or praise particular individuals and groups in order to advance or undermine their position within the political arena. In practice, many policies suc-ceed or fail due to luck rather than judgement but few critics of policy outcomes, especially within the media, are inclined to assign policy success or failure to the many unexpected and unpredictable turns of events within an unstable world.

The position that most policy issues are based on subjective values should not, however, rule out the extent to which positivist scientific and evidence-based research may also influence individuals' subjective values. An important example may be atti-tudes towards gender and women's rights. Many societies have evolved over time, often based on a sense that 'physical might is right' or that women should be subordinated to the interests of men as they have a lesser capacity to determine effective policy deci-sions. However, positivist analysis of the capacity of women and men to reason and to understand complex environmental and social situations does not suggest that in this context women are inferior to men. Moreover, even if this were the case it in no way shows that an individual from one group is necessarily inferior in some regard to members of a group that statistically is thought as a whole in some way to be superior. In more educated societies these positivist findings can and ought to help colour the subjective attitudes concerning the extent to which gender should, if at all, be regarded as an issue that determines differential access to involvement in the policy process.

Despite the reservation that positivist methodology may create facts that are difficult to ignore and hence may inform our subjective values, assessing the success or failure of a policy cannot be limited to simply ascertaining whether a proposal by a network of policy advocates has secured any of their goals. As Fischer (2009: 272) eloquently points out, 'People seldom enter the political fray without emotional convictions of one sort or another, whether they involve passionate political beliefs, deep-seated animosities towards foreign enemies, ethnic cultural commitments or religious faith'. For most people who reflect on public policy the central element of its success or failure is not so much whether it fully achieves its stated goals but whether they approved of its aims and the motives that drive its aims. Indeed few would argue that a policy that successfully resolved a problem that was based on wholly unethical grounds was in itself a satisfactory outcome.

> The policies of ethnic cleansing that, for example, transported Jews to their death in concentration camps may have been successful in terms that it was implemented and used relatively few resources and in a totalitarian society occasioned little opposition, but no one could seriously consider it to be overall a good policy.

Policy, as indicated in the opening chapters of this book, must be and is widely assessed in terms of its success or failure in its intrinsic moral worth and the motives behind what the policy seeks to secure. These assessments are, of course, inevitably subjective. One observer's attitude to a particular policy may, therefore, differ greatly from another's and cannot be dismissed as wrong on factual grounds.

Nevertheless, at the heart of many of the most intractable and bitterly fought over issues concerning public policy are disagreements over what are acceptable policy aims in terms of their moral standing. It is, therefore, not possible to develop public policy without at some point having to confront the differing values of those who may support or oppose a policy solution. Within this context, simply arguing that this is an issue that must be ignored makes no practical sense in respect to the most divisive policy problems.

> Should all societies be governed by Sharia Law based on the writings and sayings of the Prophet Mohammed? Ought the Jewish residents of Israel compensate the Palestinian families displaced by their settlement in the region and also be prepared to offer the Palestinians equal rights to the government of that territory? Should Catalonia become independent of Spain or Scotland independent of the United Kingdom? Should treason against the state in time of war be punished by the death penalty? Is it right to develop economic policies in which there are no limits on the extent to which individuals can accumulate wealth?

The solution to such deeply felt conflicts that underlie much of the intractable wicked issues that face policy makers needs resolution not within the field of objective positivist analysis but in resolving as well as possible how far we should tolerate beha-viour and policies that we believe are unethical. The basis of resolving such disputes is to find, as far as this is feasible, common ground on which a substantial number of citizens can agree concerning the ethical foundations of policy aims and to develop a society which exhibits some tolerance and understanding of opposing minority values. Within this context the means to establish policy decisions which at least satisfice as far as is possible the aims, ambitions and motives of as many of those affected by the policy as is possible, require both further consideration of ethical beliefs within a society and also how to institutionally structure the decision making machinery to take full account of such values. This element of determining the success or failings of the subjective foundations of policy is the subject of the following chapter.

Conclusion

It is possible in a rather limited sense to argue that a government has made a number of political blunders and that certain policies can be regarded as a failure because they never achieve the stated aims of their advocates. It may be argued that some policies appear to be successful as they achieve the gains that have publicly been set for them and even become so embedded in the civic structure and ideas of a society that they become permanent features of a polity and as such are rarely seen as the outcome of policy rather than simply part of the unchanging furniture of that society. However, in any wider sense of the term the pursuit of the perfect policy or the demonising of blunders is a highly subjective issue and will resonate very differently in the minds of individuals with widely different attitudes to ethics and ideology. Any attempt to secure the perfect policy solution, in as much as this is at all possible must, as the next chapter considers, require some form of ethical underpinning rationale for the greatest possible number of citizens following the opening up of discourse on a global basis.

17 Deliberative policy making

This penultimate chapter continues a discussion on how far it may be possible to develop effective policy decisions within a world divided by ideological and ethical disagreement and riven by self-interest. Frameworks for determining more rigorous means of creating workable public policies have been suggested, as outlined in Chapter 2, by pioneers of policy studies such as Harold Lasswell and in the analysis of the factors that may presage success or failure of policy initiatives in the previous chapter. Many of these arguments, however, have a largely positivist direction in that they tend to counsel better evaluation techniques or more comprehensive dovetailing of the resources and information required to ensure policy can get off the ground. Far less attention is directed to subjective issues even though, as this study has emphasised, a central issue in the development of effective public policies is that the content of any output has been established with due regard to rational thought in relation to the balance of ethical and ideological values and preservation of legitimate self-interest. This chapter outlines some of the possible directions in which the subjective differences between individuals, societies and nations may be evened out to provide a more democratic form of policy making and hence governance than is currently provided by the liberal democratic ethic.

Discourse theory

The unsatisfactory outcomes of rational, positivist policy debate based on factual evidence and the problems associated with subjective policy content ranging from ideological belief to self-interest and moral and ethical values have generated a substantial literature on how to resolve policy problems. Philippe Zittoun (2014: 54) observes 'that a decision is never a man, a place, a moment; rather, it is a complex process that is notably constituted of multiple discussions which structure all agreements and organise conflict'. It is the organisation of such discourse that is crucial to any semblance of equity and effectiveness within the policy process. A widely canvassed theoretical and, in many communities, normatively acceptable route to effective and democratic policy making is through the enhancing of liberal democracy towards a decision making process that involves more citizens interacting on an equal basis in terms of resources of power and knowledge. Such a strategy involves a capacity to widely discuss policy problems and objectives through commonly accepted principles, described by Habermas (1990) as discourse ethics. This argues for the development of a more common understanding, although not necessarily agreement, to forge the means of processing policy from ideas to implementation through what is most widely termed deliberation and in ideal society deliberative democracy. As with much of subjective and critical thought, the role of language is an important element in developing any possibility of an effective policy process that brings together the interests of professional groups, including political professionals, in line with the concerns of civil society. The means of understanding lies with the development of principles for common discourse. Habermas argues that such a common understanding must be forged through discursive ethics that set basic principles that should regulate debate. This requires that on any issue participants should have the right to communicate their ideas including their attitudes, desires and needs, and to critically question any assertion put forward by others (Habermas 1990: 89; Edgar 2005: 158). From a positivist perspective, debate, for example, on understanding human biology, with the aid of experimentation linked to theory, can create considerable consensus on how many aspects of the human body work. It can also be claimed this may be the way forward for subjective issues. On the basis of such open discussion, Habermas considers that the validity of normative values, that is, issues on which there is a high level of consensus, can be secured when they 'meet (or could meet) with the approval of all affected in their capacity as participants in a practical discourse' (Habermas 1990: 66; Edgar 2005: 160). These principles are much influenced by enlightenment European philosophers such as Jean Jacques Rousseau and Immanuel Kant. Following Kant, it is essentially a universalist theory, although, by requiring participation of those concerned, it might lend itself to the development of differing norms being followed by wholly separate communities. However, in an increasingly interconnected globalised society few basic moral demands such as respecting the right to life or property cannot but be seen as universal requirements. In contrast to modern universalist ethical theories such as those proposed by John Rawls (1971), the view of Habermas is not so much derived from logical values deriving from a relationship where each person is simply considered to have equal importance to all others, but through a capacity for individuals to accept through reasoned debate the ideas of others as well as exerting their right to try to influence others.

One of the leading writers of the twenty-first century to relate the practice of deliberative democracy to the policy process, Frank Fischer (2003: 30), defines discourse as 'the communicative interactions among political actors that translate problems into policy issues'. Discourse thus requires substantial deliberation between those who devise policy and the publics who will be subject to its demands. In this context discourse practice should apply to attempts by policy activists to view policy demands and potential solutions in a wider context than afforded by positivist 'fact based' empirical research. The activity requires policy proponents not only to review evidence in support of or against policy solutions from experts in the field but to understand and take account of the epistemological and social basis of the positivist research and subjective values on which a policy proposal is based. In addition to the more positivist issues involved in debate, there must, therefore, be a capacity for contending interests to discuss subjective issues from a rational position of understanding and where possible tolerating different emotional and motivational standpoints.

Deliberative democracy

Since the 1990s there has developed a substantial sub-discipline concerned with emphasising the importance of deliberative democracy and how institutionally the central theoretical and ethical values behind the idea may be put into practice.

The idea has gained serious attention among politicians and enters the mind-set of President Obama (2006: 92) who observes that 'What the framework of our Constitution can do is to organize the way in which we argue about our future. All of its machinery – its separation of power and checks and balances and federalist principles and Bill of Rights – are designed to force us into a conversation, a "deliberative democracy" in which all citizens are required to engage in a process of testing their ideas against an external reality, persuading others of their point of view, and building shifting alliances of consent.'

Over the last twenty years there has been considerable interest in deliberative democracy as a means of enhancing democratic systems so as to ensure widely accepted policies aimed at enhancing the general good of all rather than narrower sectional interests (Dryzek 2010: 3–4). What is required is a more open form of democracy in which the capacity to determine policy involves informed comment and assent from a much wider number of citizens. It can be suggested that new technologies have in the last fifty years greatly contributed to the possibility of involving citizens much more directly in the policy making process. Referenda in many liberal democracies are now established as a means of ensuring that all citizens are given the capacity to accept or reject proposals for constitutional change. However, referenda are used rarely and reserved for major constitutional changes and then sanctioned by a government in power only when they expect the result to emerge in their favour. More promising is the use of the internet and the related social media such as Facebook and Twitter to allow individuals to post opinions and ideas that relate to policy change on a worldwide stage. Technologically it is now possible through the internet to allow every citizen the capacity to comment on policy as it emerges on the public agenda, and is refined and implemented. These procedures may serve as an informal guide to public interest and support or rejection of policy ideas but they are not embedded into the formal methods of agenda setting, refinement or legitimation of policy ideas. Moreover free access to the internet may be blocked within many autocratic states and within capitalist economies is as much subject to the demands for profitability from multi-national companies such as Google or Amazon as are more traditional means of communication (Curran 2012: 9–12). It would also be technologically possible for citizens to vote through electronic means on any matter that in most liberal democracies today is subject only to the vote of politicians elected to a legislature. Whether such a system would on its own facilitate a stronger democracy is, however, questionable, as opinions expressed on social media can be manipulated to favour the demands of well-resourced professional interests and professionalised politicians and parties whilst the tweets of those not seen to have 'a personality' by the mass media are little read by those who most influence policy. Internet surfers are moreover drawn to those sites and contributions that favour their views rather than seek a dispassionate exchange of opinion and such bias is created by the power of the established, more conventional media owned by well-resourced business interests. In that context it may be wondered why there is in liberal democracies little enthusiasm to set up such a system. In part this may be because representatives wish to represent their own rather than their electorate's views.

Concern to enhance the practical possibilities of deliberative democracy began to emerge in the 1960s through both positivist theorists such as Carole Pateman and

Benjamin Barber and from a rather different perspective from critical realists such as Habermas. Pateman's (1970) work *Participation and Democratic Theory* criticised the development of liberal democracies into organisations that highlighted representation as opposed to participation. Furthering these developments Barber attempted to establish what the institutional basis of what he has termed 'strong democracy' might entail. Barber's vision (Barber 1984: 267–307) emphasises the need for extensive participatory community governance to resolve local concerns and that such governments could communicate their concerns to higher levels of regional, state and national governance with the expectation they would be given serious consideration. He also, like Pateman, argued for greater participation in the work place. Feminist writers, including Pateman (1988), similarly point to the need to ensure equality between the sexes in respect to representation and to ensure women gain the resources to be effective in influencing the policy process. To develop the effectiveness of such a system Barber also realised the need for more substantive civic education. Many educational systems are geared to providing young people with the capacity to be literate and numerate to enable them to find employment. However, most educational systems provide little capacity for children to learn how to live in a complex political and economic society, to enable them to be effective socially literate and open minded citizens.

Dryzek (2000: 1) defines deliberation broadly:

> As a social process (that) is distinguished from other kinds of communication in that deliberators are amenable to changing their judgements, preference and views during the course of their interactions, which involve persuasion rather than coercion, manipulation or deception.

If the moral values implicit within these definitions are practised, not only would decisions directly and effectively involve a wider number of citizens but also it may be more likely that authoritative policy decisions will be implemented as envisaged by those participating in the policy outcome, as citizens will be more likely to be persuaded rather than coerced into following the policy as a decision on which they were consulted and on which they had the power to make a contribution. Moreover, policies that bring together the ideas and experiences of a wide number of individuals who would be subject to their dictates may be less likely to fail due to a policy making elite misunderstanding the concerns of most members of a civil society or seeking to benefit their own group self-interest at the expense of those whom they govern. Such exchanges of ideas in a framework of equality of power would create, if not the best policy, the policies that 'satisfice', by revealing Rousseau's enigmatic concept of the 'general will' within a community (Rousseau 1966: 12–17). Whilst the resultant policy may be a compromise between different views and different discourses, nevertheless, if agreed following debate and deliberation by consensus between all parties, it creates a platform for establishing policy to be implemented for the good of all within the consenting community.

Deliberative democracy can in practice be illustrated most clearly in relation to small communities or as Dryzek (2010: 156) has termed them 'citizen based mini-publics'.

In the context of institutionalised political systems perhaps the most lauded and researched frameworks for deliberative democracy are township governments in the New England States of North Eastern USA that were much admired by the nineteenth century commentator on American democracy, Alexis de Tocqueville (1994). The small townships hold open meetings to determine policy that are open to all residents in their communities and annually vote into power their officers, who arrange the meetings and ensure policy is implemented. Any citizen resident in these community meetings may raise an issue for discussion and can join in subsequent debates on an issue until a majority vote is taken on the final resolution to enact policy for the community.

However, the New England local township is not widely practised in local government systems. Most local government systems in the United States rely on representative rather than participative governance. In Britain major local authorities are far too large in terms of population to allow direct participative democracy by all their citizens and are currently being deconstructed through privatisation of many local services and the establishment of city regions under directly elected mayors to undertake planning and business development roles for substantive urban conurbations. Arguably deliberative democracy is most widely practised within the centre of some public and private sector agencies where a small group of professionals who regard themselves as equals will determine the policy of an organisation within the limits allowed them by external rules and demands.

Deliberative democracy was often observed in the decision making processes for awarding degrees in which academics on an exam board may argue at length over the standard of degree that may be awarded to a student on the margins of a particular level of award until a consensus is reached among the board. Rarely are such matters put to the vote as many participants in the discussion amend their views in regard to the arguments advanced by their colleagues.

This is, however, far from being deliberative democracy in any wider scenario of democratic decision making, rather than being a recognition of common interests within a professional body.

The challenges to deliberative democracy

Few individuals, at least in Western liberal democratic societies, will disagree with the moral sentiments behind deliberative democracy but many can question how far this can institutionally be realised within an unequal and globalising society. Whilst deliberative democracy appears to suggest more egalitarian and effective principles for guiding policy development, it is recognised that there are serious institutional and cultural problems that beset its achievement. It should be clear from previous discussions in this study that liberal democracies within a capitalist economy are not sufficient to establish an ethical framework for discourse. Institutions are frequently established in liberal democracies with the aim of creating a wider basis of open discussion through, for example, public–private partnerships on policy, but, in practice, provide the appearance of popular informed consent rather than discursive reality. Thomas Zittel in an edited study of political participation in democratic systems observes that:

Many of the policies analyzed in the chapters of this volume aim to stimulate engagement within the existing institutional framework of liberal democracy. They focus on marginal institutional changes that alter details of liberal democracy without changing its core elements and that stress strategies of cost-efficient democratization at best.

(Zittel 2007: 223)

Similarly, in the conclusion summarising research on public–private policy partnerships, Pauline Rosenau concludes that:

When cost considerations are the main concern, and when externalities are expected to be limited and a short time frame is in place, public-private policy partnerships may be appropriate. When one or more of these conditions do not hold, when partnership is minimalist in form, when accountability is critical, and when vulnerable populations are the policy focus, when cost shifting creates problems, and when societal normative choices are more important than costs, public private partnering may not be the best approach to policy.

(Rosenau 2000: 235)

Where new schemes of partnership are developed, the power relationships remain the same and a wider group of participants are welcomed only in so far as they can promote cost savings to the advantage of the existing players. Liberal democracy that permits wealth to be unevenly distributed creates a similarly uneven distribution in the capacity of citizens to gain a sound education and opportunities for lifestyle choices and hence an uneven capacity to receive an understanding of the world. This problem creates a tendency to perpetuate a hegemony of acceptable values that advantage the existing sources of power within the policy making process. Equity and ethical goodwill in discourse must require adherence to democratic principles but the establishment of national liberal democratic polities does not go far enough to establish these conditions.

A central problem within a globalising world is whether any but a few politicised individuals can feel that they have substantive freedom in respect to the decisions that affect them. Even the argument that deliberative democracy can at least be practised in 'mini publics' can be questioned. There are serious problems that confront any individual citizen seeking a direct impact on decision making as was mythologised in classical Athenian democracy or pictured by Tocqueville within the New England township. In the context of local governance there is much to be said for a principle that where a decision affects only those within that community it should be the right of members of that community to resolve that problem to the exclusion of others who are personally unaffected or but marginally affected by that issue (Chandler 2010). However, it has to be questioned how many decisions can be made in a specific community that do not have major repercussions beyond its borders. Within a village the siting of a play area for the children or the allocation of allotments for gardeners may be community specific issues, but more substantive concerns such as access to secondary and higher levels of education or the location of major industrial sites or the framework of criminal law cannot practically or ethically be left to a community rather than the decision making machinery covering regional, national or international boundaries. Moreover, the understanding of society and the values of each citizen within a local authority are moulded by the weight of comment that emanates not from within a community but from the wider social groups within the political systems that govern them and the resource unequal society which surrounds and even defines the shape of the locality.

An alternative vision such as that which has been an important theme in Habermas' more recent thinking is the creation of ethical and institutional practices that can operate at a macro level (Habermas 2001, 2008; Outhwaite 2009: 154–7). The European Union has for Habermas suggested a possible template for ensuring discursive dialogue among once warring nations that may produce both a tolerance of differences in society but at the same time a means of ensuring common understanding among groups sufficient to create a peaceful and progressive society. However, as later Habermas realised, the exceptionalism sought by many nations within the European Union, Britain in particular, provides no surety that such a situation will emerge. Moreover, without perhaps a strong emphasis on subsidiarity, that is handing local and regional decision making to the smallest units capable of dealing with an issue that affects their inhabitants, it is unlikely that citizens of a European State would feel they are included within the decision making process.

Establishing institutional forums both at the local level and more problematically the regional, national and international levels is an important aspect of approximating towards the goal of deliberative democracy. However, institutions alone, as discussed above, cannot create the framework needed for common understanding, tolerance and policy resolution. Underlying these reservations are more deep-seated problems recognised by critical theorists concerning the hegemony exerted over societies through capitalist values. As writers such as Jonathan Joseph (2010) or Davies (2011) have pointed out, the development of networks linking elements in a globalised society does not describe a necessarily more open and democratic society since networks that exert collective power in a society are still imbued with values supporting capitalism and its attendant inequalities in terms of resources to bargain within the process of setting the policy agenda and its outcomes. Such a consensus may not be in the interest of the disadvantaged due to the capacity of an elite to manipulate popular culture even in the most democratic of current liberal democracies. In less consensual societies especially those riven by deep rooted ideological conflict and struggles for power as in Syria, it is impossible without root and branch social and normative change to effectively implant any semblance of discursive or deliberative politics.

Ethics as the foundation of institutions

This study has attempted to elucidate the factors that influence the policy process in the early twenty-first century but it would require another book rather than a chapter to discuss in any detail how to create a better ethical system for determining appropriate systems for devising public policy. It is essential that those within a decision making system can adopt agreed ethical values that enable open and effective consensus building within a polity. This must involve not only unfettered access to sources of information and understanding of theory that allow a positivist scientific debate on the consequences of a policy proposal. There must also be a capacity to understand normative judgements and when toleration of other lifestyles is appropriate or universally unsupportable. As Frank Fischer (2009: 298) concludes in his study of the interface between democracy and expertise, societies are:

still largely dominated by an outmoded conception of scientific knowledge, the social and policy sciences ill-equip their doctoral students for the world they are sent out to confront. Armed with empirical research designs and statistical methods, many have little or no training in understanding either the normative and inter-pretive foundations of the tools they have learned to rely upon, or the social and political settings to which these techniques are to be applied.

A further problem that faces discursive politics is how to deal with the issues thrown up by self-interest and the inequalities of power within any society. Means need to be developed in such a society to identify policy advocates who are concerned largely with their personal development rather than seeking to forge a common interest. Once empowered through a favoured capacity to advance their views, such interests may use the trust placed in them to favour and also hide their own personal enrichment.

The process of untangling deep-seated division in society through the attainment of workable policy compromise may be possible it is argued by enhancing the suggestion, embedded in the Advocacy Coalitions Framework, that institutional arrangements can be developed to ensure states or super-state international frameworks act as brokers between contending interests. Ideally this requires the development of discursive policy analysis as the accepted mode of debate between citizens within any polity but such practice needs self-knowledge and the adoption of specialist techniques for debate and is not an activity that can immediately be used in most societies. Con-sequently, it is argued that the development of policy debate should be enhanced by deliberative practitioners who are not themselves concerned with securing policy objectives but act as neutral facilitators of debate among policy interests striving to resolve a policy problem. As Forester (2013: 6) points out, 'A critical pragmatist would treat very skeptically, if not reject out right, that attention to process alone or outcomes alone, could be justified pragmatically in a planning of public policy con-text'. The facilitator needs therefore to ensure contending parties in any policy decision are fully aware of the values and arguments of each side in a conflict and seek to diffuse tension by finding common ground between interests and the dan-gers that may result from continued intolerance by all parties in the dispute. Much of the literature on the role of policy mediators emerges from discussions over conflicts on town planning where in practice the professionals involved in implementing planning laws are frequently required to find some common understanding between clearly defined interests on a clearly defined objective. However, some concerns may be raised as to how the techniques of neutrality as practised by the facilitator and their ability to ensure contending interests can understand the position of their opponents can be applied to more complex problems faced by politicians working on national or inter-national divisions. Can politicians engaged in controlling debates at such a level ever fully escape being themselves biased by self-interest and ideological or moral straitjackets?

Decisions on whether to build a waste incinerator or nuclear power station near a particular community may be assisted by an enquiry led by a neutral facilitator not directly affected by the outcome of the discussion, but this is less likely to be secured in a debate, for example, on the sacrifices that need to be made in relation to individual freedom to decrease carbon emissions for the sake of future generations.

On basic issues of morality and ideology neutrality is impossible except for the uninformed. Once enlightened on the issue the facilitator would cease to hold a neutral stance. Moreover, many a would-be facilitator will have personal interests to contend with, such as whether to please the interests of the powerful to further their career or side with the less resourced.

What may be more germane to the development of discursive discussion on policy is that there is a widely established working ethos within the whole of a polity to accept the rules of debate. This would involve not just the acceptance of the rules outlined for discourse by Habermas but also a more thorough education within society concerning the nature of evidence and proof of policy solutions from a positivist perspective and, from a subjective direction, some understanding of the point of view of others including an element of tolerance of differences that do not substantially affect the liberties of others, and an attitude of empathy and goodwill to others. It may be concluded that whilst liberal democracy can be established to emphasise the value of equality in decision making over and above personal freedom, there are serious limits to the extent that this can be achieved simply by making institutional changes. What is required is the development of more entrenched acceptance of the ethical beliefs that must underlie democratic policy making and the use made of institutions in which democracy is practised.

Tolerance is one of the more neglected elements in discourse theory. The issue was of central importance in seventeenth century Britain, given the tensions between catholic and protestant values. John Locke (Milton and Milton 2010) wrote extensively on the issue. Through the development of British utilitarianism the issue of tolerance remains a central if somewhat submerged issue. However, the doctrine that individuals should be free to carry out their lives without interference from others, provided their actions do not seriously harm others, is in effect a call for tolerance. Such a doctrine can be criticised as being unclear as to what constitutes harm, although it is widely accepted that this at least is meant to entail physical and permanent psychological harm (Hampsher-Monk 1992: 361–83). The position also needs to be clarified concerning how far the state, assuming it is based on liberal democratic principles, can tolerate those who do not abide by its dictates, such as paying taxes. There are strong grounds for suggesting that a community can only operate successfully if its members cooperate in the many roles that are required to maintain the advantages such a structure provides. Those who, left to their own devices, freeload on a society may be subject to an obligation to provide sufficient input into the system. Nevertheless, on many issues where no physical harm is being meted out by one person to another and where each person who is an incomer into a community provides in return for the advantages they gain an appropriate input from their resources and abilities, there does not seem any rational, moral reason to erect further barriers against their involvement in that society. Thus, tolerance requires us to accept that differences in religion, for example, which in itself does not harm others or diminish fair input to that community, should be left to individual choice.

In such a scenario there can be no justification for communities and hence governments to determine styles of dress codes, let alone styles of religious observance or education, for others in that society.

It is after all for many religions the role of deities to punish those, after their death on this planet, who may have wilfully disobeyed what the gods may regard as our fashions of dress or rituals in their honour, rather than for mere mortal mankind to interfere in inter-preting their will. Similarly, for those who are atheist or agnostic, there can be no cause for not practising religious tolerance. The importance to moral society of tolerance as indi-cated in relation to religion may also be applied to all others forms of social belief and interaction, not only on the level of individual treatment of fellow individuals but also in the behaviour and power given to communities and hence to the realm of political governance.

Toleration is only one aspect of the ethical armoury that needs to be brought into consideration to develop a fully discursive democratic system to resolve policy issues. Many complex policy issues cannot simply be resolved by allowing each person to develop their own interests to the detriment of their fellow humans. As argued strongly in utilitarian thought and implicit in Kantian ideas it is clearly immoral to further one's own interests in such a way that it directly harms others. Many such problems that have a central bearing on public policy in this context relate to situations in which indivi-duals, by claiming rights to secure their interest, whilst not directly intending to damage others, contribute harm by their unregulated actions to their community and even the life chances of those as yet unborn. This problem has been called the 'tragedy of the commons'.

The tragedy of the commons was a phenomenon first recognised in the late nine-teenth century and further developed in the 1960s as a critique against the view that individuals should be free to exploit without regulation the resources of planet Earth. It was pointed out that where common land was made available to all farmers in a community, unless the usage of this land was regulated, individuals would continue to add to the numbers of cattle or sheep grazing on the common land which would as a consequence deteriorate in terms of its productivity and become of little use to anyone. This metaphor can relate not just to land but to the deterioration in fish stocks in the oceans, essential minerals in the earth and also the overuse of fossil fuels. Thus the issue lies at the heart of resolving some of the most central issues facing public policy on a world scale, such as global warming or immigration.

It was pointed out by Nobel Prize-winning economist Elinor Ostrom (1999) that in practice many small communities established among themselves rules and regulations, often in democratic conclaves, to resolve how much of the common land could be used without harming its productivity in the interests of all entitled to use the resource. Problems tended to arise when communities involved in such a situation were too large to allow effective democratic decisions to be made. Resolution of these issues cannot be made on a global scale by simply building up institutions such as the United Nations or the International Monetary Fund, but by ensuring that these institutions and their member states ascribe to common ethical objectives. Without such a foundation supra-national organisations simply become a further negotiating forum for politicians play-ing the games of *realpolitik* to suit the self-interest of their nation and hence their own self-interest to secure power and resources of wealth and esteem within their country. One important message that is made within this study in the chapters on political power is that 'might is not right' and that might, in the sense of the capacity to influence public policy, is a function of inequality.

The tragedy of the commons also points to a further problem that needs to be resolved concerning democratic and discursive problem solving by raising the issue of how large on any issue the commons may be. Within the context of the majority of major public policy decisions the assumed sovereign entity that determines policy is the nation state. In many cases the nation state as in the United States of America or Russia can be a federated structure in which the national government is con-stitutionally obliged to leave some substantive areas of decision making to sub-territorial governments or even to local communities. Nevertheless, the continued dominance of nation states in itself reflects the strong ideological values of nationalism and this in turn may create unethical values concerning the worth of differing nationalities. Despite growing inter-dependence through the process of globalisation, there is rela-tively little concern to develop much needed policies on issues such as global warming largely due to the pursuit of self-interested and national interests.

The ethical foundation for discursive decision making

There is, as should be clear from preceding arguments, no undisputable answer to how such a formula for ethical policy making can be constructed, but there are formulae as to what could be a widely accepted rational approach to determining public policy. These can be based on accepting that many ethical and religious foundations for moral action have strong points on which they may, albeit for differing reasons, be in agree-ment. These may be from a utilitarian standpoint that individuals should not seek to pursue their own interest in such a way that it harms others or from a Kantian per-spective that we should act only as we would wish others to behave towards us. Few modern and widely established religious doctrines would dissent from such edicts. Moreover, most ethical codes would suggest that these values and the rational resolu-tion of issues in the category of the 'tragedy of the commons' require a concern for establishing rules of equity in the treatment of all the societies of the world. Most ethical systems accept that individuals should not be harmed physically or imprisoned unless this is a consequence of community sanctioned punishment for transgressions of others' rights to freedom and life. The problematic area of ethical presentation of public policy is in the arena of regulating the community so that it serves as a means that enhances through cooperation the lives of all its members without undermining any individual's human rights. In this context Rawls' ideas are perhaps most pertinent. We should arrange society through public policy that ensures fairness in the distribu-tion of resources within a community such that they are distributed evenly to those who can make use of what they may receive. Rawls argues that, given those principles, in the context of public policy making everyone should have equal freedom, should they wish, to gain the capacity to involve themselves in decision making, as opposed to a system of liberal democracy that in capitalist societies will always tend to benefit the resource rich rather than the poor in the task of public policy development.

The ideal discursive ethic should also be based on the principle of subsidiarity, that is, that decisions should be made by those who are seriously affected by that decision. This would be institutionally managed by an effective system of subsidiarity, which is in theory required but not effectively applied in the European Union. Thus, small com-munity based systems of governance that may be organised using principles of direct democracy should be able to make decisions on issues such as local development, entertainments or town planning, whilst larger district and municipal communities consider wider but localised decisions on strategic planning or education. If it is impractical in such areas to make decisions through democratic means then institutionally each community within that district could elect representatives to represent its views in a district based decision making discursive congress. From the district level decisions may be made using similar principles for representation to deal with substantive issues covering a region or a nation. However, it is at these levels and in particular the national level that attempts to forge a bottom up discursive decision making system are likely to break down. As discussed in earlier chapters, nation states are normally too populous to be controlled by any form of direct democracy and even more seriously will fall under the sway of those interest networks in their unequal societies that command the greatest financial resources and hence access to education and social advancement. In many respects the concept of nationalism as developed in Western Europe during the Enlightenment was predicated on an exclusivist ethic that prevented a worldwide humanitarian consensus on individualist values. Nationalism is based on a view that the patriotic citizen ought to forward policies favouring the advantage of their nation over other, presumed competitive, states. At its worst, as in the case of fascism or states based on religious extremism, the nationalist ethic wills citizens to be predatory against different weaker states or religious, racial or ethnic groups.

> The campaigns concerning the referendum on the United Kingdom's membership of the European Union have from both sides been fought predominantly in terms of whether those living in Britain will benefit economically or through influence in global politics by remaining in or leaving the Union. Few political commentators have suggested that British membership may be of value not to Britain itself but altruistically to the benefit of the poorer or more oppressed individuals and communities in Europe.

Nationalist self-interest has been and continues to be the sticking point in resolving the many problems now facing a globalised world community, such as climate change and unacceptable resource inequalities between differing areas of the globe. In the long term, as Habermas speculated, decline in nationalism in a globalised world may, as in the development of the European Union, begin to undermine the exclusivist proclivities within the nationalist ethic. However, there is in the present decade little sign of progress within this area and even less in the possibility that other large super-national state organisations will form and then join within a restructured United Nations a cooperative discursive environment capable of developing policies that can anticipate future global problems rather than fitfully and usually belatedly react to catastrophes that emanate from an inability to prevent tragedies of the commons.

Institutions, either on a community or global level, will not on their own resolve these problems, rather than the development of global ethical values on which the necessary institution can be accepted and allowed to flourish. It is impossible to spell out in detail here what this ethic may be and the rationale on which it is founded but some sketch of what may be needed to create ethical public policy has been provided in Chapter 6 and can be further integrated here. That ethic will require accountable forms of democracy at any level of policy making and wherever possible opportunities for those affected by a decision to engage in discursive debate on major issues. Moreover, the form of debate should adhere to the principles of discourse as developed by

Habermas (1990: 89) that are outlined earlier in this chapter. The required ethical framework will place considerable emphasis on establishing the allocation of decision making through the principle of subsidiarity, which places the responsibility for determining policy at the lowest level of community that is substantially affected by the policy. The extent that public policy making should however determine the conduct of all members of a community should be restricted by the principles for tolerance of emotions, values and aesthetic temperament of others in that community, which do not physically harm the well-being and opportunities of others. Thus, there would be freedom of religion but not freedom to impose those beliefs on others. Moreover, whilst communities should be permeable and embrace other cultures, there must also be an awareness both within and external to communities of the problems that may afflict them in terms of the tragedy of the commons if there is no restraint on the acceptable use of the Earth's finite resources. Where policy issues affect greater populations than can in any form be classed as community, there needs to be a much greater development of forms of global governance which would by-pass the inherently divisive self-interests bound up within nationalist sentiment. Within such a context discursive ethics will also necessitate, on a global scale and within small communities, a concern for equality along the path of the *Theory of Justice* developed by John Rawls. This would undermine the tendency, emphasised in much of this study, that those who have the greatest resources of money and capital can secure the education and connections to form elites that will eventually dominate any process of policy making within even liberal democratic systems.

Implementing global ethics

It is not possible in this book or probably any academic study to pre-judge how we can dismantle the barriers to the development of a discursive ethic. Indeed as suggested in the critique of a scientific approach to public policy development in the earlier chapters of this book, we cannot understand much of the mechanics that create the social problems of the present, let alone what may flow from new policies and unanticipated events that will shape the future. There is no system that can force a discursive ethic on individuals. The fear of imposed institutionalised sanctions for those who do not follow an official ethical path or concern over social exclusion may prompt individuals to profess loyalty to ethical principles but this does not mean that their will to self-interest and personal advantage may not override practical conformity. A discursive ethic and hence globalised systems of deliberative democracy may only emerge when through global discourse it appears to individuals rational for them to accept the underlying ethical principles.

It would be wholly naive to believe that a particular formulation of a discursive ethic might sweep away the countervailing factors that lie in its path or that some institutionalised global solution can be conjured up to enforce such an ethic. It can only be an exercise in speculation as to whether certain trends will be likely to push the cultural values within societies nearer to a tolerant and egalitarian discursive ethic. In respect to discrimination between the sexes or in relation to consenting sexual relationships there has been a revolution, yet to be completed, among attitudes within the last fifty years towards a more tolerant and fair position. Over the last hundred years the capacity for those with religious beliefs to work together on their common values, and to leave to the gods rather than humans the award of favour or punishment after death, has progressed even though there remain intolerable outbreaks of violence in the name of faith. Perhaps more deeply inherent in the human psyche, nationalism is giving way within a globalising world to an acceptance that there should be standard basic ethical principles regarding how government leaders and individuals should respect each other. Maybe the early twenty-first century will also be seen as a high water mark in the acceptance of inequality within society and rational values of the majority will prevail upon the over-resourced beneficiaries of capital to create an egalitarian society and avoid creating on a global scale a tragedy of the commons. However, whether any of these developments progress in the evolution of human society, either and ideally through evolution in ethical thought founded on globalised access to social discourse, or more dangerously through violent revolutions or natural disasters caused by the despoliation of the finite resources on which our civilisations depend, it is essential at the present time for as many as possible in the world's societies to use the media at their disposal to enter their positions on the vital debates affecting their lives on either a global or community scale to bring forward better and, both positively and subjectively, more rational approaches to public policy.

Conclusion

This chapter has considered arguments concerning discourse theory as an approach to a global methodology that can form the basis for more democratic and widely acceptable management of the public policy process. The central message of discourse theory is that the varied parties concerned with the resolution of a public problem must seek, through a mutual exchange of views, to understand the many differing opinions that are voiced and empirically verify facts that surround debate on the issues within a spirit of tolerance and morally good intentions. It is argued that the development of a normative system of discursive interests must be the basis of any more acceptable institutional arrangements for public policy making. Without a widely accepted ethical basis, institutions, however democratic they may appear, can be subverted to the self-interests of the most powerfully resourced elites within any society.

18 Conclusion

Public policy is shown in Chapter 1 to be a multi-disciplinary study closely linked to the social sciences that considers the process of making, legitimating and implementing policy made under the auspices of national governments and their agencies and through the growing array of inter-governmental organisations. It is pointed out in Chapter 2 that policy studies in its infancy was an attempt to develop a more scientific methodology for securing the best outcomes for policy problems. The discipline emerged as a separate sub-field in the social sciences primarily as an attempt to develop rational means to scientifically establish processes and attitudes of mind that could create the optimum solutions to problems that needed to be resolved for the benefit of society. These well intentioned ideas of the mid-twentieth century have never fulfilled their original aims but importantly raised controversies that have produced a more sophisticated understanding of how public policy is formed and processed. However, further advances in understanding and improving policy content and processes must lie in the better development of subjective as well as positivist answers to many continuing problems. This will also lead to a less inward and self-referential approach to the study by connecting to the wider theories of social sciences.

The positivist and subjective arenas of public policy

Policy content and policy motives are argued in Chapter 3 to be central to determining the differing fortunes and processes through which public policy evolves. Whilst policy content may be a rational response for some advocates of a solution to what is seen as a social problem or opportunity, it is not necessarily a rational response for others. This is because policy content and hence the motive behind policy suggestions are in a large part based on subjective values and attitudes that cannot be subject to proof or falsification as is the requirement in the dominant paradigm of the physical sciences. This is not, however, to denigrate the importance of positivist evidence and theory in establishing policy outcomes to 'satisfice' subjectivist aims. Both epistemological frameworks should be seen as complementary but in this study the subjectivist element has been emphasised as a counterweight to the many more studies, deriving from Lasswell's hope of a science of policy by sweeping subjective elements under the carpet.

Within this study, the subjective values that motivate policy advocates have, for simplification, been classified as ideological, self-interested and ethical, although it is accepted that it is impossible to wholly separate these broad arrangements of ideas and emotions. Rarely is a policy idea forwarded by its advocates with a purely altruistic motive but is usually propelled forward by a mixture of subjective emotions, aims and objectives. The reality of policy advocacy is thus never a matter of scientific method and, in as much as they can in one sense be rational, many policies may be rational for some, but by no means all in society. Chapters 4 to 6 discuss in more detail the emotional and subjective motives of ideology, self-interest and ethics that frame policy content and the extent to which they may structure the policy process and the institutions of the state.

The complexity of policy development is further exacerbated by the environmental structures in which societies operate. These structures take many forms such as institutional arrangements framed usually in constitutional law that are in themselves the outcome of public policies. Societies are also built through less formal cultural understandings that differentiate individuals and groups by economic class, habitus or life worlds and wealth, gender or family and clan loyalties. The juxtaposition of many environmental variables with the many aspects of public policy content driven by ethics, ideology and self-interest ensures that public policy forms a highly complex area for analysis. The development of policy consequently encounters differing treatments in differing societies to the extent that generalisations and hence predictions on how any specific policy may be developed are at best tentative sketches.

The capacity of individuals or groups to make a mark on the arena of public policy is in itself less impenetrable and as discussed in Chapter 7 is predominantly to be seen as a consequence of the distribution of power within society. Such a capacity is based on the resources that individuals and groups have at their disposal to communicate their ideas, isolate their opponents and thus develop their interests. The most effective organisations and individuals who steer the policy process on any subject are those with the most substantial resources of wealth, education and social connections. In practice these elements of power are manifested in the resources held within networks of social connections or advocacy coalitions. It is argued in this study that policy is developed only when it is seen as a problem by the largely autocratic professionalised elites and particularly professional political elites, who dominate their communities as centres of knowledge, understanding and expertise in the many subject areas that are of interest and value to complex societies. Policy networks or advocacy coalitions can encompass farmers, military personnel, scientists, economists, social theorists, including experts on public policy, but also the political activists whose leading members can act as gatekeepers who may not necessarily develop and make policy ideas, but are in a position to determine whether a policy initiative is enacted. Most professional elites are autocratic by nature be they political parties or centres of expertise. They tend to create among their members an *esprit de corps* by separating their source of influence obtained through their expertise from the rest of society in order to further their self-interest and sense of esteem. Hence professional groups are apt to create their own languages, ceremonies, and ideologies peculiar to their trade. They attempt, usually with some success, to determine who should enter their profession or calling. In many professions seniority is acquired through co-option to the policy making circles of their organisation by those established within the existing policy circles. In less autocratic societies this process may be legitimated through formal elections but in many cases claims of expertise and loyalty to the values of their profession are the major factors securing support for high office.

A distinctive form of professionalism that is central to the issue of public policy development, is that which surrounds the community of political activists. The role requires members to join communities with a common ideological understanding which are divided in many liberal democracies into competing political parties. Despite differences in ideology, a common self-interest to retain their position can edge politicians to defend the institutions that place them in a privileged and often lucrative position. Political parties are consequently by and large autocratic in form and usually require loyalty to their leaders who are selected from their politically most successful members. Such loyalty is often forthcoming as a divided party will court electoral failure and within an autocracy apostates may court expulsion and even elimination.

Chapters 8 to 10 discuss the institutionalised structuring of largely inegalitarian forms of governance in terms of political power that are consequent on differing resources of financial capital and expertise within large-scale societies. It is pointed out that although there are significant differences between most autocracies and liberal democracies in terms of political and economic freedom, many of the institutions of governance in liberal democracies, let alone their economic structures, are autocratic in form. Autocracies, discussed in Chapter 8, vary in format from totalitarian regimes premising their dominance through division, surveillance and violence to looser organisations in which a small politicised minority monopolise power but leave their poorly resourced citizens to fend for themselves. Networks of professional interest in many such regimes are likely to be dominated and controlled by the state, although it is likely that from such interests rebellion against the regime would be most potent. Although it has been claimed by the elites who rule in such regimes that policy is made for the benefit of the public, rarely does this appear to the case. The idea that an autocratic regime represents, for example, a vanguard of the proletariat, as claimed by Lenin with reference to the Bolshevik takeover of what emerged as the Soviet Union, was never put into practice. Can any autocratic leader or small oligarchy fully understand and empathise with the needs and desires of all their citizens? Ideology and ethics as explained in the opening chapters of this study are subjective and can all too easily be linked to self-interest rather than altruism.

Within liberal democracies as discussed in Chapters 9 and 10, an attachment to liberal principles allows individuals and groups greater freedom requiring the dominant gate-keepers of the core executive to tolerate opposition and to compromise their preferred policy choices largely through a process of making small adjustments to their ideas, which may be seen as a form of muddling through. Nevertheless, in developed liberal democracies there is more emphasis on liberty than there is on democracy. The leaders of dominant political parties in liberal democracies have a considerable number of means to stack decisions in their favour. Ethically it is widely argued that public policy should be made within a democratic context but in practice governance in any polity that has a significant population falls far short of any such ideal. Firstly this is a consequence of the size of most governed communities. Most of the inhabitants of any civic society are unlikely to meet or even know of the existence of their fellow compatriots and hence the final decisions on the legitimation of policy are made by policy gate-keepers in a core executive who are influenced by a relatively small population of networked interests working through predominantly autocratic arrangements. Within a large population it is impossible to give weight to the interests and comments of each member of the polity affected by a policy issue and, moreover, it may be argued that the views of most citizens come from individuals who have little interest in the problem or capacity to understand the issue and should be discounted. This is not usually because they lack the mental capacity to understand policy problems but often because their time is limited and often focused on personal problems. Most individuals including policy gate-keepers can but concern themselves with a few issues at any one time. Freedom of thought and expression allows individuals with the motivation and education to shape their world to force their ideas onto the policy agenda and, with luck, allow themselves to become part of the ruling elite. However, luck in particular only shines its light on a relatively small cohort in any substantial society and these are largely those who have inherited greater resources of wealth, education and networked connections from their families.

Many policy decisions also require specialised theories and research that empower the groups who have acknowledged expertise in these issues. The number of contending solutions and possible outcomes of any problem means that a process of what Etzioni referred to as mixed scanning must take place to sift out a few policy alternatives for extensive consideration. Only individuals who regard policy making as part of their profession or mainstream concern can become particularly expert in this activity. The decisions are, therefore, predominantly influenced by the views of professionals either directly given their authority to represent accepted wisdom on technical issues, but also the relatively few professional interests that purport to represent to interest networks what they believe to be the public interest and have the resources to ensure that without their consent it is impossible for societies to engage in vital tasks that require their expertise.

The capacity for public policy to be determined democratically is further undermined by the underlying difficulty of reconciling the value of liberalism as seen within the context of a right to property with that of democracy. Whilst democracy suggests that every person in a community has an equal opportunity to involve themselves in policy development, liberalism suggests each person is free to develop their own interests without interference by others as long as their actions do not harm or undermine the liberties of fellow citizens. There are many debates concerning the extent to which any claim to have a right to freedom may always be damaging to the liberty of others but, in practice in liberal democracies, there is a tendency to follow the values first promulgated by John Locke that individuals have a right to life, liberty and, most problematically for democracy, a right to property. As has been shown earlier, the inequalities between the resources to obtain power within any society largely relate to the capacity and also the good fortune to amass resources of wealth, education and connections and pass these benefits on to descendants. Thus in liberal democracies those with property in terms of fixed and disposal assets have the resources to be significantly more dominant in the policy making process.

Public policy in these circumstances becomes unduly influenced not just by a few individuals but also by private collective interests. Given that in liberal democracies citizens have a right to own and inherit property, wealth gradually accumulates unevenly into the hands of a relatively small number of wealthy individuals of whom many have had a well-resourced upbringing enabling them to secure greater wealth than the majority of citizens. The political leaders that have risen to elite positions in competitive political parties in many cases obtain their position through co-option and the patronage of existing members of a core executive who have reached this position through a similar process. It may be argued that personal liberty afforded by liberal democracies does in theory allow every citizen to seek out such favoured status but few can be chosen to reach such political heights and those that succeed will frequently adopt the mannerisms and values of the 'life world' of their newly acquired elite status. In contrast the vast majority realise or accept with little thought that even attempting to become the gate-keepers or successful advocates of policy is beyond their resources.

In effect the liberal element of liberal democracy, that is freedom of personal choice, dominates over any democratic concern to ensure power is evenly allocated. Under such a system there is hardly a level playing field in which the needs of the resource poor are altruistically understood and considered by the resource rich, let alone any capacity to help form policies that determine their lifestyle. Fischer (2003: 205) also points out that Western societies, and it may be added, the rapidly developing societies of East Asia and Latin America, value the positivist vision of scientific methodology that runs counter to the concept of developing policy through majority agreement but ensures that professional experts can reveal unchallengeable certainties that cannot easily be set aside by the lay majority of citizens. Such a conclusion has led a number of political theorists to rethink the possibilities for a more egalitarian democracy in terms of both the influence that those affected by a policy can exert on its development and also who should be considered to be materially affected by a policy.

The policy process

Chapters 11 to 14 discuss the policy process from the development of policy initiatives to their implementation and subsequent evolution. A summary of the policy process that is presented in this volume appears to have reached generally pessimistic conclusions, particularly in terms of the practicality of public policy achieving rational and predictable outcomes as envisaged by policy advocates. Many policy ideas are canvassed within civil societies but very few enter a wider public consciousness at a time when the social and material environment allows them a chance to receive serious attention from those with the power to advance the idea onto a national political stage. Those policies that emerge on the political agenda may then fail to progress to legitimation as contending networks of interest seek to bury the idea or to push the policy idea from its original goals to more closely suit their own interests. Few policies that are legitimated are other than compromises between the interests that have the resources to influence their development. Once established as a public policy the outcome may be very different from the aims of its advocates. As indicated in Chapter 10, the outcomes of the policy process are largely created through the interaction of highly politicised networks. They are not only characterised by communication on matters of agreement but may also harbour similar objectives for different reasons and also create serious rivalries among personnel bidding for power. Policy objectives may, therefore, have different values and different meanings for those who advocate change. There are, as shown in Chapters 12 to 14, serious pitfalls when policy is implemented through misinterpretation, either wilfully or as a result of poor communication, between the policy advocates and gate-keepers and the street level bureaucrats who must manage the implementation of the idea. Implementation may also reveal that some policy ideas are flawed either technically or in their capacity to be accepted by the societies or networks that are supposed to be the subjects of the policy. The extent to which it is even possible to determine whether a policy that has reached the stage of being a legitimated aim of a polity has been successful or a complete failure is also usually subject to unsettled debate. As emphasised in Chapter 12, evaluation is in reality as much an attempt by policy advocates and political gate-keepers to validate their policy choices and their outcomes within the framework of their subjective and often self-interested aims, as a dispassionate review.

The possibility of partial or total failure is present in the many processes within the cyclical evolution of public policy development, as shown in Chapter 15. As discussed in Chapter 16 there is an extensive literature on why policies fail but often these pay little heed to the argument from complexity theory that it is virtually impossible to engineer in one attempt a successful policy outcome. Where possible it makes sense for most policy initiatives to be tested in pilot studies before being imposed on a wider society. Failures may then be mitigated by learning from mistakes and seeking a different path to resolve a problem.

Strong discursive democracy

Winston Churchill is reported as saying that democracy is the worst form of government apart from all the others. Critics of the domination of capital within the policy making process variously argue for greater democracy and more substantive political education of civic society to enable an ethic of discourse as suggested by Habermas and institutions through subsidiarity, referenda and ethical will to create what may be termed a strong democracy. It may better be said in the context of effective and ethical policy making that deliberative democracy is the worst form of policy development and implementation apart from all other frameworks. Discursive, deliberative democracy would in theory mitigate the inequalities in the distribution of power within liberal democracies, but it is difficult within capitalist liberal democracies to establish the normative values and institutional structures that can form the foundation for such practice, especially outside the confines of small communities. Deliberative democracy requires the development of a more educated public as regards social, economic and political argument and above all ethical understanding than is normally encouraged in school or tertiary systems of education. However, professionals may operate within the confines of acknowledged positivist expertise concerning a specific subject area, whereas the professional politicians who serve as the gate-keepers of the policy process, in general, must determine the way forward on a wide range of issues. If the politicised elite have a specialism, it is the darker arts of validating, communicating and compelling others to follow their subjective interests. A serious problem that stalks liberal democratic systems is the trend for the development of political elites based on the recruitment of able candidates to positions that allow them eventual access and membership of core executive positions through the patronage of those who already hold power at this level. Through such means those in power may be detached from the societies they govern and also remain motivated to keep the system of patron–clientelism at the heart of the political system.

Why attempt to make policy at all?

Despite these pessimistic and unsatisfactory conclusions it is, nevertheless, nonsense to suggest that policy solutions should never be attempted. When faced by a domestic or international crisis, doing nothing because it is impossible to predict the consequences of a policy, is in itself a policy decision. Whilst policy cannot be reduced to a science in which it is possible to devise strategies whose outcomes can be reliably predictable, the possibilities of failure can be diminished by reference to experience and carefully thought through experimentation and debate. There are also a wide variety of techniques and disciplines that can help to remove the chances of error and failure in building the foundations and implementation of policy. Many of these factors are reflected in established methodologies within the social studies that, whilst not guaranteeing certainty in predicting the success of policies, can be claimed to establish a rational basis for attempting to resolve a policy problem or opportunity. Such practices ought, through effective systems for education, to be made widely accessible to anyone with the motivation to shape their world to influence the policy agenda and, with luck, allow themselves to enter the ruling elite. However, luck in particular only shines its light on a relatively small cohort in any substantial society and these are largely those who have inherited greater resources of wealth, education and networked connections. They include the capacity to develop ideas based on thorough research into the social environment that impinges on the policy area in question. An understanding of the history of the issue is essential to understand feasible solutions to a problem and to quickly reject ideas and behaviours that have been widely agreed to have failed in the past. An understanding of ethical and moral values will also be essential. Such activity, similar to Etzioni's idea of mixed scanning, must be based on policy activists having the capacity to understand what may be convincing evidence of policy interests and wider public opinion towards particular aspects of a solution. As Pawson (2013) emphasises in his attempts to secure what he has termed realistic evaluation, interpretation of data requires the capacity to link evidence with theory to approximate to a plausible explanation of past events that may give guidance to future development. Effective social scientific methodology requires minds that are willing at all times to question their conclusions and to be prepared, as has been argued by theorists of complexity, to change direction when they perceive that their ideas ceased to be supported by either evidence or practice.

As this study argues, public policy making is only partially rooted in the capacity to develop through positivist scientific methodology ideal solutions to policy problems, since most policy solutions are based on the subjective interests as to what policy gatekeepers, advocates and those who implement policy decide to impose on the great majority of citizens who are subject to the consequences of policy outcomes rather than its development. Strong democratic decision making is, as discussed in Chapter 17, best implemented in small communities and becomes increasingly less effective the greater the population of a community. Ensuring public policy that is in the interest of as many individuals as possible therefore requires the development of widely held ethical principles concerning the conduct of debate and discourse and societies throughout the world that accept fundamental rational values of tolerance, equality and above all from a Kantian perspective goodwill and empathy for others as well as for self. Such a change would be a much needed assault on nationalism as a largely divisive concept. Perhaps, despite its many wars, tragedies of the commons such as climate change, and growing inequality between rich and poor, there can be found in the development of both community ethics and a global ethic the basis for a more humane world society.

Glossary

Agency The individuals or institutions that actively cause or attempt to cause or prevent political change

Altruism Living or acting for the interest of others

Behaviouralism A social and psychological theory that all human action can be interpreted through observation of human behaviour

Capital Economic wealth measured in terms of ownership of property or saved transferrable cash

Civic Society The interactions and thoughts within the whole population of a political system

Complexity Theory Theories that attempt to understand and model social organisations activities as a consequence of the interaction of a large number of independent physical and subjective variables

Core executive The politicians and civil servants who compose the central leaders of a government

Deliberative democracy A system of democracy built on widespread discussion on ideas and values in which those concerned are willing to change their views through absorbing the persuasive views of others

Discourse Theory Theories concerning communication and debate between individuals and between groups of individuals

Ethics The moral relationships between individuals and groups

Functionalism A theory arguing that living organisations and society are best understood and described as inter-related systems in which recognisable elements should be viewed as performing essential functions that retain the integrity of that system

Government The agencies and individuals who collectively have the authority to develop and ensure the implementation of public policy within a sovereign state

Governance Those organisations in society whether public, private or third sector (qv) that are involved in influencing policy and the action of government

Habitus Termed used by Pierre Bourdieu to describe the values and social environment of individuals and groups

Hegemony A situation in which ruling elites could develop myths, values and language that were so penetrated into civil society that the majority of citizens could not accept any form of governance and control other than that implanted by the ruling class

Ideology 'Any more or less coherent systems of beliefs or views on politics and society' (Leach 1991: 10)

Interpretive Theory   An approach to understanding society by consideration of the meaning given to the beliefs and attitudes of individuals in relation to their actions and actions of others

Iron Triangles   Closely integrated interests such as, in the United States, the Presidential executive and bureaucracy, Congress, and business interests that dominate the policy making process

Life World   Term used by Jürgen Habermas to denote the totality of the social, cultural and ideological world view of individuals and social groups

Macro level   The study of social phenomena acting or operating on a large, often global scale

Meso level   The study of social phenomena acting on a scale between micro and macro levels. For example, explanations of policy making in specific governments

Micro level   The study of social phenomena relating to inter-personal behaviour between individuals or between individuals and organisations

New Right Theory   The term is used differently in differing countries and areas of study but for the purposes of this book it is based on the mainstream development of the term in the United Kingdom as the theory and ideology that individual and group actions can be modelled on the assumption that individuals seek to maximise their income and wealth for the least amount of effort. As an ideology it also argues that governments should base their policies predominantly on this assumption. These ideas developed by economists such as Friedrich Hayek and Milton Friedman re-shaped in the 1970s the values of the Conservative Party under the leadership of Margaret Thatcher and continue as of now to be a central pillar of modern Conservative thought. As public choice, new-liberalism or rational choice theory the view is also substantially held within the United States policy system

Participatory democracy   A view that studies direct democracy and models how liberal democracy may be deepened by allowing as many citizens as possible to directly vote and express opinions on all issues that affect or interest them

Pluralism   Political systems in which a large number of interest groups have the capacity and freedom to influence decision making

Policy   'A purposive course of action followed by an actor or set of actors in dealing with a problem or matter of concern' (Anderson 1975: 3)

Policy entrepreneurs   Individuals and, collectively, the institutions that analyse and develop policy solutions (Kingdon 2006: 122)

Policy advocates   The individuals and groups who favour and promote a particular policy

Policy gate-keepers   The political leaders with the power to accept and legitimate or reject a policy proposal

Policy networks   Institutionalised groups that communicate with one another in the determination of policy

Policy process   The activity of developing policy proposals from their early development to, if an idea gets that far, its becoming an item on a government's agenda implementation and further evolution

Policy soup   A termed established by John Kingdon (1995) to describe the amorphous environment of public opinion from which policy ideas emerge

Politics   The study and practice of creating, managing and resolving social conflict

Political power   The capacity in individuals and groups to ensure that other individuals or groups act in their interest

Polity   The individuals, groups and institutions that make up the totality of a public political arrangement

Positivism   The belief that there is an observable world independent of human observation whose content may be discovered through deductive and intuitive logic and can be developed into explanatory theories that are capable of falsification

Public Choice Theory   A theory, which may be broadly based in the category of New-Right thinking, that models human actions as largely economically self-interested

Rationality   A capacity to develop thoughts and arguments based on observation and theory rather than unsupported intuition

Rational Choice Theory   A theory and basis for modelling society on the premise that individuals wish to maximise their well-being for the least possible cost in time, effort and resource

Self-interest   Acting for one's personal interest or that of one's close dependants

Social capital   The accumulated store of ideology, value and support within a society that can be drawn on by governments to ensure peaceful cooperation within that society

Subjectivism   Those ideas which are created within the mind that are not capable of being demonstrated to be objectively true or false

Third sector organisations   Organisations that are involved in the political system that are neither part of government nor are privately owned

Bibliography

Afari-Adomah, A. (2009) Health Sector Reforms: A Study of Mutual Health Organisations in Ghana, PhD Thesis, Sheffield: Sheffield Hallam University.

Allison, G. (1971) *Essence of Decision Making: Explaining the Cuban Missile Crisis*, Boston, MA: Little Brown.

Almond, G. and Verba, S. (1963) *The Civic Culture*, Princeton, NJ: Princeton University Press.

Almond, G. and Powell, G. B. (1966) *Comparative Politics: A Developmental Approach*, Boston, MA: Little Brown.

Amy, D. J. (1984) 'Why Policy Analysis and Ethics are Incompatible', *Journal of Policy Analysis and Management*, 3(4): 573–591.

Anderson, J. (1975) *Public Policy Making*, London: Nelson.

Arendt, H. (1967) *The Origins of Totalitarianism*, 3rd edn, London: George Allen and Unwin.

Ashworth, P. (2000) *Psychology and Human Nature*, London: Psychology Press.

Atkinson, H., (2015) 'Planetary Challenges: The Agenda Laid Bare' in Atkinson, H. and Wade, R. (eds) *The Challenge of Sustainability*, Bristol: Policy Press.

Ayer, A. J. (1936) *Language Truth and Logic*, London: Gollancz.

Bachrach, P. and Baratz, M. S. (1962) 'Two Faces of Power', *American Political Science Review*, 56: 947–952.

Bagehot, W. (1867) *The English Constitution*, 2nd edn, http://socserv.mcmaster.ca/econ/ugcm/3ll3/bagehot/constitution.pdf.

Banfield, E. (1958) *The Moral Basis of a Backward Society*, Glencoe, IL: Free Press.

Barber, B. (1984) *Strong Democracy: Participatory Politics for a New Age*, Berkeley, CA: California University Press.

Barker, E. (ed. and translator) (1946) *The Politics of Aristotle*, Oxford: Oxford University Press.

Barrett, S. and Fudge, C. (1981) 'Reconstructing the Field of Analysis' in Barrett, S. and Fudge, C. (eds) *Policy and Action*, London: Methuen, pp. 249–278.

Bauman, Z. (2006) *Liquid Fear*, Cambridge: Polity Press.

Baumgartner, F. and Jones, B. (1991) 'Agenda Dynamics and Policy Sub-systems'. *Journal of Politics*, 53(4): 1044–1074.

Baumgartner, F. and Jones, B. (1993) *Agendas and Instability in American Politics*, Chicago, IL: University of Chicago Press.

Baumgartner, F., Jones, B. and Mortensen, P. (2014) 'Punctuated Equilibrium Theory: Explaining Stability and Change in Public Policy Making' in Sabatier, P. and Weible, C. M. (eds) *Theories of the Policy Process*, 3rd edn, Boulder, CO: Westview Press, pp. 59–103.

Beard, M. (2015) *SPQR: A History of Ancient Rome*, London: Profile Books.

Beck, U. (1992) *Risk Society: Towards a New Modernity* (trans. Mark Ritter), London: Sage.

Bell, D. (1960) *The End of Ideology: On the Exhaustion of Political Ideas in the Fifties*, Glencoe, IL: Free Press.

Benn, T. (2002) *Tony Benn Free at Last, Diaries 1991–2001*, London: Hutchinson.

Benson, D. and Jordan, A. (2011) 'What have we learned from Policy Transfer Research? Dolowitz and Marsh re-visited', *Political Studies Review*, 9: 366–378.

Benson, J. K. (1975) 'The Interorganizational Network as a Political Economy', *Administrative Science Quarterly*, 20(2): 229–249.

Benson, J. K. (1982) 'A Framework for Policy Analysis' in Rogers, D. and D. Whetten and Associates, *Interorganizational Coordination, Theory, Research and Implementation*, Ames: Iowa State University Press, pp. 132–176.

Bentham, J. (1779) 'A Fragment on Government' in Harrison, W. (ed.) (1948) *A Fragment on Government*, Oxford: Basil Blackwell.

Bentley, A. (1908) *The Process of Government*, Chicago, IL: University of Chicago Press.

Beverige, W. (1942) *Social Insurance and Allied Services*, Cmd. 6404, London: His Majesty's Stationery Office.

Bevir, M. and Rhodes, R. A. W. (2003) *Interpreting British Governance*, London: Routledge.

Birch, A. H. (1959) *Small Town Politics: A Study of Political Life in Glossop*, Oxford: Oxford University Press.

Blair, T. (2010) *A Journey*, London: Hutchinson.

Blake, R. (1970) *The Conservative Party from Peel to Churchill*, London: Eyre and Spottiswoode.

Bourdieu, P. (1998) *Practical Reason*, Stanford, CA: Stanford University Press.

Bovens, M. and t'Hart, P. (1996) *Understanding Policy Fiascoes*, New Brunswick, NJ: Transaction Books.

Bovens, M., t'Hart, P. and Peters, B. G. (eds) (2001) *Success and Failure in Public Governance: A Comparative Analysis*, Cheltenham: Edward Elgar.

Bowen, E. R. (1982) 'The Pressman-Wildavsky paradox: four addenda on why models based on probability theory can predict implementation success and suggest useful tactical advice for implementers', *Journal of Public Policy*, 2: 1–22.

Boydstun, A. (2013) *Making the News*, Chicago, IL: Chicago University Press

Braybrooke, D. and Lindblom, C. E. (1963) *A Strategy of Decision*, New York: The Free Press.

Breckon, J. (2015) *Better Services through Experimental Government*, London: Alliance for Useful Evidence.

British Broadcasting Corporation (2014) *Profile: Silvio Berlusconi: Italian ex-Prime Minister*, www.bbc.co.uk/news/world-europe-11981754 (accessed 2 September 2014).

Brown, G. (2010) *Beyond the Crash: Overcoming the First Crisis of Globalisation*, New York: Free Press.

Bullock, A. (1990) *Hitler: A Study in Tyranny*, London: Penguin.

Burke, E. (1790) *Reflections on the Revolution in France*, ed. Conor Cruise O'Brien (1968) Harmondsworth: Pelican Classics.

Burnham, J. (1941) *The Managerial Revolution*, Bloomington: Indiana University Press.

Butler, D., Adonis, A. and Travers, T. (1994) *Failure in British Government: The Politics of the Poll Tax*, Oxford: Oxford University Press.

Butler, D. and Stokes, D. (1969) *Political Change in Britain*, London: Macmillan.

Cairney, P. (2012) *Understanding Public Policy*, Basingstoke: Palgrave Macmillan.

Calhoun, C. (1995) *Critical Social Theory*, Oxford: Blackwell.

Carr, E. H. (1939) *The Twenty Years Crisis 1919–1939: An Introduction to the Study of International Relations*, London: Macmillan.

Carr, R. and Fusi, J. (1981) *Spain: Dictatorship to Democracy*, 2nd edn, London: George Allen and Unwin.

Carter, N., Klein, R. and Day, P. (1992) *How Organisations Measure Success*, London: Routledge.

Castells, M. (1977) *The Urban Question*, London: Edward Arnold.

Castells, M. (2000) 'Materials for an exploratory theory of the network society', *British Journal of Sociology*, 51(1): 5–24.

Catlin, G. (1927) *The Science and Method of Politics*, New York: Knopf.

Chandler, J. A. (1988) *Public Policy Making for Local Government*, London: Croom Helm.

Chandler, J. A. (2007) *Explaining Local Government*, Manchester: Manchester University Press.

Chandler, J. A. (2009) *Local Government Today*, 4th edn, Manchester: Manchester University Press.

Chandler, J. A. (2010) 'A Rationale for Local Government', *Local Government Studies*, 36(1): 5–20.

Chandler, J. A. (2014) *Comparative Public Administration*, 2nd edn, London: Routledge.

Chase, W. (2007) 'Stalin as producer: The Moscow Show Trials and the Construction of Mortal Threats' in Davies, S. and Harris, J. (eds) *Stalin*, Cambridge: Cambridge University Press.

Checkland, S. G. and Checkland, E. O. A. (eds) (1974) *The Poor Law Reports of 1834*, Harmondsworth: Penguin.

Christoff, P. and Eckersley, R. (2013) *Globalization and the Environment*, Lanham, MD: Rowman and Littlefield.

Cohen, M. D., March, J. G. and Olsen, J. P. (1972) 'A Garbage Can Model of Organizational Choice', *Administrative Science Quarterly*, 17: 1–25

Colebatch, H. K. (2002) *Policy*, 2nd edn, Basingstoke: Macmillan.

Constantine, S. (1992) *Lloyd George*, London: Routledge.

Copus, C. (2006) *Leading the Localities: Executive Mayors in English Local Governance*, Manchester: Manchester University Press.

Coveney, P. and Highfield, R. (1995) *Frontiers of Complexity: The Search for Order in a Chaotic World*, London: Faber and Faber.

Crick, B. (1962) *In Defence of Politics*, London: Penguin.

Crosland, C. A. R. (1964) *The Future of Socialism*, London: Jonathon Cape.

Crossman, R. H. S. (1975) *The Diaries of a Cabinet Minister: Volume One: Minister of Housing*, London: Hamish Hamilton and Jonathan Cape.

Curran, J. (2012) 'Re-interpreting the Internet' in Curran, J., Fenton, N. and Freedman, D. (eds) *Misunderstanding the Internet*, Abingdon: Routledge.

Dahl, R. A. (1961) *Who Governs? Democracy and Power in an American City*, New Haven, CT: Yale University Press.

Dahl, R. A. (1989) *Democracy and its Critics*, New Haven, CT: Yale University Press.

Davies, J. S. (2011) *Challenging Governance Theory: From Networks to Hegemony*, Bristol: The Policy Press.

De Leon, P. (1999) 'The Stages Approach to the Policy Process' in Sabatier, P. (ed.) *Theories of the Policy Process*, Boulder, CO: Westview Press.

De Leon, P. (2006) 'The Historical Roots of the Field' in Moran, M., Rein, M., and Goodin, R. (eds) *The Oxford Handbook of Public Policy*, Oxford: Oxford University Press.

Derthick, M. (1970) *The Influence of Federal Grants*, Cambridge, MA: Harvard University Press.

Derthick, M. (1972) *New Towns in Town: Why a Federal Program Failed*, Washington, DC: Urban Institute.

De Tocqueville, A. (1994) *Democracy in America*, ed. J. P. Mayer, London: Fontana Press.

Deutscher, I. (1966) *Stalin*, London: Penguin Press.

Diamond, J. (2001) 'Managing Change or Coping with Conflict: Mapping the Experience of a Local Regeneration Partnership', *Local Economy*, 16(4): 272–285.

Dewey, J. (1998) *The Essential Dewey Vol. 1 Pragmatism, Education and Bureaucracy*, ed. L. Hickman and T. Alexander, Bloomington: University of Indiana Press.

Disraeli, B. (1948) (first published 1844) *Coningsby*, London: John Lehmann.

Disraeli, B. (1981) (first published 1845) *Sybil or The Two Nations*, Oxford: Oxford University Press.

Dobson, A. (2007) *Green Political Thought*, 4th edn, London: Routledge.

Dolowitz, D. P. (2000) 'Introduction', *Governance*, 13(1): 1–4.

Dolowitz, D. P. and Marsh, D. (1996) 'Who Learns What from Whom? A Review of the Policy Transfer Literature', *Political Studies*, 44(2): 343–357.

Dolton, P. and Chung, T. (2004) 'The Rate of Return to Teaching: How does it Compare to other Graduate Jobs', *National Institute Economic Preview*, 190: 89–103.

Downs, A. (1957) *An Economic Theory of Democracy*, New York: Harper and Row.

Drolet, M. (2004) 'Introduction' in Drolet, M. (ed.) *The Post Modernism Reader*, London: Routledge.

Dror, Y. (1964) 'Muddling Through – Science or Inertia?' *Public Administration Review*, 24: 153–157.

Drucker, P. F. (1954) *The Practice of Management*, New York: Harper Brothers.

Dryzek, J. (2000) *Deliberative Democracy and Beyond*, Oxford: Oxford University Press.

Dryzek, J. (2010) *Foundations and Frontiers of Deliberative Governance*, Oxford: Oxford University Press.

Dryzek, J. and Dunleavy, P. (2009) *Theories of the Democratic State*, Basingstoke: Macmillan.

Dunleavy, P. (1991) *Democracy, Bureaucracy and Public Choice*, London: Harvester Wheatsheaf.

Dunleavy, P. (1995) 'Policy disasters: Explaining the UK's record', *Public Policy and Administration*, 10(2): 2–70.

Dunsire, A. (1978) *Implementation in a Bureaucracy: The Execution Process*, Vol. 1, Oxford: Martin Robertson.

Dye, T. R. (1995) *Understanding Public Policy*, 8th edn, Englewood Cliffs, NJ: Simon and Schuster.

Easton, D. (1965) *The Political System*, New York: Knopf.

Easton, G. (2013) 'How is Iain Duncan Smith still in his job', *New Statesman*, www.newstatesman.com/politics/2013/11/how-iain-duncan-smith-still-in-his-job (accessed 1 September 2014).

Edgar, A. (2005) *The Philosophy of Habermas*, Chesham: Acumen.

Eisenhower, D. (1961) *Farewell Address, January 17th*, www.youtube.com/watch?=8y06NSBBRtY.

Elcock, H. (1990) 'Implementing Management Change: Leading and Following' in Younis, T. (ed.) *Implementation in Public Policy*, Aldershot: Dartmouth.

Espeland, W. N. (1998) *The Struggle for Water: Politics, Rationality and Identity*, Chicago, IL: Chicago University Press.

Etzioni, A. (1964) *Modern Organizations*, Englewood Cliffs, NJ: Prentice-Hall.

Etzioni, A. (1967) 'Mixed Scanning, a third approach to decision making', *Public Administration Review*, 27: 385–392.

Etzioni, A. (1968) *The Active Society*, London: Collier-Macmillan.

Farr, J., Hacker, J. and Kazee, N. (2006) 'The Policy Scientist of Democracy: The Discipline of Harold D. Lasswell', *American Political Science Review*, 100(4): 579–587.

Finer, S. E. (1958) *Anonymous Empire: A Study of the Lobby in Great Britain*, London: Pall Mall Press.

Finer, S. E. (1970) *Comparative Government*, London: Allen Lane.

Fischer, F. (1983) 'Ethical Discourse in Public Administration', *Administration and Society*, 15(1): 5–42.

Fischer, F. (1995) *Evaluating Public Policy*, Chicago, IL: Nelson-Hall.

Fischer, F. (2003) *Reframing Public Policy, Discursive Politics and Deliberative Practices*, Oxford: Oxford University Press.

Fischer, F. (2009) *Democracy and Expertise: Re-orientating Policy Inquiry*, Oxford: Oxford University Press.

Fiske, S. T. (2010) *Social Beings: Core Motives in Social Psychology*, 2nd edn, Hoboken, NJ: Wiley.

Flynn, P. (2012) *How to be an MP*, London: Biteback Publishing.

Forester, J. (2013) 'On the theory and practice of critical pragmatism: Deliberative practice and creative negotiations', *Planning Theory*, 12(1): 5–22.

Foucault, M. (1980) *Power/Knowledge: Selected Interviews and Other Writing 1972–1977*, ed. C. Gordon, Brighton: Harvester Press.

Foucault, M. (1982) 'Subject and Power', *Critical Inquiry*, 8(4): 777–795.

Foucault, M. (1991) 'Governability' in Buchell, C., Gordon, C. and Miller, P. (eds) *The Foucault Effect: Studies in Governability*, Chicago, IL: University of Chicago Press, pp. 85–103.

Fraser, D. (1984) *The Evolution of the British Welfare State*, 2nd edn, Basingstoke: Macmillan.

Freedman, D. (2012) 'Outsourcing internet regulation' in J. Curran, N. Fenton and D. Freedman, *Misunderstanding the Internet*, Abingdon: Routledge.

Freeman, R. (2008) 'Learning in Public Policy' in Moran, M., Rein, M. and Goodin, R. (eds) *The Oxford Handbook of Public Policy*, Oxford: Oxford University Press, pp. 367–388.

Friedrich, C. and Brzezinski, Z. (1965) *Totalitarian Dictatorship and Autocracy*, 2nd edn, London: Praeger.

Friedman, M. (1970) 'The Social Responsibility of Business is to Increase its Profits', *New York Times Magazine*, 13 September.

Fukuyama, F. (1992) *The End of History*, London: Hamish Hamilton.

Fukuyama, F. (1995) *Trust: The Social Virtues and the Creation of Prosperity*, London: Hamish Hamilton.

Gamble, A. (1988) *The Free Economy and the Strong State: The Politics of Thatcherism*, Basingstoke: Macmillan.

Gerth, H. and Wright-Mills, C. (eds) (1948) *From Max Weber*, London: Routledge, Kegan Paul.

Geyer, R. and Rihani, S. (2010) *Complexity and Public Policy*, London: Routledge.

Giddens, A. (1998) *The Third Way: The Renewal of Social Democracy*, Cambridge: Polity Press.

Gilley, B. (2012) 'Authoritarian Environmentalism and China's response to climate change', *Environmental Politics*, 21(2): 287–307.

Graham, E., Shipan, C. and Volden, G. (2012) 'The Diffusion of Policy Diffusion Research in Political Science', *British Journal of Political Science*, 43(03): 673–701.

Gramsci, A. (1971) *Selections from the Prison Notebooks*, ed. and trans. Q. Hoare and G. Nowell Smith, London: Lawrence and Wishart.

Gray, P. and t'Hart, P. (eds) (1998) *Public Policy Disasters in Western Europe*, London: Routledge.

Green, D. G. (1981) *Power and Party in an English City*, London: George Allen and Unwin.

Greenberg, D., Linkz, D. and Mandell, M. (2003) *Social Experimentation and Public Policymaking*, Washington, DC: The Urban Institute Press.

Gulick, L. (1937) 'Notes on the Theory of Organization' in Gulick, L. and Urwick, L. (eds) *Papers on the Science of Administration*, New York: Columbia University.

Gunn, L. (1978) 'Why is implementation so difficult?' *Management Services in Government*, 33: 169–176.

Habermas, J. (1990) *Moral Consciousness and Communicative Action*, trans. C. Lenhardt and S. Weber, Cambridge, MA: MIT Press.

Habermas, J. (2001) *The Post-national Constellation*, trans. M. Pensky, Cambridge: Polity Press.

Habermas, J. (2008) *Ach Europa*, Frankfurt: Suhrkamp.

Hampsher-Monk, I. (1992) *A History of Modern Political Thought*, Oxford: Basil Blackwell.

Hancock, M. (1972) *Sweden: The Politics of Post-Industrial Change*, London: The Dryden Press.

Hansard Society (2014) *Audit of Political Engagement 11: The 2014 Report*, www.hansardsociety. org.uk/wp-content/uploads/2014/04/Audit-of-Political-Engagement-11-2014-pdf (accessed 29 July 2015).

Hattersley, R. (1987) *Choose Freedom: The Future of Democratic Socialism*, London: Penguin.

Hayek, F. (1944) *The Road to Serfdom*, London: Routledge.

Hayek, F. (1960) *The Constitution of Liberty*, London: Routledge and Kegan Paul.

Heclo, H. (1978) 'Issue Networks and the Executive Establishment' in King, A. (ed.), *The New American Political System*, Washington, DC: American Enterprise Institute, pp. 87–124.

Heclo, H. and Wildavsky, A. (1974) *The Private Government of Public Money*, Basingstoke: Macmillan.

Hennessy, P. (1989) *Whitehall*, London: Secker and Warburg.

Heywood, A. (2012) *Political Ideologies: An introduction*, 5th edn, Basingstoke: Palgrave Macmillan.

Hill, J. N. C. (2012) *Nigeria since Independence*, Basingstoke: Palgrave.

Hill, M. (2014) *The Public Policy Process*, Abington: Routledge

Hirschman, A. O. (1970) *Exit, Voice and Loyalty*, Cambridge, MA: Harvard University Press.

Hobbes, T. (1965) (first published 1651) *Leviathan*, ed. A. D. Lindsay, London: Dent, Dutton, Everyman's Library.

Hobsbawm, E. (1987) *The Age of Empire 1875–1914*, London: Weidenfeld and Nicolson.

Hogwood, B. and Gunn, L. (1984) *Policy for the Real World*, Oxford: Oxford University Press.

Hood, C. C. (1976) *The Limits of Administration*, London: John Wiley.

Hood, C. (1991) 'A Public Management for all Seasons', *Public Administration*, 69: 3–19.

Howlett, M. (2012) 'The Lessons of Failure: Learning and blame avoidance in public policy-making', *International Political Science Review*, 33(5): 539–554.

Howlett, M. and Ramesh, M. (2003) *Studying Public Policy*, 2nd edn, Oxford: Oxford University Press.

Hume, D. (1962) *A Treatise of Human Nature*, Vol. II, ed. A. D. Lindsay,London: Dent Dutton.

Hunter, F. (1953) *Community Power Structure*, Chapel Hill: University of North Carolina Press.

Hutchings, K. (2010) 'Global Justice' in Hay, C. (ed.) *New Directions in Political Science*, Basingstoke: Palgrave.

Hutton, W. (2015) *How Good Can We Be*, London: Abacus.

Hyder, M. (1984) 'Implementation: The evolutionary model' in Lewis, D. and Wallace, H. (eds) *Policies into Practice: National and International Case Studies in Implementation*, London: Heinemann.

Ingram, H. (1977) 'Policy Implementation through Bargaining: The Case of Federal Grants in Aid', *Public Policy*, 25: 499–526.

Jackson, J. E. and Kingdon, J. W. (1992) 'Interest Group Scores and Legislative Votes', *American Journal of Political Science*, 36(3): 805–823.

Jaeger, M. (2006) 'What Makes People Support Public Responsibility for Welfare Provision: Self-interest or Political Ideology?' *Acta Sociologica*, 49(3): 321–338.

Jameson, F. (1991) *Postmodernism or The Cultural Logic of Late Capitalism*, Durham, NC: Duke University Press.

Jenkins, W. I. (1978) *Policy Analysis*, London: Martin Robertson.

Jenkins-Smith, H. and Sabatier, P. (1994) 'Evaluating the Advocacy Coalition Framework', *Journal of Public Policy*, 14(2): 175–203.

Jenkins-Smith, H. C., Nohrstedt, D., Weible, C. and Sabatier, P. (2014) 'The Advocacy Coalition Framework: Foundations, Evolution and ongoing Research' in Sabatier P. and Weible, C. (eds) *Theories of the Policy Process*, 3rd edn, Boulder, CO: Westview Press, pp. 183–224.

John, P. (1998) *Analysing Public Policy*, 1st edn, London: Continuum.

Jones, M. A. (1995) *The Limits of Liberty: American History 1607–1992*, 2nd edn, Oxford: Oxford University Press.

Jones, O. (2014) *The Establishment*, Harmondsworth: Penguin.

Jones, R. A. (2001) *The Politics and Economics of the European Union*, 2nd edn, Cheltenham: Edward Elgar.

Joseph, J. (2010) 'The Problem with Networks Theory', *Labour History*, 51(1): 127–144.

Katz, R. S. and Mair, P. (1995) 'Changing Models of Party Organization and Party Democracy', *Party Politics*, 1(1): 5–28.

Kauffman, S. (1995) *At Home in the Universe*, London: Viking.

Kimmel, M. (1990) *Revolution: A Sociological Interpretation*, Philadelphia, PA: Temple University Press.

King, A. (1975) 'Overload: Problems of Governing in the 1970s', *Political Studies*, 23(2–3): 284–296.

King, A. and Crewe, I. (2013) *The Blunders of our Governments*, London: One World.

Kingdom, J. E. (2014) *Government and Politics in Britain*, 4th edn, Cambridge: Polity Press.

Kingdon, J. (1995) *Agendas, Alternatives and Public Policies*, 2nd edn, New York: Harper Collins (first published 1984).

Kingdon, J. (2006) *Agendas, Alternatives and Public Policies*, 2nd edn, Peking: Pearson Education Asia and Peking University.

Kirchheimer, O. (1966) 'The transformation of the West European party systems' in Palombara, J. La and Weiner, M. (eds) *Political Parties and Political Development*, Princeton, NJ: Princeton University Press.

Knill, C. and Tosun, J. (2012) *Public Policy: A New Introduction*, Basingstoke: Palgrave Macmillan.

Kohlberg, L. (1973) 'The Claim to Moral Adequacy of a Highest Stage of Moral Judgement', *Journal of Philosophy*, 70(18): 630–646.

Labour List (2015) labourlist.org/2015/10/10@of-the-best-denis-healey-quotes (ccessed 12 June 2016).

Lane, J. (1993) *The Public Sector: Concepts, Models and Approaches*, London: Sage.

Lasswell, H. (1948) *Power and Personality*, New York: W. W. Norton.

Lasswell, H. (1951) 'The Policy Orientation' in Lerner D. and H. D. Lasswell (eds), *The Policy Sciences*, Stanford, CA: Stanford University Press.

Lasswell, H. (1971) *A Pre-View of Policy Sciences*, New York: American Elsevier Publishing Company.

Laws, D. and Hajer, M. (2008) 'Policy in Practice' in Moran, M., Rein, M., and Goodin, R. (eds) *The Oxford Handbook of Public Policy*, Oxford: Oxford University Press, pp. 409–425.

Leach, R. (1991) *British Political Ideologies*, London: Phillip Allen.

Le Grand, J. (2003) *Motivation, Agency and Public Policy*, Oxford: Oxford University Press.

Lembruch, G. and Schmitter, P. (1982) *Patterns of Corporatist Policy Making*, London: Sage.

Lerner, D. and Lasswell, H. D. (eds) (1951) *The Policy Sciences*, Stanford, CA: Stanford University Press.

Lewis, N. (1992) *Inner City Regeneration*, Buckingham: Open University Press.

Lewis Silkin Journal (2014) *The Tories Strike Back*, http://journal.lewissilkin.com/Journal/2014/July/The-Tories-strike-back.aspx#.V8VcH_krLIU (accessed 4 September 2014).

Lindblom, C. E. (1965) *The Intelligence of Democracy*, New York: The Free Press.

Lindblom, C. E. and Woodhouse, E. J. (1993) *The Policy Making Process*, 3rd edn, Englewood Cliffs, NJ: Prentice Hall.

Lipset, S. M. (1981) *Political Man*, 2nd edn, Baltimore, MD: The Johns Hopkins University Press.

Lipsky, M. (1971) 'Street Level Bureaucracy and the Analysis of Urban Reforms', *Urban Affairs Quarterly*, 6: 391–409.

Lipsky, M. (1980) *Street Level Bureaucracy*, New York: Russell Sage Foundation.

Locke, J. (1924) *Two Treatises of Civil Government*, London: Dent and Sons.

Lowi, T. (1972) 'Four Systems of Policy, Politics and Choice', *Public Administration Review*, 32(4): 298–310.

Lukes, S. (2005) *Power: A Radical View*, 2nd edn, Basingstoke: Palgrave Press (1st edn published 1974).

Lynd, R. and Lynd, H. (1929) *Middletown: A Study of Modern American Culture*, New York: Harcourt Brace.

Machiavelli, N. (1950) *The Prince* and *The Discourses*, trans. Luigi Ricci, New York: Random House.

McBeth, M., Jones, M. D. and Shanahan, S. (2014) 'The Narrative Policy Framework' in Sabatier, P. and Weible, C. (eds) *Theories of the Policy Process*, Boulder, CO: Westview Press.

McConnell, A. (2010a) *Understanding Policy Success*, Basingstoke: Palgrave.

McConnell, A. (2010b) 'Policy Success, Policy Failure and Grey Areas In-Between', *Journal of Public Policy*, 30(3): 351.

McMenamin, I. and Gwiazda, A. (2011) 'Three roads to institutionalisation: Vote, office and policy seeking explanations of party switching in Poland', *European Journal of Political Research*, 50: 838–866.

McNair, B. (2003) *An Introduction to Political Communication*, 3rd edn, Abingdon: Routledge.

Majone, G. and Wildavsky, A. (1984) 'Implementation as Evolution' in Pressman, J. and Wildavsky, A., 1984, *Implementation*, 3rd edn, Berkeley, CA: University of California Press.

Major, J. (2000) *The Autobiography*, London: Harper Collins.

Mantel, H. (2009) *Wolf Hall*, London: Fourth Estate.

Mantel, H. (2015) *Bring Up the Bodies*, London: HarperCollins.

Marx, K. and Engels, F. (1962a) 'The Communist Manifesto' in Marx, K. and Engels, F., *Selected Works*, Vol. I, Moscow: Foreign Languages Publishing House, pp. 34–64.

Marx, K. and Engels, F. (1962b) 'Letter of Engels to C. Schmidt August 5th 1890' in Marx, K. and Engels, F., *Selected Works*, Vol. II, Moscow: Foreign Languages Publishing House, pp. 486–487.

Marx, K. and Engels, F. (1962c) 'Critique of the Gotha Programme' in Marx, K. and Engels, F., *Selected Works*, Vol. II, Moscow: Foreign Languages Publishing House, pp. 18–42.

Maslow, A. H. (1970) *Motivation and Personality*, 3rd edn, Harlow: Longman.

Mazmanian, D. and Sabatier, P. (eds) (1981) *Effective Policy Implementation*, Lexington, MA: D. C. Heath.

Mazmanian, D. and Sabatier, P. (1983) *Implementation and Public Policy*, Glenview, IL: Scott, Foresman and Company.

Medhurst, K. (1973) *Government in Spain: The Executive at Work*, Oxford: Pergamon Press.

Miliband, R. (1968) *The State in Capitalist Society*, London: Weidenfeld and Nicolson.

Mill, J. S. (1861) *Considerations on Representative Government* in Wollheim, R. (ed.) (1975) *John Stuart Mill: Three Essays*, Oxford: Oxford University Press.

Mill, J. S. (1863) *Utilitarianism*, ed. Warnock, M. (1962) London: Fontana, Collins.

Mill, J. S. (1869) *Essay on the Subjection of Women* in Wollheim R. (ed.) (1975) *John Stuart Mill: Three Essays*, Oxford: Oxford University Press.

Miller, H. and Fox, C. (2007) *Postmodern Public Administration*, 2nd edn, New York: M. E. Sharpe.

Mills, S. (2003) *Michel Foucault*, London: Routledge.

Milton, J. R. and Milton, P. (eds) (2010) *John Locke: An Essay concerning Toleration and other writings on Law and Politics 1667–1683*, Oxford: Oxford University Press.

Moise, E. (2008) *Modern China: A History*, 3rd edn, Harlow: Longman.

Moore, Barrington (1966) *Social Origins of Dictatorship and Democracy*, London: Allen Lane.

Moran, M. (2009) *Business, Politics and Society*, Oxford: Oxford University Press.

Moran, M. (2010) 'Policy Making in an Inter-dependent World' in Hay, C. (ed.) *New Directions in Political Science*, Basingstoke: Palgrave, pp. 25–42.

Moran, M., Rein, M. and Goodin, R. (eds) (2006) *The Oxford Handbook of Public Policy*, Oxford: Oxford University Press.

Morgenthau, K. (1948) *Politics among Nations: The Struggle for Power and Peace*, 1st edn, New York: Alfred A. Knopf.

Mosca, G. (1939) *The Ruling Class*, ed. A. Livingstone, New York: McGraw Hill.

Mullin, C. (2009) *A View from the Foothills*, London: Profile Books.

Nagel, S. (2000) *Creativity and Public Policy: Generating Super-Optimum Solutions*, Aldershot: Ashgate.

Nelson, R. R. and Winter, S. G. (1982) *An Evolutionary Theory of Economic Change*, Cambridge, MA: Harvard University Press.

Newton, K. (1976) *Second City Politics*, Oxford: Oxford University Press.

Niskanen, W. A. (1971) *Bureaucracy and Representative Government*, Chicago, IL: Aldine-Atherton.

Nolutshungu, S. (1983) *Changing South Africa*, Cape Town: David Philip.

Nozick, R. (1974) *Anarchy, State and Utopia*, Oxford: Basil Blackwell.

Nye, J. S. (1967) 'Corruption and Political Development: A Cost Benefit Analysis', *American Political Science Review*, 61(2): 417–427.

Oakeshott, M. (1962) 'Rationalism in Politics' in M. Oakeshott (ed.) *Rationalism in Politics and Other Essays*, London: Methuen.

Obama, B. (2006) *The Audacity of Hope: Thoughts on Reclaiming the American Dream*, New York: Crown Publishers.

O'Conner, J. (1973) *The Fiscal Crisis of the State*, New York: St Martins Press.

Offe, C. (1984) *Contradictions of the Welfare State*, London: Hutchinson.

Orwell, G. (1949) *1984*, London: Secker and Warburg.

Ostrom, E. (1999) 'Coping with the Tragedies of the Commons', *Annual Review of Political Science*, 2: 493–535.

Outhwaite, W. (2009) *Habermas*, 2nd edn, Cambridge: Polity Press.

Palumbo, D. J. (1988) *Public Policy in America: Government in Action*, Orlando, FL: Harcourt, Brace and Jovanovich.

Parekh, B. (ed.) (1973) *Bentham's Political Thought*, London: Croom Helm.

Pareto, V. (1966) *Sociological Writings*, ed. S. E. Finer, London: Pall Mall.

Parkinson, M. and Evans, R. (1990) 'Urban Development Corporations' in Campbell, M. (ed.) *Local Economic Policy*, London: Cassell, pp. 65–84.

Parry, G. (1969) *Political Elites*, London: George, Allen and Unwin.

Parsons, W. (1995) *Public Policy*, Cheltenham: Edward Elgar.

Pateman, C. (1970) *Participation and Democratic Theory*, Cambridge: Cambridge University Press.

Pateman, C. (1988) *The Sexual Contract*, Stanford, CA: Stanford University Press.

Pawson, R. (2002) 'Evidence and Policy and Naming and Shaming', *Policy Studies*, 23(3/4): 211–230.

Pawson, R. (2006) *Evidence-based Policy*, London: Sage.

Pawson, R. (2013) *The Science of Evaluation: A Realist Manifesto*, London: Sage.

Pawson, R. and Tilley, N. (1997) *Realistic Evaluation*, London: Sage.

Peardon, T. P. (1974) 'Bentham's Ideal Republic' in Parekh, B. (ed.) *Jeremy Bentham: Ten Critical Essays*, London: Frank Cass.

Peters, T. and Waterman, R. (1982) *In Search of Excellence: Lessons from America's Best Run Companies*, New York: Harper and Row.

Piaget, J. (1977) *The Origins of Intelligence in the Child*, London: Penguin.

Poulantzes, N. (1968) *Political Parties and Social Classes*, London: New Left Books.

Poulantzes, N. (1978) *State, Power, Socialism*, London: New Left Books.

Piketty, T. (2014) *Capital in the Twenty-First Century*, Cambridge, MA: The Belknap Press of Harvard University Press.

Popper, K. (1957) *The Poverty of Historicism*, London: Routledge.

Posner, P. (2007) *The Politics of Unfunded Mandates: Wither Federalism?* Washington, DC: Georgetown University Press.

Pressman, J. and Wildavsky, A. (1973) *Implementation*, Berkeley, CA: University of California Press.

Pressman, J. and Wildavsky, A. (1984) *Implementation*, 3rd edn, Berkeley, CA: University of California Press.

Prest, J. (1990) *Liberty and Locality: Parliament, Permissive Legislation and Ratepayer Democracies in the Nineteenth Century*, Oxford: Clarendon Press.

Preston, P. (1995) *Franco: A Biography*, London: Fontana Press.

Putnam, R. D. with Leonardi, R. and Nanetti, R. (1994) *Making Democracy Work: Civic Traditions in Modern Italy*, Princeton, NJ: Princeton University Press.

Rawls, J. (1971) *A Theory of Justice*, Oxford: Oxford University Press.

Reeves, R. (2007) *John Stuart Mill: Victorian Firebrand*, London: Atlantic Books.

Reynolds, J. (2004) 'Decision' in Reynolds, J. and Roffe J., *Understanding Derrida*, London: Continuum.

Rhodes, R. A. W. (1981) *Control and Power in Central-Local Government*, Farnborough: Gower.

Rhodes, R. A. W. (1991) 'Theory and Methods in British Public Administration: The View from Political Science', *Political Studies*, 39(3): 533–554.

Rhodes, R. A. W. (1994) 'The Hollowing Out of the State: The Changing Nature of the Public Service in Britain', *Political Quarterly*, 65(2): 138–151.

Rhodes, R. A. W. (1997) *Understanding Governance*, Buckingham: Open University Press.

Rhodes, R. A. W. (1999) *Control and Power in Central-Local Government*, 2nd edn, Aldershot: Ashgate.

Rhodes, R. A. W. (2006) 'Policy Network Analysis' in Moran, M., Rein, M. and Goodin, R. (eds) *The Oxford Handbook of Public Policy*, Oxford: Oxford University Press.

Rhodes, R. A. W. and Marsh, D. (1992) 'Policy Networks in British Politics: A Critique of Existing Approaches' in Marsh, D. and Rhodes, R. A. W. (eds) *Policy Networks in British Government*, Oxford: Clarendon Press, pp. 2–26.

Richards, D. (2008) *New Labour and the Civil Service*, Basingstoke: Palgrave.

Richardson, J. (2000) 'Government, Interest Groups and Policy Change', *Political Studies*, 48: 1006–1025.

Richardson, J. J. and Jordan, A. G. (1979) *Governing under Pressure*, Oxford: Blackwell.

Room, G. (2011) *Complexity, Institutions and Public Policy*, Cheltenham: Edward Elgar.

Rose, R. (1993) *Lesson Drawing in Public Policy*, Chatham, NJ: Chatham House.

Rosenau, P. V. (2000) 'Strengths and Weaknesses of Public-Private Partnerships' in Rosenau, P. V., *Public Policy Partnerships*, Cambridge, MA: MIT Press, pp. 217–242.

Rossi, P. H. and Freeman, H. (1993) *Evaluation: A Systematic Approach*, 2nd edn, Newbury Park, CA: Sage.

Rousseau, J. J. (1966) *The Social Contract and Discourses*, ed. G. D. H. Cole, London: Everyman's Library.

Rule, J. B. (1973) *Private Lives and Public Surveillance*, London: Allen Lane.

Sabatier, P. (1986) 'Top-down and Bottom-up Approaches to Implementation Research: A Critical Analysis and Suggested Synthesis', *Journal of Public Policy*, 6(1): 21–48.

Sabatier, P. (1993) 'Policy Change over a Decade or More' in Sabatier, P. and Jenkins-Smith, H. (eds) *Policy Change and Learning: An Advocacy Coalition Approach*, Boulder, CO: Westview Press.

Sabatier, P. (1998) 'The Advocacy Coalition Framework: Revisions and Relevance for Europe', *Journal of European Public Policy*, 5(1): 98–130.

Sabatier, P. and Jenkins-Smith, H. C. (eds) (1993) *Policy Change and Learning*, Boulder, CO: Westview.

Sayre, W. and Kaufman, H. (1960) *Governing New York City*, New York: Russell Safe Foundation.

Schreurs, M. (2010) 'Federalism and the Climate: Canada and the EU', *International Journal*, 66 (1): 91–108.

Schumpeter, J. A. (2010) (First published 1943) *Capitalism, Socialism and Democracy*, London: Taylor and Francis.

Scruton, R. (2001a) *The Meaning of Conservatism*, 3rd edn, Basingstoke: Palgrave.

Scruton, R. (2001b) *Kant: A Very Short Introduction*, Oxford: Oxford University Press.

Sears, D. and Funk, C. (1990) 'The Limit Effect of Economic Self-interest on the Political Attitudes of the Mass Public', *The Journal of Behavioural Economics*, 19(3): 247–271.

Seligman, J. (2003) *The Transformation of Wall Street: A History of the Securities and Exchange Commission in Modern Corporate Finance*, New York: Aspen.

Selznick, P. (1949) *TVA and the Grass Roots: A Study in the Sociology of Formal Organisation*, Berkeley, CA: University of California Press.

Service, R. (2004) *Stalin: A Biography*, Basingstoke: Macmillan.

Sheldon, O. (1925) 'Policy and Policy Making', *Harvard Business Review*, 4(1): 1–6.

Simon, H. A. (1976) *Administrative Behaviour: A Study of Decision Making Processes in Administrative Organization*, 3rd edn, New York: The Free Press.

Simon, H. A. (1997) *Administrative Behaviour: A Study of Decision Making Processes in Administrative Organization*, 4th edn, New York: The Free Press.

Skocpol, T. (1979) *States and Social Revolutions*, Cambridge: Cambridge University Press.

Skocpol, T. (1985) 'Bringing the State Back In: Current Research' in Evans, R., Rueschemeyer, D. and Skocpol, T. (eds) *Bringing the State Back In*, Cambridge: Cambridge University Press, pp. 4–37.

Smart, B. (2002) *Michel Foucault*, London: Routledge.

Smith, A. (1999) (first published 1776) *The Wealth of Nations*, ed. A. Skinner, London: Penguin Books.

Spence, R. (2014) 'Italy' in Chandler, J. A. (ed.) *Comparative Public Administration*, 2nd edn, London: Routledge, pp. 97–112.

Stacey, R. (2000) *Strategic Management and Organisational Dynamics*, Harlow: Pearson Education.

Stoker, G. (2002) 'Life is a Lottery: New Labour's Strategy for the Reform of Devolved Governance', *Public Administration*, 80(3): 417–434.

Taylor, A. J. P. (1969) *War by Timetable: How the First World War Began*, London: Macdonald and Co.

Taylor, F. W. (1911) *Principles of Scientific Management*, New York: Harper and Brothers.

Thatcher, M. (1995) *The Path to Power*, London: Harper Collins.

Thomas, R. (1978) *The British Philosophy of Administration: A Comparison of British and American Ideas 1900–1939*, London: Longman.

Tilly, C. (1978) *From Mobilization to Revolution*, New York: McGraw-Hill.

Truman, D. (1951) *The Governmental Process*, New York: Knopf.

Wallas, G. (1934) *Social Judgement*, London: George Allen and Unwin.

Waltz, K. (1979) *Theory of International Politics*, New York: McGraw-Hill.

Weale, S. (2015) 'Teacher shortage and Pupils surge creating Perfect Storm in UK Schools', *The Guardian*, 5 October: www.theguardian.com/education/2015/Oct/05/teacher-shortage-pupils-surge-perfect-storm-uk-schools.

Weber, M. (1948) 'Bureaucracy' in Gerth, H. H. and Wright Mills, C. (eds) *From Max Weber: Essays in Sociology*, London: Routledge and Kegan Paul, pp. 196–266.

Weible, C., Heikkila, T., de Leon, P. and Sabatier, P. A. (2011) 'Understanding and Influencing the Policy Process', *Policy Sciences*, 45(1): 1–21.

Weible, C., Sabatier, P. and McQueen, K. (2009) 'Themes and Variations: Taking Stock of the Advocacy Coalition Framework', *Policy Studies Journal*, 37(1): 121–141.

Weiss, C. and Birckmayer, J. (2006) 'Social Experimentation for Public Policy' in Moran, M., Rein, M. and Goodin, R. (eds) *The Oxford Handbook of Public Policy*, Oxford: Oxford University, pp. 806–832.

Wilks-Heeg, S. (2015) 'The politics of sustainability: democracy and the limits of policy action' in Atkinson, H. and Wade, R. *The Challenge of Sustainability: Linking Politics, Education and Learning*, Bristol: Policy Press, pp. 43–62.

Wilks-Heeg, S., Blick, A. and Crone, S. (2016) 'The political affiliations of the UK's national newspapers have shifted but there is again a heavy Tory predominance' at www.blogs.lse.ac.uk/politicsandpolicy/the-political-affiliations-of-the-uks-national-newspapers-have-shifted-but-there-is-again-a-heavy-tory-predominance (accessed 29 June 2016).

Williams, L. (2014) 'What is TTIP? And six reasons why this should scare you', *The Independent* at www.independent.co.uk/voices/comment/what-is-ttip-why-the-answer-should-scare-you-9779688.html (accessed 28 August 2015).

Williams, M. (2013) 'Obama and Clinton's TV love-in fuels talk of White House run', *The Guardian*, 28 January, p. 12.

Wilson, J. Q. (1989) *Bureaucracy*, New York: Basic Books.

Wilson, T. and Skidmore, H. (2008) 'Overview' in Skidmore, H. and Wilson, T. (eds) *Dictatorship, Disorder and Decline in Myanmar*, Canberra: Australian National University Press, pp. 1–9.

Wilson, W. (1887) 'The Study of Administration', *Political Science Quarterly*, 2(2): 197–222.

Winkler, J. (1976) 'Corporatism', *Archives Européenes de Sociologie*, 17: 100–136.

Winship, C. (2006) 'Policy Analysis as Puzzle Solving' in Moran, M., Rein, M. and Goodin, R. *The Oxford Handbook of Public Policy*, Oxford: Oxford University Press, pp. 109–123.

Wittgenstein, L. (1958) *Philosophical Investigations*, trans. G. E. M. Anscombe, Oxford: Basil Blackwell.

Wollmann, H. (2003) 'Evaluation in public rector reform: Towards a "third wave" of evaluation?' in Wollmann, H. (ed.) *Evaluation in Public Sector Reform*, Cheltenham: Edward Elgar.

Wright-Mills, C. (1959) *The Power Elite*, New York: Oxford University Press.

Yanow, D. (1995) 'Built Space as Story: The Policy Stories Buildings Tell', *Policy Studies Journal*, 23(3): 407.

Yanow, D. (2000) *Conducting Interpretive Policy Analysis*, London: Sage.

Young, H. (1989) *One of Us: A Biography of Margaret Thatcher*, London: Macmillan.

Zittel, T. (2007) 'Conclusion' in Zittel, T. and Fuchs D. (eds) *Participatory Democracy and Political Participation*, London: Routledge.

Zittoun, P. (2014) *The Political Process of Policymaking: A Pragmatic Approach to Public Policy*, Basingstoke: Palgrave.

Index

Abbott, Diane 75
acquisitive dictatorships 102, 114, 182
Adonis, Andrew 124
Adorno, Theodor 27
Advocacy Coalition Framework 19, 115, 120–5, 128, 174, 176, 179,186, 210, 218; limitations 122–5
Afghanistan 71
agencies 89, 92, 94, 96 126; arms length 144; bureaucratic 60; government 4, 44, 72, 84, 97, 109,119,135, 144, 154,170, 174, 178; professional 103; voluntary 131
agents 15, 37, 59, 84, 127, 178, 179, 191
agile policy making toolkit 192
Amazon 205
alienation 51–2, 86
altruism 1, 219
Allison, Graham 7,
Almond, Gabriel 112, 155
ambassadors 154
ambition 33,
Amin, Idi 102
Amy, Douglas, 66
anarchism 42
Anderson, James 3
apartheid 48, 101
Arab Spring 136
Arendt, Hannah 97
Aristotle 11, 67
Atkinson, Hugh, 177
Atlanta 108
Attlee, Clement 38; government 44
audit 143, 156,
Australia 159
authoritarian regimes 59, 92–102
authority 82–3, 85
autocracies 4, 92–102, 157,182, 219
autocracy 92–102, 96, 99, 156–7, 218
Ayer, A. J. 23

Bacharach, P. and Baratz, M. 86, 126
Bagehot, Walter 169
Bakunin, Mikhail 42

balance of powers 41, 93, 104–5, 107, 159, 162, 205
Banfield, Edward 32
bankers 94
banks 5, 47, 113, 135; 2008 crisis 5, 35, 47, 119, 162, 166
Bank of England 119, 162
Barber, Benjamin 38, 87, 206
Barrett, Susan and Fudge, Colin 171
Bashkar, Roy 24
Bauman, Zygmunt 41
Baumgartner, Frank 180–1, 191, 198
Bay of Pigs 74
Beck, Ulrich 128
behaviouralism 11, 50
Bell, Daniel 32, 112
Benn, Tony 74
Benn, Hilary 74
Benson, J. K. 116
Bentham, Jeremy 10, 21, 45, 68–9, 105, 107
Bentley, Arthur 112
Berlusconi, Silvio 63
Beveridge, William 44, 197
Bevir, Mark 29, 117
Bin Laden, Osma 73
Blair, Tony 25, 34, 55, 57, 59, 66, 67, 123, 152, 91; governments 35, 38, 144, 146
bounded rationality 14–16
Bovens, Mark and t'Hart, Paul 193, 200
Bourdieu, Pierre 24, 44, 87–8, 126
Boydstun, Amber 127
'Brexit' 214
Brzezinski, Zbigniew 97
bribery 61, 169
BSE 138
Buddhism 67
Brown, Gordon 35, 37, 55, 162
bureaucracy 46, 94–5, 157
bureaucrats 60, 92, 94
bureau shaping model 46
Burke, Edmund 16, 41
Burnham, James 110
Bush, George W. 36, 56, 66, 139, 152

Butler, David 111, 124, 193
business interests 2, 3, 4–5, 81–83, 85, 91, 94, 101–3,108–10, 119, 148, 154

Calhoun, Craig 27
Cameron, David, 37, 54, 131, 153; 'big society' 178
Campbell, Alastair 59
capitalism 34, 41, 42, 85–90, 209, 220
cadre party 60–1
Canada 53, 159
Carr, E. H. 74
Carter Presidency 139
Castells, Manuel, 111
catch-all party 60
categorical imperatives 70–1
Catlin, George 112
census 143
charities 5, 94
Charles I 41
Chartists 122
checks and balances 105,107, 162, 205
China (Peoples Republic of) 1, 43, 76, 95, 96, 157, 182
Christian beliefs 73
Christians 40
Churchill, Winston 222
civic culture 32–3, 61, 62, 86, 112, 140, 155, 183, 194
civic education 127, 206, 222
civil servants 24, 46, 47, 62, 139, 143, 154
civil service 19, 91, 154, 157, 161, 164
civil society 32, 80, 85–90, 112, 140, 158, 183, 219
class 22, 28, 41, 42, 46, 87–9, 111, 128, 185–6.
climate change, 163, 177
Clinton, Bill 139
Clinton, Hillary 54
coalitions 21, 121, 196
coercion 30, 31
Cohen, Michael 132
Colebatch, Hal 19
command economies 96
commodification 27, 88 126
communication 47, 86, 88, 103, 127, 150, 16, 219
communities 47, 92, 107, 218
community charge; *see* poll tax
community studies 108, 113
complexity theory 45, 188–191
conservatism 16, 40–1,
Conservative Party 55, 58, 123, 131, 185
contractual agreements 82, 85
Cook, Robin 66
Corbyn, Jeremy 123
corporatism 108–10
correlation 146, 148
corruption 61–3, 67, 97, 143, 177; defined 61

counter-revolution 184
coup de état 100
Crewe, Ivor 193, 198
Crick, Bernard 3
crime 138
critical realism 27, 70
Cromwell, Thomas 1, 93
Crossman, Richard 37, 124–5, 153, 87
Cuba, 66, 74
Cuban missile crisis, 7, 66, 74
cult of personality 98, 99

Dahl, Robert 112–4, 115
Davies, Jonathan 126, 209
decrees 161–2
deductive logic
Deities 40, 45, 68, 99, 133, 212, 215
deliberative democracy 204–9
deliberative policy making, 203–16; defined 206
democracy 9, 21, 26, 34, 44–5, 48, 61, 78, 94–5, 111–4, 121–3, 214, 219, 220; direct democracy 105, 107, 205–7, 214; *see* also liberal democracies
Derrida, Jacques 27
Derthick, Martha 170
Descartes, Rene 24
Dewey, John 73
Diamond, John 126
dictators 92
Diggers 41
discourse 114, 204
discourse theory 204
discretion
Disraeli, Benjamin 41, 123, 185
distributive justice
Dolowitz, 135
Downs, Antony 111, 115
doxa 87
Dror, Yehezkel 17
Drucker, Henry 144
Dryzek, John 25, 206
Ducan-Smith, Iain 55
Dunleavy, Patrick, 46, 53
Dunsire, Andrew 171
Dye, Thomas 4

Easton, David 18, 121, 122
ebola 25, 194
economic crash 2008, 119, 152
economics 97, 134
economic policy 138, 152–3
education 44, 72, 75, 110–1, 127, 175, 194, 206, 211, 220
effectiveness of policy 9, 23, 138, 142–5, 151, 154, 170
efficiency of policy 7, 12, 14, 144–7, 148
Eisenhower, Dwight 110

Elcock, Howard 172
elite theory 107–111, 220
empathy 57
emotions 3, 28, 201
Engels, Friedrich, 42–3, 110
English Civil War 3, 41
environment 77–8, 218
environmentalism 35, 36, 89
equality 21, 72, 207, 215–6
ethics viii, 8, 29, 65–79, 136, 148, 209–15, 219;
    defined 65; and ideology 65; and policy
    content 65–67, 73, 201
ethnic cleansing 201
ethnic divisions 101
Etzioni, Amatai 17, 21, 37, 137, 145, 148,
    193–4, 220, 223
Euro 177
European Union 54, 135, 136, 138, 158, 177,
    209, 213, 214
evaluation 7, 17, 19–20, 21, 143–155, 196, 221,
    223; realistic 149–1; what can be evaluated
    147–9; see also policy evaluation
evolution 40, 88, 173, 179–91, 216
executives, 161
exit, voice and loyalty 171

Facebook 205
failed sates 186
fairness 31, 63, 72–3, 76, 213
Falange 95, 100
Fascism 48, 95
Fayol, Henri 12
Federalists 104
federalism 164, 213
feedback 138
feminism 48
freedom from the state 45
freedom of association 103, 130
freedom of speech 103
Finer, Samuel 81, 109
First World War 4
Fischer, Frank 51, 66, 89, 151, 175, 201, 204,
    219, 221
Fiske, Susan 31–2
fitness landscape 202
Foucault, Michel 26, 89, 176, 198
fox hunting 25, 147, 191
France 21, 47, 93, 103–4, 106, 160–1; civil
    service 161; President 160, 166
Franco, Francisco 83, 93, 95, 100
Frankfurt School 27
freedom of speech 103, 215
Freidman, Milton, 5, 135
Friedrich, Carl 97
French Revolution 41
fudging 172
Fukayama, Francis 32, 34, 155

functional theory 18
funding 5, 120, 126, 143, 174, 175, 177

Gamble, Andrew 78
garbage can model 132–3, 134, 137, 140
general will 107, 206
Germany 4, 97, 109
Ghana 174–5
Giddens, Anthony 34
globalisation, 5, 86, 89, 100, 136, 204,
    213
global warming 77–8, 163, 177, 180
Google 205
Gorbachev, Mikhail 196
governance, 118–120, 128
government ministers 19, 55
government by lottery 178
Greece 135
Green Movements 6, 48, 156, 177
Green, Thomas Hill 43, 72
Gramsci, Antonio 85, 126, 155
Gulick, Luther 12
Guantanamo Bay 71
Gunn, Lewis 16, 19, 170

Habermas, Jürgen 24, 27, 86–7, 89, 126,
    203–4, 209, 211, 214
habitus 87, 126
Haldane, Richard 12
Hamilton, Alexander 104
Hayek, Friedrich von 35, 46, 76
heads of state 166
health care 36, 44, 101, 131, 151, 174–5, 181;
    see also United States and United Kingdom
    health care
health insurance 134, 139, 151
Heath, Edward 124
Heclo, Hugh 116
Hegel, Georg F. 70, 80
hegemony 125–8, 140–1, 155
Henry VIII, 93
Hill, Michael 7
Hirschman, Albert 171
Hitler, Adolf 4, 48, 49, 97
Hobbes, Thomas 3, 24, 45, 65, 70, 76
Hobsbawm, Eric 72
Hobhouse, Lionel T. 43
Hogwood, Brian 16, 19, 170
hollowing out of the state 46, 119
Hood, Christopher 144, 170
Howlett, Michael 194, 196, 198
human nature 68
human rights 68, 104, 213
Hume, David 10, 11, 23, 70
Hunter, Floyd 108, 113
Hussein, Saddam 57
Hyder, Massof 178

ideology, 6, 34–49, 51, 120, 122, 135; content, 39–41; definition, 39, 65;end of 34–35, 103, 112; impact on policy 36–9, 96–7, 126, 167
immigration 40, 212
implementation 166–178; top down/bottom up 171–4; stages in process 173
incremental change 16–17
industrial decline 177
inference 10, 23, 151
information technology 132, 182
Ingram, Helen 10
institutions 212, 214, 218, 219
interest groups 21,28, 32, 59, 84–5, 94, 109, 112, 119, 130–2, 139, 218–9
International Monetary Fund, 5, 135, 136, 212
internet, 95, 136, 205
interpretivism 28–9
inspectorates 143
irrationality 2
Iraq, 66, 97
Ireland 159
Iron triangles 109, 111
ISIS 67
issue networks 116
Italy 63, 135, 161

Jackson, J. E., 53
Jaeger, Mads 53
Jameson, Frederic, 88
Jay, John, 104
Jaures, Jean 43
Jenkins, Bill 18
Jenkins-Smith, Hank 19, 115, 120, 174
Jews 40, 201
John, Peter 16, 19, 179–80
Johnston, Boris 54
Johnston, Lyndon 36, 116, 170, 178
Jones, Bryan D. 180–1, 191,198
Jordan 99
Jordan, Grant, 109
Joseph, Jonathan 209
journalists 138, 139
judges 165
justice 72–3
justice as fairness 72

Kant, Immanuel 24, 27, 70–2, 212, 213, 223
Katz, Richard and Mair, Peter 60
Kennedy, John F. 66, 71, 161–2; administration 36, 116
Kennedy, Joseph 154
Keynes, John Maynard 11
Kimmel, Michael 184
King, Anthony 140, 193, 198
Kingdon, John 53, 94, 134, 137–40
Kingdom, John 81
Kirchheimer, Otto 60

Kohlberg, Lawrence 51
Knill, Chrisoff and Tosun, Jale 21

Labour Party 38, 59, 123, 124, 126, 156
Lane, Jan-Erik 148
language 25–28
Lasswell, Harold 13, 14, 21, 29, 50, 192, 203, 217
lawyers 83, 85, 94
Le Grand, Julian 53
legislatures 58, 162
legitimation 142, 166, 219, 221
Lehmann Brothers, 138, 162
Lembruch, Phillippe 109
Lenin 44, 98, 219
lesson drawing 134
Levenson Enquiry 163
liberal autocracies 99–100
liberal democracies 1, 21, 91, 103–14, 181–2, 219–20
liberalism 41–2, 104, 106, 114, 220
libetarianism 40
liberty 103, 107, 220
Libya 186
life world 86, 220
Likert scales 146
Lindblom, Charles E. 16–17, 114, 115, 137, 179, 181
lions and foxes 108
Lipset, S. M. 46, 112, 155
Lipsky, Michael 171, 172
Lloyd George, David 62–3
local government 84,103, 105, 107, 117, 119, 135, 153, 213; *see also* United Kingdom and United States local government
lottery 187
Locke, John 10, 41, 68, 99, 104, 211, 220
London 166; dockland 148, 149; underground 198
Louis XIV 93
Lowi, Theodore 29–30,
Lukes, Stephen 86, 126
luck 77, 83, 12, 153, 175, 190, 200, 220, 223
Lynd, Robert and Helen 108, 112

Machiavelli, Niccolo 73, 76, 108
MacMillan, Harold 138
McConnell, Allan 194, 195–8
Madison, James 104
Majone, Giandomenico 171
Major, John 56, 138
management by objectives 144
management theory 12–13
Mao Tze Tung 76, 95, 100
March, James 132
market economy 48, 128
market forces 6, 16, 43, 128

marketing 85, 88
Marsh, David 116
Marx, Karl 35, 39, 42–3, 110–1, 122, 184
Marxist-Leninism 5, 95
Marxist theory, 85–6, 89, 110–1; *see also*
   Neo-Marxism
marxists 85, 88, 89, 184
Maslow, A. H. 31, 51, 59
mayors 147
Mazmanian, Paul 172, 173
media 95–6, 127, 205
meso level theory 5, 129, 186
Michels, Roberto, 108
Middle East 35, 40, 66, 188
Miliband, Ralph
Mill, James 105
Mill, John Stuart 61, 69, 78, 105–6, 169
Miller and Fox, 113–4
ministers 19, 55, 92, 93, 125, 159
military 83, 98
military regimes 83, 100–1, 183
monarchy 41, 42
Montesquieu 41
Moore, Barrington 184
moral dilemmas 74–6
morality 36, 65–79, 211; *see also* ethics
Moran, Michael 119, 122
Morgenthou, Hans 74
Mosca, Gaetano 108
Milburn, Alan 55
Miliband, Ralph 85
Miller, Hugh and Fox, Charles 44, 113, 140
mixed scanning 17
muddling through 16, 179, 181
Mugabe, Robert 92
Mullin, Chris, 55, 57, 65, 67
multi-national corporations 5, 96, 99, 119,
   125, 158, 163
multi-variant analysis 149
Muslims 40
Muslim fundamentalism 66
Myanmar 97, 101

Nagel, Stuart 192
Narrative Policy Framework 186
narratives 28, 29, 184, 186, 195
National Health Service 30, 44, 131, 194
nationalisation 38
nationalism 35, 47–8, 51, 99, 214
natural rights 76
natural selection180
Neo-Marxism 30, 111
network theory 115–118, 128
networks 24, 38, 60, 87, 92, 115–8, 150, 180–1,
   191, 196, 218–221
New Deal 17
New England townships 206–7

New Haven 112–3
New Labour 38, 59, 144
New Liberalism 43–4
New Public Management 46, 119, 144
New Right 6, 38, 45–7, 72, 76–7, 132, 135,
   165; theory 119
New York 113
newspapers 127, 163
Nigeria 102, 183
Niskanen, William 46, 53
Nixon, Richard 56, 187
non-decisions 86, 126
Non-Governmental Organisations 4, 5
normative values 204
North Korea 98, 99 101, 155, 182
'Northern Power House' 177
Nosick, Robert 46, 68, 72
nuclear power 180, 210
nuclear weapons 66
nuclear war 74, 134, 193

Oakland, 170
Oakshott, Michael 16, 41
Obama, Barak 54, 139, 153, 160, 181, 205;
   Obama administration 134, 151; health care
   policy 151
O'Conner, James 30
Offe, Claus 31
office holding 54–8
oligarchies 2, 35, 43, 91, 93, 95–99, 101–2
Olsen, Johan 132
Orwell, George 97
Osborne, George 55
Ostrom, Elinor 212
overload thesis 140

Palumbo, Dennis 144
Pareto, Villfredo 108
parliamentary systems 37, 42, 55, 67, 105
Parsons, Wayne 13
partisanship 59
partnerships 126
participation 42, 51–2, 175, 206–8
Pateman, Carole 38, 205–6
patronage 32, 222
Pawson, Ray 150–1, 223
perestroika 196
persuasion 81–2
Peters, Thomas and Waterman, Robert 190
pharmaceutical industry 25, 190
phenomenology 28, 50
Piaget, 51
pilot studies 149, 180, 191, 222
Piketty, Thomas 47
Plato 24, 67
pluralism 4, 17, 21, 4, 60–1, 85, 109, 111–4,
   125, 128, 139 141, 175

Poland 59, 177
police 172
policy advisors 93
policy analysis viii, 7, 11, 18, 46, 186
policy agenda 130–141
policy blunders 193, 195–6
policy brokers 121, 210
policy categories 29–33
policy communities 117, 118, 174
policy cycle 18, 19, 142, 155
policy definition of, 3, 7
policy diffusion 134, 136
policy entrepreneurs 57, 94, 138, 171, 191
policy evaluation 7, 20, 140–55; development
    of 143–5; and rationality 145–151
policy evolution 21, 141, 179–91
policy failure 193–5, 196, 200–2
policy facilitators 210
policy gatekeepers 39, 74, 92–4, 102, 123, 125,
    140–1, 158, 167, 176
policy implementation 164,168–78, 199, 200,
    215
policy landscapes 189–91
policy legitimation 166
policy mediators 120–1, 210
policy narratives 186
policy and power 80–90
policy problems and opportunities 24, 131–3
policy process 1–3, 7, 9, 17–20, 24, 29, 33, 39
    80, 91,112, 115, 121, 130, 134, 137, 198,
    218, 220; alienation from 61–62; discourse
    203–4; evaluation 147, 150, 152, 155,
    implementation 169–74; refining 156–7,
    162
policy puzzles 187
policy refinement 154–6
policy roles 92–4
policy soup 137
policy stages 18–20
policy streams 137–40
policy success 195–202
policy transfers 134
policy validation 151–5
political education 94, 99, 127, 138, 206, 214,
    222
political institutions 1,24, 28, 47, 77, 83, 89,
    94–6, 113, 117,132, 178, 207, 209, 212, 219;
    effect of 33, 47, 58–60, 141
political participation 42, 51–2, 175, 206–8
political parties 48, 59, 60, 91,100, 131, 153–4,
    161 197, 219
poll-tax 19, 56, 58, 123–4, 128, 146–7, 187
Poor Law Act 1834, 143, 197
Popper, Karl 23, 150
positivism 1–2, 10, 21, 23, 50, 145, 203–4, 217
post-modernism 27, 87–88
Poulantzes, Nicos 85, 111

power 1, 37, 80–90, 121, 174, 218; as authority
    82; as a capacity 83; defined 81; sources of
    83–4
power dependence model 84, 171
pragmatism 73–4, 210
press 96, 127–8
Pressman, Jeffery 122, 166, 170
prime ministers 62, 91, 141, 190
private education 7
private sector 4, 5, 81, 144, 198
privatisation 35, 47, 135, 165–6
professionals 60, 66, 83, 85, 92, 96, 100, 108,
    110, 175, 218
public choice theory 44–7
public finance 113
public-private partnerships 198
punctuated equilibrium 180–1
Putnam, Robert 82–3
puzzle solving 187

Quakers 40

racism 42, 99
RAND Corporation 146
rational choice theory 44–7
rationality 23–5, 36–37, 145–7, 203–4, 218
Rawls, John 70, 72–3, 204, 213, 215
Reagan, Ronald 47
realistic evaluation 149–51
realist politics 73–4
realpolitik 73–4, 143, 151, 193, 212
Redcliffe-Maud Commission 37, 124–5, 153,
    163
referenda 164, 205
regulation 119; light touch 119, 162
religious beliefs 40, 67–8, 211
rendition 69
Republicans 36
resources 84, 218
revolt, 181–84
revolution 3, 97, 181, 184–86
Rhodes, R. A. W. 28, 46, 84, 116–9
Richelieu, 93
Richardson, Jeremy 109, 118
rights 3, 31, 66, 68, 76, 104–5, 200–1, 212, 213
Rio conferences on sustainability 77–8
Room, Graham 192
Roosevelt, Franklyn, D. 12, 17, 44, 154, 169
Rose, Richard 134
Rosenau, Pauline 208
Rossi, Peter 145
Rotherham 172
Rousseau, Jean Jaques 3, 106–7, 129, 206
Rule, James, 170
rule of law 62
rule utilitarianism 70
Russia 17, 219; *see also* Soviet Russia

Sabatier, Paul 19, 115, 120–21, 172, 173, 174
Samuelson, Paul 11
satisfice 15, 81, 217
Saudi Arabia 99, 136
Sayre and Kaufman 113
Schmitter, Gerhard 109
Schumpeter, Joseph 111, 113, 179
scientific methodology 2, 10–12, 217
Scotland 56, 201
Scottish Independence Referendum, 118
Scottish Parliament
Scruton, Roger 41, 70
Second Gulf War 57, 152, 188
Second World War 4
self-esteem 31, 33, 57, 123
self-interest 1, 24, 50–64, 96–7, 202, 217–8;
    defined 50, 51; institutional consequences
    60–1, 212, 221; quantifying 53
Selznick, Phillip 170
separation of powers 37, 159
Sharia Law 201
Sheffield 172
Sheldon, Oliver 13, 169
Simon, Herbert 14–16, 20–1, 23, 81
Skocpol, Theda 184, 186
slavery 42, 105, 122
Smith, Adam 45, 59
socialisation 63, 128; *see also* political
    education
social benefits
social democracy 43–4, 85–6
social deprivation 138
social sciences 2, 7, 11–13, 16, 28–9, 33, 45,
    146, 148–9, 151, 155, 180, 188, 217
socialism 28, 38, 42–3, 110–1
sociology 126, 127, 181
Somalia 186
South Africa 48, 101
sovereignty 135
Soviet Russia 37, 43, 66, 76, 93, 97, 98, 182
Spain 83, 100–1, 135, 176, 201
Spanish Civil War 95, 100
Stacey, Ralph 188–9
Stalin, Joseph 57, 63, 93, 98
stalinism 48
Stamp, Josiah 13,
state 42–3, 81, 85–8
statistics 145, 210
street level bureaucrats 171
strong democracy
Stoker, Gerry 178
Stokes, Donald 111
strong democracy 87, 129, 206
subjective classifications 29–33
subjectivism 1–2, 20–2, 23–33, 80–1,147, 191,
    200–1, 217–218
subsidiarity 213

super optimum solutions 193
surveys 146, 164
sustainable development
Sweden 109
symbolic capital 87
Syria 96, 166
surveillance 26, 132, 182, 219
systems theory 17–18

taxation 44, 47, 67, 135
tax payers 26
Taylor, A. J. P. 6–7
Taylor, F. W. 12
terrorism 181
television 127
Tennessee Valley Authority 170
Thatcher, Margaret 19, 56, 58, 123, 185;
    governments 35, 47, 118, 148
'thick skin' 57
think tanks 94, 164
third sector organisations 5, 119, 170
Third Way 34, 38
Tilly, Charles 185–6
Tilley, Nick 150
tolerance 201–2
Toqueville, Alexis de 107, 207
totalitarian regimes 52, 94, 97–9
trade unions 84, 139
tragedy of the commons 212, 213, 216
Transatlantic trade and investment partnership
    158
Travers, Tony 193
trickle-down effect 45, 76
Trotsky, Leon 44, 98
Truman, David 112, 115
trust 32, 56
truth 72
Twitter 96, 205
'tyranny of the majority' 106

Uganda 102
United Kingdom 51; aristocracy 41, 42; Audit
    Commission 145; 'Big Society' 83, 178;
    British Broadcasting Corporation 154;
    Cabinet 105, 125; Census 143; civil service
    153, 161; 172 coalition government 2010;
    devolution 164; Education Acts 194; elec-
    toral reform Acts 196; electoral system 159;
    expenses scandal 62, 16; Head of State 166;
    House of Lords 62–3; industrial regenera-
    tion; Labour Party 59; local government 19,
    37, 109, 124–5, 135, 145, 149, 153, 164,
    172, 176, 184, 187; *Modernising Govern-
    ment 1999*; Members of Parliament 58, 62,
    165; National Health Service 30, 44,
    131,139, 206; National Office for Statistics
    143; OFSTED 145, 176; Parliament 37, 58,

62, 105, 159; Prime Minister 37, 56, 159;
Secretaries of State, 159; social services
evolution 197; Trade Unions 84;
Treasury 116, 198; Urban Development
Corporations 149, 177, 198
United Nations, 5, 68, 163, 212; charter of
human rights 68
United States 158, 160; Bill of Rights 104,
205; *Brown vs Board of Education Topeka*
165; Civil War 35; Confederate States 196;
Congress, 5, 53, 104, 109, 160; Constitution
35, 104; executive orders 161; Federal
Census 143; Federal States 164; foreign
policy 131; General Accounting Office 144;
gun control 181, 191; health care 36, 134,
139, 146, 151, 181; health insurance 36;
local government 36, 108, 164, 170, 207;
New Deal 44; Planning, Programme and
Budgeting Systems 144; President, 5, 83,
160; prohibition 169; Republicans 36;
Supreme Court 35, 104, 164, 165; Tea Party
67; Twin Towers 69; War of Independence
42; War on Poverty 170, 178; White House
93, 169
Utilitarianism, 45, 68–70, 75, 105
Urwick, Lyndall 13

validation 151–5
Verba, Sidney 112
violence 63, 81
Virginia School 46
voting systems 53, 107, 51–2, 175,
206–8

Wales 56, 164
Wallas, Graham 169
Waltz, Kenneth 74
Water Gate 56, 187
weapons of mass destruction 67
Webbs Sydney and Beatrice 43
Weber, Max 81, 94, 110
Weible, Christopher, 121
Weimar Republic 49
welfare state 30, 38, 44, 46, 53, 72, 85–6, 111, 116
Westminster systems 159, 160
wicked issues 66, 178
Winkler, J. T. 109
Winship, Christopher 187
Wiki-Leaks 96
Wildavsky, Aaron 116, 122, 166, 170, 171
Wilks-Heeg, Stuart 78, 156
Wilson, Harold 124–5
Wilson, James Q. 30
Wittgenstein, Ludwig 23, 26
Wollmann, Hellmut 144
womens' rights 35, 105, 136, 200
Woodrow Wilson, Thomas 11–12
World Health Organisation 194
Wotton, Henry 154
world wide web 134, 182
Wright-Mills, C. 110, 116

Yanow, Dvora 28, 9

zero-sum games 193
Zittel, Thomas 207–8
Zittoun, Philippe 133, 203